ULTIMATE

Road Trips

AUSTRALIA

LEE ATKINSON

Hardie Grant

EXPLORE

Great Ocean Road, Victoria

Introduction

Australians and tourists alike have always loved a good road trip. Whether it's a leisurely Sunday drive through the wineries or to the beaches near our capital cities, a quick weekend getaway to the mountains, a summer family holiday travelling our beautiful coastline or roughing it on a remote outback track, hitting the road is our favourite way to spend our holiday time. So to help you get the most out of your time on the road, we've put together a collection of 40 of the best driving holiday routes in Australia.

In this guide you'll find everything you need to know to plan your next driving holiday. To help make the planning easier we've organised *Ultimate Road Trips Australia* into eight themed sections: bucket-list drives, long weekends and short breaks, gourmet getaways, coastal road trips, capital city to capital city trips, country drives, outback adventures and epic journeys. Each of the 40 road trip chapters includes things to see and do, route maps and a handy list of distances to help you plan your trip, as well as useful advice on family-friendly attractions, where to eat and the best hotels, guesthouses, caravan parks and camping spots. You'll also find details on weather conditions and where to find more information.

Keep this book in the car for when you're out on the road, or curl up with it at home and dream about your next journey. Bon voyage, and have a safe trip!

HELPFUL INFORMATION

DRIVING ON UNSEALED ROADS

Many of the roads in country areas are unsealed; they can be bumpy and dusty, but unless otherwise signposted are generally fine for conventional 2WD vehicles when conditions have been dry. After heavy rains, however, they may take days to dry out. Travelling on roads that have a 'closed road' sign, even if you are in a 4WD vehicle, may incur a substantial fine.

TOWING A CARAVAN

Unless otherwise noted in the text, most of the roads covered in this guide are suitable for caravans, but road conditions can and do change, so always check local conditions before setting out, particularly if it has been raining recently.

Be aware of your van's height and weight – you'll often come across low-level bridges in country areas. Before you leave home, measure the height of your van or motorhome, including any rooftop airconditioners and so on, and put it on a sticker on your windscreen or dashboard to remind you. Do the same with your total laden weight, as some bridges have a 3 tonne limit – as do some country roads after rain.

DRIVING IN SNOW

Snow chains must be carried on certain roads between 1 June and 10 October in alpine areas of New South Wales and Victoria. Unless you intend to do a lot of driving in snow- and ice-affected regions, the best option is to hire chains, which are widely available in these areas in winter. Make sure you ask for a demonstration of how to correctly fit your chains before you leave.

DRIVING IN THE OUTBACK

Outback driving can be challenging and potentially hazardous, but the following tips should help you plan and stay safe.

- The most important thing to remember when driving on remote tracks in the outback is to ensure you are carrying enough water, basic spare parts, food and fuel. Remember fuel and supply outlets in remote areas are not often open after hours or on weekends.

- If you do get into trouble, *never ever* leave your vehicle. Most people who have perished in the outback died while trying to walk to help. Wait until help comes to you.

- Station properties are often unfenced in the outback, so watch for cattle and wildlife on roads and avoid driving at night. Always leave gates as you found them.

- When driving over sandhills or through drifts of sand, lower your tyre pressure to approximately 15 psi to help avoid getting bogged (but don't go below 10 psi, as it's very easy to roll the tyre off the rim when making turns or stake the tyre on sharp wood hidden in the sand).

- Bulldust is a superfine sand a bit like red talcum powder and it's everywhere in the outback. It's slippery and hard to see, so you'll often hit a patch when you least expect it. Aside from handling difficulties, it can make following, overtaking or passing oncoming vehicles very difficult as your windscreen will be swamped by dust. Shift down a gear quickly if you hit a patch and steer carefully. Watch for the end of the dust patch because a sudden hard edge can deflate your tyres or even bend rims.

- Do not enter dips at high speed. Brake on entry and accelerate again as you exit to gain maximum clearance.

- Check tracks across creeks for clear passage and water depth.

- Do not camp in dry creek beds. Flash floods can occur without warning.

- Give road trains a wide berth. Slow down and, if there is an escort vehicle, watch for signals. If you move off the road, reduce speed and watch for guide posts and soft edges.

Opposite Rainbow Beach, Queensland

ROAD READY

Before you leave home, give your car the ten-step once-over.

1. Service please – get your vehicle serviced by a licensed mechanic before you leave home.

2. The good oil – engines like fresh oil, so treat your engine to a lube. And check it regularly while on your trip to make sure it doesn't get low.

3. Keep your cool – check your radiator coolant level and top it up if necessary. If you're heading a long way from help, carry some spare hoses and a bottle of coolant with you.

4. Power rangers – you'd be amazed how many people get stranded with a flat battery, especially if they are running portable fridges, chargers or night lights. Carry a spare and turn off appliances overnight.

5. Keep the pressure on – most of us forget to check tyre pressure. Carry, and use, a tyre gauge. Before you leave, check the tread and make sure you have a spare in good condition.

6. The right tools – a basic tool kit should include a jack, jacking plate and wheel-replacement tools, spare tyre, fire extinguisher, emergency fuel supplies if heading off the beaten track, engine oil, coolant, jumper leads, spare radiator hoses and fan belts and the tools you'll need to replace them.

7. First aid – never travel without a first-aid kit, and always carry extra drinking water.

8. Pack it in – don't overload your car or carry unrestrained items in the backseat (even a flying book can cause serious injury in a crash). If it won't fit in the boot, either don't take it or make sure it is well secured. If you're travelling in a wagon or 4WD, install a cargo barrier.

9. Take the right maps or a good sat nav – fighting over which is the right way to go is a major cause of holiday (and relationship) breakdowns.

10. Play it safe – make sure your vehicle and home insurance policies are up to date. Cancel any home deliveries, get the neighbours to collect your mail and install a timer switch on a light or two. Join your state auto club, such as the RAA or NRMA, to help you out in the event of a breakdown.

FAMILY ROAD TRIP SURVIVAL GUIDE

Road tripping with kids can be fun. Here are six tips on how to make sure everyone enjoys the drive.

1. Plan ahead – the secret to successful road tripping with kids is not to be too ambitious in terms of how far you think you can get in one session. Allow twice as long for the journey as you normally would, allocating plenty of time for rest breaks (plan them in advance). Take the time to get off the highway and stop at a park or swimming pool rather than a roadhouse. It goes without saying that wherever you choose to stop should have toilets, but try to choose places with playgrounds or at least an expanse of grass where the kids can run around and burn off some energy. Bring games (inflatable balls are a good space saver) to play with on these breaks.

2. Map it out – get the kids involved in planning your trip. Make a map of your trip before you leave home, letting them pick a couple of things they'd like to see and do along the way. Decorating the map with drawings or stickers of what they see (or keeping a journal/scrapbook) as you travel is a great way to keep them occupied. Collect postcards at each town you drive through – buy a book of stamps before you leave home and the kids can post them off on the spot. Another option is to create a treasure list of things to find at each stop. If the kids are old enough, let them navigate – then they can answer your 'are we there yet?' questions.

3. Staying healthy – make sure you have enough medication if your kids get car sick (dose them up before you hit the road, not once they feel unwell). Carry a plastic bucket (with a lid) and plenty of wet wipes just in case. Roadhouse food is usually atrocious, unhealthy and expensive. Pack a bag of healthy snacks, sandwiches and drinks – but go easy on the sugar and anything that can spill or stain.

4. Keeping kids amused – pack some toys and games but don't even think about asking them to share: let each child have their own bag of things to play with. Avoid books if your kids are prone to motion sickness and avoid anything hard, sharp or tricky to clean if spilt (or doodled) on upholstery. Have a storytelling competition or make it a team effort, where each person adds a line. Read them a book, listen to an audio book or podcast some children's stories. Don't underestimate the power of old-fashioned games like I-spy, spelling bees, word games, 'who am I?' and so on – the internet is full of quirky suggestions, just google 'road trip games'. If all else fails, tablets and portable DVD players are a lot cheaper than they used to be and most run via the 12-volt outlet in the car – don't forget headphones.

5. Pack a survival bag – put everything you might need, like a change of clothes, towel, swimmers, jumpers, torch, medication and, even pyjamas, in a bag to carry in the car to save repacking the boot every time you need something.

6. Avoid driving at night – in theory the idea that driving through the night will mean the kids sleep while you motor in peace is a tempting proposition, but in reality you'll just end up dog-tired the next day while they are full of beans. Driving in the dark on country roads also means that the chance of colliding with wildlife is high.

Opposite Paluma Range National Park, Queensland

Map Legend

Road trip with distance markers and distance

125

Sidetrack route

Road network

Arterial   Major   Minor   Ferry

Federal & state route numbering

A1   1   1   M31   A15   B37   C425   72

🍴 Best eats

🛏 Best sleeps

⛺ Camping area

🎋 Picnic area

BRISBANE ○ State capital city

WOLLONGONG ○ Major city/town

Paynesville ○ Town

Austinmer ○ Other population centres/localities

ℹ Visitor information

Caravan park

● Attractions

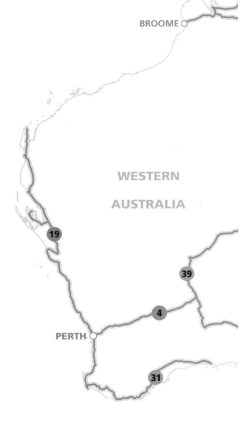

BROOME ○

WESTERN AUSTRALIA

19

39

4

PERTH ○

31

Bucket-list drives

Take one of these once-in-a-lifetime road trips on Australia's most iconic roads.

It's one of the world's greatest coastal drives, following the south-west coast of Victoria and taking in countless beaches, stunning sections of cliff-top road, lush rainforest and, of course, those famous rocky sea stacks known as the Twelve Apostles.

Great Ocean Road, Vic.

HOW LONG?

You can easily drive the Great Ocean Road in one day – and many people even do the return trip to Melbourne in one (very long) day – but this is a drive best taken slowly, allowing time to explore the many beaches and coastal towns along the way, so make it a two- or three-day trip. If you are short of time, hook up with the A1 back to Melbourne about 12km east of Warrnambool.

WHEN TO GO

If you can, try to avoid holidays and weekends, when the heavy traffic can be frustrating. Midweek in mid-winter is a glorious time to drive the route, as you'll have the road almost to yourself, although it's too cold to swim. Summers are dry and warm; most rain falls during winter, when temperatures can be quite chilly.

NEED TO KNOW

Book accommodation ahead if you are planning on driving the Great Ocean Road during school holidays or on a weekend. Most people drive the route from east to west: go against the flow and you'll have less traffic, but watch out for vehicles, including tour buses and caravans, drifting into your lane on tight bends. You'll also miss out on many of the roadside lookouts, as the only places to pull off are on the sea side of the road and crossing the double lines is both foolhardy and illegal.

Drive rating
Easy. Sealed roads with extensive winding sections

Distances
Total distance, Geelong to Port Fairy: 282km
- Melbourne to Torquay: 94km
- Torquay to Port Campbell: 165km
- Port Campbell to Port Fairy: 95km
- Port Fairy to Melbourne via the A1: 295km

Temperatures
January: 14–21°C
July: 4–13°C

More information
- Great Ocean Road Visitor Information Centre, 100 Great Ocean Rd, Apollo Bay; 1300 689 297; iamapollobay.com.au
- Lorne Visitor Centre, 15 Mountjoy Pde, Lorne; (03) 5289 1152; lovelorne.com.au
- Warrnambool Visitor Information Centre, 89 Merri St, Warrnambool; 1800 637 725
- visitgreatoceanroad.org.au

Snapshot
Top of any list of great Australian drives is the Great Ocean Road. Built between 1919 and 1932, the cliff-hugging road was hewn from the rock using picks, crowbars and shovels by 3000 returned World War I soldiers, who dedicated the 14-year project as a memorial to their comrades who died in the war. The Great Ocean Road officially runs from Torquay for 195km to Warrnambool, but many people continue along the coast to Port Fairy.

Previous Coastline along the Great Ocean Road, near Lorne, Victoria *Opposite top left* Exploring Great Otway National Park *Top right* Griffiths Island Lighthouse, Port Fairy *Bottom left* Enjoying the beach at Peterborough *Bottom right* Port Fairy Coastal Reserve

Great Ocean Road, Vic.

TORQUAY TO APOLLO BAY

The starting point of the Great Ocean Road, Torquay (22km south of Geelong) could easily claim to be Australia's surfing capital – Bells Beach, one of the most famous surf beaches in the country and home of the world's longest running professional surfing event, the Rip Curl Pro, is just down the road. Two of the world's leading surfwear brands, Rip Curl and Quiksilver, were born here, and there's even a museum that claims to be the largest surfing museum in the world, the Australian National Surfing Museum, which encompasses interactive exhibits, memorabilia, a Surfing Hall of Fame and lots of surf art and kitsch (77 Beach Rd, Torquay; (03) 5261 4606; open Mon–Sun 9am–5pm).

From Torquay head south, along what is known as the 'surf coast', to Anglesea, where the road hits the coast and you first enjoy the spectacular views that make the Great Ocean Road famous. Stop at Aireys Inlet and drive up to the lighthouse for a fine coastal panorama. At Eastern View, just a few kilometres on from Aireys Inlet, is the Great Ocean Road Memorial Arch – a nice place to stop for a souvenir photo. The stylish resort town of Lorne is not far away; it's great for a stroll, a spot of boutique shopping and coffee or lunch at one of the many restaurants that line the main street. Pop into the Great Ocean Road Heritage Centre inside the Lorne Visitor Centre to see the Great Ocean Road Story, a fascinating exhibition that tells the story of how the famous road was built (15 Mountjoy Pde, Lorne; (03) 5289 1152; open Mon–Sun 9am–5pm).

SIDETRACK

Wedged between the coast and the Otway forests, Lorne is also a good base for short excursions into the hinterland. Erskine Falls is just a few minutes' drive from the village centre and there are well-made walking tracks through the rainforest past the falls, huge tree ferns and towering trees. Further afield the former logging town of Forrest has a network of forest and waterfall walking trails and is one of the state's best mountain-biking destinations – hire bikes from Forrest Hire Bikes (33 Grant St; 0448 843 236; forresthirebikes.com.au). Don't leave town without a hot chocolate from Platypi Chocolate (73 Grant St; 0433 362 639).

Apollo Bay is about an hour's drive from Lorne, and the road hugs the coast the whole way. Drive through the pretty hamlets of Wye River and Kennett River and pull over at Cape Patton Lookout for a fantastic coastline view and yet another great photograph.

The town of Apollo Bay curves around the beach and is, like Lorne, full of boutiques, cafes and restaurants. It is also home to a lively fishing industry and you can watch the fleet unloading its catch at the wharf, or buy some of the local speciality (crayfish and lobster) at the fishermen's co-op, at the edge of the wharf, to eat on the beach.

APOLLO BAY TO PORT CAMPBELL

After Apollo Bay the road leaves the coast and cuts through lush green farmland and the dense rainforest of Great Otway National Park, before the ocean emerges again on the western side of the Cape Otway headland at Princetown.

SIDETRACK

Maits Rest Rainforest Trail in Great Otway National Park is a 30-minute boardwalk stroll through beautiful rainforest, where giant myrtle beeches tower above a delicate understorey of tree ferns, lichens and mosses. It's just off the Great Ocean Road, approximately 16km from Apollo Bay.

SIDETRACK

Take the turn-off to the tip of Cape Otway, about 12km from the Great Ocean Road. It's the site of one of the best preserved groups of historic lighthouse buildings in Australia, built in 1848. The lighthouse is open (Mon–Sun 9am–5pm) for self-guided tours, or join one of the guided history tours that depart regularly throughout the day (usually when there are enough people) and include climbing the spiral staircase to the top of the light tower (see lightstation.com for details). Keep a lookout on the drive in, as you will often see koalas asleep in the trees beside the road.

😊 KIDS' SPOT

Fly through the tree-tops at the fabulous Otway Fly, a must-see attraction on this stretch. Take the one-hour rainforest walk that includes an elevated boardwalk through the rainforest canopy, 25m above the ground. If you have a head for heights, climb the 47m high lookout tower for stunning views. Thrill-seekers can join a two-and-a-half-hour zipline tour that zooms through the tree-tops. 360 Phillips Track, Beech Forest, 12km from Lavers Hill; (03) 5235 9200; open Mon–Sun 9am–5pm (last entry 4pm); otwayfly.com.au.

Opposite Take a break at one of Lorne's many cafes *Right* The Arch, Port Campbell National Park

The road now cuts across a heath-covered plateau to Princetown, where the coastal plain borders sheer cliffs, sometimes just metres from the edge of the road. Highlights along this stretch include the Twelve Apostles rock formations – there are actually only eight left – which were carved out of the adjacent cliffs by wind and wave erosion. The cliffs rise to nearly 70m in some places and the highest Apostle is about 50m from base to tip. A great way to see them is on a short helicopter flight, available near the Interpretive Centre at the Twelve Apostles (a 15-minute flight will cost around $150; 12apostleshelicopters.com.au).

The grand views continue as you head to Loch Ard Gorge, site of a tragic shipwreck in 1878 that left just two survivors out of 54 passengers and crew; then on to London Bridge, which dramatically lost one of its arches in 1990, stranding two startled sightseers on the newly formed tower; and then to Bay of Islands Coastal Park. All of these major natural attractions are well signposted and offer great lookout points and boardwalks.

☺ KIDS' SPOT

With wild and dramatic stories of the more than 180 shipwrecks along this section of coast, Flagstaff Hill is a fascinating open-air museum and village created around the original lighthouses and fortifications that gave rise to Warrnambool in 1859. One star exhibit is the Loch Ard Peacock, a Minton porcelain peacock – one of only nine in the world – that was destined for the Melbourne International Exhibition in 1880 and miraculously washed up unscathed after the *Loch Ard* came to grief near Port Campbell in 1878. Kids will enjoy the brilliant nightly sound-and-laser show, *Tales of the Shipwreck Coast*, which tells the story of the shipwreck. Merri St, Warrnambool; (03) 5559 4620; open Mon–Sun 9am–5pm, show times vary; flagstaffhill.com.

PORT CAMPBELL TO PORT FAIRY

After Peterborough, the road leaves the coast once more to meander through beautiful pastoral lands and rich dairy country before returning to the coast at Warrnambool. If you are here between June and September, head for Logans Beach, where you might be lucky enough to see one of the many female southern right whales that come here each year to give birth – this is one of the best shore-based places to see these whales and their calves in winter. The whales stay in the bay for around two or three months, so frequent visitors to the whale-watching platform in the dunes can watch the calves, which are about 5–6m long when they are born, grow. By the time they head back to the Southern Ocean they are almost double that size. Though the whales come close to shore, you'll get a much better look if you have binoculars.

There's still buried treasure hidden in the sand dunes west of Warrnambool, or so the legend goes. In the 1830s some shipwrecked sealers found a decaying wreck in the Armstrong Bay area, and a story grew that it was the remains of a 16th-century Spanish or Portuguese galleon full of treasure. Sometime in the 1880s the wreck seems to have disappeared, possibly covered by shifting sands, and ever since the story of the so-called Mahogany Ship has become more mysterious with each retelling. If you fancy a bit of treasure hunting, follow the Mahogany Ship Walking Track, which traces the coast between Warrnambool and Port Fairy and passes sites where the mythical ship may rest. The trail is 22km long and is mostly on the beach, but if you want to concentrate your search efforts head to the area east of Gormans Road and west of Levys Point near Dennington – at least that's what the treasure hunters on the online forums suggest!

Port Fairy is about 30 minutes away and is a pretty town with many historic buildings housing restaurants, boutiques and art galleries – more than 50 of the buildings are classified by the National Trust – and a streetscape that looks much as it would have done 100 years ago. Take an early morning walk along the historic wharf and watch the fishing boats unload their catch of crayfish and abalone among the bobbing cruising boats and racing yachts, and chat to some of the anglers who line the riverside boardwalk, all hoping to catch their own breakfast fresh from the sea. Continue on past the wharf towards the harbour, following the track to Griffiths Island, where you can walk out to the historic lighthouse or wander through the shearwater colony.

From Port Fairy it is 295km back to Melbourne via the Princes Highway (A1).

BEST EATS

- **Wye River General Store** This relaxed cafe opposite the beach serves very good coffee and all-day brunch, along with wine and cocktails. 35 Great Ocean Rd, Wye River; (03) 5289 0247; open Mon–Sun for breakfast and lunch; thewyegeneral.com.
- **Chris's Beacon Point Restaurant** Located in the hills above Skenes Creek overlooking Apollo Bay and a Great Ocean Road institution since 1979, Chris's is the place to go for Greek-inspired meals and fresh seafood served with a sublime view. 280 Skenes Creek Rd, Skenes Creek; (03) 5237 6411; open Mon–Sun for dinner, Sat–Sun for lunch.
- **Forage on the Foreshore** Warm up in this cosy beachside cafe in Port Campbell – the fireside seats are perfect on a cold, blustery day – with lots of organic, gluten-free and vegetarian options. Try the green egg soufflé or the milled spelt hotcakes with rhubarb and coconut. 32 Cairns St, Port Campbell; (03) 5598 6202; open Mon–Sun for breakfast and lunch; forageontheforeshore.com.au.
- **Brae** Allow three or four hours to eat at Victoria's best regional restaurant – one of only two Australian restaurants to make it into the world's top 100. It's a set menu of 14 or 15 small courses that changes daily according to what chef Dan Hunter has harvested from the organic garden adjacent to the farmhouse dining room. It's a 30-minute detour from the coast but worth it if you enjoy your food. For drivers the non-alcoholic drinks that match each course are arguably more exciting than the wine, and there are six suites on-site if you want to stay overnight. It's a bucket-list experience worth every cent but you'll need to book several weeks in advance. 4285 Cape Otway Rd, Birregurra; (03) 5236 2226; open Thurs and Sat for dinner, Fri–Mon for lunch; braerestaurant.com.

BEST SLEEPS

- **La Perouse Lorne** Charming French-inspired B&B with three ensuite rooms, all with private terraces, high on the hill above Lorne – it's an easy five-minute walk into town, a little longer coming back up the hill after dinner. 26a William St, Lorne; 0418 534 422; laperouselorne.com.
- **Chris's Beacon Point Villas** Perched in high bushland above the Great Ocean Road, near Apollo Bay, these villas offer spectacular views of the ocean and Otway Ranges, with an on-site restaurant (*see* Best eats). 280 Skenes Creek Rd, Skenes Creek; (03) 5237 6411; chriss.com.au.
- **Deep Blue Hotel and Hot Springs** You don't have to be a guest to enjoy a therapeutic soak in one of the geothermal mineral pools at this Warrnambool hotel, but if you are it's nice not having to stumble too far back to your room. Worm Bay Rd, Warrnambool; (03) 5559 2000; thedeepblue.com.au.
- **Hearns Beachside Villas** Fall asleep listening to the booming waves and wake up to an ocean view in one of these contemporary villas on the southern edge of Port Fairy. With a fully equipped kitchen and laundry and lots of room to move, they are ideal for longer stays. 13–17 Thistle Pl, Port Fairy; (03) 5568 3150; hearnsbeachsidevillas.com.au.
- **Caravanning and camping** There are caravan parks at Geelong, Port Fairy, Aireys Inlet, Anglesea, Torquay, Warrnambool and Lorne, but two of the best spots are the Cumberland River Reserve, 7km west of Lorne, where you'll find a lovely grassy camping area set beside the river (unpowered sites only), and beachfront Kennett River Foreshore Reserve, beside the Kennett River between Lorne and Apollo Bay, where powered sites are available.

Opposite Go back in time at the open-air museum Flagstaff Hill in Warrnambool
Right One of the delicious small courses at Brae

Traversing one of the most isolated corners of the country and Australia's most celebrated outback track, the Gibb River Road in Western Australia is a road trip for those who like wild adventures, travelling through some of the most magnificent country you'll ever see.

Gibb River Road, WA

HOW LONG?

Technically you could drive the 700 or so kilometres between Kununurra and Derby in two or three days, but you really need at least two weeks, especially if it's your first time. If you are short of time, forgo the side trip up to the Mitchell Plateau.

WHEN TO GO

May through to November (the dry season) is the best time to travel the Gibb, which can be cut by flooded rivers during the wet season. Most of the stations that offer accommodation and tours are also closed during the wet season. Campsites can be busy during the July school holidays.

NEED TO KNOW

To drive the Gibb you'll need a 4WD. If you are towing, your caravan or camper trailer will need to be very robust – the roadside is littered with abandoned vans and trailers that have been shaken to bits by the corrugations. You'll need to be pretty much self-sufficient, carry spares and tools and be willing to camp most nights. There are two roadhouses on the Gibb (Mount Barnett and Imintji), and fuel is also available at Drysdale River Station on the way to Mitchell Plateau. The longest distance between fuel stops for petrol vehicles is approximately 470km (from Derby to Mount Barnett Roadhouse via Windjana Gorge and Bell Gorge) as Imintji Roadhouse sells diesel only. The longest distance between diesel fuel stops is 395km (Derby to Imintji via the above gorges along the way). There is no LPG gas and no supermarkets on the Gibb. The two roadhouses sell very basic supplies, like UHT milk and frozen bread, but that's about it. There is also no mobile phone coverage on the Gibb anywhere. If you are planning on visiting the Mitchell Plateau you will need to purchase a Ngauwudu Road Zone pass for each adult in your vehicle before you travel: look under 'visiting country' at wunambalgaambera.org.au.

Opposite Enjoy dramatic views of the Cockburn Ranges along the Gibb River Road

Drive rating
Hard. 4WD only. Remote, unsealed roads with corrugations and bulldust

Distances
Total distance, Kununurra to Broome: 932km
- Kununurra to Wyndham: 101km
- Kununurra to El Questro: 110km
- El Questro to Mount Barnett: 331km
- Gibb River Road intersection to Mitchell Falls: 246km
- Mount Barnett to Derby: 304km
- Derby to Broome: 220km

Temperatures
January: 24–37°C
July: 11–33°C

More information
- Broome Visitor Centre, 1 Hamersley St, Broome; (08) 9195 2200; visitbroome.com.au
- Kununurra Visitor Centre, 75 Coolibah Dr, Kununurra; 1800 586 868; visitkununurra.com
- australiasnorthwest.com
- kimberleyaustraliaguide.com
- parks.dpaw.wa.gov.au

Snapshot
The Gibb River Road starts just west of Kununurra, and spears through the heart of the Kimberley to meet the sea at Derby. It's a dusty trail of almost 700km that takes you across boab-studded savannah lands, past weather-beaten ranges where rivers tumble down cliffs and wind their way through deep rock gorges that are billions of years old, and over wide waterways that can only be crossed during the dry season between May and November. It's crocodile country, but there are plenty of places to cool off – floating in a waterhole surrounded by rock walls decorated in ancient rock art after a long, hot dusty drive is one of the things that makes this extraordinary part of the world so special.

INDIAN OCEAN

ALBERT ISLANDS

Bigge Island

NORTH KIMBERLEY MARINE PARK

ADMIRALTY GULF

Lamarck Island

Coronation Island

CORONATION ISLANDS

Cape Wellington

NORTH LALANG-GARRAM MARINE PARK

PRINCE REGENT NATIONAL PARK

CHAMPAGNY ISLANDS

Jungulu Island

Augustus Island

Adele Island

ADELE ISLAND NATURE RESERVE

LALANG-GARRAM/ CAMDEN SOUND MARINE PARK

PRINCE REGENT NATIONAL PARK

KUNMUNYA

Conway Island

MACLEAY ISLANDS

MONTGOMERY ISLANDS

Storr Island

Macleay Island

Caffarelli Island

BUCCANEER ARCHIPELAGO

Cockatoo Island

Koolan Island

Koolan

Kingfisher Islands

LALANG-GARRAM/ HORIZONTAL FALLS MARINE PARK

MUNJA

KIMBERLEY

WOTJALUM

Fletcher Islands

Walcott Inlet

Cape Leveque

Sunday Island

SUNDAY STRAIT

Kooljaman

One Arm Point

Lombadina

KING SOUND

Dillie Gorge

KING LEOPOLD RANGES CONSERVATION PARK

Bell Gorge

West Island

East Island

Lacepede Islands

LACEPEDE ISLANDS NATURE RESERVE

Beagle Bay

BEAGLE BAY

BEAGLE BAY CARNOT BAY

Derby

Birdwood Downs

306

WINDJANA GORGE NP

Windjana Gorge

COULOMB POINT NATURE RESERVE

TUNNEL CREEK NP

DEVONIAN REEF CONSERVATION PARK

1 216

RH Willare Bridge Roadhouse

1

Roebuck Roadhouse

RH

Camballin

Cable Beach

BROOME

Looma

LOOMA

1

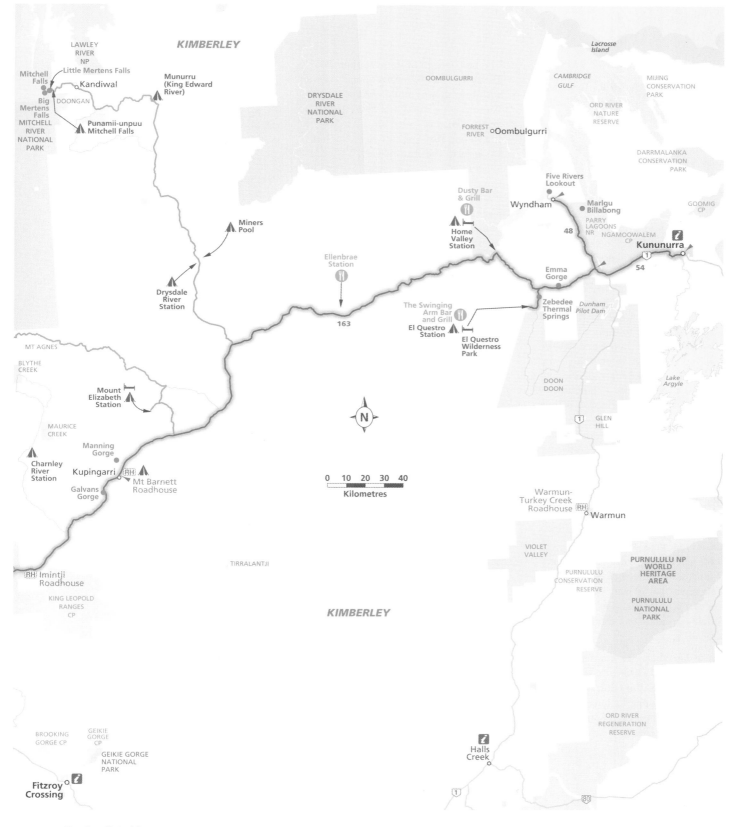

KIMBERLEY

LAWLEY
RIVER
NP
Little Mertens Falls
Mitchell Falls
Kandiwal
Munurru (King Edward River)
Big Mertens Falls
DOONGAN
MITCHELL RIVER NATIONAL PARK
Punamii-unpuu Mitchell Falls

Lacrosse Island

OOMBULGURRI

CAMBRIDGE GULF

MIJING CONSERVATION PARK

DRYSDALE RIVER NATIONAL PARK

ORD RIVER NATURE RESERVE

FORREST RIVER
Oombulgurri

DARRMALANKA CONSERVATION PARK

GOOMIG CP

Miners Pool

Drysdale River Station

Five Rivers Lookout

Dusty Bar & Grill

Wyndham

Marlgu Billabong

PARRY LAGOONS NR

NGAMOOWALEM CP

Kununurra

Ellenbrae Station

Home Valley Station

48

Emma Gorge

54

1

MT AGNES

BLYTHE CREEK

163

The Swinging Arm Bar and Grill
El Questro Station

El Questro Wilderness Park

Zebedee Thermal Springs

Dunham
Pilot Dam

Lake Argyle

Mount Elizabeth Station

MAURICE CREEK

N

DOON DOON

Manning Gorge

Charnley River Station

Kupingarri

RH

Mt Barnett Roadhouse

Galvans Gorge

0 10 20 30 40
Kilometres

GLEN HILL

1

Warmun-Turkey Creek Roadhouse
RH
Warmun

RH Imintji Roadhouse

KING LEOPOLD RANGES CP

TIRRALANTJI

KIMBERLEY

VIOLET VALLEY

PURNULULU NP WORLD HERITAGE AREA

PURNULULU CONSERVATION RESERVE

PURNULULU NATIONAL PARK

BROOKING GORGE CP

GEIKIE GORGE CP

GEIKIE GORGE NATIONAL PARK

ORD RIVER REGENERATION RESERVE

Fitzroy Crossing

Halls Creek

1

80

KUNUNURRA TO MOUNT BARNETT

For most people the Gibb River Road starts (or ends) in Kununurra, but technically it starts at the port at Wyndham, about 100km to the west. The Kimberley is cattle country and the Gibb River Road was originally built to link the vast cattle stations along it to meatworks and port facilities in Derby and Wyndham at either end.

Take the back road from Kununurra to Wyndham via Parry Creek to see some impressive boabs. Related to, but not the same as, the African baobab, the boab is found only in the Kimberley and can live for more than 1500 years. Unlike Kununurra, which was built in the 1960s to service the Ord River Irrigation Scheme and is very neat and tidy, Wyndham, which was established in 1886 after gold was found in Halls Creek, reeks with character. The ramshackle historic port is lined with boabs and crumbling wooden shopfronts emblazoned with the fading names of Chinese shopkeepers from the past – it's easy to imagine that this was what Broome might have been like in the 1970s before the tourism boom.

Drive up to the Five Rivers Lookout at the top of the Bastion Range for a sensational view over the Cambridge Gulf, where the Ord, Forest, King, Durack and Pentecost rivers converge – it's a great spot to watch the sunset. If you're a birdwatcher you'll love Marlgu Billabong, home to a fabulous array of birdlife.

These days there are more camper trailers and off-road caravans than cattle trucks on the Gibb and almost every station along its length welcomes visitors, and most offer some truly spectacular gorges and swimming holes.

The best known of these stations is El Questro, a 283,000ha spread popular with tour groups and daytrippers from Kununurra – it's 110km from town and the road is sealed all the way to the station turn-off, although the last 16km from the entrance is 4WD only. With four levels of accommodation, plus three restaurants, bars, swimming pools, 4WD tours, fishing trips, horse treks, river cruises and helicopter flights, it's more resort than cattle station. Must-see spots include Emma Gorge, an achingly beautiful pool surrounded by towering 120m high red-rock walls over which spills Emma Falls from high above, and Zebedee Thermal Springs, naturally warm pools hidden among sheer cliffs and ancient palms, perfect for a long soak. (1 Gibb River Rd; 1800 837 168; open April – late Oct; elquestro.com.au.)

Just across the Pentecost River from El Questro, Home Valley Station is owned and operated by the Indigenous Land Corporation and serves as a training academy for locals in both tourism and cattle management. It's huge – 248,934ha – and activities include horseriding, helicopter flights, fishing, gorge walks and 4WD tours. Like El Questro, Home Valley offers a range of accommodation as well as a campground, all clustered around the Dusty Bar & Grill. Don't be surprised if the landscape looks kind of familiar – Baz Luhrmann filmed much of his epic movie *Australia* here. (Gibb River Rd, on the western side of the Pentecost River; (08) 9161 4322; open May–Oct; hvstation.com.au.) If you enjoy tours and creature comforts, it's worth allowing a couple of days at each station.

 KIDS' SPOT

If your kids love to run wild in the bush, sign them up to El Questro's Junior Ranger program, which teaches them all about crocodiles, snakes and bush survival tips, and includes lots of fun activities like fishing and birdwatching. Led by El Questro rangers, sessions last 90 minutes and are held daily from June through to late August. 1 Gibb River Rd; 1800 837 168; elquestro.com.au.

Above Found only in the Kimberley, the Australian boab is also known as the upside-down tree *Opposite* Negotiating the infamous Munja Track

You'll need to allow two days travelling time each way to drive the 240km track to the Mitchell Plateau over several creek crossings, through thick red bulldust and across corrugations that can shake even the toughest gear to bits (air down your tyres), but the dramatic three-tiered Mitchell Falls is a highlight of any trip along the Gibb River Road.

The five-hour walk to Mitchells Falls from the camping area is a strenuous trek across rough and rocky country, passing Little Mertens Falls and Big Mertens Falls along the way – carry more water than you think you'll need. Saltwater crocodiles inhabit the area, so the pools below the falls are off limits, but you can swim at Little Mertens Falls. You can also take a scenic helicopter flight over the plateau and the falls – the office and helipad are at the campground ((08) 9161 4512; helispirit.com.au).

Camping is available en route at Drysdale River Station – home to one of Australia's most remote beer gardens – and at Munurru (King Edward River). This campground is managed by the Traditional Owners, has good swimming and is a short drive from two very impressive rock-art sites with both Wandjina figures (wide-eyed, lightning-crowned spirits who control the weather and created the landscape of the far north-west) and Gwion Gwion figures (previously called Bradshaw figures); they pre-date European rock art by thousands of years.

Back on the Gibb there's more extraordinary rock art to be found at Mount Elizabeth Station, a working cattle station about 40km east of Mount Barnett Roadhouse – the homestead is 30km from the turn-off. The 10km track from the homestead to Wunnamurra Gorge is not for the faint-hearted – it's rocky and gnarly and very steep in sections – although it's really only the last kilometre and a half that is seriously daunting, and plenty of people pull over and walk in. It's worth it: the gorge, which you climb down into by a ladder, is a large semicircular basin flanked by a sandy beach with a deep pool fed by a waterfall that you can swim beneath. There's no clearly marked track, but if you follow the river downstream on the left-hand side for a few hundred metres (you'll need to rockhop a bit) you will come to a large rocky overhang covered with sacred Wandjina figures, kangaroos and other beasts. Another gorgeous spot to cool off – and much easier to get to – is the sandy beach on the Hann River, a short drive from the homestead.

Mount Elizabeth Station is home to one of the best, and toughest, 4WD tracks in the Kimberley: the Munja Track. It runs 220km north to Walcott Inlet on the coast, and it will take at least three days each way due to the deep mud, soft sand, tricky water crossings and steep rocky jump-ups along the way. It costs $100 to get a key to access the track, but you can stay on the track as long as you want – most people spend between four and ten days and you can bush camp anywhere you like along the way.

MOUNT BARNETT TO DERBY

The Gibb has some of the country's best natural swimming pools with dozens scattered all along its length, many on private property. Mount Barnett Roadhouse, one of just two roadhouses along the Gibb that sell fuel and basic supplies, is also home to Manning Gorge. It's at the end of a fairly strenuous one-hour walk that includes crossing the Manning Creek – either by swimming the 100m length or using a rope-guided dinghy – along the way. It's private property, so you'll need to pay an entrance fee at the Mount Barnett Roadhouse before you head to the gorge.

If that sounds like too much hard work, Galvans Gorge is a 15-minute drive west of the roadhouse. It is free to visit and just a five-minute walk from the Gibb. The gorge features the full Kimberley trifecta with a waterfall, boabs and an Aboriginal rock-art gallery.

About 55km further west down the Gibb is the turn-off to Charnley River Station. A working cattle farm until 2010, it's now owned by the Australian Wildlife Conservancy and is one of the few places where you might be lucky enough to see an endangered northern quoll. As a guest you're given a mud map of 4WD tracks, and must-see spots include Donkey Hole, a cascading series of three lily-covered waterholes; Grevillea Gorge, which you access via climbing down a ladder then rockhopping down the side of a waterfall; and Dillie Gorge, a big river gorge with several swimming spots. Finding Charnley River Station can be tricky if you're using an old map – it used to be called Beverley Springs Station. Like all the stations on the Gibb, it's worth spending a few days exploring the property, rather than just overnighting. (43km north of the Gibb, about halfway between Mount Barnett Roadhouse and Bell Gorge; (08) 9191 4646; open dry season only; australianwildlife.org.)

Another lovely swimming spot is at Bell Gorge in King Leopold Ranges Conservation Park, where the Isdell River slashes its way through the mountains forming a series of cascading waterfalls and deep plunge pools.

Windjana Gorge, 95km further east, is an ancient coral reef, eroded by the Lennard River to create a wide, 100m high gorge that cuts through the limestone of the Napier Range exposing countless fossils. There is a lovely 7km return walk along the length of the gorge beside the river, where you can get a close-up look at the gorge's resident fruit bats, corellas and freshwater crocodiles.

From Windjana Gorge it's roughly 145km to Derby, and the Gibb turns to bitumen about halfway along, which can feel super smooth and very fast after the bumps and bulldust of the unsealed Gibb.

Don't be tempted to just hightail it to Broome though: Derby is a good base for scenic flights over the magnificent Buccaneer Archipelago, a beautiful area consisting of some 800 to 1000 rocky islands surrounded by turquoise water, part of a drowned coastline. The area has huge tidal ranges – up to 12m – creating such natural phenomena as the famous horizontal waterfall in Talbot Bay, caused by the differential created when the tide flows between narrow island gaps. Accessible only by boat or plane, it makes a fitting finale to one of outback Australia's great driving adventures.

BEST EATS

- **The Swinging Arm Bar and Grill** The Saturday night barbecues and wood-fired pizzas are popular at this convivial outback pub in the Station 'township' at El Questro, with live music, open mic nights and singalongs. 1 Gibb River Rd via Great Northern Hwy; (08) 9161 4318; open Mon–Sun for lunch and dinner Apr–Oct; elquestro.com.au.
- **Dusty Bar & Grill** The social heart of Home Valley Station, 'the Dusty' offers steak, barramundi and other pub-style classics, along with cold beer and live entertainment. Gibb River Rd, on the western side of the Pentecost River; (08) 9161 4322; open Mon–Sun for lunch and dinner.
- **Ellenbrae Station** Should the craving for a cup of tea with scones, jam and cream strike you, Ellenbrae serves them in the garden of the cattle station homestead. 230km west of Kununurra (70km from the Gibb River Rd/Kalumburu Rd intersection); (08) 9161 4325; open Mon–Sun 8am–4pm Apr–Oct.

BEST SLEEPS

- **El Questro Wilderness Park** Four levels of accommodation are on offer here: camping, family-friendly cabins, safari-style tented cabins and the ultra luxe homestead. 1 Gibb River Rd via Great Northern Hwy; 1800 837 168; elquestro.com.au.
- **Home Valley Station** Home Valley offers stylish 'Grass Castle' bungalows overlooking the boab-lined Bindoola Creek, motel-style guesthouse rooms and permanent tents with raised wooden floors and queen-sized beds. Alternatively, set up your own camp at one of the powered sites or roll out your swag beside the Pentecost River. Gibb River Rd, on the western side of the Pentecost River; (08) 9161 4322; hvstation.com.au.
- **Mount Elizabeth Station** There's basic accommodation in the homestead, or you can camp. If you are after an authentic taste of the Kimberley station life, this is the place. Mount Elizabeth Rd, Gibb; (08) 9191 4644; mtelizabethstationstay.com.au.
- **Birdwood Downs** The focus of this small-scale (by Kimberley standards) station not far from Derby is on pastoral regeneration and horsemanship, which means that activities centre around ecological tours, horseriding lessons and trail-rides. Of course, you don't have to join in: you could just chill out beneath a boab in the pocket-sized bush campground (no caravans) or rustic bungalows (shared bathrooms). Gibb River Rd, 210km north-east of Derby; (08) 9191 1275; birdwooddowns.com.

Opposite Cooling off at Dillie Gorge on Charnley River Station
Right The luxury lodges of El Questro Homestead

- **Caravanning and camping** At El Questro camping is at the Station (the resort's main hub with store, restaurant, bar, helipad and swimming hole, 26km from Emma Gorge) where there are powered and unpowered sites – you'll need to book if you want one of the 48 powered sites. For those wanting a quieter camp there are also 30 riverside sites beside the Pentecost River, about a 10-minute drive from the facilities at the Station. (See above; elquestro.com.au.) Home Valley Station has powered sites (book ahead) at the homestead camp, or bush camp beside the Pentecost River (see above; hvstation.com.au). You can also camp at Drysdale River Station (drysdaleriver.com.au), Mount Elizabeth Station (mtelizabethstationstay.com.au), Manning Gorge on Mount Barnett Station and Charnley River Station (australianwildlife.org), and at Imintji Roadhouse. There are national park campgrounds at Mitchell Falls and Munurru (King Edward River). The campgrounds at Bell Gorge (King Leopold Ranges Conservation Park) and Windjana Gorge National Park have hot showers and flush toilets, but fill quickly during busy school holiday periods.

This drive will take you to all the icons of the Australian outback: Alice Springs, Kings Canyon and Uluṟu.

Red Centre, NT

HOW LONG?

You'll need to spend about four days driving; however, as there is so much to see and do in the Red Centre, you should plan to spend at least two or three days in each place. If you only have time to stop at one of the gorges in the Tjoritja–West MacDonnell Ranges, make it Ellery Creek Big Hole, a perfect spot for a swim.

WHEN TO GO

The temperature range is extreme and travelling through the Red Centre in summer can be uncomfortable, with flies in plague proportions. The best time to go is April through to October. Winter days may be warm, but nights (and early mornings) can be very cold, so take warm clothes.

NEED TO KNOW

The unsealed Mereenie Loop Road, from Kings Canyon to Alice Springs, is 330km. Much of the land is Aboriginal owned, so you need a permit to travel through it. Permits costs $5 and are available from the visitor centre in Alice Springs, Hermannsburg, Glen Helen Gorge, Kings Canyon Service Station and the Central Land Office in Alice Springs (27 Stuart Hwy). The permit must be carried with you at all times while travelling through Aboriginal land. No alcohol is permitted in Aboriginal communities.

Drive rating
Moderate. Some unsealed roads with corrugations and bulldust – 4WD or SUV recommended – and some sections not suitable for caravans

Distances
Total distance, return loop from Alice Springs: approximately 1080km
- Alice Springs to Kings Canyon: 330km
- Kings Canyon to Ayers Rock Resort: 305km
- Ayers Rock Resort to Uluṟu: 18km
- Ayers Rock Resort to Alice Springs: 445km

Temperatures
January: 22–37°C
July: 4–19°C

More information
- Alice Springs Visitor Information Centre, cnr Parsons St and Todd Mall, Alice Springs; (08) 8952 5800; discovercentralaustralia.com

Snapshot
The Red Centre is a place of endless surprises. The bush stories and legends of Australia's harsh outback fail to prepare most people for its stark beauty; similarly, tales of starving pioneers and dying explorers mean many are surprised by the feast of bush tucker available. And these days staying in the desert can be as luxurious, or as rough, as you want to make it.

Opposite top left Local skink blends into the landscape *Top right* Camel tours offer a welcome break from driving *Bottom left* The dramatic hues of Walpa Gorge, Uluṟu–Kata Tjuṯa National Park *Bottom right* Magnificent Uluṟu sunrise

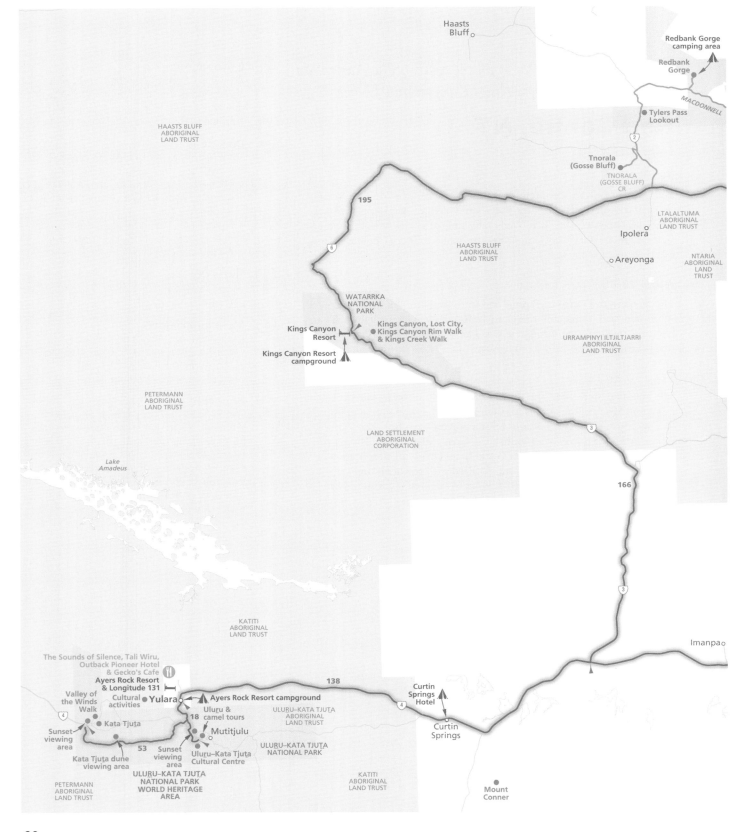

Red Centre, NT

Haasts
Bluff

Redbank Gorge
camping area

Redbank
Gorge

MACDONNELL

Tylers Pass
Lookout

HAASTS BLUFF
ABORIGINAL
LAND TRUST

2

Tnorala
(Gosse Bluff)

TNORALA
(GOSSE BLUFF)
CR

LTALALTUMA
ABORIGINAL
LAND TRUST

Ipolera

195

HAASTS BLUFF
ABORIGINAL
LAND TRUST

Areyonga

NTARIA
ABORIGINAL
LAND
TRUST

6

WATARRKA
NATIONAL
PARK

Kings Canyon
Resort

Kings Canyon, Lost City,
Kings Canyon Rim Walk
& Kings Creek Walk

URRAMPINYI ILTJILTJARRI
ABORIGINAL
LAND TRUST

Kings Canyon Resort
campground

3

PETERMANN
ABORIGINAL
LAND TRUST

LAND SETTLEMENT
ABORIGINAL
CORPORATION

166

Lake
Amadeus

3

Imanpa

KATITI
ABORIGINAL
LAND TRUST

The Sounds of Silence, Tali Wiru,
Outback Pioneer Hotel
& Gecko's Cafe

Ayers Rock Resort
& Longitude 131

Valley of
the Winds
Walk

Cultural
activities

Yulara

4

Kata Tjuṯa

Sunset
viewing
area

Kata Tjuṯa dune
viewing area

18

Ayers Rock Resort campground

Uluṟu &
camel tours

Mutitjulu

Sunset
viewing
area

53

Uluṟu–Kata Tjuṯa
Cultural Centre

ULUṞU–KATA TJUṮA
NATIONAL PARK
WORLD HERITAGE
AREA

138

ULUṞU–KATA TJUṮA
ABORIGINAL
LAND TRUST

ULUṞU–KATA TJUṮA
NATIONAL PARK

Curtin
Springs
Hotel

4

Curtin
Springs

KATITI
ABORIGINAL
LAND TRUST

PETERMANN
ABORIGINAL
LAND TRUST

Mount
Conner

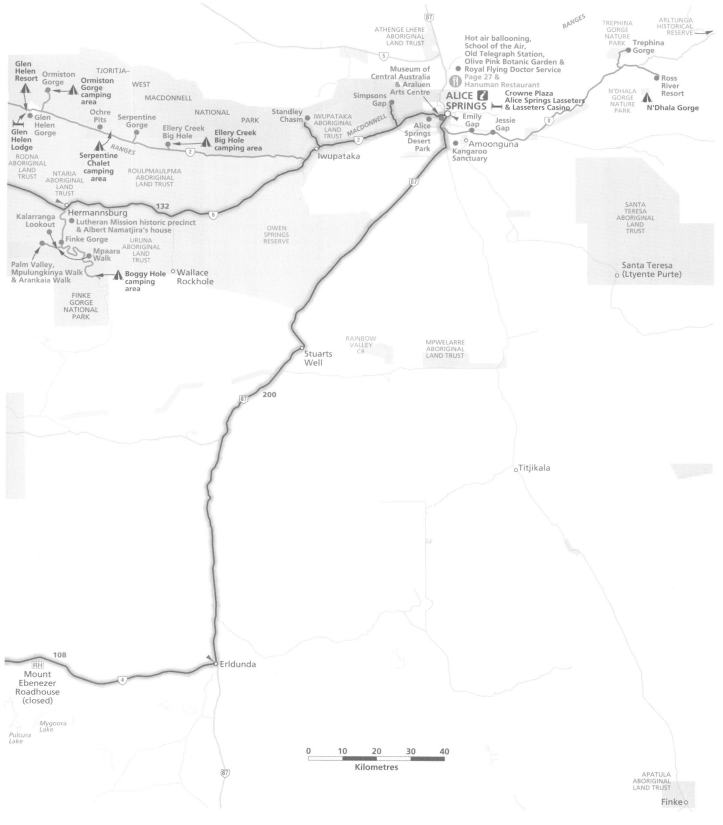

Glen
Helen
Resort

Ormiston Gorge

**Ormiston
Gorge camping
area**

TJORITJA–

WEST

MACDONNELL

Ochre
Pits

Serpentine
Gorge

Glen Helen
Gorge

**Glen
Helen
Lodge**

NATIONAL

Ellery Creek
Big Hole

PARK

**Ellery Creek
Big Hole
camping area**

Standley
Chasm

IWUPATAKA
ABORIGINAL
LAND
TRUST

Simpsons
Gap

ATHENGE LHERE
ABORIGINAL
LAND TRUST

Hot air ballooning,
School of the Air,
Old Telegraph Station,
Olive Pink Botanic Garden &
Royal Flying Doctor Service
Page 27 &
Hanuman Restaurant

**ALICE
SPRINGS**

Crowne Plaza
Alice Springs Lasseters
& Lasseters Casino

RANGES

TREPHINA
GORGE
NATURE
PARK

Trephina
Gorge

ARLTUNGA
HISTORICAL
RESERVE

N'DHALA
GORGE
NATURE
PARK

Ross
River
Resort

N'Dhala Gorge

Museum of
Central Australia
& Araluen
Arts Centre

Alice
Springs
Desert
Park

Emily
Gap

Jessie
Gap

Amoonguna

Kangaroo
Sanctuary

RODNA
ABORIGINAL
LAND
TRUST

RANGES

NTARIA
ABORIGINAL
LAND
TRUST

Serpentine
Chalet
camping
area

ROULPMAULPMA
ABORIGINAL
LAND TRUST

132

Hermannsburg

Lutheran Mission historic precinct
& Albert Namatjira's house

Kalarranga
Lookout

Finke Gorge

Mpaara
Walk

**Palm Valley,
Mpulungkinya Walk
& Arankaia Walk**

URUNA
ABORIGINAL
LAND
TRUST

Boggy Hole
camping
area

Wallace
Rockhole

FINKE
GORGE
NATIONAL
PARK

OWEN
SPRINGS
RESERVE

Iwupataka

MACDONNELL

SANTA
TERESA
ABORIGINAL
LAND
TRUST

RAINBOW
VALLEY
CR

MPWELARRE
ABORIGINAL
LAND TRUST

Santa Teresa
(Ltyente Purte)

Stuarts
Well

200

Titjikala

Erldunda

108

Mount
Ebenezer
Roadhouse
(closed)

Mygoora
Lake

Pulcura
Lake

0   10   20   30   40
Kilometres

APATULA
ABORIGINAL
LAND TRUST

Finke

Bucket-list drives

ALICE SPRINGS TO KINGS CANYON

'The Alice' is the gateway to Uluṟu, but many people are surprised to discover once they get there that Uluṟu is still a five-hour drive away. This drive loop takes the long-but-beautiful way there. Before you head off though, spend a couple of days exploring this iconic outback town.

Must-see attractions in Alice Springs include the Alice Springs Desert Park, a zoo, botanic garden and museum all wrapped up in one superb arid-landscape park (871 Larapinta Dr; (08) 8951 8788; open Mon–Sun 7.30am–6pm, last entry 4.30pm; alicespringsdesertpark.com.au). Another highlight is the old telegraph station beside the original Alice Springs waterhole (Alice Springs Telegraph Station Historical Reserve, Herbert Heritage Dr, 4km north of town via the Stuart Hwy; (08) 8952 3993; open Mon–Sun 8.30am–5pm). The Araluen Arts Centre has several galleries of central Australian Aboriginal Art as well as one of the country's largest collection of works by Albert Namatjira. If you're here in September or October, don't miss the annual Desert Mob exhibition. (61 Larapinta Dr; (08) 8951 1120; open Mon–Sun 10am–4pm; araluenartscentre.nt.gov.au.)

Just nearby is the Museum of Central Australia (4 Memorial Ave; (08) 8951 1121; open Mon–Sun 10am–4pm). You can also take a tour of Kangaroo Sanctuary, set up by TV's Kangaroo Dundee (by guided tour only; (08) 8965 0038; kangaroosanctuary.com); watch the sunrise over the desert in a hot-air balloon (outbackballooning.com.au); and visit the Royal Flying Doctor Service Tourist Facility, where you can see inside a flying-doctor plane (8 Stuart Tce; (08) 8958 8411; Mon–Sat 9am–5pm, Sun 1–5pm, tours run every half-hour 9am–4pm; flyingdoctor.org.au). Founded by local character and Aboriginal Rights activist Olive Pink, at the ripe old age of 72, the Olive Pink Botanic Garden features more than 2500 plantings of almost 500 central Australian plants, as well as a sculpture trail (Tuncks Rd; (08) 8952 2154; open Mon–Sun 8am–6pm; opbg.com.au).

From the Alice, head west on Larapinta Drive, driving across the desert plains beside the ancient Tjoritja–West MacDonnell Ranges, also known as the West Macs. The landscape here is all about colour – red rocks and sand, blue sky, yellow spinifex and purple hills. Just 18km from Alice Springs is Simpsons Gap, a spectacular cleft in the red rocky range. A few kilometres further on is Standley Chasm, less than 9m wide yet towering to a height of 80m. The best time to see it is at midday, when the sun, directly overhead, lights up the walls and floor of the rocky chasm. Don't leave without trying the mango ice-cream at the kiosk cafe.

Continue south-west on Larapinta Drive. Travelling this road, also known as the Mereenie Loop Road, it feels as if you have stepped inside the frame of a classic outback landscape painting. Appropriately, you'll pass by the former Lutheran mission, Hermannsburg, that was the birthplace and home of Aboriginal artist Albert Namatjira, whose paintings of red rocks and dunes, hazy purple mountains and tall desert oaks are some of the most familiar images of outback Australia. His tiny two-room house is just a kilometre or two west of the Hermannsburg community and is open for self-guided tours; you can also tour the old mission buildings in Hermannsburg, including the church and school, mess house, manse and sleeping quarters (Hermannsburg Historic Precinct; (08) 8956 7402; open Mon–Sun 9am–5pm; hermannsburg.com.au).

An alternative route is to drive deeper into the West Macs along Namatjira Drive and link up with the Mereenie Loop Road 100km west of Hermannsburg. The Namatjira Drive turn-off is a few kilometres west of Standley Chasm; the road is sealed to Glen Helen Gorge, but beyond there you'll need a 4WD. It's a stunning drive, one of the outback's best. Highlights include a number of waterholes framed by red rocky gorge walls, including Ellery Creek Big Hole; Serpentine Gorge; the Ochre Pits, where Arrernte people have long mined ochre for ceremonies and trade; Ormiston Gorge; Glen Helen Gorge; and Redbank Gorge. South-west of the ranges, Tnorala (Gosse Bluff) is a huge crater formed by an asteroid or a comet more than 130 million years ago. The Aboriginal Creation story for the crater mirrors the scientific one: a group of women were dancing across the sky as the Milky Way, when a mother put her baby in a wooden baby-carrier. The carrier toppled over the edge of the dancing area and crashed to earth, where it was transformed into the circular rock walls of Tnorala. There is a good lookout over the crater at Tylers Pass or you can drive (4WD only) into the crater reserve. There's so much to see and do along this stretch of road that you might want to consider overnighting along the way at one of the gorge campgrounds or at Glen Helen Lodge.

From Hermannsburg to Kings Canyon, the road is unsealed and not suitable for caravans (off-road camper trailers are fine, but there are a lot of corrugations), and a 4WD is recommended.

South of Hermannsburg is Finke Gorge National Park, where the highlight is Palm Valley, a beautiful oasis of about 3000 red cabbage palm trees. The last 16km of the road into the park follows the sandy bed of the usually dry Finke River, which means it may be inaccessible after heavy rains. This track can be hard going and is only for experienced 4WD tourers who have a high-clearance vehicle or a robust off-road motorhome (if you have a trailer, don't try to take it all the way in to Palm Valley: unhitch it at the campground). The two-hour Mpaara Walk takes you up onto rocky ridgetops for fantastic views of a natural amphitheatre; storyboards along the way recount an Arrernte legend told to young Aboriginal children to discourage them from walking in these hills alone. A shorter 45-minute walk takes you to Kalarranga Lookout for similar views of the amphitheatre from the opposite side. In Palm Valley, walk through the oasis of palm trees and cycads on the two-hour Mpulungkinya Walk or the shorter one-hour Arankaia Walk.

From the Finke Gorge turn-off, continue west then south to Watarrka National Park, which will take about three hours. The park protects Kings Canyon and its breathtaking 300m sheer cliffs. The three-hour, 6km walk around the rim of the canyon taking you through spectacular rock formations, such as the Lost City, and by palm-fringed waterholes is a must. The best time to tackle it is either early in the morning, before the heat and flies begin to fray tempers, or late in the afternoon, when the setting sun lights up the sheer sandstone walls of the canyon to their best advantage. The first half-hour or so is a lung-busting, muscle-destroying climb up the side of the canyon, but, if you can make it that far, the remainder of the walk is an easy stroll around the rim. A less strenuous alternative is the one-hour Kings Creek Walk into the floor of the canyon.

Opposite Walking the rim of of Kings Canyon
Left Taking a dip at Ellery Creek Big Hole

KINGS CANYON TO ULURU

From Kings Canyon it's bitumen all the way to Uluru, and the drive will take roughly three hours. Look out along the way for Mount Connor, a huge flat-topped mesa rising from the desert plains that is so often mistaken for Uluru by first-time visitors that tour guides have nicknamed it 'fooluru'. You'll start to see your first glimpses of Uluru about 50km or so from Yulara, the resort village near the rock. And it doesn't matter how many times you've seen it before, it's always mesmerising.

For the Traditional Owners, the Anangu people, Uluru and nearby Kata Tjuta (the Olgas) are fundamental to their spiritual beliefs and you can learn about the Creation stories and ceremonies associated with the land at the Cultural Centre inside Uluru–Kata Tjuta National Park. The climbing route to the top of Uluru was closed, in accordance with the wishes of the Anangu, in October 2019, but there are many wonderful walks, waterholes and rock-art galleries around its base worth exploring – allow three and a half hours to walk the track that circumnavigates the rock and carry plenty of water.

The most spectacular times to visit Uluru are sunrise and sunset, when the red rock takes on different colours in the changing light, and there are special viewing areas inside the park and at various locations around Ayers Rock Resort. Tours and other activities are available, including guided walks, stargazing tours, special breakfasts and dinners served outdoors in sight of the rock, and camel rides (ulurucameltours.com.au).

The huge, weathered domes of Kata Tjuta, which lie 53km from Yulara, are just as impressive as Uluru. The 8km Valley of the Winds Walk winds along a rocky trail past sheer rock faces and unusual rock formations to a magnificent lookout, but if that's too long for you the Walpa Gorge Walk is a gentle one-hour-return hike into a serene canyon.

If you are returning to Alice Springs, it's an easy run of about 445km on an all-sealed road.

SIDETRACK

The rocky ramparts and spectacular gorges of the East Macs are every bit as spectacular as the West Macs but are overlooked by most travellers. Emily Gap and Jesse Gap are only a few minutes' drive from Alice Springs on the Ross Highway and are great picnic spots. Emily Gap is an important place in the local caterpillar (Yeperenye) Creation story and there are some amazing examples of caterpillar rock art here. At Trephina Gorge, 85km east of Alice on a sealed road (the last 5km is unsealed but fine for 2WD), there are some fantastic walking trails along the floor and around the rim of the large semicircular canyon. About 12km further on, the Ross River Resort serves up monster-sized burgers for lunch (7829 Ross Hwy, Hale; (08) 8956 9711; rossriverresort.com.au). If you have a 4WD, N'Dhala Gorge is one of the most impressive rock-art sites in the Red Centre, with more than 5900 Aboriginal petroglyphs (rock engravings). Two distinct styles of engravings – pecked and pounded – represent two time periods, somewhere between 2000 and 10,000 years ago. The turn-off is just before Ross River Resort and there is a deep water crossing on the way in that can get tricky if there have been recent rains. The ghost town of Arltunga is 46km east of Ross River Resort (114km east of Alice Springs) and was a thriving gold-rush town back in the 1890s and the first official town in central Australia. These days it's an outdoor museum: wander around the government battery, cyanide works, old police station, mines and homes, or fossick for gold in the adjacent reserve.

KIDS' SPOT

The Red Centre offers heaps of fabulous activities for kids. Walk with kangaroos and watch the free-flying bird-of-prey shows at Alice Springs Desert Park (871 Larapinta Dr; (08) 8951 8788; open Mon–Sun 7.30am–6pm, last entry 4.30pm; alicespringsdesertpark.com.au). See how bush kids do school at the School of the Air (80 Head St; (08) 8951 6834; open Mon–Sat 8.30am–4.30pm, Sun 1–4.30pm). Ride the camels at Uluru, and explore Indigenous culture with the family-friendly activities (many of them free) at Ayers Rock Resort (see Best sleeps), including dot-painting classes (popular with both adults and kids), didgeridoo playing, spear and boomerang throwing, storytelling and stargazing.

BEST EATS

- **Hanuman Restaurant** This restaurant has some of the best food in Alice Springs, most of it a spicy mix of Thai, Indian and Nyonya dishes. At the Hilton Doubletree Hotel, 82 Barrett Dr, Alice Springs; (08) 8953 7188; open Mon–Sun for dinner, Mon–Fri for lunch, bookings essential.
- **Page 27** This buzzy cafe is a little bit of Melbourne laneway cool in the middle of Alice Springs, serving good coffee and light lunches, with lots of vegan and gluten-free options. 3 Fan Arcade, off Todd Mall, Alice Springs; 0429 003 874; open Tues–Sun for breakfast and lunch.
- **Ayers Rock Resort** Each of the four hotels at Ayres Rock Resort has restaurants and bars (there are also a number in the Yulara town centre), but the best value-for-money option (and one of the most convivial) is the cook-it-yourself barbecue at the bar in the Outback Pioneer Hotel. Another good-value spot is Gecko's Cafe in the town square, which serves gourmet pizzas, pastas and salads. The Sounds of Silence dinner atop a sand dune near Ayers Rock Resort is not your average bush barbecue: after a buffet dinner of fresh barramundi, lamb, kangaroo or emu steaks and delicious desserts, the lanterns are dimmed, the port poured and the legends of the southern sky explained by a local astronomer. For a more intimate experience, the Tali Wiru dinner (April–Oct) caters for just 20 guests at a time, serving champagne and a four-course table d'hôte dinner with matching wines, followed by port and cognac served around a fire while a guide tells Indigenous stories. Neither is recommended for children under 10 and both are expensive, but they are absolutely worth the splurge. 1300 134 044; ayersrockresort.com.au.

BEST SLEEPS

- **Crowne Plaza Alice Springs Lasseters** The best beds in Alice Springs are the premium rooms here; there's a great swimming pool and Lasseters Casino, with its late-night bars, restaurants and entertainment, is just next door. 93 Barrett Dr, Alice Springs; (08) 8950 7777; ihg.com.
- **Glen Helen Lodge** The basic airconditioned ensuite rooms are a bit overpriced for what you get, but unless you are set up to camp there's not much choice out here – and the resort is in a beautiful spot beside the gorge. Avoid rooms 10–17 as they are next door to a noisy diesel generator, which runs all night. Pets are welcome in the campground and campers can use the pool and other resort facilities. Namatjira Dr, Glen Helen; (08) 8956 7208; glenhelenlodge.com.au.
- **Kings Canyon Resort** The resort has hotel rooms with shaded verandahs and desert views, as well as lodge rooms, glamping tents and powered caravan sites (the caravan sites have sensational sunset views). Luritja Rd, Watarrka National Park; 1800 837 168; kingscanyonresort.com.au.
- **Ayers Rock Resort** Six accommodation options are available here to suit varying budgets: the five-star Sails in the Desert; Desert Gardens (some rooms have views of Uluṟu); the family-friendly Emu Walk apartments; the mid-range Lost Camel and the Outback Pioneer Hotel for those on a budget; and the pet-friendly Ayers Rock campground with drive-through powered caravan sites and airconditioned cabins (shared bathrooms). 1300 134 044; ayersrockresort.com.au.
- **Longitude 131** If money is no object, or you're celebrating a special occasion, this super-luxury wilderness camp is worth the splash-out. You can even see Uluṟu from your bed! It doesn't come cheap though – more than $3000 a night for two – but it does include all food, drinks and tours. Yulara Dr, Yulara; (08) 8296 8010; longitude131.com.au.
- **Caravanning and camping** There are camping and caravan facilities at Glen Helen Lodge, Kings Canyon Resort and Ayers Rock Resort, and free camping and caravan sites at Curtin Springs Hotel, about an hour's drive east of Yulara. There are also basic camping facilities at Ellery Creek Big Hole and Redbank Gorge in Tjoritja–West MacDonnell National Park, and you can bush camp at Serpentine Chalet and 2-Mile (also in Tjoritja–West MacDonnell National Park but 4WD only), but there are no facilities. Ormiston Gorge has camping and caravan facilities with showers and toilets, and the campground beside the Finke River in Finke Gorge also has hot showers – neither campground has power, however.

Fine dining with a view at Ayers Rock Resort's Tali Wiru dinner

Drive across the famous Nullarbor Plain, where camels roam and you feel as if you can see forever, on one of the longest, straightest pieces of road in the world.

Across the Nullarbor, WA and SA

HOW LONG?

It's at least a five- or six-day drive, one way, capital to capital. If you want to get across the same country in a hurry while sitting back and taking it easy, consider putting your car on the Indian Pacific's Motorail service – see journeybeyondrail.com.au.

WHEN TO GO

Summer can be extremely hot. The best time to travel is during the winter months, when days are dry and warm, though nights can be freezing. Whale season is between June and October.

NEED TO KNOW

Don't drive at night: wandering stock are a real hazard, as are wild camels. The longest sections without fuel are about 200km. Carry plenty of drinking water: if caravanning or camping, make sure you have enough water to last the trip, particularly as most roadhouses along the way rely on tank water and will not allow you to fill up your water tanks for free. Stock up on tinned food because you'll have to surrender all fresh fruit and vegetables, nuts and honey at the South Australia–Western Australia border; cooked food is okay though, so have a cook-up the night before to get you through the next couple of nights if you don't fancy eating out of a tin. Carry some snacks: most of the roadhouse food is less than gourmet. Roadhouses along the way sell frozen bread, long-life milk and a limited selection of over-priced basics.

Drive rating
Moderate. Sealed roads with long distances between stops

Distances
Total distance, Perth to Adelaide (without detours): approximately 2700km
- Perth to Kalgoorlie: 596km
- Kalgoorlie to Norseman: 187km
- Norseman to Balladonia: 191km
- Balladonia to Cocklebiddy: 247km
- Cocklebiddy to Eucla: 260km
- Eucla to Nullarbor Roadhouse: 186km
- Nullarbor Roadhouse to Ceduna: 297km
- Ceduna to Gawler Ranges (Wudinna): 210km
- Gawler Ranges to Adelaide: 565km

Temperatures
January: 10–40°C
July: 4–25°C

More information
- Ceduna Visitor Information Centre, 58 Poynton St, Ceduna; (08) 8625 3343; cedunatourism.com.au
- Kalgoorlie Goldfields Visitor Centre, 316 Hannan St, Kalgoorlie; (08) 9021 1966; kalgoorlietourism.com
- nullarbornet.com.au

Snapshot
The drive from Perth to Adelaide across the Nullarbor is a long trip – it will take you at least four days just to get to Ceduna, which is still two days away from Adelaide. And there's no denying it's flat, with long sections of empty, straight road between tiny settlements where shopping, nightlife and good coffee just don't exist. But once you've done the trip, you could never argue that it was boring, nor could you say there was nothing to see. And as for the driving – well, quite simply, it's Australia's greatest road trip.

Opposite Flat landscape, endless sky and plenty of wildlife on the Nullarbor

PERTH TO KALGOORLIE

It's almost 600km from Perth to Kalgoorlie, through the wheat belt and goldfields of south-western Western Australia, following, for much of the drive, the so-called Golden Pipeline. An incredible feat of engineering, the pipeline was the vision of Charles Yelverton O'Connor, Chief Engineer of Western Australia from 1891 to 1902, who managed what many people considered impossible: pumping 22,700 cubic metres of water from Mundaring Weir near Perth, lifting it 355m using only eight pumping stations, and delivering it to the thirsty goldfield towns 600km away. Sadly, both the pipeline and his work were subjected to prolonged criticism and scepticism by parliament and the press, and he took his own life in March 1902 – just before the water was turned on.

Gold was first discovered in this region in 1892 and in a few months the rush was in full swing, with thousands of men swarming to the outback to try their luck. The towns along this stretch – Southern Cross, Coolgardie and Kalgoorlie – are full of grand gold-rush-era buildings that testify to the riches found. In Kalgoorlie, keep an eye out for the statue of Paddy Hannan on the corner opposite the Kalgoorlie Hotel. After he and his mates Tom Flanagan and Daniel Shea were forced to camp out when their horse lost a shoe, they stumbled across some alluvial gold nuggets, sparking the gold rush to beat all other gold rushes.

Western Australia still supplies the vast majority of Australia's total gold production. Much of it is dug from the ground along Kalgoorlie's Golden Mile, which has more than 3000km of old underground workings and has yielded more than 49 million ounces of gold so far. See the workings of the modern-day mining industry from the lookout over the Super Pit on the outskirts of Kalgoorlie. This is Australia's largest open-pit goldmine; at 3km long, 1.4km wide and 330m deep, it makes the huge trucks that carry the ore, which are themselves more than 6m high and 7m wide, look like tiny toys.

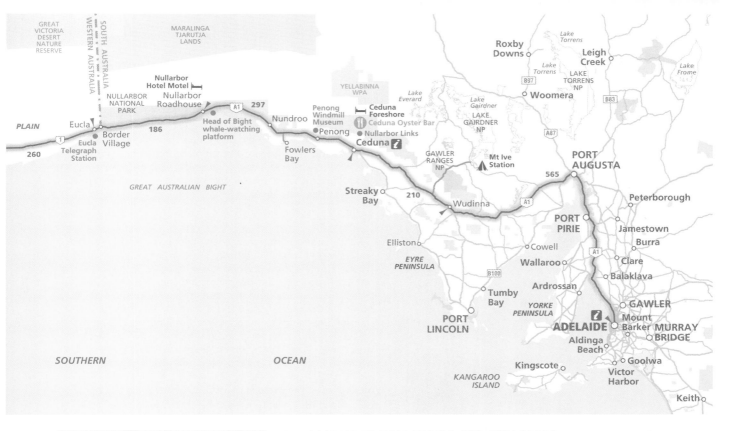

KALGOORLIE TO BALLADONIA AND NULLARBOR

Kalgoorlie is a good place to stock up on fresh fruit and snacks. Once you leave, you begin to hit the true outback; the road gets straighter and the gaps between stops get longer. Norseman, named after a horse who pawed the ground in 1894 and uncovered a gold nugget, is the last 'town' as such until you reach Penong, 1127km away to the east, and your last chance to stock up on any supplies at reasonable prices.

Balladonia was the site of the dramatic crash landing of the US Skylab Space Station in 1979. According to the locals, the Dundas Shire Council presented NASA with a littering fine, and President Jimmy Carter even rang the Balladonia Roadhouse to make his apologies. Indeed, the event caused a (good-natured) diplomatic incident, with the US ambassador to Australia visiting the region to inspect the damage. Parts of the space station are displayed in a museum at the roadhouse.

Beyond Balladonia you are on the Nullarbor Plain, where the road runs due east with hardly a turn or hill along the way and the only stops are roadhouses – now's the time to break out your picnic supplies. The road across the plain includes the longest straight section of sealed road in the country – almost 147km – known as the 90 Mile Straight (although it's actually closer to 91).

Toy-sized monster truck at the Kalgoorlie Super Pit

SIDETRACK

Surrounded by the Nuytsland Nature Reserve, the Eyre Bird Observatory is home to more than 240 species of birds, many rare and endangered. Established in 1977 by Birds Australia, it was, at the time, the first bird observatory in the country. Access is 17km off the highway from Cocklebiddy. To drive all the way to the observatory you'll need a 4WD; trailers and caravans can travel along the access road as far as the carpark at the microwave tower. ((08) 9039 3450; open Mon–Sun during daylight hours; birdlife.org.au/visit-us/observatories/eyre.)

SIDETRACK

Eucla Telegraph Station was established in 1887 and was a bustling (if lonely) little town, but a rabbit plague in the 1890s saw the town abandoned and, by 1927, the telegraph station – one of the most important links in the overland telegraph line that kept the west in touch with the rest of the country – was closed. Since then large sand drifts have repeatedly covered and uncovered the stone buildings, and it's quite eerie wandering around the ruins, half buried in the dunes. They may soon be covered entirely, so see them while you still can. It's signposted just west of the border.

After crossing the Western Australia–South Australia border, you'll reach the section of highway closest to the sea. Tracks veer off to the right, each leading to a lookout over the Bunda Cliffs, where the immense, treeless Nullarbor Plain abruptly meets the Southern Ocean and the Great Australian Bight along an unbroken 200km line of spectacular cliffs, the longest line of sea cliffs in the world.

The world's longest golf course

We all know that the walking you do around a golf course is good exercise, but even the fittest golfer might find they need a set of wheels to complete a round on Nullarbor Links, the longest golf course in the world. Spread across two states and two time zones, the 18-hole, par-72 course spans a mind-boggling 1365km, with one hole in each town or roadhouse along the Eyre Highway, from Kalgoorlie in Western Australia to Ceduna in South Australia. Distances aside, the course has a unique set of challenges. Seven of the holes are on existing golf courses, but 11 have been purpose built and their fairways are just the natural scrub. Crows have been known to steal balls, headwinds can be ferocious and you need to keep an eye out for snakes when you go looking for any lost balls. (Nullarbor Links; 0407 990 049; nullarborlinks.com.)

NULLARBOR TO CEDUNA

At Head of Bight, a dip in the coastline 20km east of Nullarbor Roadhouse, there is a whale-viewing platform where, during the whale season (between June and October), you can see up to 100 southern right whales and their calves lolling in the water at the foot of the cliffs below. The whales come here each year during winter from the freezing Antarctic waters to give birth and it's one of the best whale-watching places in the world.

The lands surrounding the highway east of Nullarbor Roadhouse until almost as far as Nundroo, 145km to the east, are owned by the Anangu people who live in remote communities scattered across the treeless plain. According to their Creation stories, the Head of Bight landscape was formed by Wanampi, the Rainbow Serpent, on a journey from the desert to the sea.

SIDETRACK

Take a short detour off the highway to tranquil Fowlers Bay, a tiny fishing village by the sea with a general store, a few holiday shacks and not much else. It's perfect, however, for dozing in the sun and taking a lazy walk along the long jetty that juts into the ocean. Before road trains took over, grain ships would load up here with the wheat that is still the area's main crop.

From the Fowlers Bay turn-off it's 140km to Ceduna and the beginning of the Eyre Peninsula. You are now travelling through a much lusher landscape, as the saltbush gives way to vast undulating fields of wheat. Stretch your legs at the tiny township of Penong roughly halfway. There has been an assortment of old windmills on the outskirts of Penong for years, but the growing collection – all rescued and restored by local volunteers who call themselves the 'windmill warriors' – officially became the Penong Windmill Museum in late 2016 (West Terrace; open Mon–Sun, free entry). A highlight of the outdoor collection, which currently stands at about 20, includes Bruce, a Comet windpump thought to be the biggest windmill in the country and originally used by the railways to pump water to steam trains.

Appropriately, the name 'Ceduna' comes from the Aboriginal word *chedoona*, which means 'resting place', and the township's services are often a welcome sight after the vast expanse of nothing on the Nullarbor. Take a walk along the jetty and try some of the local oysters (*see* Best eats, p. 33).

Opposite top Historic streetscape, Kalgoorlie *Opposite bottom* A symbol of Australia's outback, windmills at Penong Windmill Museum

CEDUNA TO ADELAIDE

You could take the long way to Adelaide by following the Eyre Peninsula drive (*see* p. 137), but if you stick to Highway 1 you'll skirt the edges of the Gawler Ranges (40km north of Wudinna), one of Australia's oldest mountain ranges at a mind-boggling 1.5 billion years old. Originally more than three times their current height, they have been eroded over millions of years to become a small ridge of weathered hills that rarely rise more than 450m (the highest point is Nukey Bluff at 465m). Rough, rugged and remote, the battered ranges were formed by a massive volcanic eruption that spewed more than 3700 cubic kilometres of lava out of the earth in one massive eruption, leaving behind a dramatic landscape of rock formations, including one of the largest examples of volcanic rhyolite (commonly known as an organ-pipe formation) in the world. Expect to see plenty of wildlife too, particularly kangaroos, wallabies, wombats and emus.

From Wudinna, it's about a six-hour drive to Adelaide via Port Augusta. To cut out some of the distance, you can catch the car ferry from Cowell on the Eyre Peninsula to Wallaroo on the Yorke Peninsula (see seasa.com.au).

SIDETRACK

Lake Gairdner, in the northern reaches of the Gawler Ranges, is the fourth biggest salt lake in the country. It's immensely impressive, a vast empty expanse of sun-baked, white-hot salt that stretches from horizon to horizon under a huge cloudless sky, the desert shoreline a deep blood red. Aside from the annual Dry Lake Racers land-speed event held in March, when motor enthusiasts from all around the world hit the flats in the hope of setting a new world record, Lake Gairdner is a relatively unknown and unvisited area, so, if you like to have your wilderness pretty much to yourself, you'll love it. Lake Gairdner is a surprisingly easy area to visit; the roads are unsealed, but you don't need a 4WD. And there are plenty of places to camp (many of them free) and lots of interesting ruins to explore. It's still remote enough to make you feel you are really out there in the outback – which, of course, you are. It also offers a fascinating alternative to the well-travelled Stuart Highway if you want to get from Port Augusta to Coober Pedy or the Red Centre.

BEST EATS

- **Kalgoorlie Hotel** Overlooking the main street, the restaurant on the verandah of the Kalgoorlie Hotel serves huge steaks and wood-fired pizzas. 319 Hannan St, Kalgoorlie; (08) 9021 3046; open Mon–Sun for lunch and dinner.
- **Balcony Bar and Restaurant** This rather swish restaurant (by Kalgoorlie standards) does especially good steaks and has a selection of fresh seafood. Palace Hotel, 137 Hannan St, Kalgoorlie; (08) 9021 2788; open Mon–Sun for dinner.
- **Balladonia Hotel Motel** Most of the roadhouses on the Nullarbor are justifiably (in)famous for their inedible food, but the cafe at the roadhouse and the restaurant in the adjoining motel (*see* Best sleeps) are the best for miles (literally). Eyre Hwy, Balladonia; (08) 9039 3453; open Mon–Sun for dinner; balladoniahotelmotel.com.au.
- **Ceduna Oyster Bar** Enjoy freshly shucked oysters and a glass of wine under an umbrella on the roof of the oyster shed overlooking the bay. Lot 20 Eyre Hwy; 0497 085 549; open Tues–Sun 10am–6.30pm.

Opposite The stark white landscape of Lake Gairdner *Above* Nullarbor Roadhouse is a welcome sight for tired travellers, offering food, fuel and accommodation

BEST SLEEPS

- **Quest Yelverton Kalgoorlie** This comfortable apartment hotel is within easy walking distance of the centre of town. 210 Egan St, Kalgoorlie; (08) 9022 8181; questkalgoorlie.com.au.
- **Nullarbor roadhouses** Basic hotel, motel and caravan park accommodation is available at all roadhouses along the Nullarbor. The best choices are the Balladonia Hotel Motel (Eyre Hwy, Balladonia; (08) 9039 3453; balladoniahotelmotel.com.au) and the Nullarbor Hotel Motel (Eyre Hwy, 184km east of the Western Australia–South Australia border; (08) 8625 6271). It pays to book during the busy winter season. Most roadhouses on the Nullarbor will allow pets on leashes in the caravan and camping areas; however, you should check before leaving home, as this may change.
- **Ceduna Foreshore** Enjoy ocean views from this waterfront hotel motel. 32 O'Loughlin Tce, Ceduna; (08) 8625 2008; cedunahotel.com.au.
- **Caravanning and camping** No camping is permitted in Nullarbor National Park. There are, however, designated camping areas at roadhouses and you can bush camp at rest areas. In the Gawler Ranges there are several nice, reasonably shady campgrounds with views to red rocky outcrops, although you will need a 4WD to access all of them and there are no facilities. Mount Ive Station near Lake Gairdner has powered and unpowered sites as well as a few bush campsites if you'd prefer to camp without neighbours ((08) 8648 1817; mtive.com.au).

Long weekends and short breaks

*These great spots are perfect for quick getaways,
weekends away and city escapes.*

Explore the magnificent plateaus, gorges and waterfalls of the Blue Mountains, just a short drive from Sydney.

Blue Mountains, NSW

HOW LONG?

You can do this loop in one day, or stretch it out over two or three days by taking all the sidetracks and doing some bushwalks. Taking the Great Western Highway from Sydney is a quicker route than the Bells Line of Road; if you are really short of time, simply head to Katoomba and then come home.

WHEN TO GO

The Blue Mountains region is appealing year-round. During winter it's a great place to go to snuggle up beside a roaring fire on a romantic weekend away. In summer it's the place to go to escape the heat. In autumn it is painted with the fiery hues of the turning leaves, and in spring hundreds of private and public gardens burst into bloom.

NEED TO KNOW

Roads can get icy in winter, particularly early in the morning, so take care. If you are heading to Jenolan Caves there is no fuel available at the caves – fill up at Mount Victoria, Lithgow or Oberon.

Drive rating
Easy. Sealed roads with some winding sections

Distances
Total distance, return to Sydney: 292km
- Sydney to Lithgow via Bells Line of Road: 140km
- Lithgow to Katoomba: 40km
- Katoomba to Sydney: 112km

Temperatures
January: 13–23°C
July: 2–9°C

More information
Visitor Information Centre, Echo Point, Katoomba; 1300 653 408; visitbluemountains.com.au

Snapshot
The massive ridge of mountainous wilderness known as the Blue Mountains is about two hours by car from the centre of Sydney. It's an area of dramatic mountain scenery, home to the well-photographed Three Sisters rock formation and a fantastic place to do some bushwalking.

Previous A quiet spot in Lamington National Park, Queensland *Opposite* Aerial view of the Blue Mountains and Heritage-listed Hydro Majestic Hotel

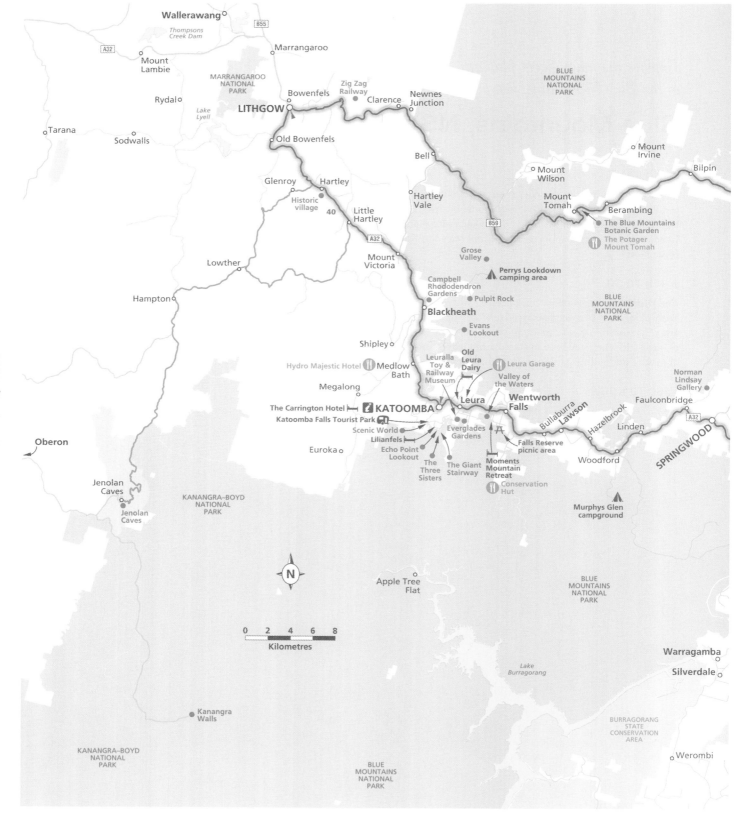

Blue Mountains, NSW

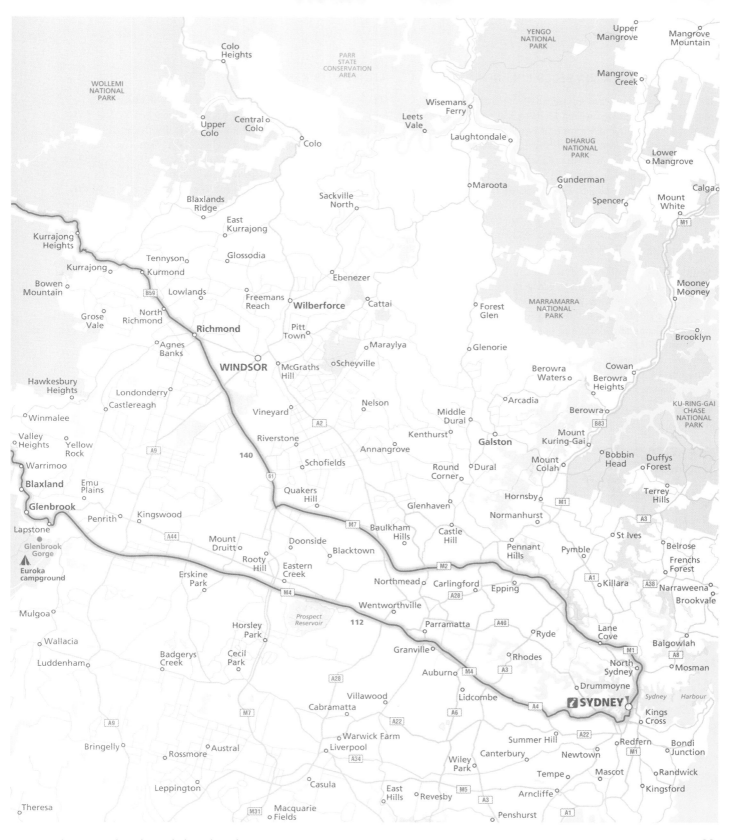

SYDNEY TO LITHGOW VIA BELLS LINE OF ROAD

Most people head into the mountains from Sydney on the Great Western Highway, which leads to Katoomba. However, Bells Line of Road from Richmond is a slower, more scenic and less busy route. You'll travel through Bilpin, a large apple- and stone-fruit-growing area where can you buy fresh fruit from farmgate stalls in season, and then on to Mount Tomah, where the Blue Mountains Botanic Garden has one of the world's finest collections of cool-climate plants (Bells Line of Road, Mount Tomah; (02) 4567 3000; open Mon–Fri 9am–5.30pm, Sat–Sun 9.30am–5.30pm; bluemountainsbotanicgarden.com.au).

If you're a history buff or trainspotter, or have kids in tow, a ride on a steam train on the Zig Zag Railway at Clarence is a must. The railway was built between 1866 and 1869 in a series of sloping tracks forming the letter Z, with reversing stations at the top and bottom. The volunteer-run railway was closed due to damage caused by bushfires in 2013 but is due to reopen in late 2019, so check the website for the latest news. (Chifley Rd, Clarence; 1300 944 924; zigzagrailway.com.au.)

From the Zig Zag Railway it's just 10km to Lithgow, the turning point on our loop.

LITHGOW TO KATOOMBA

The historic village of Hartley, 11km south of Lithgow, was one of the first colonial settlements west of the Blue Mountains and appears today much as it did in the 1870s. The village was settled in 1837 when the courthouse was built as a police centre. The Bathurst gold rush in the 1850s brought about enormous growth and Hartley became a bustling judicial and administrative centre. Take tours of the village (ask at the information centre in the old Farmers Inn) or walk around the site on your own – interpretive boards detail the history of the buildings. This is also a great spot for a picnic: there are tables beside the courthouse.

SIDETRACK

Follow the road signposted to Oberon and Jenolan Caves. It's a steep, narrow and winding road and is not suitable for caravans, but it is simply spectacular – allow at least an hour to get from the highway to the caves. The last section of the road down into the Jenolan Valley is one-way from 11.45am to 1.15pm every day (so the tour coaches can safely negotiate the narrow road), which means that if you want to leave Jenolan Caves in the middle of the day you'll need to go via Oberon. No fuel is available in Jenolan, so make sure you fill your tank at Mount Victoria, Lithgow or Oberon.

There are 280 known caves in the Jenolan Reserve, many richly decorated with stunning limestone formations. Nine of the caves are open to the public and tours leave regularly, ranging from one to two hours. There are also candlelit ghost tours at night and adventure caving tours (jenolancaves.org.au). If you prefer to stay above ground there are many bushwalking tracks – climb up to Carlotta's Arch and the Devil's Coach House Lookdown or stroll beside the river to the cyan-coloured Blue Lake. Jenolan Caves is also a great starting point for the stunning cliff-top walks at Kanangra Walls, a 30-minute drive away in Kanangra–Boyd National Park.

Soon after leaving Hartley the road begins to climb up steep Victoria Pass into the mountains again. At Blackheath, check out Evans Lookout, the Campbell Rhododendron Gardens (in Bacchante Street) and Pulpit Rock, or escape into the Grose Valley for a full-day bushwalk.

Opposite Hiking through the dense Blue Mountains National Park *Left* Passing through the Grand Arch cave at Jenolan Caves

KATOOMBA TO SYDNEY

Katoomba is home to one of the most photographed spots in the state: the Three Sisters. More than two million people come to ogle the rock formation each year. The best view is from Echo Point Lookout, which is also the starting point of the half-hour walk out to the first sister. Another great walk that starts from here is the Giant Stairway. This track, which takes about three hours to complete, descends some 900 steps into the valley and along the base of the cliffs. What goes down must come up, of course, but you can take the easy way and ride back to the top on the Scenic Cableway or the Scenic Railway, both part of the Scenic World complex (1 Violet St, Katoomba; 1300 SKYWAY or (02) 4780 0200; open Mon–Sun 9am–5pm; scenicworld.com.au).

The Scenic Railway is the steepest passenger railway in the world, with a rather startling 52-degree incline. It was originally built in the 1880s as part of a network of tramlines that hauled coal and kerosene shale from mines in the valley up to the main railway. An all-day discovery pass includes unlimited rides on the Scenic Railway, Skyway (the highest cable car in Australia), Cableway (the biggest in Australia) and Walkway (the longest elevated boardwalk in the country).

Cliff Drive winds its way along the cliff edge from Katoomba to Leura. Leura is known as the garden village and its annual Gardens Festival is in October. Everglades Gardens, created by Paul Sorenson in the 1930s, is a magnificent cold-climate heritage garden with formal terraces, Jamison Valley views and a tearoom in the Art Deco house (37 Everglades Ave; (02) 4784 1938; open Mon–Sun 10am–5pm Oct–Mar, 10am–4pm Apr–Sept; nationaltrust.org.au/places/everglades-house-gardens).

Continue east to Wentworth Falls, turn into Falls Road and follow the walk from the Falls Reserve picnic area to the Valley of the Waters. Here spectacular lookouts along the walking tracks offers dramatic views of cliff-top escarpments, waterfalls and the Jamison Valley below.

Another excellent place to stop is the Norman Lindsay Gallery at Faulconbridge. The former home of Australian artist and author Norman Lindsay houses a collection of his oil paintings, watercolours, etchings, drawings, novels, sculptures, ship models and memorabilia, and is set in extensive gardens. (14 Norman Lindsay Cres, Faulconbridge; (02) 4751 1067; open Mon–Sun 10am–4pm; nationaltrust.org.au/places/norman-lindsay-gallery.)

East of Faulconbridge the highway winds to Glenbrook then descends towards Penrith, on the western edge of the Sydney suburban sprawl.

☺ KIDS' SPOT

You don't have to be a kid to enjoy the Leuralla Toy and Railway Museum – after all, we were all kids once. It likes to boast it's the largest collection of toys and trains in the Southern Hemisphere, and it seems to live up to that claim. There's a vast range of antique tin toys, dolls, teddy bears and trains, and the heritage-listed house is surrounded by 5ha of beautiful gardens. 36 Olympian Pde, Leura; (02) 4784 1169; open Mon–Sun 10am–5pm; toyandrailwaymuseum.com.au.

Opposite No trip to the Blue Mountains is complete without stopping to see the Three Sisters at Katoomba *Below* Great coffee and eats at The Potager, Mount Tomah

BEST EATS

- **The Potager Mount Tomah** This cafe is set in the beautiful Blue Mountains Botanic Garden. Bells Line of Road; (02) 4567 2575; open Wed–Sun for breakfast and lunch, bookings recommended on weekends.
- **Hydro Majestic Hotel** Built in 1904 as a health retreat at Medlow Bath, this grand hotel – a rambling mix of Art Deco and castellated Edwardian architecture that stretches more than a kilometre along the cliff-top overlooking the Jamison Valley – is the place to go for afternoon high tea (if you don't like scones opt for the dumplings). 52–88 Great Western Hwy, Medlow Bath; (02) 4782 6885; afternoon tea served Mon–Fri 11am–3pm, Sat–Sun 10.30am–3pm; hydromajestic.com.au.
- **Leura Garage** Housed in an old garage and decorated with miscellaneous bits of old engines, this restaurant has an all-day dining menu meaning you don't have to panic if you get distracted by the scenery on the drive there and turn up late. 84 Railway Pde, Leura; (02) 4784 3391; open Mon–Sun 12pm until late; leuragarage.com.au.
- **Conservation Hut** Relax by the open fire here and enjoy views over the edge of the escarpment. Fletcher St, Wentworth Falls; (02) 4757 3827; open Mon–Sun for breakfast and lunch.

BEST SLEEPS

- **Lilianfels** Hard to beat if you want to splurge for a night or two of indulgence, Lilianfels has superb Jamison Valley views, romantic decor, a day spa, the award-winning Darley's restaurant and resort-style facilities. Lilianfels Ave, Katoomba; (02) 4780 1200; lilianfels.com.au.
- **The Carrington Hotel** Take a step back in time at the first hotel built in Katoomba, back in 1882. The heritage-listed hotel has been restored to reflect its original grandeur. 15–47 Katoomba St, Katoomba; (02) 4782 1111; thecarrington.com.au.
- **Old Leura Dairy** This relaxed, chintz-free, rustic retreat offers a range of luxurious accommodation in beautifully renovated buildings. 61 Kings Rd (cnr Eastview Ave), Leura; (02) 4782 0700; oldleuradairy.com.
- **Moments Mountain Retreat** A luxuriously appointed country house in Wentworth Falls with spectacular views from all rooms. 86 Fletcher St, Wentworth Falls; (02) 4757 4455; moments.com.au.
- **Caravanning and camping** The best campsites are in Blue Mountains National Park; the most popular is Euroka at Glenbrook Gorge. Other good camping spots can be found at Murphys Glen south of Woodford and Perrys Lookdown north of Blackheath. Caravanners should try Katoomba Falls Tourist Park in Katoomba (Katoomba Falls Rd, Katoomba; (02) 4782 1835; bmtp.com.au).

Wind your way through some of the most beautiful rainforest and gorge scenery in Australia, between Coffs Harbour and Armidale in New South Wales.

Waterfall Way, NSW

Since going to print, some of the areas featured in this trip were affected by flooding. Some of the information, particularly about roads in national parks and camping areas, may have since changed – contact local visitor information centres for updates before travelling.

HOW LONG?

It's a full-day drive, one way, plus you should allow a day in Armidale for sightseeing. And you'll need another day if you loop back to the coast via Port Macquarie. If your time is tight and you only have time to stop at one waterfall, make it Ebor Falls, roughly halfway on the drive.

WHEN TO GO

Any time of the year is a good time to do this drive, although Armidale gets very cold in winter, and late summer rains can close sections of the road near Dorrigo (the waterfalls are truly spectacular after rain, however). Autumn (April and early May) is fantastic, as the many deciduous trees in Armidale are ablaze with colour.

NEED TO KNOW

The first section of the road from Coffs Harbour to Dorrigo is narrow and winding; if you suffer from travel sickness, take some medication before you set off – likewise for the final section from Walcha to Wauchope if you take the Oxley Highway home. Dogs are not allowed in the national parks along the way, even if you are only dropping in for half an hour or so to visit a lookout or unpack a picnic.

Opposite top left WWII tank traps near Ebor *Top right* Enjoying the scenery along the Crystal Shower Falls walk in Dorrigo National Park *Bottom left* Lyrebird Circuit, New England National Park *Bottom right* Ellenborough Falls

Drive rating
Easy. Sealed roads with some winding sections

Distances
Total distance, Coffs Harbour to Armidale: 190km
- Coffs Harbour to Dorrigo: 65km
- Dorrigo to Ebor: 37km
- Ebor to Armidale: 88km
- Armidale to Port Macquarie via Oxley Hwy extension: 250km

Temperatures
January: 16–31°C
July: 3–16°C

Note: These temperatures are for the Armidale region. The coast is much milder during winter, when minimum temperatures rarely fall below 7 or 8°C.

More information
- Armidale Visitor Information Centre, 82 Marsh St, Armidale; (02) 6770 3888; armidaletourism.com.au
- Coffs Coast Visitor Information Centre, Park Beach Plaza, 253 Pacific Hwy, Coffs Harbour; (02) 6552 4366; coffscoast.com.au
- Port Macquarie Visitor Information Centre, inside the Glasshouse, cnr Clarence and Hay sts, Port Macquarie; 1300 303 155; portmacquarieinfo.com.au

Snapshot
This classic touring drive starts on the mid-north coast at the banana-clad beach-resort town of Coffs Harbour and coils its way up through the luxuriant World Heritage rainforest of the Great Divide to the New England tablelands, finishing in Armidale. Although you could do the whole drive in less than a day, to do so would mean missing out on several of the very good short walks in the national parks and zooming past countless perfect picnic spots. This is one trip where the road itself really is the destination, not just a way to get somewhere else.

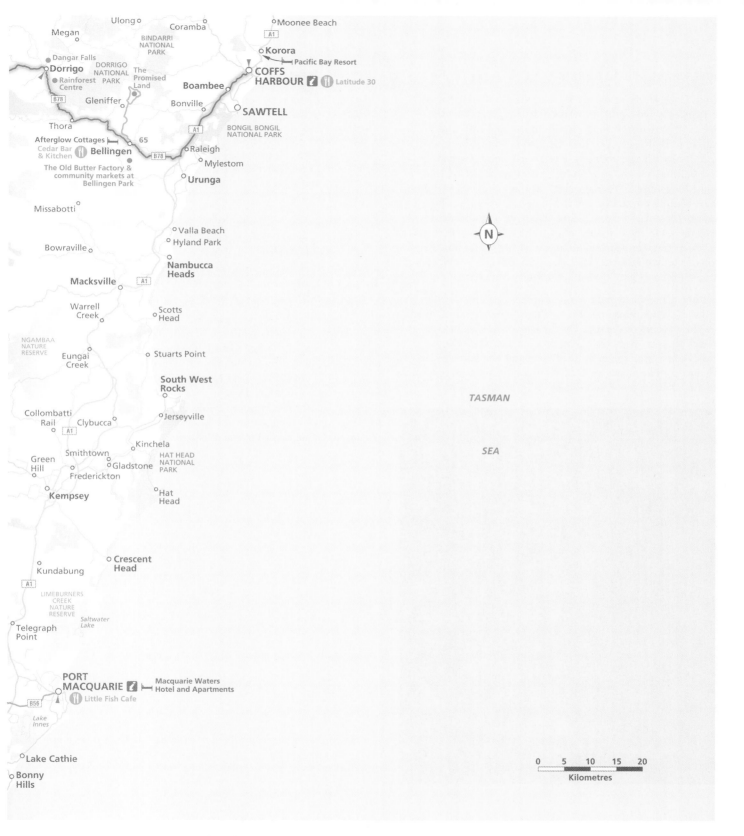

COFFS HARBOUR TO DORRIGO

From Coffs Harbour, head south on the Pacific Highway to the sleepy river estuary town of Urunga, then take the Waterfall Way west into the fertile hinterland hills and valleys to Bellingen. The lush farmlands around here were once covered in great forests of red cedar and rosewood, and Bellingen began as a timber-getting town during the mid-19th century. The red cedar was soon all gone, and the town became the centre of a rich dairying industry. These days Bellingen is a lively centre for artists and alternative lifestylers. On the east side of town the Old Butter Factory has been transformed into an arts retailing centre and is a popular tourist attraction (1 Doepel St; (02) 6655 2150; open Mon–Sun 9am–5pm; theoldbutterfactory.com.au).

Bellingen's historic main street is an eclectic mix of cafes, galleries, restaurants and shops, where free-range and organic are the flavours of the day. On the third Saturday of each month the very popular community markets in Bellingen Park have a wide range of handmade and homegrown produce and local arts and crafts, and are a great place to pick up a bargain or some interesting valley-made souvenirs.

SIDETRACK

Although it's not officially part of the Waterfall Way, the beautiful short loop drive just north of Bellingen through the peaceful farming valley called the Promised Land is well worth doing. From the centre of town cross the Bellinger River and follow the signs to Gleniffer, where you'll see the sign pointing the way to the Promised Land (how can you resist?). The whimsy continues as you follow the course of Never Never Creek, through lush rainforest and bucolic green valleys. The drive will take about 45 minutes return to Bellingen.

From Bellingen the Waterfall Way winds up through the rainforest to the mountain-top town of Dorrigo, passing several roadside waterfalls and lookouts along the way. As you climb, the humid coastal air gets cooler and the forests denser, until the steep, often narrow road finally reaches the Dorrigo Plateau, 762m above sea level.

Situated just before Dorrigo township, Dorrigo National Park is a great place to explore, whether it's for a quick one-hour visit or an entire day spent following one of the longer bushwalks. Don't miss the Rainforest Centre (142 Dome Rd, Dorrigo; (02) 6657 2309; open Mon–Sun 9am–4.30pm), which has an excellent interpretive display, and the Skywalk, a dramatic boardwalk above the rainforest canopy that leads out over the edge of the escarpment for spectacular views across the rainforest and down to the coast.

Opposite Bucolic views at Petersons Guesthouse and Winery in Armidale *Left* Epic views of Crystal Shower Falls

DORRIGO TO ARMIDALE

Just out of Dorrigo is stunning Dangar Falls, on the eastern edge of the high-plateau gorge country. The viewing area is an easy walk from the carpark, or take the 30-minute-return bushwalk to the Bielsdown River.

From Dorrigo the road rolls across the tablelands through open grazing country. In summer the air is cool and dry; in winter expect very chilly conditions, frequent fog and mist and even occasional snow. At Ebor, a blink-and-you'll-miss-it whistlestop about half an hour down the road, you'll find Ebor Falls. At 1500m above sea level, the Guy Fawkes River rarely runs dry, making these spectacular double falls one of the most reliable of all the falls on the Waterfall Way.

Another 10km or so further south, it's worth taking the detour on the left to drive 15km to Point Lookout. Enjoy the short walk here through the misty, moss-covered, high-altitude rainforest to two viewing platforms that provide magnificent panoramic views to the north, east and south. On clear days you will see as far as the coast, 70km away, although mist and fog can roll in at a minute's notice. You'll also find a lovely picnic area and day shelter here and a number of good bushwalking trails.

Back on the Waterfall Way, the road skirts the edge of Oxley Wild Rivers National Park, home to two more magnificent waterfalls and rugged gorge country. There is a waterfall lookout at Wollomombi Gorge, where the spectacular single fall (one of the highest in Australia) is at its most impressive after heavy rain – the falls stop during dry periods.

Armidale, the finishing point of the Waterfall Way, is about half an hour's drive from the national park across rolling high-country plains. It's a lively regional city with a vibrant university and many grand historical buildings, testament to the town's importance as a centre for the surrounding wealthy pastoral grazing properties. Armidale is especially beautiful in autumn (mid to late April), when the turning leaves of the deciduous trees in the many parks and avenues paint the town red, yellow and orange.

Taste some local wines at Petersons Armidale Winery (345 Dangarsleigh Rd; (02) 6772 0422; open Sun–Fri 10am–4pm, Sat 10am–5pm); visit NERAM, the New England Regional Art Museum, home to one of the most significant collections of late-19th- and early-20th-century Australian art outside a capital city (106–114 Kentucky St; (02) 6772 5255; open Tues–Sun 10am–4pm; phone ahead to book a guided tour; neram.com.au); and travel back in time at Saumarez Homestead, where each room remains exactly as it was when the original owners left town, got married or passed away, resulting in a 30-room snapshot of Edwardian life and times (230 Saumarez Rd; (02) 9258 0123; open Sat–Sun and public holidays 10am–5pm, end Aug – mid-June; nationaltrust.org.au/places/saumarez-homestead). You could even splurge on a spectacular helicopter flight over the rugged gorge country of Oxley Wild Rivers National Park (fleethelicopters.com.au).

SIDETRACK

Head south down the New England Highway to Uralla. This is Thunderbolt country, and you've as much chance of escaping the clutches of this cavalier bushranger as the police had of capturing him when he roamed the countryside around Uralla in the 1860s (the rocks he used as a lookout are just south of town). There are all sorts of Thunderbolt artefacts in the McCrossin's Mill Museum (31 Salisbury St; (02) 6778 3022; open Mon–Sun 10am–5pm) and almost every business in town makes the most of the Thunderbolt connection with pies, motels, cafes and monuments all proudly sporting the outlaw's name. Circle back to Armidale via Tourist Drive 19 across the Salisbury Plain, stopping at Gostwyck's little ivy-covered church – in autumn the ivy turns a brilliant red and makes for great photographs. Also stop at the waterfall lookout at Dangars Gorge. The full loop is about 70km.

Take the long way home

For more dramatic waterfalls, loop back to the coast on the Oxley Highway via Uralla, Walcha and Wauchope to Port Macquarie, which is about two hours' drive south of Coffs Harbour. One of the state's most popular motorcycle touring routes, its highlights include Apsley Falls, where the Apsley River spills down a 65m drop into a circular gorge, and Tia Falls, just a few kilometres further on; in both cases, you'll need to take one of the short walks to get a lovely view of the falls.

Take a break in Walcha at either the Royal Cafe in the old bank building or Cafe Graze on the main street – both serve great coffee. Walcha's a bit of an arts hub and there are 41 sculptures scattered around town, as well as a couple of interesting galleries in the main street. It's a lovely drive across the high plains before winding down the range, a slow but incredibly scenic trip through towering tree ferns and dense rainforest. Stop at Gingers Creek Roadhouse around halfway for a drink on the back verandah, looking out over the mountains, then make your way to Wauchope and on to the beaches of Port Macquarie.

SIDETRACK

There's a great detour that turns off the highway about 10km from Wauchope: follow the signs to Ellenborough Falls, just beyond the very pretty mountain-top village of Comboyne. The falls are reputed to be the largest single drop of water in the Southern Hemisphere (the devil's in the detail, as Wollomombi makes the same claim – it all depends on where the water is considered to really 'fall'); take the 642 steps to the bottom or follow the much easier walk through the rainforest to view the falls from the other side of the gorge.

😃 KIDS' SPOT

Parents, be forewarned: the Waterfall Way is not a great drive to do with young kids – it's so twisty that even if they don't normally get car sick they might on this drive. If you do brave the trip with littlies, treat them to a steam-train ride at Wauchope's Timbertown (see p. 182) at the end of the drive. Oxley Hwy, Wauchope; (02) 6586 1940; open Mon–Sun 9.30am–4pm; timbertown.com.au.

BEST EATS

- **Latitude 30** Perched on the edge of the breakwall in the Coffs Harbour marina, Latitude 30 offers great seafood with even greater views, especially if you're lucky enough to be there when dolphins or whales cruise by. 1 Marina Dr, Coffs Harbour; (02) 6651 6888; open Mon–Sun for lunch and dinner.
- **Cedar Bar & Kitchen** Enjoy relaxed regional dining in this lovely old weatherboard former church. 8 Church St, Bellingen; (02) 6655 1001; open Sat–Sun for breakfast, Wed–Sun for lunch, Wed–Sat for dinner; cedarbar.com.au.
- **Fusspots at Ebor** Treat yourself to the homemade buttermilk scones at this quirky little tea shop. They also serve good steak sandwiches and burgers. 33 Ebor St, Ebor; (02) 6775 9299; open Mon–Sun for breakfast and lunch.
- **Archie's on the Park** Snuggle up by the blazing fire in this 1860s homestead. The menu makes use of local lamb, beef and rabbit. Moore Park Inn, Uralla Rd, Armidale; (02) 6772 2358; open Mon–Sun for dinner; mooreparkinn.com.au.
- **Little Fish Cafe** At the end of your drive you could spend a lazy afternoon in this winery cafe, sipping wine and dining under the shade of a spreading jacaranda tree while enjoying the view over vineyards. Innes Lake Vineyards, 147 The Ruins Way, Port Macquarie; (02) 6581 1332; open Mon–Sun for lunch and morning and afternoon tea (cellar door open Mon–Sun); inneslake.com.au.

BEST SLEEPS

- **Pacific Bay Resort** This beachfront resort at Charlesworth Bay, 3km north of Coffs Harbour, has a nine-hole, par-3 golf course, three heated swimming pools, tennis courts, walking and jogging trails, a fitness centre and the Bayside Spa Centre. Cnr Pacific Hwy and Bay Dr, Coffs Harbour; (02) 6659 7000; pacificbayresort.com.au.
- **Afterglow Cottages** Soak in the view from your bathtub on the deck of a self-contained luxury cottage, situated on the edge of the rainforest just a few minutes' drive from Bellingen. 259 Kalang Rd, Bellingen; (02) 6655 2215; afterglowcottages.com.au.
- **Lindsay House** Relax in style in this gracious old country house full of lovely antiques close to the centre of Armidale. 128 Faulkner St, Armidale; (02) 6771 4554; lindsayhouse.com.au.
- **Petersons Guesthouse** This was once the summer home of the Dangar family, one of the great New England pastoral dynasties. Petersons Winery, 345 Dangarsleigh Rd, Armidale; (02) 6772 0422; petersonsguesthouse.com.au.
- **Macquarie Waters Hotel and Apartments** This boutique hotel in the heart of Port Macquarie has a mix of hotel rooms and apartments, many with ocean views. 11 Clarence St, Port Macquarie; (02) 6584 5755; macquariewaters.com.au.
- **Caravanning and camping** There are plenty of good camping sites within cooee of waterfalls in Oxley Wild Rivers National Park at Wollomombi Gorge (caravan access for smaller vans), Dangar Falls, Apsley Gorge and Tia Gorge. Styx River campground on the edge of New England National Park (Point Lookout Rd) has room for camper trailers and caravans and is free and pet friendly, but has no power.

Opposite Apsley Falls in full flood *Left* An inviting bed at Petersons Guesthouse

Relive the glory days of the great Victorian gold rush in grand cities full of magnificent architecture and historic towns that look much the same as they would have 165 years ago.

Goldfields, Vic.

HOW LONG?

You can do this drive in a day, but allow a day or two in both Bendigo and Ballarat to explore the many museums and art galleries. To cut the trip short, take the A300 from Ballarat straight to Bendigo via Daylesford and Castlemaine.

WHEN TO GO

Summers are warm and dry – most rain falls during winter, when temperatures can be quite low.

NEED TO KNOW

Many of the shops, cafes and attractions in the smaller towns and villages are closed during the week: the best time to visit is on the weekend.

Drive rating
Easy. Sealed roads

Distances
Total distance, Ballarat to Bendigo
(with detours): 205km
- Ballarat to Clunes: 35km
- Clunes to Maryborough via Avoca: 70km
- Maldon to Castlemaine: 18km
- Castlemaine to Bendigo: 38km

Temperatures
January: 10–25°C
July: 3–10°C

More information
- Ballarat Visitor Information Centre,
  225 Sturt St, Ballarat; 1800 446 633;
  visitballarat.com.au
- Bendigo Visitor Centre,
  51–67 Pall Mall, Bendigo; 1800 813 153;
  bendigoregion.com.au

Snapshot
The goldfields of Central Victoria, around the Ballarat and Bendigo areas, were once the richest goldfields in the world, attracting hundreds of thousands of hopeful fossickers and miners to the district. In just one decade, from 1851 to 1861, the population of Victoria swelled from 97,000 to almost 540,000. During the same period, the diggings yielded almost 2.6 million ounces of gold each year. The discovery of gold left a rich and lasting legacy of grand hotels and public buildings, historic gardens and homesteads, and quaint shopfronts and miners' cottages.

Opposite top left Many of Ballarat's buildings date back to the 1860s *Top right* Golden leaves line the road to Castlemaine *Bottom left* Gold-rush-era architecture *Bottom right* Detail of Bendigo's Alexandra Fountain

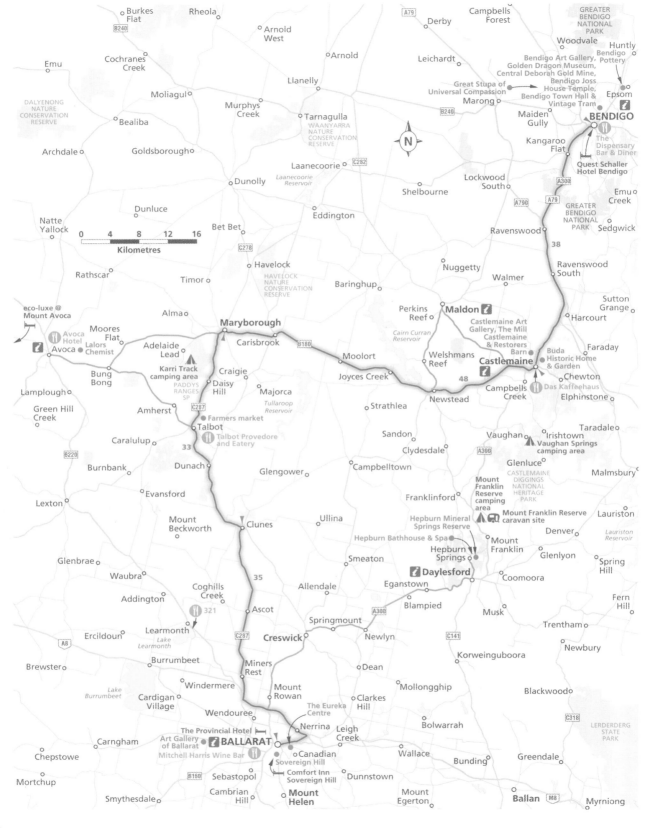

Goldfields, Vic.

BALLARAT TO MARYBOROUGH

Begin your drive tour in Ballarat, site of one of the most significant events in Australian history: the Eureka Rebellion. Gold was first discovered in Ballarat in 1851 and it didn't take long for the pretty little valley with its meandering stream and surrounding ironbark forests to be transformed into a sea of mud, tree stumps and canvas tents. In 1854 ongoing grievances regarding the unfair licence system and government corruption, coupled with the murder of one of the diggers, sparked Australia's first armed rebellion. The events leading up to the short-lived battle are masterfully retold each night in the spectacular outdoor sound-and-light show *Blood on the Southern Cross* at Sovereign Hill, a huge outdoor museum that re-creates Ballarat in the years between 1850 and 1860. Most of the show takes place outside, so rug up! (39 Magpie St, Ballarat; (03) 5337 1199; open Mon–Sun 10am–5pm, bookings essential for the sound-and-light show; sovereignhill.com.au.)

The original, rather tattered Eureka flag is on display at the Eureka Centre on the site of the 1854 Eureka Stockade (102 Stawell St South, Eureka; (03) 5333 0333; open Mon–Sun 10am–5pm).

Below Enjoy the serenity inside and out at popular spa destination Daylesford

The most obvious legacy of the riches that poured into the town is a stunning streetscape of grand Victorian buildings and it is worth spending some time wandering the main streets. The Art Gallery of Ballarat is one of the best regional art galleries in the country (40 Lydiard St North, Ballarat; (03) 5320 5858; open Mon–Sun 10am–5pm; artgalleryofballarat.com.au).

SIDETRACK

Victoria's spa capitals, Daylesford and Hepburn Springs, are only a 40-minute drive from Ballarat. The area, discovered by goldminers in the 1850s, has Australia's richest concentration of mineral springs. But these are no ordinary mineral springs. They are, if you believe the locals, so rich in therapeutic powers that they can relieve just about any ill. You can take the waters by drinking them – there are a number of springs (with lovely old-fashioned hand-operated pumps) in the Hepburn Mineral Springs Reserve where you can fill up as many containers as you can carry, for free. Or soak in them at a number of day spas or the historic Hepburn Bathhouse, which has been going since 1895 (Mineral Springs Reserve Rd, Hepburn Springs; (03) 5321 6000; open Sun–Thurs 9am–6.30pm, Fri–Sat 9am–9pm; hepburnbathhouse.com).

From Ballarat head north to Clunes, a sleepy little place that was once the fifth largest town in the colony but has remained pretty much unchanged for the past 100 years or so. Clunes is also Australia's only official 'booktown'. There are several bookshops in town, selling mostly second-hand volumes, and the village attracts thousands of booklovers to its annual Booktown Festival in early May, when streets are closed to traffic and booksellers and traders from all around the country set up stalls and the old buildings host a program of literary events and writers' workshops.

Continue north to Maryborough. Its historic railway station is a grand monument to a golden age – it's so large that in 1895 writer Mark Twain declared that 'you can put the whole population of Maryborough into it, and give them a sofa apiece, and have room for more'. Today it houses a nice cafe and antiques store.

SIDETRACK

Avoca is your classic goldfields town, with a main street so wide you could turn a bullock team in it. The middle of the main street is now a pretty park, complete with an imposing Art Deco war-memorial rotunda and a tree propagated from the seeds of a pine cone brought back from the Lone Pine battlefield at Gallipoli. Many of the shopfronts retain their historic facades. Some haven't changed at all: Lalors Chemist, established in 1854, is believed to be the oldest continuously operating chemist shop in Victoria.

Below Book lovers unite at Fraser Street Book Bazaar in Clunes

MARYBOROUGH TO BENDIGO

Head east from Maryborough to Castlemaine, regarded as the artistic heart of the goldfields. Its main street is, like those of most of the towns in the region, lined with grand shopfronts, these days housing galleries, cafes and antiques stores. The Theatre Royal is the oldest continuously operating theatre in mainland Australia. Castlemaine Art Gallery was one of the first Art Deco buildings to be built outside Melbourne and houses a strong collection of Australian art, with works by many of the big names, such as Tom Roberts, Frederick McCubbin, Arthur Streeton, Margaret Preston and Jeffrey Smart, on show (14 Lyttleton St, Castlemaine; (03) 5472 2292; open Thurs–Sun 12–5pm; castlemainegallery. com). Just down the road is the Restorers Barn, a Tardis-like antique-cum-hardware store that stocks more than 280,000 individual items (129–133 Mostyn St, Castlemaine; (03) 5470 5669; Mon–Fri 10am–5.30pm, Sat–Sun 10am–4pm).

Opposite the lovely Botanic Gardens – a stroll around the lake is a great way to stretch the legs – a former woollen mill has been transformed into a food and arts hub with furniture makers, blacksmiths, art spaces, a sprawling vintage bazaar, an artisan smokehouse, a craft brewery and coffee roaster, and a speciality ice creamery (1–9 Walker St, Castlemaine; Mon–Sun, individual business hours vary; millcastlemaine.com.au).

Don't miss Buda Historic Home and Garden. Built in 1861, it was the home of silversmith Ernest Leviny, but it was his five unmarried daughters who filled it up with stunning art and craft, much of which they made (they lived in the house until the 1980s). (42 Hunter St, Castlemaine; (03) 5472 1032; open Wed–Sat 12–5pm, Sun 10am–5pm; budacastlemaine.org.)

Bendigo is built on gold – quite literally. More gold has been found under and around Bendigo than anywhere else in Victoria – a colossal 22 million ounces since 1851, worth approximately $9 billion today. To get to the source of all this wealth, take the mine tour at the Central Deborah Gold Mine, the last commercial mine that operated in the city. Almost a tonne of gold was extracted from this mine before it closed in 1954. The 75-minute tour gives a first-hand glimpse of the life of a miner and the huge efforts required to extract gold from the earth. A number of tours are available, including the four-hour Nine Levels of Darkness tour, which is said to be Australia's deepest underground mine tour. (76 Violet St, Bendigo; (03) 5443 8322; open Mon–Sun 9am–5pm; central-deborah.com.)

Like most of the Australian goldfields, the Bendigo diggings attracted thousands of Chinese prospectors and the city is home to five ceremonial dragons, including Loong, the world's oldest Chinese imperial dragon, who made his first appearance on Bendigo streets in 1892, and Sun Loong, the world's longest imperial dragon at more than 100m (which comes out to play during the Bendigo Easter Festival parade, on Easter Sunday). All five are displayed in the Golden Dragon Museum, which explores the Chinese history and culture of the city and surrounding goldfields. The museum complex also contains a Chinese tearoom, a classical Chinese garden, a temple and a very grand Chinese gate. (5–13 Bridge St, Bendigo; (03) 5441 5044; open Mon–Sun 9.30am–5pm; goldendragonmuseum.org.)

SIDETRACK

Bendigo is about half an hour's drive north of Castlemaine via the Midland Highway but make sure to detour on the way to visit Maldon. Like Clunes, Maldon is a town that time seems to have forgotten: miners' cottages stand cheek by jowl with restored mansions, and the shopfronts along the crooked main street look like they have come straight from a movie set. Today Maldon's historic buildings host a number of cafes, galleries, antiques stores and other shops, and the town is very popular with browsing shoppers on weekends.

☺ KIDS' SPOT

Get your hands dirty at the renowned Bendigo Pottery. Established in 1858, Bendigo Pottery has been making acid jars, ginger-beer bottles and all manner of ceramic items on the same site for the past century and a half. The fascinating museum, built around the old kilns, details the history of the pottery and the current production processes with an interesting display of old products. Little kids can play with clay in the potters' workshops, and older kids and adults can have a go at shaping a vase on the wheel under the expert eye of a master potter – your pot will be fired and sent home to you. The complex also has a cafe, large antiques centre and four art galleries with resident artists. 146 Midland Hwy, Epsom; (03) 5448 4404; open Mon–Sun 9am–5pm; bendigopottery.com.au.

At the height of the rush, there were hundreds of Chinese temples in the goldfields. Today only one survives – the Bendigo Joss House Temple – and it is still a working temple. The bright red (for luck) building is dedicated to the god of prosperity (naturally), the rooms inside are redolent with burning incense and the shrines are laden with offerings of fruit and sweets. Don't forget to rub the lion's head beside the door when you leave and roll the marble in his mouth three times for good luck. (Finn St, North Bendigo; (03) 5442 1685; open Mon–Sun 11am–3pm; bendigojosshouse.com.)

A fun way to get to the temple is to ride the vintage tram, a hop-on, hop-off tour with recorded commentary that visits all of the major tourist attractions in the city, including the tram depot – the oldest operating one in the country, where old trams salvaged from around the world are painstakingly restored. A full circuit of the six stops will take about half an hour. (Trams depart hourly 10am–5pm; bendigotramways.com.)

Bendigo has one of the finest collections of Victorian-era buildings of any Australian inland city. Take a stroll after dark, as most are beautifully illuminated at night. The grandest of them all is Bendigo Town Hall. It's impressive enough from the outside, with its colonnade and three towers, but inside it is a fairytale confection of elaborate plasterwork, most of it handpainted or covered in gold leaf. Frolicking golden cherubs abound, as do bunches of flowers and feathers, birds, beasts and gargoyles. (Guided tours Wed 2pm, Sun 11am; book at the visitor centre in the (equally grand) Old Post Office building on Pall Mall or call 1800 813 153.) And like Ballarat and Castlemaine, Bendigo has an outstanding art gallery with an impressive collection of Australian art, and often hosts travelling blockbuster exhibitions (42 View St, Bendigo; (03) 5434 6088; open Mon–Sun 10am–5pm; bendigoregion.com.au).

It's still under construction, but when it's finished the 50m high Great Stupa of Universal Compassion at Myers Flat just outside Bendigo will be the largest stupa in the Western world. It will include extensive gardens and be home to the world's largest jade buddha, which is currently on a world tour. The precise completion date of the $20 million stupa is uncertain, as it depends on donations, but even if it isn't finished you can see the building taking shape from a viewing platform and explore the visitor centre with its large collection of sacred Buddhist relics. (25 Sandhurst Town Rd, Myers Flat; (03) 5446 7568; open Mon–Fri 9am–5pm, Sat–Sun and public holidays 10.30am–5pm; stupa.org.au.)

From Bendigo, it is 150km – about a two-hour drive – back to Melbourne.

BEST EATS

- **Mitchell Harris Wine Bar** As well as a quality menu, the wine bar offers a wide selection of wines from central and western Victoria, more than 20 of which can be bought by the glass. With its exposed beams and worn brick walls featuring some fabulous modern art, it's a cosy spot for a drink and a bite to eat. 38 Doveton St North, Ballarat; (03) 5331 8931; open Mon–Sun for lunch and dinner; mitchellharris.com.au.
- **Talbot Provedore and Eatery** The tiny town of Talbot is famous for its weekly farmers' markets on the third Sunday of each month when more than 80 stalls stretch down the main street, but if you miss the markets you can still get a taste of the local produce at this fabulous food shop and bistro, next door to the immaculately tended community gardens. The food is very good. 42 Scandinavian Cres, Talbot; (03) 5463 2008; open Thurs–Sun for lunch, Sat for dinner; talbotprovedore.com.au.
- **Avoca Hotel** The front bar is a typical old-style country pub, but head out the back and you'll find the recently refurbished dining room. The menu has a strong regional focus and the wine list too is local – in fact, unless the grapes were grown locally they won't stock a wine, even if it was made in the region. 115 High St, Avoca; (03) 5465 3018; open Thurs–Sun for lunch, Wed–Sun for dinner; theavocahotel.com.au.
- **Das Kaffeehaus** This opulent Viennese-style coffee house and cafe, complete with crystal chandeliers and velvet booths, in an old mill in Castlemaine serves great schnitzels and sausages (all handcrafted in the smokehouse next door) and delicious cakes. 9 Walker St, Castlemaine; (03) 5470 6270; open Mon–Sun for breakfast and lunch; coffeebasics.com.
- **The Dispensary Bar & Diner** Situated in a Melbourne-style laneway, this place serves up great food in an old chemist shop decorated with colourful graffiti and paste-up art. 9 Chancery La (off Pall Mall between Williamson and Bull sts), Bendigo; (03) 5444 5885; open Tues–Sun for lunch, Mon–Sat for dinner; dispensarybendigo.com.

BEST SLEEPS

- **Comfort Inn Sovereign Hill** Situated within the grounds of the Sovereign Hill complex, this motel-style establishment is a good option if you are travelling with kids and plan on seeing the sound-and-light show. Accommodation, dinner and show packages are available. 39 Magpie St, Ballarat; (03) 5337 1199; sovereignhill.com.au.
- **The Provincial Hotel** Built in 1909 this grand Art Nouveau hotel lay derelict for years before a meticulous restoration saw it reborn as a boutique 23-room hotel. Each of the bespoke suites and rooms features a mix of contemporary and antique furniture, beautiful fabrics and the work of local female artists. There's also an excellent restaurant, called Lola, on the ground floor. 121 Lydiard St North, Ballarat; (03) 5331 3399; theprovincialballarat.com.au.
- **eco luxe @ Mount Avoca** From the comfort of your bed in one of the luxury eco-sensitive cabins, you can watch kangaroos and sheep graze as the sun rises over Mount Avoca's grapevines, just a few kilometres from Avoca. Moates La via Vinoca Rd, Avoca; (03) 5465 3282; eco-luxe.com.au.
- **Quest Schaller Hotel Bendigo** Enjoy a modern stay in a historic city in this contemporary hotel named for Melbourne-based artist Mark Schaller, whose bold and colourful work features throughout the hotel. Standard rooms are small but it's reasonably priced; superior rooms offer more space. 60 Lucan St, Bendigo; (03) 4433 6100; questapartments.com.au.
- **Caravanning and camping** There is a bush-camping ground along Karri Track in Paddy Ranges State Park; the track also leads to a walking track loop that links up with the day picnic area. You can also camp at Vaughan Mineral Springs in Castlemaine Diggings National Heritage Park, and there is a camping and (unpowered) caravan area at Mount Franklin in Hepburn Regional Park with basic facilities.

Opposite Bendigo Art Gallery is one of Australia's oldest and largest regional galleries

Explore the wilder side of life on this trip through the Grampians (Gariwerd). The combination of wilderness and fine dining makes the rugged Grampian Range a great spot for a short break.

Grampians (Gariwerd), Vic.

HOW LONG?

It's a full-day drive, one way, plus a day at each end if you are travelling from Melbourne. To cut the drive short, head back to Melbourne from Dunkeld, skipping Hamilton.

WHEN TO GO

Summers are dry and warm; most rain falls during winter, when temperatures can get very chilly. In spring vast areas are blanketed with wildflowers.

NEED TO KNOW

Dogs are not allowed in Grampians (Gariwerd) National Park, even if you are only dropping in for half an hour or so to visit a lookout or unpack a picnic.

Drive rating
Easy. Sealed roads

Distances
Total distance, return to Melbourne (with detours): approximately 700km
- Melbourne to Halls Gap: 266km
- Halls Gap to Hamilton: 101km
- Hamilton to Melbourne: 286km

Temperatures
January: 13–29°C
July: 4–12°C

More information
Halls Gap and Grampians Visitor Information Centre, 117 Grampians Rd, Halls Gap; 1800 065 599; visitgrampians.com.au

Snapshot
This road trip through the Grampian Range is all about the wilder side of life. Grampians (Gariwerd) National Park, in western Victoria between Dunkeld and Halls Gap, is made up of four spectacular tilted sandstone ridges, rising gently on the western side and falling abruptly in a series of ragged overhangs and rocky bluffs on the eastern side. The photogenic ridges are crisscrossed with walking trails, dotted with lookouts and threaded by clear streams cascading down some of Victoria's largest waterfalls, and provide excellent places for rock climbing, abseiling and other adventure activities. The landscape might be rugged, but the dining's certainly not, and the fields and townships huddled in the shadow of the mountains produce some fantastic food and wine.

Opposite The drive to Mount Abrupt, the highest peak in the Southern Grampians

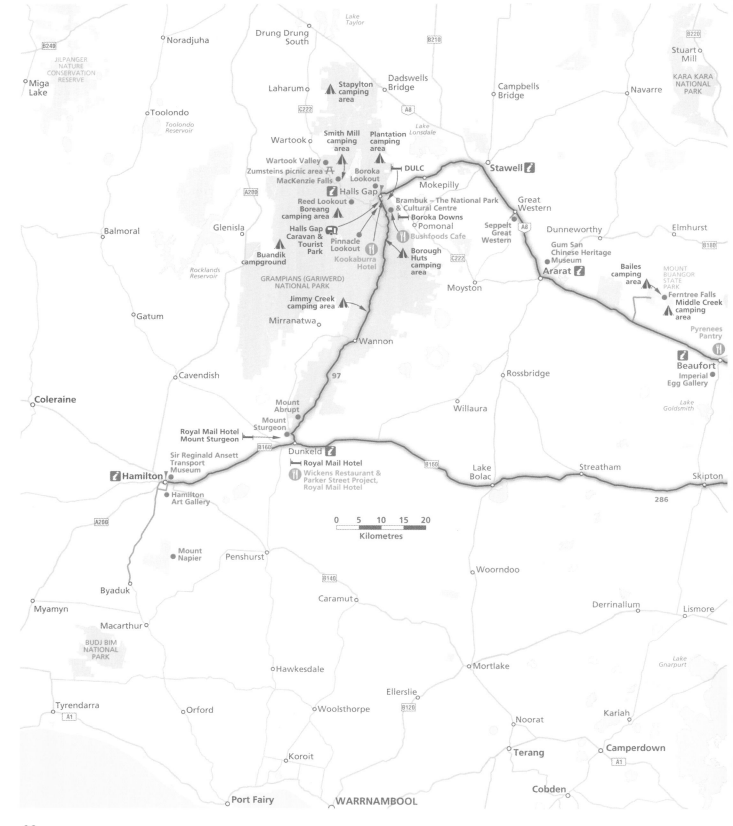

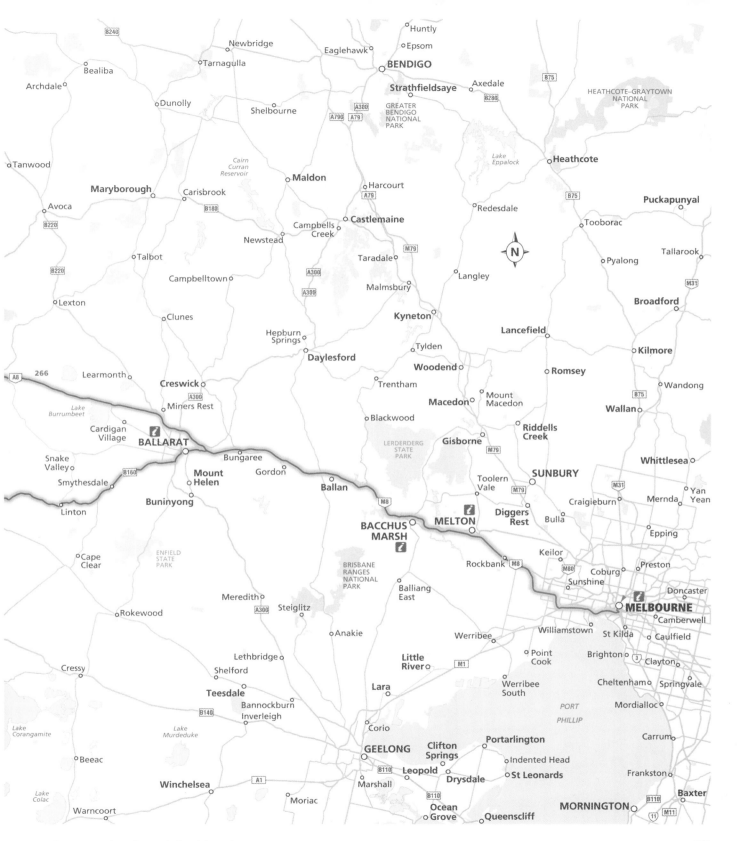

MELBOURNE TO HALLS GAP VIA BEAUFORT

The main town in the Grampians is Halls Gap, which is situated in a tight valley between the southern tip of the Mount Difficult Range and the northern tip of the Mount William Range, just beyond the border of Grampians (Gariwerd) National Park. To get there from Melbourne will take about three hours via the M8 (Western Freeway) and Ballarat (*see* p. 53).

Stretch your legs in Beaufort. The Imperial Egg Gallery in the middle of the main street is reputed to be the largest collection of eggs in the Southern Hemisphere, with more than 4000 on display at any one time. It's all the work of one woman, Margaret Saunders, who has been collecting eggy things for more than 60 years. There are carved, painted, enamelled and bejewelled emu eggs; ostrich, duck, goose and dove eggs; as well as egg-shell lamps, eggs within eggs, clocks within eggs, fairies within eggs and sculptures made from hundreds of eggs. The most treasured pieces are eight replica Fabergé eggs encrusted with semiprecious stones and gilded with gold leaf – the original eggs were made for Russian nobility between 1885 and 1917, and most are now in art museums. It is, if you'll excuse the pun, a cracker of a collection. (18 Neill St, Beaufort; (03) 5349 2297; open Mon–Sun 10am–4pm.)

SIDETRACK

Just a few kilometres off the road between Beaufort and Ararat is Mount Buangor State Park. It's a top spot for a picnic and there is an easy five-minute walk to Ferntree Falls, a lovely little waterfall in a lush fern gully.

Ararat has the distinction of being the only town in Australia founded by Chinese. The Gum San Chinese Heritage Museum tells the story of how most of the Chinese diggers walked overland from Robe in South Australia to the goldfields, and displays cultural artefacts and interesting relics. Kids will also love playing traditional Chinese games and learning how to pan for gold. (31-33 Lambert St, Ararat; (03) 5352 1078; open Mon–Sun 11am–4pm.)

SIDETRACK

Established in 1865, Seppelt Great Western is one of Australia's best known producers of sparkling wine. If you've ever wondered how they get those lovely little bubbles into the wine, this is the place to find out, on a guided tour of the 3km of underground cellars – called the Drives – where the wine is matured. There are barbecue and picnic facilities in the beautiful gardens. (36 Cemetery Rd, Great Western; 1300 761 649; open Mon–Sun 10am–5pm, tours depart every hour 11am–3pm and bookings are essential; seppelt.com.au.)

Grampians (Gariwerd), Vic.

HALLS GAP TO DUNKELD

Brambuk – The National Park and Cultural Centre has information about Grampians (Gariwerd) National Park and a range of activities great for kids, including didgeridoo workshops and boomerang painting and throwing. It also runs guided tours of many of the Indigenous sites in the park. (Grampians Tourist Rd, 2.5km south of Halls Gap; (03) 5361 4000; open Mon–Sun 9am–5pm.)

There are more than 50 walking trails in the national park, but most of the best walks are based in the park's northern section. The Wonderland Walk is a wonderful five-hour loop from Halls Gap around the spectacular Pinnacle Lookout. Highlights include the high-walled Grand Canyon, the sandstone rock face named 'Elephant Hide' and the Venus Bath Rock Pools. And don't miss Mackenzie Falls, widely considered to be the largest in Victoria. There's a lookout from the top, but they are best seen from below – it's a half-hour walk to get to the beautiful waterhole at the foot of the falls. If you don't fancy tackling the 265 steps to get there (much harder coming back up!), try the three-hour river walk from Zumsteins picnic area, which leads you to the bottom of MacKenzie Falls along the river – it's much longer, but much easier on the knees.

☺ KIDS' SPOT

Your children may not remember *Skippy* (and neither may you!), but they no doubt like kangaroos. Wartook Valley, at the northern entrance of the national park (follow the Northern Grampians Road from Halls Gap towards Horsham), is a great place for them to see large mobs of kangaroos in the wild.

The park is also home to the largest number of Indigenous rock-art sites in south-eastern Australia – there are more than 60 art sites scattered around the park, decorating the rocky bluffs and ragged overhangs. Billiminia Shelter in the southern section of the park is one of the easiest to find. It's a 20-minute walk from Buandik campground.

But one of the great things about the Grampians is that you don't have to pull on hiking boots or engage 4WD to see the best of the park. The sealed road between Halls Gap and Dunkeld through the middle of the national park is one of most scenic mountain drives on sealed roads in the country, and many of the most vertigo-inducing views are from easily accessible lookouts – don't miss Boroka Lookout, Reed Lookout and the Balconies.

The pretty village of Dunkeld, at the southern entrance to the Grampians, stands in the shade of Mount Sturgeon and Mount Abrupt, the highest mountain in the southern Grampians.

Opposite Traditional Chinese statues line the roof of Gum San Chinese Heritage Centre in Ararat
Right The walk to Pinnacle Lookout rewards with amazing views

DUNKELD TO MELBOURNE VIA HAMILTON

From Dunkeld, continue south-west to Hamilton, which was one of the first areas of pastoral settlement in Victoria and has claims to being the wool capital of the world – roughly six million sheep graze within an 80km radius of the town. The Hamilton Art Gallery has a renowned collection of silver, glass, porcelain and oriental ceramics, many of which were gifts from country homesteads in the area. The permanent collection of more than 7000 items is complemented by a program of temporary exhibitions. (107 Brown St, Hamilton; (03) 5573 0460; open Mon–Fri 10am–5pm, Sat 10am–12pm and 2–5pm, Sun 2–5pm; hamiltongallery.org.)

Commercial aviation pioneer Sir Reginald Ansett lived in Hamilton and his relocated company hangar is now a museum of the earliest days of commercial flight (cnr Ballarat Rd and Riley St; (03) 5571 2767; open Mon–Sun 10am–4pm; ansettmuseum.com.au).

SIDETRACK

The southern Grampians sit atop one of the largest volcanic plains in the world, and Mount Napier, just south of Dunkeld, is Victoria's youngest volcano. The last activity was only about 8000 years ago, which means it is classified as dormant rather than extinct. Trek up to the crater's edge, explore lava tubes near Byaduk and climb tumuli, or lava blisters, in the nearby paddocks.

From Hamilton, allow about three and a half hours to get back to Melbourne.

Grampians (Gariwerd), Vic.

BEST EATS

- **Brambuk – The National Park and Cultural Centre** Try some bushfoods at the cafe here. 277 Grampians Tourist Rd, just south of Halls Gap; (03) 5361 4000; open Mon–Sun 9am–5pm.
- **Kookaburra Hotel** The menu focuses on local produce and offers an extensive wine list, including most of the local wines. 125–127 Grampians Rd, Halls Gap; (03) 5356 4222; open Tues–Sun for dinner, Sat–Sun for lunch.
- **Pyrenees Pantry** The pantry specialises in local produce and is famous in the area for its delicious handmade pies. 44 Neil St, Beaufort; (03) 5349 2002; open Mon–Sun 9am–4.30pm.
- **Royal Mail Hotel** People come from as far away as Melbourne just to eat at this hotel's highly awarded restaurant, Wickens, so book well ahead. It can be hard to get a booking; if you miss out, try its more casual eatery called Parker Street Project. 98 Parker St, Dunkeld; (03) 5577 2241; Wickens open Wed–Sat for dinner, Sat for lunch, Parker Street Project open Mon–Sun for breakfast, lunch and dinner; royalmail.com.au.

BEST SLEEPS

- **Boroka Downs** Luxury accommodation is available here in any of five 'residences', 7km from Halls Gap. Each one has polished wooden floors, wall-to-ceiling windows, a full-size spa bath, a fully equipped kitchen, an espresso machine and views of the Grampian Mountains. 51 Birdswing Rd, Halls Gap; (03) 5356 6243; borokadowns.com.au.
- **DULC** These lovely timber cabins on the outskirts of Halls Gap offer surrounded-by-bushland seclusion with lots of luxurious touches: spa baths, beautiful beds, private decks, espresso machines, swish decor and floor-to-ceiling windows (the shower even has a glass ceiling) that blur the boundaries between outside and in. Thryptomene Ct, Halls Gap; (03) 5356 4711; dulc.com.au.
- **Royal Mail Hotel** If you don't fancy getting back in your car after a long lunch or dinner at the hotel (see Best eats), stay in one of the motel units with mountain views or in a self-contained apartment. The hotel also offers accommodation at Mount Sturgeon, near Dunkeld, in historic bluestone cottages, originally built by Chinese workers during the gold rush. Complimentary transfers to and from the hotel are included in the tariffs. 98 Parker St, Dunkeld; (03) 5577 2241; royalmail.com.au.
- **Caravanning and camping** There are seven car-friendly camping areas in Grampians National Park, all with toilets, fireplaces and picnic tables, but you'll need to bring your own drinking water. All of these areas are busy during Easter, long weekends and summer holidays. There are a number of caravan parks in and around Halls Gap, but a favourite is the Halls Gap Caravan and Tourist Park (Grampians Rd; (03) 5356 4251). Mount Buangor State Park, 15km west of Beaufort on the Western Highway, has two campgrounds suitable for caravans: Bailes and Middle Creek. Facilities include toilets, water, fireplaces, tables and a picnic shelter. Grampians and Mount Buangor sites must be pre-booked before arrival at parkstay.vic.gov.au.

Opposite Mount Sturgeon and Mount Abrupt peak out from the rural landscape *Left* Fresh produce from the garden goes into delicious meals at Royal Mail Hotel

A drive around South Australia's wild and rugged Kangaroo Island is a wildlife safari in your own backyard.

Kangaroo Island, SA

Since going to print, some of the areas featured in this trip were affected by the 2020 bushfires. Some of the information, particularly about national park camping areas, may have since changed – contact local visitor information centres for updates before travelling.

HOW LONG?

The best way to explore the island is in three separate daytrips to three corners of the island: Cape Willoughby, Cape du Couedic and Cape Borda. To save time you can fly directly to Kangaroo Island from Adelaide and hire a car on the island. See below and tourkangarooisland.com.au.

WHEN TO GO

Any time of year is a great time to do this drive – temperatures are relatively mild during both summer and winter. At times, cool ocean breezes make windproof clothing necessary, while central areas of the island occasionally experience temperatures of 35–40°C in mid-summer.

NEED TO KNOW

Take care when driving on the island's unsealed roads: they are made from ironstone, a loose, floating material that can feel like you are driving on a mat of ball bearings. A sudden swerve to avoid a wallaby or kangaroo (of which there are plenty, especially in the late afternoon or at dusk) can end in disaster. Avoid driving at night.

Kangaroo Island SeaLink (13 1301; sealink.com.au) and Kangaroo Island Connect fast ferries (0419 100 100; kic.com.au) depart several times each day between Cape Jervis on the Fleurieu Peninsula (about a 90-minute drive south of Adelaide) and Penneshaw on the island, and the trip takes around 30–45 minutes, depending on which ferry you take.

Regional Express (REX) has regular 30-minute flights from Adelaide to Kangaroo Island (regionalexpress.com.au). Qantas also operates flights from Adelaide and Melbourne (qantas.com).

Pets are not allowed in national or conservation parks on Kangaroo Island. Although there are boarding kennels on the island and some tourist accommodation is pet friendly, it's probably best to leave your pets at home.

Opposite top left Pelican keeps watch at Emu Bay *Top right* Lookout at Admiral's Arch in Flinders Chase National Park *Bottom left* Remarkable Rocks have earned their name *Bottom right* Sea lion on the rocks of Cape du Couedic

Drive rating
Moderate. Unsealed roads with loose gravel

Distances
Total distance, returning to Kingscote each day: approximately 660km. Base point, Kingscote, is 186km from Adelaide, including the ferry crossing.
- Kingscote to Penneshaw: 58km
- Penneshaw to Cape Willoughby: 27km
- Kingscote to Seal Bay: 60km
- Seal Bay to Cape du Couedic: 82km
- Cape du Couedic to Cape Borda: 55km
- Kingscote to Cape Borda: 103km

Temperatures
January: 14–24°C
July: 9–15°C

More information
Gateway Visitor Information Centre, Howard Dr, Penneshaw; 1800 811 080; tourkangarooisland.com.au

Snapshot
Kangaroo Island's gentle rolling hills, covered in rich pasture and dotted with grazing sheep and cattle, belie a wilder heart. Close to half of the island is either natural bushland or national park, and it is home to some of the most diverse wildlife you'll find concentrated in one area anywhere in Australia – 6000 fur seals, 600 rare Australian sea lions, 5000 koalas, 15,000 kangaroos, 254 species of birdlife and somewhere between 500,000 and one million tammar wallabies. If you can't spot wildlife here, then you simply aren't trying.

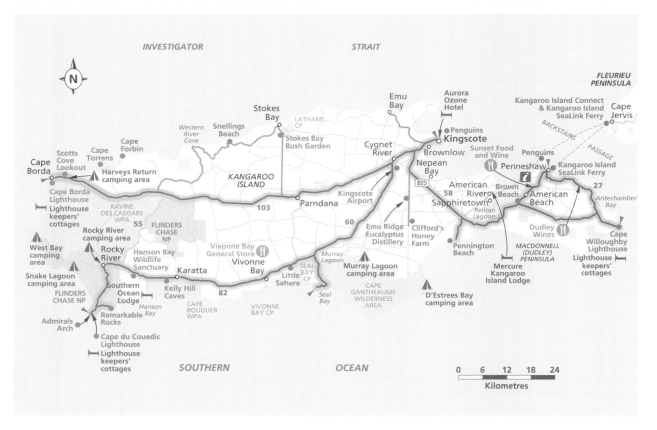

KINGSCOTE TO PENNESHAW AND CAPE WILLOUGHBY

Kingscote is the biggest town on KI, as the locals call the island, with about 2500 people, so it is a good place to use as a base. It is also where flights arrive and depart for Adelaide. If you've travelled over on the ferry, you'll arrive and depart from the slightly sleepier town of Penneshaw, which is about 45 minutes' drive from Kingscote.

Head east from Kingscote along Hog Bay Road, through the pastoral heart of the island to Penneshaw.

SIDETRACK

Emu Ridge Eucalyptus Distillery is the only commercial eucalyptus distillery in operation in South Australia. The oil is reputed to be excellent for soothing arthritic aches and pains. (691 Willsons Rd, Macgillivray; (08) 8553 8228; open Mon–Sat 9am–4pm, Sun 10am–1pm; emuridge.com.au.)

Stop at Pennington Beach, a long expanse of white sand edged up against rugged limestone cliffs at the narrowest point on the island. From here continue east through Penneshaw and onto the unsealed road that leads 30km out to Cape Willoughby on the far eastern tip of the island. The lighthouse here is one of four on the island and was also the first built in South Australia. The 27m high tower is open for tours (Thurs–Mon 11am, 12.30pm, 2pm; Mon–Sun during school holidays with extra tours at 3pm and 4pm) and from its top you can see across the rather descriptively named Backstairs Passage towards the mainland.

Both Kingscote and Penneshaw have small penguin colonies, and the best way to see them is on the guided boardwalk tour in Penneshaw. Adult penguins spend most of the day feeding out at sea and return to land just after dark. You can watch as they come waddling out of the water and clamber up the rocky beach to their burrow-like nests in the sand dunes to feed their hungry chicks. The penguins are in residence at the colony all year, except for the month of February when they go out to sea, but sightings are not guaranteed. (Penneshaw Penguin Centre, cnr Middle and Bay tces; (08) 8553 7407; tours Fri–Tues; penneshawpenguincentre.com.)

KINGSCOTE TO CAPE DU COUEDIC

On your second day, head south to Flinders Chase National Park and Cape du Couedic along the South Coast Road. At misnamed Seal Bay, 60km from Kingscote, join a tour and stroll along the high-water mark on the beach among dozens of huge, sleepy sea lions resting after spending three days at sea hunting for food. Seal Bay is the only place in Australia where you will get this close to sea lions; all other colonies are perched on inaccessible rocky headlands. If you don't want to join a tour, there is a self-guided boardwalk, but it does not allow you to get onto the sand or as close to the sea lions.

SIDETRACK

Part of Seal Bay Conservation Park, the area known as Little Sahara (7km west of the Seal Bay turn-off on South Coast Road) is a place of massive inland sand dunes. It's a tough climb up, but it only takes seconds to slide down on a well-waxed board and is almost too much fun. Just resist the urge to squeal or you'll end up with a mouthful of sand. Sandboards and toboggans are available for hire from KI Outdoor Action, 188 Jetty Rd, Vivonne Bay; (08) 8559 4296; kioutdooraction.com.au.

From Seal Bay, drive on to the far western reaches of the island in Flinders Chase National Park. Wander among Remarkable Rocks, a cluster of huge weather-sculpted granite boulders perched on a granite dome that swoops 75m down to the sea, then head south-west to Cape du Couedic. The rock platforms below the lighthouse are home to a colony of New Zealand fur seals; look for them wallowing in the sun or frolicking in the surf under the dramatic rock arc of Admirals Arch.

On the way back to Kingscote, watch for dawdling echidnas crossing in front of your car, and, of course, the wallabies and kangaroos that are ubiquitous on the island. Although you have a good chance of seeing koalas in the trees just about anywhere on the island, you're guaranteed to see them at the Hanson Bay Wildlife Sanctuary (7797 South Coast Rd, between Kelly Hill Caves and Flinders Chase National Park; (08) 8559 7344; open Mon–Sun from 9am; hansonbay.com.au).

 KIDS' SPOT

Kangaroo Island may only be 20km from the mainland, but that's way too far for a bee to fly. As a result, the island is one of the world's oldest bee sanctuaries. And, despite being just about as far away from Italy as you can get, the island is home to the only genetically pure population of Ligurian bees in the world. You can check them out in the glass hives at Clifford's Honey Farm, which is worth visiting for its sinfully good honey ice-cream alone. 1157 Elsegood Rd; (08) 8553 8295; open Mon–Sun 9am–5pm; entry is free.

Above Sandboarding down the dunes of Little Sahara

Kangaroo Island, SA

KINGSCOTE TO CAPE BORDA

The third driving route on KI is to the far north-western tip at Cape Borda, with a side trip to the north coast. From Kingscote, head west on the Playford Highway through Parndana, where in late winter and spring the roadside is carpeted with wildflowers, to Cape Borda; the last 38km or so of the road cuts through the wilderness of Flinders Chase National Park. The rather squat, square lighthouse at Cape Borda is 155m above sea level. Four kilometres to the east is Scotts Cove Lookout, where you can see the spectacular cliffs of Cape Torrens and Cape Forbin.

SIDETRACK

Good side trips on the way back to Kingscote include Western River Cove, which is ideal for swimming, rock fishing and surf fishing; picture-perfect Snellings Beach, at the mouth of Middle River; and Stokes Bay, where a walk through a headland of boulders brings you to a fine, white sandy beach surrounded by cliffs. If you're a garden lover, visit Stokes Bay Bush Garden, which displays an extensive collection of KI and Australian native plants in a beautiful bush-garden setting (Stokes Bay Rd, Stokes Bay; (08) 8559 2244; check opening times before visiting). Emu Bay is another worthwhile detour: a lovely 3km long beach with vehicle access onto the hard sand. Anglers can try their luck from the jetty or launch their boats from the ramp. Any of these spots is a great place for a picnic lunch with a million-dollar view – and chances are you'll have it all to yourself.

Money-saving pass

Great value if you are planning on visiting all (or most) of the parks on KI, the Kangaroo Island Tour Pass provides entry to the island's parks as well as guided tours at most of its popular nature-based tourist attractions, such as Seal Bay and the lighthouses of Flinders Chase National Park. It's available at the visitor centre in Penneshaw.

BEST EATS

- **Dudley Wines** Enjoy expansive ocean views from the deck while enjoying some of the winery's award-winning wine, along with a pizza or a cheese board. Here you can learn about yabby and marron (freshwater crayfish) farming then try some of the harvest at the cafe, with a glass of local wine. 1153 Cape Willoughby Rd, Cuttlefish Bay; (08) 8553 1333; open Mon–Sun for lunch; dudleywines.com.au.
- **Sunset Food and Wine** This is the place to go when you want to eat out in style: the food is just as spectacular as the view overlooking American Beach. The seasonal menu has a strong focus on the island's produce and seafood as well as a stellar wine list. 4564 Hog Bay Rd, Kangaroo Head; (08) 8553 1378; open Tues–Sat for lunch, Thurs–Sat for dinner; sunsetfoodandwine.com.
- **Vivonne Bay General Store** Situated not far from Seal Bay, the store is locally famous for its fresh whiting burgers and does a good coffee. South Coast Rd, Vivonne Bay; (08) 8559 4285; open Mon–Sun 9am–5.30pm.

BEST SLEEPS

- **Aurora Ozone Hotel** Overlooking the beach in the centre of Kingscote, this hotel has good-value motel-style rooms and apartments. The Foreshore, Kingscote; (08) 8553 2011; auroraresorts.com.au.
- **Mercure Kangaroo Island Lodge** Ideal for those on tighter budgets, this older-style motel offers affordable rooms with a pool and waterfront views. Kids will love watching the wallabies graze on the lawn and the pelicans on the beach in front of the hotel. 73 Scenic Dr, American River; 1800 355 581; kilodge.com.au.
- **Lighthouse keepers' cottages** Accommodation is available in the lighthouse keepers' cottages at Cape du Couedic, Cape Borda and Cape Willoughby. The cottages sleep between six and eight and there is a minimum two-night stay. (08) 8553 4410 or email kiparksaccom@sa.gov.au.
- **Caravanning and camping** The following beaches have caravan sites: Nepean Bay (Kingscote), Penneshaw, Antechamber Bay, Browns Beach, Stokes Bay, Emu Bay, Vivonne Bay and Western River. The best camping in Flinders Chase National Park is at Rocky River, near the visitor centre, where facilities include showers and gas barbecues, and there are also (unpowered) caravan sites. You can bush camp at Snake Lagoon, Harveys Return and West Bay (4WD only), and at Murrays Lagoon or D'Estrees Bay in Cape Gantheaume Wilderness Area.

Opposite Follow the paved road along the coastline of Flinders Chase National Park to Remarkable Rocks *Right* Pitch a tent and get back to nature on Kangaroo Island

Explore the Gold Coast's wilder side in the rainforest-clad mountains and valleys of the Scenic Rim hinterland.

Scenic Rim, Qld

Since going to print, some of the areas featured in this trip were affected by bushfires and flooding. Some of the information, particularly about roads in national parks and camping areas, may have since changed – contact local visitor information centres for updates before travelling.

HOW LONG?

This can be a two- or three-day drive. Alternatively, you can cut the route into two one-day drives, doing the Lamington National Park section and the Boonah loop separately.

WHEN TO GO

Summer is temperate, with the ranges being much cooler than the coast, but the area is prone to violent storms in that season. Winter is more likely to be dry and sunny.

NEED TO KNOW

Some of the steep, narrow roads around Nerang and Canungra are unsuitable for caravans and trailers. Check with local visitor centres before travelling.

Drive rating
Moderate. Sealed roads with some steep, winding sections

Distances
Total distance, return loop (with detours): approximately 500km
- Gold Coast to Warwick: 190km
- Gold Coast to Tamborine: 56km
- Tamborine to Lamington National Park: 51km
- Tamborine to Boonah: 60km
- Boonah to Warwick: 88km
- Boonah to Warwick via Killarney: 106km

Temperatures
January: 17–26°C
July: 8–17°C

More information
- Boonah Visitor Information Centre, Bicentennial Park, 20 Boonah Fassifern Rd, Boonah; (07) 5463 2233
- Canungra Visitor Information Centre, 12–14 Kidston St, Canungra; (07) 5543 5156; canungrainformationcentre.com.au
- Tamborine Mountain Visitor Information Centre, Doughty Park, 2 Main Western Rd, North Tamborine; (07) 5545 3200
- Warwick Visitor Information Centre, 72 Palmerin St, Warwick; (07) 4661 3122
- southerndownsandgranitebelt.com.au
- visitscenicrim.com.au

Snapshot
The beauty of south-east Queensland is that no matter where you are, even if it's in the middle of the Brisbane CBD or the high-rise strip of the Gold Coast, you're never very far from the wilder side of life. Just one hour from Brisbane, and half an hour from the Gold Coast, is an altogether different world: mountains, rainforests, valleys, wide plains and World Heritage wilderness – the green behind the gold. Known as the Scenic Rim, this region is a chain of craggy mountains and high plateaus cut through with rich, fertile river valleys and dotted with historic townships and magnificent rainforests.

Opposite Enjoy lakeside camping at Lake Moogerah (don't forget the marshmallows)

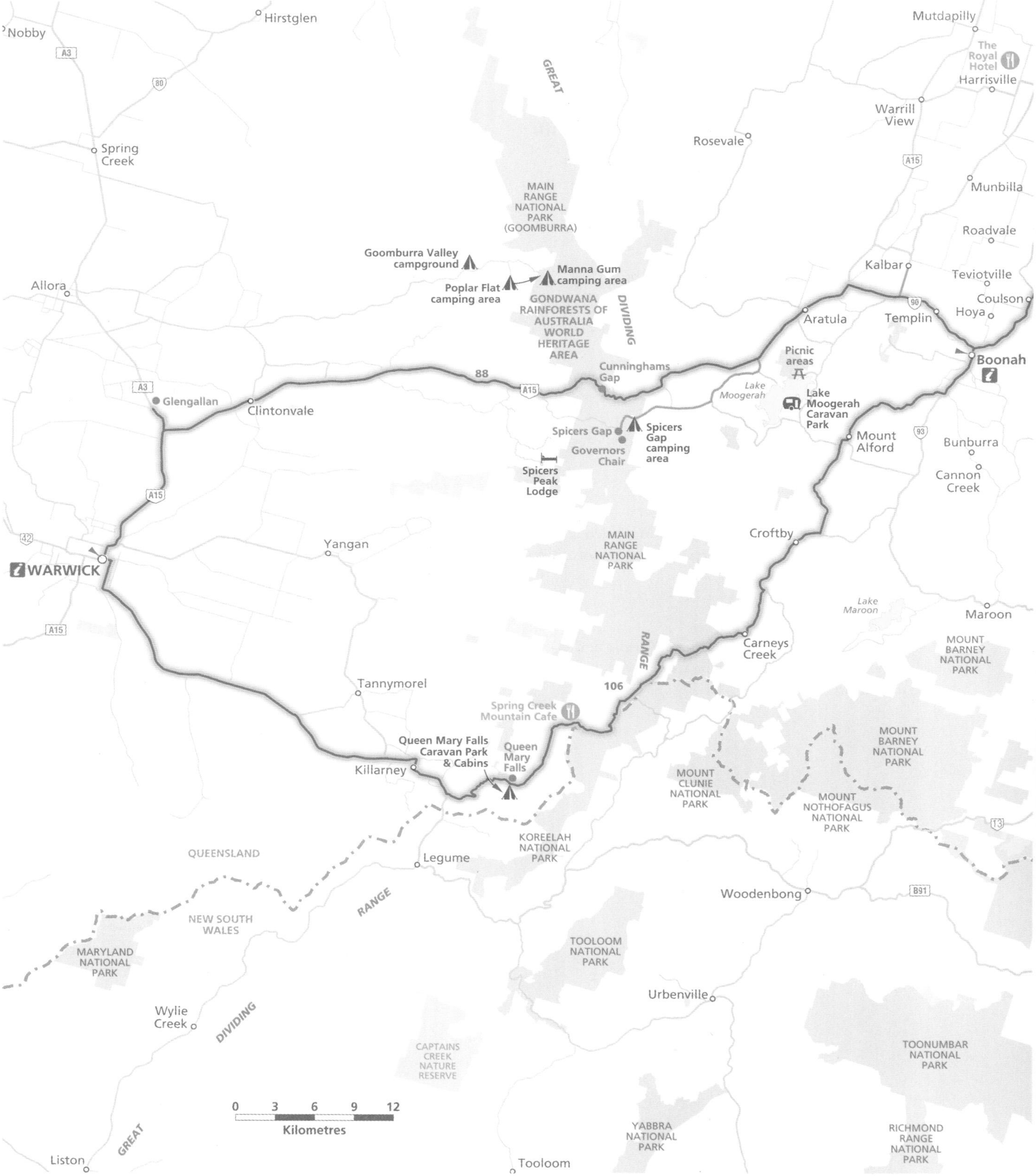

Nobby
Hirstglen
A3
80
Spring Creek
GREAT
DIVIDING
RANGE
MAIN RANGE NATIONAL PARK (GOOMBURRA)
Goomburra Valley campground
Poplar Flat camping area
Manna Gum camping area
GONDWANA RAINFORESTS OF AUSTRALIA WORLD HERITAGE AREA
Mutdapilly
The Royal Hotel
Harrisville
Warrill View
Rosevale
A15
Munbilla
Roadvale
Kalbar
Teviotville
Coulson
Hoya
Templin
90
Aratula
Boonah
Picnic areas
Lake Moogerah
Lake Moogerah Caravan Park
Allora
A3
Glengallan
Clintonvale
88
A15
Cunninghams Gap
Spicers Gap
Governors Chair
Spicers Gap camping area
Spicers Peak Lodge
Mount Alford
93
Bunburra
Cannon Creek
A15
42
WARWICK
Yangan
MAIN RANGE NATIONAL PARK
Croftby
Lake Maroon
Maroon
A15
Carneys Creek
MOUNT BARNEY NATIONAL PARK
Tannymorel
106
Spring Creek Mountain Cafe
Queen Mary Falls Caravan Park & Cabins
Queen Mary Falls
Killarney
MOUNT BARNEY NATIONAL PARK
MOUNT CLUNIE NATIONAL PARK
MOUNT NOTHOFAGUS NATIONAL PARK
13
QUEENSLAND
KOREELAH NATIONAL PARK
Legume
NEW SOUTH WALES
RANGE
Woodenbong
B91
MARYLAND NATIONAL PARK
TOOLOOM NATIONAL PARK
Urbenville
Wylie Creek
DIVIDING
CAPTAINS CREEK NATURE RESERVE
TOONUMBAR NATIONAL PARK
0 3 6 9 12
Kilometres
GREAT
Liston
YABBRA NATIONAL PARK
Tooloom
RICHMOND RANGE NATIONAL PARK

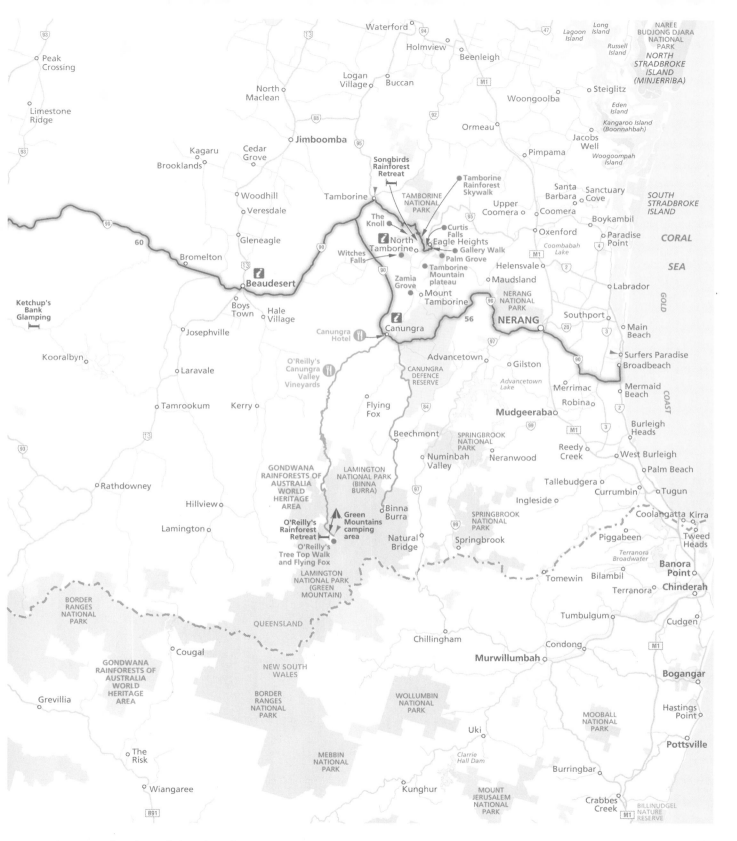

KIDS' SPOT

Let your kids become park rangers at the Eco Rangers school holiday program at O'Reilly's Rainforest Retreat (for kids over five). It includes twice-daily activities such as campfire cookouts, rainforest art, scavenger hunts and after-dark wildlife spotting, as well as eco-detective games, wacky chemistry classes, adventure racing and kid-friendly bush survival courses. Afternoon activities include dinner. Lamington National Park Rd via Canungra; (07) 5544 0644; oreillys.com.au.

GOLD COAST TO TAMBORINE MOUNTAIN

Your first stop should be Tamborine Mountain, about a 45-minute drive from Surfers Paradise via the Nerang–Broadbeach/Beaudesert–Nerang Road (State Road 90). The air up here is cooler and the views from the plateau are fantastic, but the drive is steep, winding and narrow. Stop and explore the villages of Mount Tamborine, Tamborine Village, North Tamborine and Eagle Heights. Shoppers should head for Gallery Walk on Long Road, a string of galleries, craft shops, antiques stores, cafes and eateries.

Queensland's first national park was established at Witches Falls in 1908, and since then additional reserves of subtropical rainforest on the Tamborine plateau have been added to it, making up what is now known as Tamborine National Park. There are 22km of graded walking tracks, with most walks taking less than half a day and almost all easily reached from Tamborine Mountain township. Most are either wheelchair accessible or graded as easy, so they are great for kids and families with strollers. Palm Grove, Witches Falls and the Knoll have spectacular views, and Zamia Grove has ancient cycads, relics of plants that flourished 150 million years ago. There are also lovely waterfalls and rockpools throughout the park, including Curtis Falls, one of the prettiest – and most popular – waterfalls on the mountain, an easy 1.5km return walk from the carpark on Dapsang Drive at Eagle Heights.

Tamborine Rainforest Skywalk is a privately owned canopy walk with a 40m long cantilevered bridge suspended 30m above the forest floor. It's a great way to get a bird's-eye view of the rainforest and is suitable for wheelchairs and strollers. (333 Geissmann Dr, North Tamborine; (07) 5545 2222; open Mon–Sun 9.30am–5pm, last entry 4pm; rainforestskywalk.com.au.)

If you'd like to really give your hiking boots a workout, detour south to Lamington National Park. This World Heritage–listed park has more than 160km of walking tracks, some over 20km long. Highlights include many of the 150 waterfalls and stands of 15,000-year-old Antarctic beech trees. If you need an adrenalin rush, try the Flying Fox Adventure, a 180m long zipline that takes you zooming 25m above the rainforest, at O'Reilly's Rainforest Retreat.

Also at O'Reilly's is a tree-top canopy walk: it might seem a little tame by today's standards but 25 years ago it was the first of its kind in Australia. O'Reilly's Rainforest Retreat is in the Green Mountain section of the park (Lamington National Park Rd via Canungra; (07) 5544 0644; oreillys. com.au). There are two entrances to Lamington: the Green Mountains entrance is 115km south of Brisbane via Canungra, or 70km from Surfers via Nerang and Canungra, while Binna Burra is 107km from Brisbane via Canungra, and 55km from the Gold Coast. The historic Binna Burra mountain lodge was destroyed in the 2019 bushfires but there are plans to rebuild. (1040 Binna Burra Rd, Beechmont; (07) 5533 3622; binnaburralodge.com.au). Both routes are fully sealed, but the road to Green Mountains is too steep and winding for caravans.

Opposite Treetops seen from Tamborine Rainforest Skywalk *Above top* Regent bowerbird finds food among the trees of Lamington National Park *Above bottom* O'Reilly's Tree Top Walk

Long weekends and short breaks

MOUNT TAMBORINE TO WARWICK AND BOONAH

Keep following the main road west, through Beaudesert, for another 45 minutes or so, to Boonah. This great little drive loop around the Boonah area will take about four or five hours, depending on how much you dawdle along the way at places like Kalbar – full of classic Queensland architecture (think lots of white-washed wood, big verandahs and ornate trims) – or Lake Moogerah, with its extensive lakeside picnic areas.

Next, head west along the highway towards Warwick, climbing up and over the Great Dividing Range at Cunninghams Gap in the middle of Main Range National Park.

SIDETRACK

Although the highway cuts through the middle of Main Range National Park at Cunninghams Gap, the best views are to be had from Spicers Gap. Get there via the Lake Moogerah and Spicers Gap roads. (The western approach is 4WD only; the eastern approach is unsealed and very steep and rocky, but generally okay for conventional cars.) The short walk from the carpark leads to Governors Chair and has superb views.

Don't miss Glengallan, 18km north of Warwick on the New England Highway – just look for the big half-house on the hill. This great stone house was started in 1867 but was never finished, and lay in ruins for most of the 20th century. Downstairs has been restored; upstairs is pretty grim, but it's still a great place to wander around. Keep an eye out for the mummified cat that was buried beneath the floor for good luck. The rose gardens are beautiful in spring. (18515 New England Hwy; (07) 4667 3866; open Wed–Sun and public holidays 10am-4pm.)

Stop in Warwick to admire the grand town hall and other buildings. Then head east across rolling hills and through pretty villages to Killarney, and follow the signs to Queen Mary Falls. There's a terrific 45-minute walk that takes you from a lookout at the top of the falls down into the gorge, along to the bottom of the falls 40m below and back up again. A tip: start at the track on the left-hand side of the picnic area to avoid the stairs.

The final section of the loop back to Boonah via Spring Creek and Carneys Creek Road winds through beautiful rainforest and has some great lookouts along the way.

BEST EATS

- **Canungra Hotel** Good-value meals are served up daily in the shady courtyard. 18 Kidston St, Canungra; (07) 5543 5233; open Mon–Sun for lunch and dinner.
- **O'Reilly's Canungra Valley Vineyards** Enjoy lunch on the verandah of the old homestead or order a picnic basket to have down near the creek. 852 Lamington National Park Rd; (07) 5543 4011; open Mon–Sun 10am–4.30pm.
- **Royal Hotel** This Harrisville hotel does a great porterhouse steak. 1 Queen St, Harrisville; (07) 5467 1882; open Wed–Sun for lunch, Tues–Sun for dinner.
- **Spring Creek Mountain Cafe** This is a great spot to stop for lunch or an afternoon coffee and slice of cake, and the views from the deck are sublime. If you have the appetite, try the Killarney beef or lamb. 1503 Spring Creek Rd, Killarney; (07) 4664 7101; open Wed–Fri 10am–5pm, Sat–Sun 8am–5pm.

BEST SLEEPS

- **O'Reilly's Rainforest Retreat** O'Reilly's has been welcoming guests to Lamington National Park for more than 100 years. It has a range of accommodation, from a guesthouse to self-contained villas, a licensed restaurant and the Lost World Spa, and it also offers guided tours. End of Lamington National Park Rd via Canungra; (07) 5544 0644; oreillys.com.au.
- **Songbirds Rainforest Retreat** Enjoy the birdsong from your deck at this luxe 23ha forest retreat on Tamborine Mountain, just a few minutes' drive from the main township. Each of the six private villas has a king-size bed, gas fireplace, spa bath, huge lounge and a large outdoor deck. A range of pampering and relaxation massages are available in your villa, along with yoga and meditation classes. 10 Tamborine Mountain Rd, North Tamborine; (07) 5545 2563; songbirds.com.au.
- **Ketchups Bank Glamping** If you ignore the fact that the walls are made of canvas and the doors zip rather than lock, the suites here are just like hotel rooms, but in the bush. 726 Green Hills Rd, Cannon Creek, Boonah; (07) 5463 4592; ketchupsbankglamping.com.au.
- **Spicers Peak Lodge** Perfect for a special occasion getaway – or just because you feel like some pampering – this mountain-top luxury lodge has suburb food, wine, views and a wonderful day spa. 1 Wilkinson Rd, Maryvale; 1300 253 103; spicersretreats.com.
- **Caravanning and camping** Camping is permitted in the Green Mountains section of Lamington National Park. There is a caravan park on the shores of Lake Moogerah and the grassy campsites run right down to the water's edge, so if you time it right you can secure yourself the ultimate water view. The park has powered and unpowered sites for both tents and vans, and facilities include boat ramps, playground, laundry, kiosk, barbecues and all amenities (Lake Moogerah Caravan Park, Muller Park Rd, Moogerah; (07) 5463 0141; moogerah.com). In Main Range National Park, there are three camping areas with basic facilities: Spicers Gap, and Poplar Flat and Manna Gum at Goomburra. Private campgrounds (both pet friendly) are located opposite Queen Mary Falls and at Goomburra.

Opposite The grand town hall at Warwick *Left top* Stop for lunch or a coffee at Spring Creek Mountain Cafe *Left bottom* The winding road to Spicers Peak Lodge

Gourmet getaways

Enjoy these food-and-wine destinations that also offer plenty of things to do that don't involve eating and drinking.

This route winds through South Australia's picturesque ranges, pretty valleys and historic towns – and three of the country's best wine regions: the Adelaide Hills, the Barossa Valley and the Clare Valley.

Wine Country, SA

HOW LONG?

Allow four to five days, depending on how many wineries you want to visit. Alternatively, you can split the trip into three day drives from Adelaide, one to each wine region.

WHEN TO GO

Any time of year is a good time to explore these three wine regions. Summers are warm and fairly dry; most rain falls during winter. The large gardens of the Adelaide Hills look spectacular during autumn.

NEED TO KNOW

Harvest time is usually at the end of summer and a number of harvest festival events are held in autumn. See crushfestival.com.au and barossavintagefestival.com.au for details of specific events.

 Drive rating
Easy. Sealed roads with some winding sections

 Distances
Total distance, return to Adelaide (with detours): approximately 400km
- Adelaide to Hahndorf: 26km
- Hahndorf to Gumeracha: 29km
- Gumeracha to Tanunda: 48km
- Tanunda to Clare: 97km
- Clare to Burra: 41km
- Burra to Adelaide: 162km

 Temperatures
January: 15–30°C
July: 5–13°C

 More information
- Adelaide Hills Visitor Information Centre, 68 Mount Barker Rd, Hahndorf; (08) 8393 7600; adelaidehills.org.au
- Barossa Wine and Visitor Information Centre, 66–68 Murray St, Tanunda; 1300 852 982; barossa.com
- Clare Valley Visitor Information Centre, 8 Spring Gully Rd, Clare; (08) 8842 2131; clarevalley.com.au

 Snapshot
The Barossa and Clare valleys, both just an hour or two's drive from Adelaide, are among the country's most celebrated wine-producing regions. Rich in heritage, these two valleys offer a diverse range of landscapes and activities and are a popular place for a weekend gourmet getaway, with walking and cycling the main adventure activities on offer. Even closer to Adelaide, the Adelaide Hills region is a mixture of Australian bushland and European-style farmland, with historic villages and towns, beautiful gardens, galleries and vineyards.

Previous Twilight drinks at TarraWarra Estate, Yarra Valley *Opposite* The gnarled vines of South Australia's wine country

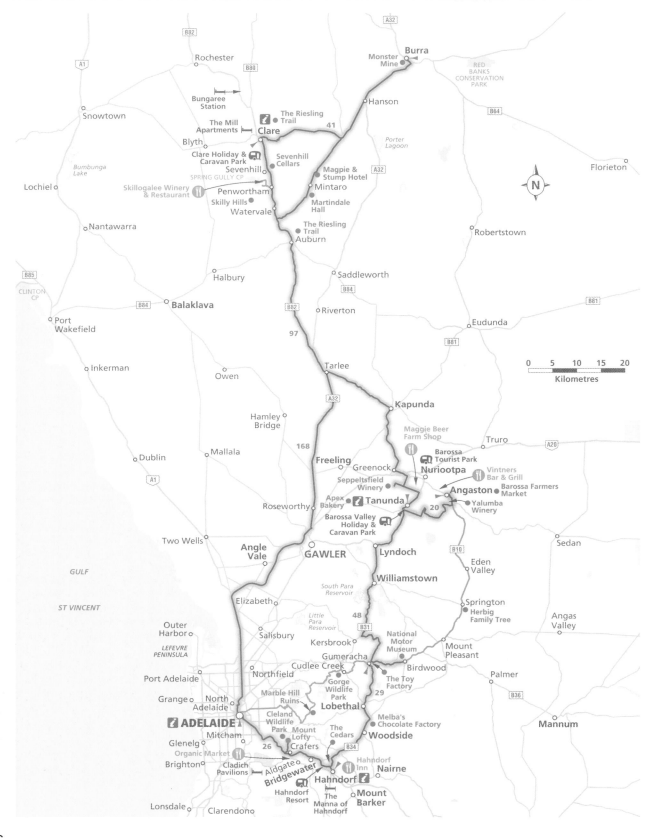

Wine Country, SA

ADELAIDE HILLS

Lying less than half an hour's drive from the city, the rugged hill-top scenery, vineyards, art galleries and historic towns of the Adelaide Hills make for a great daytrip. From the city head south-east via the freeway and the Heysen Tunnels to Crafers. From there wind up and across the top of the Mount Lofty Ranges. According to the local Aboriginal Creation story, Mount Lofty is one of two ears of the giant Urebilla, whose fallen body forms the Mount Lofty Ranges. The summit of Mount Lofty is *the* place to stop for city views; you can also visit the cafe and wander around the Botanic Gardens, where the walking trails are lined with stunning displays of native and exotic plants.

Hahndorf is the unofficial capital of the Adelaide Hills region and by far the most popular town with visitors. Settled in 1839 by Prussian and East German immigrants, Hahndorf is Australia's oldest surviving German settlement. The town's main street has about 90 historic buildings, many housing craft shops, galleries, cellar doors and restaurants. It is the ideal place to buy traditionally made German wursts and smallgoods or indulge in delicious German teacakes and strudels.

 KIDS' SPOT

Want to immerse your kids in nature? Stop off at Cleland Conservation Park on Mount Lofty, home to Cleland Wildlife Park, a lovely bushland park with native Australian animals. Join animal attendants on the animal-feed runs or on a guided night walk (bookings essential for the night walks). 365 Mount Lofty Summit Rd, Crafers; (08) 8339 2444; open Mon–Sun 9.30am–5pm; clelandwildlifepark.sa.gov.au.

The streets of picturesque Hahndorf are lined with historic buildings

Famous Australian landscape painter Hans Heysen lived in Hahndorf for more than 50 years and his former home, the Cedars, is on the outskirts of town and is open for tours. The homestead is furnished with original artefacts and is full of family treasures and paintings by Heysen, including many portraits and still-life works. His studio remains just as he left it when he died in 1968. Inside the house is the studio of his daughter, Nora, a renowned artist in her own right: she was the first woman to win the Archibald Prize and the first woman to be appointed as an Australian war artist. (Heysen Rd, Hahndorf; (08) 8388 7277; open Tues–Sun 10am–4.30pm, guided tours 11am, 1pm and 3pm; hansheysen.com.au.)

Wind your way towards Gumeracha along Onkaparinga Valley Road, past vineyards and orchards. Stop for a chocolate fix at Melba's Chocolate Factory in Woodside, where you can watch chocolate being made on historic machinery and then taste and buy the finished goods (22 Henry St, Woodside; (08) 8389 7868; open Mon–Sun 9am–4.30pm).

Head east on the Torrens Valley Road to Birdwood and spend a couple of hours in the National Motor Museum, one of the largest collections of cars, motorcycles and commercial vehicles in the world, with more than 300 vehicles dating from the late 1800s to the present day. Not just for rev heads, this museum examines the social influence of the motor car in Australia and has some fun interactive family exhibits as well as displays of hundreds of motor vehicles, motorbikes, buses and trucks. (Shannon St, Birdwood; (08) 8568 4000; open Mon–Sun 10am–5pm; motor.history.sa.gov.au.)

SIDETRACK

If you are making a daytrip of the Adelaide Hills, circle back to the city via Gorge Road, a scenic drive that follows the course of the Torrens River. Then drive across the range on the Mount Lofty Scenic Route, passing the ruins of Marble Hill, the summer home of South Australian governors until it was destroyed by bushfires in the 1950s. It's now in private ownership and is currently being rebuilt to its former glory. Open days are occasionally held; check marblehill.com.au for details. Then follow the steep, winding switchbacks down the mountainside to Adelaide.

☺ KIDS' SPOT

For old-school wooden toys, you can't go past the Toy Factory at Gumeracha, but what the kids will love the most is climbing the giant rocking horse, reputed to be the biggest in the world (453 Torrens Valley Rd, Gumeracha; (08) 8389 1085; open Mon–Sun 9am–5pm). Nearby, Gorge Wildlife Park is Australia's largest privately owned collection of native and exotic animals and birds, including American alligators, meerkats, otters and monkeys, contained in 6ha of natural bushland (30 Redden Dr, Cudlee Creek; (08) 8389 2206; open Mon–Sun 9am–5pm; gorgewildlifepark.com.au).

BAROSSA VALLEY

Despite its larger-than-life reputation in the wine world, the Barossa Valley is a snug collection of country towns surrounded by vineyards that is very easy to explore on a daytrip from Adelaide. Distances between towns are short, and many wineries sit next door to each other, so it's easy to visit a few in a very short time. Be warned, however: with all that delicious food and wine to taste, it's likely you'll want to stay overnight and indulge.

The Barossa has been famous for its rich, big-bodied shiraz for many years, but the region's heritage of growing, curing, preserving and cooking its own unique foods is less well known. The Lutheran settlers who came here 170 years ago have left not only a legacy of beautiful churches but also a bounty of wonderful small meats, sausages, preserved fruits, cheeses and delicious breads, all unique to the valley. Most restaurants and cafes pride themselves on serving as much local produce as possible, and tasting plates featuring a range of local specialities are served at many cellar doors.

The best starting point for a tour is Tanunda, about an hour's drive from the city or half an hour from Gumeracha on the B31 via Lyndoch. The Apex Bakery in Tanunda is famous for its German-style bread, pretzels and pastries. Many of the valley's best wineries are close by – take a drive along Krondorf Road or head out to Seppeltsfield, past Maggie Beer's Farm Shop, and along the avenue of 2000 date palms planted as a work scheme for winery workers during the 1930s Depression. The winery was established in 1851, and the Seppelt family were pioneers in Australian winemaking. Taste the wines at the historic cellar door, take one of several different history and tasting tours of the complex, picnic in the gardens and visit the grand Seppelt family mausoleum. (730 Seppeltsfield Rd, Seppeltsfield; (08) 8568 6200; open Mon–Sun 10.30am–5pm; seppeltsfield.com.au.)

Double back to Tanunda and take the Bethany Road to Angaston for a pretty drive through the vine-clad hills. Stop at historic Yalumba, with its distinctive clock tower. Established in 1849, it's the oldest family-owned winery still operating in Australia. Visit the nursery, cooperage and tasting room. (40 Eden Valley Rd, Angaston; (08) 8561 3200; open Mon–Sun 10am–5pm.) If you're in Angaston on a Saturday don't miss the Barossa Farmers Market, a 'food-only' market featuring produce associated with the heritage and traditions of the region (Vintners Sheds, cnr Stockwell and Nuriootpa rds, Angaston; Sat 7.30–11.30am).

SIDETRACK

If you're heading back to Adelaide from the Barossa, go via the beautiful Eden Valley (B10/Mount Pleasant Road), which is well known for its riesling. Keep an eye out for the Herbig Family Tree, a giant hollow red gum once home to Barossa settler Friedrich Herbig, his wife, Caroline, and the first two of their 16 children between 1855 and 1860. It's just south of Springton.

Opposite The former studio of landscape painter Hans Heysen in Hahndorf *Above* Planted during the 1930s Depression, 2000 date palms line Seppeltsfield Road

CLARE VALLEY

The Clare Valley, a 90-minute drive from Adelaide, has more than 40 wineries, all within 15 minutes' drive of each other, and is one of Australia's oldest wine regions. The first Europeans to settle in the area were from England, Ireland and Poland. One of their legacies was a rich architectural heritage, most of which remains, although the original village homes now tend to house restaurants and galleries. The first vines were planted in 1842 by James Green, servant to one of the district's first settlers, John Horrocks.

To get to the Clare from the Barossa (or Adelaide), follow the Main North Road to Auburn, the birthplace of C.J. Dennis, of *Sentimental Bloke* fame. The town has many beautifully maintained historical buildings, many of which now house good-value, country antiques stores.

SIDETRACK

All sorts of grapes are grown in the Clare, but the valley is best known for its riesling. The Riesling Trail is a 27km sealed walking and cycling path that follows a disused railway line between Clare and Auburn and takes about two hours to complete if you are cycling. There are three loop trails along the way for those who want to park and ride; parking is also available at Clare, Sevenhill, Watervale and Auburn. Bikes can be hired at Clare (call 0418 802 077) and free trail maps are available from visitor centres (or visit southaustraliantrails.com/trails/riesling-trail).

SIDETRACK

Spear off the main road at Penwortham and travel up through the Skilly Hills. The network of back roads is mostly unsealed and deeply potholed in places, but it will take you past many wineries, into the Spring Gully Conservation Park and through beautiful bush scenery.

Don't miss the cellars at Sevenhill. Founded in the mid-19th century by early Jesuit settlers, the winery offers tastings and sales in the old monastery cellars, as well as tours of the underground cellar, museum, St Aloysius' Church, historic cemetery, crypt and shrines. (College Rd, Sevenhill; (08) 8843 4222; open Mon–Sun 10am–5pm; sevenhill.com.au.)

You can return home to Adelaide the way you came, but a worthwhile detour is to head north-east for 43km and spend some time in historic Burra. This quaint little town is one of the world's best preserved colonial mining communities. An excellent way to fully explore the town is with a Heritage Passport, a detailed guidebook with an entry ticket to sites

along an 11km heritage trail. There are 47 sites in all, including historic cottages, the gaol, churches, museums and the Monster Mine. If that all sounds like too much serious history, you could, alternatively, spend a couple of hours browsing the many antiques shops in town.

From Burra, head back to Adelaide via the historic hamlet of Mintaro, South Australia's first proclaimed historic town. Call into the Magpie and Stump Hotel for a cold drink or visit Martindale Hall, a historic mansion built in 1881 and located in the 18ha Martindale Hall Conservation Park, which was originally established in 1841 as a grazing property called Martindale Station (1 Manoora Rd, Mintaro; (08) 8843 9088; open Wed–Mon 11am–4pm; martindalehall-mintaro.com.au).

BEST EATS

- **Organic Market** Food store and cafe serving delicious breakfasts, light lunches, organic beer and wine, and good coffee. 5 Druid Ave, Stirling; (08) 8339 4835; open Mon–Sun 8.30am–5pm.
- **Hahndorf Inn** For the full German eating experience you can't go past this inn, with its menu of pickled pork hocks, pork knuckles, sauerkraut and a vast array of bockwurst, bratwurst, weisswurst and kransky sausages. At the very least, pop in for a stein of German beer and a monster-sized pretzel. 35 Main Rd, Hahndorf; (08) 8388 7063; open Mon–Sun 10.30am–late; hahndorfinn.com.
- **Maggie Beer Farm Shop** Try some of the celebrity chef's farm produce in the eatery or stock up for a picnic. 50 Pheasant Farm Rd, off Samuel Rd, Nuriootpa; (08) 8562 1902; open Mon–Sun for lunch; maggiebeer.com.au.
- **Vintners Bar & Grill** This Barossa dining landmark specialises in modern bistro dishes inspired by local produce. Cnr Stockwell and Angaston rds, Angaston; (08) 8564 2488; open Mon–Sun for lunch, Mon–Sat for dinner; vintners.com.au.
- **Skillogalee Winery and Restaurant** Eat inside the tiny 150-year-old Cornish miner's cottage or on the terrace under the olive tree overlooking the vineyard and Skilly Hills. Trevarrick Rd, Sevenhill; (08) 8843 4311; open Mon–Sun for breakfast and lunch, best to book on weekends; skillogalee.com.au.

BEST SLEEPS

- **Cladich Pavilions** These luxury contemporary villas are set in bushland on the outskirts of Aldgate in the Adelaide Hills. 27–29 Wilpena Tce, Aldgate; (08) 8339 8248; cladichpavilions.com.
- **The Manna of Hahndorf** If you want to stay in the heart of Hahndorf, this place offers good-value motel-style rooms (some with spas) and studio apartments at sister property the Haus. Guests have the use of a heated pool at another sister hotel, the nearby Lodge. 25 Main St, Hahndorf; (08) 8388 1000; themanna.com.au.
- **The Mill Apartments** Enjoy a leafy outlook from the cluster of luxe, self-contained one-bedroom villas surrounded by bushland, even though they are in the middle of Clare's main street. 310 Horrocks Hwy, Clare; (08) 8842 1111; themill.apartments.

Opposite Red or white? Wine-tasting at Clare Valley's Kilikanoon Wines. *Right* A blissful moment of quiet at Skillogalee Winery and Restaurant

- **Bungaree Station** One of the oldest working sheep farms in South Australia, Bungaree was established in 1841 and by the 1880s was one of the state's largest sheep stations, with more than 100,000 sheep. The property was effectively a small village, with its own church, station store, carpenter's shop, blacksmith's forge, police troopers' station, woolshed and shearing quarters and staff cottages, as well as an imposing homestead. Many of the historic buildings have been converted into accommodation, ranging from cute little studio apartments to self-contained two- and four-bedroom cabins. It's 12km north of Clare on Main North Rd/Highway B82; (08) 8842 2677; bungareestation.com.au.
- **Caravanning and camping** Camping is prohibited in most of the national and conservation parks in the region, so you are restricted to commercial caravan parks. The Hahndorf Resort has more than 100 caravan and camping sites and is a short stroll to town (145A Main St, Hahndorf; 1300 763 836; hahndorfresort.com.au). In the Barossa, the Barossa Tourist Park at Nuriootpa (Penrice Rd, Nuriootpa; (08) 8562 1404; barossatouristpark.com.au) and the Barossa Valley Holiday and Caravan Park (Barossa Valley Way, Tanunda; (08) 8218 5505) are both central to the attractions and wineries. In the Clare, try the Clare Holiday and Caravan Park (8511 Horrocks Hwy, Clare; (08) 8842 2724).

Whether you come for the golf, the gardens or the grapes, the Hunter Valley in New South Wales is a great weekend escape.

Hunter Valley, NSW

HOW LONG?

Two to three days if you do the entire loop through the Barrington Tops. If you just want to tour the wine area, head east at Singleton to Maitland and south back to Sydney on the Pacific Highway/Motorway.

WHEN TO GO

The Hunter Valley has a temperate climate with temperatures rarely reaching extremes, though it can be humid in January. March to April is harvest time with lots of special events on. Dustings of snow are not uncommon in winter in the Barrington Tops.

NEED TO KNOW

Dogs are not allowed in the national parks, even if you are only dropping in for half an hour or so to visit a lookout or unpack a picnic.

 Drive rating

Moderate. Mostly sealed roads with some winding sections. The Barrington Tops Forest Road is steep, winding and unsealed and can sometimes be rough, but is generally fine for 2WDs and smaller caravans.

 Distances

Total distance, Sydney to Newcastle via the Barrington Tops: 560km
- Sydney to Pokolbin: 164km
- Pokolbin to Singleton: 41km
- Singleton to Scone: 73km
- Scone to Gloucester: 144km
- Gloucester to Newcastle: 124km

 Temperatures

January: 16–26°C
July: 6–13°C

More information
- Gloucester Visitor Information Centre, 27 Denison St, Gloucester; (02) 6538 5252; gloucestertourism.com.au
- Hunter Valley Visitor Information Centre, 455 Wine Country Dr, Pokolbin; (02) 4993 6700; winecountry.com.au

 Snapshot

The Hunter Valley, about a two-hour drive north-west of Sydney, is home to some of Australia's best wineries and winemakers. But the Hunter Valley is not just all wine and roses. To the north-east the World Heritage–listed rainforest wilderness of the Barrington Tops sits at one of the highest points of the Great Dividing Range. The Hunter River spills into the sea at Newcastle, the state's second largest city. With a natural harbour two and half times as large as Sydney's, a string of ocean beaches and its surrounding national parks, Port Stephens is an aquatic playground.

SYDNEY TO CESSNOCK VIA WOLLOMBI

If you're driving from Sydney the quickest way to get to the Hunter is to take the Pacific Motorway (M1) north and then the Cessnock exit.

SIDETRACK

For a scenic alternative to the freeway, when you get to the Central Coast take the Peats Ridge Road exit from the motorway and follow Tourist Drive 33 through Bucketty and Wollombi. In the early 19th century the village of Wollombi, 30km south-west of Cessnock, was established on the Great North Road, a convict-built feat of road engineering still visible today. The Endeavour Museum in the old courthouse has a local history collection and is well worth the $2 entry fee (Maitland Rd; (02) 4998 3375; Mon, Wed and Thurs 11am–1.30pm, Fri 11am–3pm, Sat–Sun 11am–4pm). Pop into the Wollombi Tavern for a tasting of the infamous Dr. Jurd's Jungle Juice. This fruity fortified wine is an acquired taste, but sipping a cold drink on the verandah overlooking the creek at the back of the hotel is a nice way to spend some time.

Follow the signs to Broke, skirting the Broken Back Range, and you'll start to see more vines and fewer cattle. Broke and nearby Pokolbin and Lovedale are the heart of the main wine-producing area and there are more than 120 cellar doors in the area.

If you like golf then you'll love the Hunter. There are three premium courses in the Valley: the Hunter Valley Golf and Country Club, the Oaks Cypress Lakes (which has the Golden Door Spa for those partners who prefer massages and pampering to hacking and chipping) and the Greg Norman course 'the Vintage'. Contact the visitor centre for details.

UPPER HUNTER TO SCONE

The Upper Hunter Valley, bounded by the towns of Singleton, Denman and Muswellbrook, also features some great wineries, although not as many as the Pokolbin–Cessnock–Lovedale area. To get there from Cessnock, follow the signs to the New England Highway, travelling through Branxton and then on to Singleton.

In Singleton, visit the Australian Army Infantry Museum, just off the New England Highway on the Sydney side of town. Even pacifists will find this museum interesting as it tells the story of all Australian infantry involvements beginning with Sudanese service in 1885. There are lots of guns, but also some great exhibits giving charming snapshots of the human side of the infantry – such as the recorded tales 'told' by a pair of soldier's boots: the nightclubs they danced in, the battles they fought and the time they, and their owner, went AWOL. (Hamilton VC Dr, Singleton; (02) 6575 0257; open Wed–Sun 9am–4pm; infantrymuseum.com.au.)

☺ KIDS' SPOT

Wander down a magical garden path at the Hunter Valley Gardens. Its 8km of pathways wind through 12 themed gardens, including a storybook garden for the kids, with recorded nursery rhymes and fairytales and lots of storybook characters. In December the gardens open at night and host a spectacular Christmas light display. Broke Rd, Pokolbin; (02) 4998 4000; open Mon–Sun 9am–5pm; huntervalleygardens.com.au.

From Singleton continue north to Scone, one of the world's largest thoroughbred horse-breeding centres, eclipsed only by Kentucky in the United States. Take a drive around the district and you'll see airconditioned stables with facilities that rival many of the Hunter's five-star hotels and guesthouses.

SCONE TO GLOUCESTER

The Barrington Tops Forest Road runs from Moonan Flat near Scone (take the Gundy Road) along Tourist Drive 29 up over the mountains and through Barrington Tops National Park to emerge on the eastern side of the range not far from Gloucester. It's a must-do daytrip when in the area. While sections of it are unsealed, the road is fine for conventional cars (although it can be in rough shape after rain). The panoramic scenery along the route is breathtaking as you pass from the grassy foothills into the rainforest and up onto the plateau, and there are numerous places along the way to stop at lookouts for short walks and picnics.

SIDETRACK

The Barrington Trail is a summertime, 4WD-only track that runs off the Barrington Tops Forest Road. The 15km trail leaves the Barrington Tops Forest Road about 1.7km east of Polblue Swamp and winds through beautiful subalpine snow-gum forests to riverside camping spots and Mount Barrington picnic area. The Barrington Trail is closed each year between 1 June and 30 September.

Opposite Enjoying the good life at Pokolbin's Tinkler's Wine *Above* Spring colour at Hunter Valley Gardens

GLOUCESTER TO NEWCASTLE

From Gloucester head south down the Bucketts Way, named for the mountains behind the town, which are called the Bucketts. This is a country road in its truest sense: there are sections that are more like a goat track than a highway, most of the time there will be little traffic and the scenery is some of the prettiest you'll find in country New South Wales.

Take a break at the historic village of Stroud, home of the annual International Brick and Rolling Pin Throwing Competition in July (stroudbrickthrowing.com.au). Most of the buildings along the main street date from the 1830s and many are convict built.

Hunter Valley, NSW

SIDETRACK

Take the turn-off to Nelson Bay, just south of where the Bucketts Way joins the Pacific Highway. Port Stephens claims it is the 'Dolphin Capital of Australia' and the bay is home to a resident pod of about 150 bottlenose dolphins. There are ten operators offering dolphin cruises and in winter (late May–Nov) it's a great place to see whales. Whale- and dolphin-watching cruises depart from Nelson Bay Marina. Tomaree Headland is part of an extinct volcano that guards the southern entrance to Port Stephens. The half-hour walk from the beach at Shoal Bay to the summit is steep but not as hard as it looks and the views from the top over the bay, beaches and offshore islands make the climb worthwhile. During World War II a fort was built on the headland and you can explore the remains of gun emplacements and fortifications along the way (portstephens.org.au).

Officially still part of the Hunter Valley – the harbour is at the mouth of the Hunter River – Newcastle is one of the biggest coal-exporting ports in the world, and the city has always been best known for its hot and heavy industry, including steelmaking. Grab a stool at one of the riverside bars or cafes in Honeysuckle and watch the massive freighters being guided in and out of the harbour by tugboats. Newcastle Museum also has a good display on the industrial heritage of the city, including a (very noisy) sound-and-light show that features molten steel being poured from a furnace (Workshop Way, Honeysuckle; (02) 4974 1400; open Tues–Sun 10am–5pm, Mon–Sun during school holidays; newcastlemuseum.com.au).

You're never very far from the beach in Newcastle. Follow the waterfront promenade and walk along the convict-built breakwall up to the lighthouse on Nobbys Head at the harbour entrance for some great views. Nobbys is linked to the string of beaches to the south by the Bathers Way, a 5km coastal walk. Stop for a swim at the Art Deco Newcastle Ocean Baths or head to the Bogey Hole at the southern end of Newcastle Beach. It was carved out of the cliff face by convicts in 1819. There's another ocean pool at Merewether, the largest in the Southern Hemisphere, and most of the beachfront parks along the way have barbecue and picnic facilities. From Newcastle you can drive back to Sydney via the motorway in about two hours.

Opposite Newcastle's The Landing Bar and Kitchen is great for a casual meal or drink *Left* Take a dip in Newcastle's famous Ocean Baths

BEST EATS

- **Hunter Valley Cheese Factory** This is the place to come if you are planning your own picnic (many of the vineyards have picnic areas). It has a well-stocked produce room with local olive oils, jams, mustards, spreads, dried fruits, breads and, of course, cheeses. 447 McDonalds Rd, Pokolbin; (02) 4998 7744; open Mon–Sun 9am–5.30pm.
- **Muse** Treat yourself to a special meal surrounded by grape vines at the Hunter's best fine dining restaurant. The menu specialises in local produce. Hungerford Hill Winery, 2450 Broke Rd, Pokolbin; (02) 4998 6777; open Sat–Sun for lunch and Wed–Sat for dinner; musedining.com.au.
- **Roadies Cafe** Popular with touring motorcyclists (it's full of vintage bikes and memorabilia), this is a nice spot for lunch, and their dinners and wood-fired pizzas are pretty good too. 77 Church St, Gloucester; (02) 6558 2772; open Mon–Sun for breakfast and lunch.
- **The Landing Bar & Kitchen** This is a great option for lunch or dinner in Newcastle. The beer garden and cocktail lounge bar have a view over the working harbour. 1 Honeysuckle Dr, Honeysuckle; (02) 4927 1722; open Mon–Sun for lunch and dinner.

BEST SLEEPS

- **Oaks Cypress Lakes Resort** Accommodation is offered in 200 luxury villas with views across the 18-hole golf course or surrounding bush. Beyond the golf and day spa, facilities include tennis courts, three swimming pools, a fitness centre, bike hire, archery, petanque, bushwalking and a kids' club. Golf and spa packages are available. Cnr McDonalds and Thompsons rds, Pokolbin; (02) 4993 1555; oakshotels.com.
- **Spicers Guest House** Overlooking vineyards and bushland in Pokolbin, this luxe guesthouse has open fires in winter and an excellent restaurant. Also on-site are a swimming pool and tennis court and complimentary bicycles if you want to explore surrounding vineyards. 57 Ekerts Rd, Pokolbin; 1300 192 868; spicersretreats.com.
- **Copeland House Rainforest Retreat** Adults-only suites – all with spa baths and private balconies – on the edge of the rainforest are offered at this retreat, about a 10-minute drive from Gloucester; on-site dining available on request. 129 Old Copeland Rd, Copeland; (02) 6558 4330; copelandhouse.com.au.
- **Novotel Newcastle Beach** Most rooms have balconies with great views overlooking either Newcastle Beach or Nobbys Headland and the harbour entrance, and it's an easy walk into the centre of town. 5 King St, Newcastle; (02) 4032 3700; novotelnewcastlebeach.com.au.

- **Caravanning and camping** You can camp at Finchley camping ground in Yengo National Park and further east in Watagans National Park. The Ingenia Holidays Hunter Valley in Cessnock is the best bet for pet-friendly caravanning in the heart of the Hunter (ingeniaholidays.com.au/hunter-valley). In the Barrington Tops, Polblue camping area is a roomy campground suitable for cars and caravans, though at 1450m above sea level it can get chilly at night. Also suitable for caravans are the Horse Swamp camping area on Tubrabucca Road and Gloucester River campground off the Gloucester Tops Road. Four-wheel-drive camping spots include the Gummi Falls, Junction Pools and Little Murray Swamp. In Newcastle a great family option is NRMA Stockton Beach Holiday Park (with cabins as well as caravan and camping sites), a five-minute ferry ride from the city centre (nrmaparksandresorts.com.au).

Victoria's Dandenong Ranges and Yarra Valley are food-and-wine destinations that also offer plenty of things to do that don't involve eating and drinking, with wildlife, art and ferny forests topping the list.

Dandenong Ranges and Yarra Valley, Vic.

HOW LONG?

The drive can be done in a day, or take your time and make a weekend of it. To cut the trip short, head straight to Marysville via Yarra Glen and leave the Dandenongs for another day.

WHEN TO GO

Summer is temperate, with the ranges being much cooler than the valley. Winter is more likely to be wet.

NEED TO KNOW

Some roads in Yarra Ranges National Park are subject to seasonal road closures. Check current road conditions with Parks Victoria by looking under the Parks Management (closures and conditions) tab of parkweb.vic. gov.au, or call 13 1963.

Drive rating
Easy. Sealed roads with some winding sections

Distances
Total distance, return to Melbourne (with detours): approximately 270km
- Melbourne to Healesville via Mount Dandenong: 95km
- Healesville to Marysville: 34km
- Marysville to Melbourne via Warburton: 138km

Temperatures
January: 11–26°C
July: 4–12°C

More information
- Yarra Valley Visitor Information Centre, Harker St, Healesville; (03) 5962 2600; visityarravalley.com.au
- visitdandenongranges.com.au

Snapshot
One of the most popular weekend getaway destinations for Melburnians is the Dandenongs and Yarra Valley region. Drive through the lush rainforest and the vine-covered hills and you'll soon see why: lovely views, great food, superb wine and lots to see and do – all one hour from the city.

Opposite top left Oak barrels at Giant Steps Winery *Top right* The Black Spur Drive links the Yarra Valley with the mountain forests near Marysville *Bottom left* Quaint boutiques in Olinda *Bottom right* Modern art on show at TarraWarra Museum of Art

MELBOURNE TO HEALESVILLE VIA THE DANDENONG RANGES

Forget big concrete bananas, giant fibreglass pineapples and the big apple: the Dandenong Ranges, on the outskirts of Melbourne, are home to the tallest flowering plant on the planet: the mighty *Eucalyptus regnans*, or mountain ash. And it's not just one but whole forests of this towering tree, some more than 100m high, sheltering misty gullies of lush tree ferns and framing historic cool-climate gardens. To get to the Dandenongs, take the M1 out of Melbourne towards Belgrave or Ferntree Gully.

Garden lovers will find plenty of reasons to linger near the town of Olinda, a popular spot with boutiques, antiques stores and cafes. The Dandenong Ranges Botanic Garden on the Georgian Road is home to 15,000 rhododendrons, 12,000 azaleas, 3000 camellias and 250,000 daffodils. In spring and autumn, its gardens are cloaked in colour and perfume. They also feature moorlands, rock gardens, fern gullies and sweeping lawns. (13 1963; open Mon–Sun 10am–5pm; parkweb.vic.gov.au.)

Nearby is the William Ricketts Sanctuary, where almost 100 kiln-fired clay sculptures of Aboriginal figures are set among rocks, fern trees and mountain ash. William Ricketts bought the 1.6ha bush block on Mount Dandenong in the 1930s and called it Potter's Sanctuary. Word soon spread about the extraordinary sculptures with which Ricketts was adorning the property, and in the 1960s the Victorian Government heard about his work and bought the sanctuary, which is now managed by Parks Victoria. William Ricketts lived on at the sanctuary into his nineties and continued to create sculptures until his death in 1993. (Off Mount Dandenong Tourist Rd, Mount Dandenong; 13 1963; open Mon–Sun 10am–4.30pm; parkweb.vic.gov.au.)

☺ KIDS' SPOT

Take a ride on Puffing Billy, a century-old steam train still running on its original mountain track from Belgrave to Gembrook through some of the most picturesque scenery near Melbourne – the soaring mountain ash forests and fern gullies of the Dandenongs. Even the locals, who see the train every day, will stop to wave madly as it trundles by (your kids will be keen to wave back). Built in 1900, the narrow-gauge railway line was used to transport goods and produce from local farms to and from Melbourne. 1 Old Monbulk Rd, Belgrave; (03) 9757 0700; trains operate Mon–Sun; puffingbilly.com.au.

Head up to the summit of Mount Dandenong to the lookout at Sky High Mount Dandenong, where you'll find plenty of things to do beyond staring at the amazing view – explore the Sky High Maze, gardens, tree sculptures and forest trail or lunch at the cafe with Melbourne spread out below you.

As you head north towards Yarra Glen and Healesville on the Maroondah Highway, you'll start to see more vines covering the slopes – you're heading into the famous Yarra Valley wine region. About 6km before you get to Healesville on the Healesville–Yarra Glen Road is one of the hidden gems of the Yarra Valley, the TarraWarra Museum of Art. Housing one of the most significant collections of modern Australian art, this private gallery includes works by outstanding Australian artists from 1950 onwards, displayed in a series of seasonal exhibitions in a stunningly designed gallery space where even the view is framed as art. (311 Healesville–Yarra Glen Rd; (03) 5957 3100; open Tues–Sun 11am–5pm; twma.com.au.)

Opposite One of the striking sculptures at the William Ricketts Sanctuary *Above* The Dandenongs' famous Puffing Billy steam train

KIDS' SPOT

A favourite spot for many is the wonderful Healesville Sanctuary, Healesville's most famous attraction, which was first established in 1934. So much more than just another zoo, this conservation park is home to more than 200 species of Australian wildlife, all housed in open-air and open-range exhibits, many so cleverly constructed that it's almost impossible to see the enclosure boundaries. Highlights include the brilliant bird-of-prey flight demonstrations, a daily reptile show and the 'platypusary', where you can tickle Australia's most elusive monotreme on a Wade with Platypus tour (Mon–Sun 1pm). The sanctuary also looks after more than 2000 rescued animals each year and you can watch the vets and keepers caring for their patients. Glen Eadie Ave, Healesville; 1300 966 784; open Mon–Sun 9am–5pm; zoo.org.au/healesville.

HEALESVILLE TO MARYSVILLE

The Black Spur, between Healesville and Narbethong, is a narrow 10km section of the Maroondah Highway that winds its way up into the Great Dividing Range through towering mountain ash and lush green fern forests. This area, along with the town of Marysville, was devastated by the tragic Black Saturday bushfires of 2009, which claimed 173 lives. Although you can still see the charred remains of some trees, much of the forest is lush and green with regrowth.

Continue on to Marysville, which has been rebuilt since the fires, and visit Steavenson Falls, which, at 82m, are Victoria's highest cascades. If you are staying overnight, come back after dark when the falls are floodlit.

From Marysville, take Lady Talbot Forest Drive, a round-trip of 46km into Yarra Ranges National Park. There are several walking trails that will lead you through old-growth myrtle-beech forest to waterfalls plummeting over huge granite boulders and through dense rainforest. Unless you have a 4WD, however, it's a dry-weather road only.

Return to Melbourne via the Woods Point Road, which runs east from Marysville through Yarra Ranges National Park and along the Yarra River to Warburton.

Yarra Valley food trails

If you like eating and drinking, follow one of the Yarra Valley themed food trails that crisscross the entire region, taking in the Yarra Valley, the Warburton Ranges, the Dandenongs and Marysville. There's a cider-and-ale trail, a U-Pick trail (orchards and fruit farms where you can pick fruit), several wine trails and even a 'top picnic spot' trail. Along the way, you'll find dozens of producers whose foods feature on local and city restaurant menus – free-range eggs, honey, fruit, berries, herbs, cheeses, game, pasta, preserves, trout, clotted cream, chocolates and ice-cream. Before you set out, check the opening days of the local markets, where stalls are piled high with food, much of it organic. As for the wines, the area is one of the world's best cool-climate wine districts, specialising in sparkling wines, chardonnay and pinot noir. There are more than 160 wineries and vineyards in the valley, ranging from stunning multimillion-dollar commercial wineries to boutique, family-operated businesses – most have cellar doors offering a warm welcome to wine lovers. Download trail maps from visityarravalley.com.au and see yarravalleyfood.com.au for more information.

BEST EATS

- **Sky High Mount Dandenong** You can't beat this place for dining with a view. By day the city towers of Melbourne shimmer on the horizon; at night the plain below is a carpet of twinkling lights. 26 Observatory Rd; (03) 9751 0443; open Mon–Sun for lunch and dinner; skyhighmtdandenong.com.au.
- **Chateau Yering** Victoria's oldest vineyard offers sunny, casual dining at Sweetwater Cafe (Mon–Sun for breakfasts, coffee and cake; Fri–Sun for lunch), opulent afternoon tea and fine dining at Eleonore's Restaurant (Sat–Sun for high tea; Mon–Sun for dinner). 42 Melba Hwy, Yering; (03) 9237 3333; chateauyering.com.au.
- **Healesville Hotel** This beautifully restored 1910 hotel provides friendly country hospitality, roaring open fires, a monthly menu of fine French cooking and a stunning wine list. 256 Maroondah Hwy, Healesville; (03) 5962 4002; open Mon–Sun for lunch and dinner; yarravalleyharvest.com.au.
- **Innocent Bystander** This winery has a cellar door in the heart of town that also offers great gourmet pizzas and paella, artisan breads and local produce. 336 Maroondah Hwy, Healesville; (03) 5999 9222; open Mon–Sun for lunch and dinner; innocentbystander.com.au.

BEST SLEEPS

- **Chateau Yering** This luxurious all-suite boutique hotel occupies a historic mansion next door to Yering Station winery. Indulgence, adventure and wine packages are available. 42 Melba Hwy, Yering; (03) 9237 3333; chateauyering.com.au.
- **Balgownie Estate Vineyard Resort & Spa** Enjoy vineyard views from your luxe spa suite at Balgownie Estate. Facilities include a restaurant and cellar door wine-tasting area, Natskin Day Spa and Health Club with heated indoor pool and gym, tennis court and segway trail. Ask about the wine-lover packages. 1309 Melba Hwy, Yarra Glen; (03) 9730 0700; balgownieestate.com.au.
- **Healesville Apartments** The four apartments each have a balcony or terrace and are an easy walk from the centre of town. 18 Symons St, Healesville; 0497 999 020; healesvilleapartments.com.au.
- **Vibe Hotel Marysville** This new contemporary hotel with a pool in the heart of Marysville makes an ideal base from which to explore the region. 32–42 Murchison St, Marysville; (03) 5957 7700; vibehotels.com/hotel/marysville.
- **Caravanning and camping** Camping is permitted at Upper Yarra Reservoir Park and there are caravan parks in Warburton and Marysville. You can also camp in Cathedral Ranges State Park: advance bookings are required for Neds Gully (tents only) and Cooks Mill (suitable for a small number of caravans) at parkweb.vic.gov.au.

Opposite Pastries on offer at Innocent Bystander's Cellar Door
Above Healesville Hotel is great for a bite and a brew

Take a drive down the Mornington Peninsula, Victoria's favourite seaside escape. If the beaches aren't enough to tempt you, the array of fine wine and even finer food certainly will.

Mornington Peninsula, Vic.

HOW LONG?

You can do this drive in one day or stretch it out over two for a gourmet weekend escape. For a shortcut to Rosebud and the southern peninsula, take the M11 Mornington Peninsula Freeway from Melbourne (via the M3 Eastlink).

WHEN TO GO

Summer is mild, winter is more likely to be wet.

NEED TO KNOW

The Mornington Peninsula is a popular place, so if you're travelling on the weekend or during the summer school holidays, make sure you book accommodation and restaurants in advance.

Drive rating
Easy. Sealed roads

Distances
Total distance, return to Melbourne: approximately 265km
- Melbourne to Portsea: 107km
- Portsea to Cape Schanck: 29km
- Cape Schanck to Bittern: 37km
- Bittern to Melbourne: 80km

Temperatures
January: 13–25°C
July: 7–14°C

More information
Peninsula Visitor Information Centre, 359B Point Nepean Rd, Dromana; 1800 804 009; visitmorningtonpeninsula.org

Snapshot
About an hour's drive south of Melbourne, the Mornington Peninsula is one long beach – a 100km boot-shaped peninsula jutting into the ocean on the eastern edge of Port Phillip. Colonies of seals and bottlenose dolphins frolic in the bay and the beaches are flanked by lines of brightly coloured wooden 'bathing boxes'. In the hinterland, vineyards produce some of Victoria's best cool-climate wines, and fertile farmlands yield rich crops of olives, apples and strawberries.

Opposite You're spoilt for choice when it comes to beautiful beaches on the Mornington Peninsula

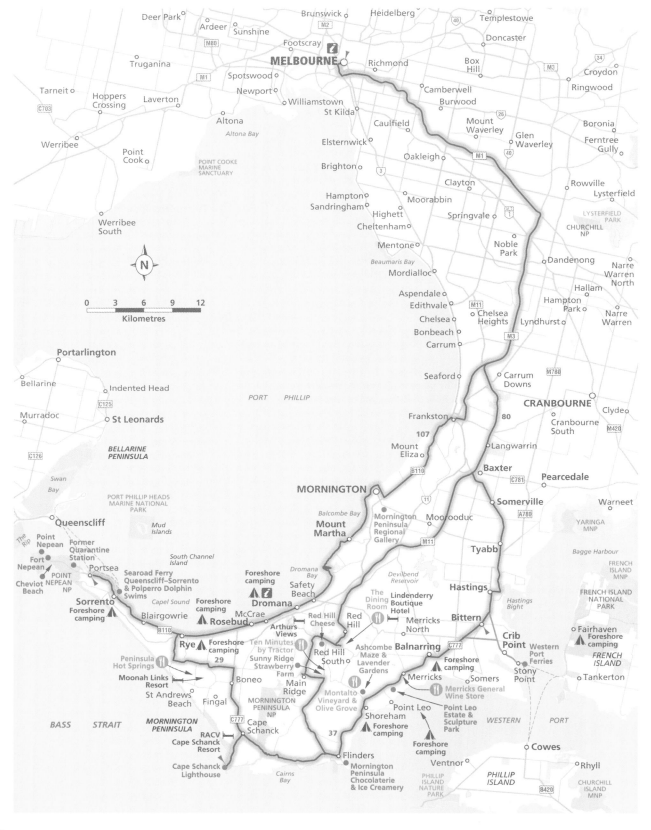

MELBOURNE TO PORTSEA

The best way to explore the peninsula is to drive along the western shore from Melbourne to Portsea, stopping on the way to explore towns like Mornington, Mount Martha, Dromana, Rosebud, Rye and Sorrento, which have attracted city people for decades. On a sunny summer day, crowds head for the sand and sea, often finishing off the afternoon in a beer garden in one of the beachside pubs or restaurants.

Visit Mornington Peninsula Regional Gallery (Civic Reserve, Dunns Rd, Mornington; (03) 5950 1580; open Tues–Sun 10am–5pm), go shopping in Sorrento or drop a fishing line from any number of small-town jetties and simply sit back and watch the pelicans drift by.

SIDETRACK

Situated at the entrance to Port Phillip and just a short, 40-minute vehicle ferry ride from Sorrento, Queenscliff started as a fishing village then became a fashionable holiday destination for Melbourne's elite in the late 19th century. Today it still attracts thousands of holidaymakers to its beaches, galleries and boutiques each year. For ferry details see searoad.com.au.

The Mornington Peninsula is a popular destination for dolphin-watching and there are about 150 bottlenose dolphins living in the bay. You can even join a summertime trip to swim with dolphins and Australian fur seals. Swimmers float in the water behind the boat, holding onto a rope while dolphins and seals approach; they are usually friendly, inquisitive and playful, and will often come very close to the swimmers. (Polperro Dolphin Swims; (03) 5988 8437; trips depart from Sorrento Pier Mon–Sun 8am and 12pm in summer and by arrangement in winter, bookings essential; polperro.com.au.)

POINT NEPEAN AND CAPE SCHANCK

Head out to Portsea and visit the former quarantine station and military fort at Point Nepean, in Point Nepean National Park. The Fort Nepean Walk is an easy 90-minute one-way walk to the tip of the peninsula; it passes Cheviot Beach, where Prime Minister Harold Holt disappeared in 1967. To the south, Mornington Peninsula National Park, with its windswept dunes and steep cliffs, stretches along the Bass Strait foreshore (the foot of the 'boot') from Portsea to Cape Schanck. It's home to grey kangaroos, southern brown bandicoots, echidnas, native rats and mice, reptiles, bats, and many forest and ocean birds. At Cape Schanck visit the 150-year-old lighthouse and learn more about its history in the museum (tours Mon–Sun between 10am and 4pm; capeschancklightstation.com.au).

 KIDS' SPOT

Get completely lost in Australia's oldest maze at Ashcombe Maze and Lavender Gardens, which also has a circular rose maze with 1200 rose bushes and a sweet-smelling lavender labyrinth. 15 Shoreham Rd, Shoreham; (03) 5989 8387; open Mon–Sun 9am–5pm; ashcombemaze.com.au.

Colourful beach boxes line the Mount Martha beachfront

FLINDERS

Take the Boneo Road from Cape Schanck east to Flinders then meander your way north through the sleepy beachside communities of Point Leo, Somers and Hastings, where koalas saunter along the tops of garden fences and the bush echoes with the call of native birds. Fine wine and fine art collide at Pt Leo Estate, home to an acclaimed fine dining restaurant, Laura, and a sculpture park with an outdoor gallery that offers changing exhibitions of more than 50 Australian and international artworks studded throughout the vineyard (3649 Frankston-Flinders Rd, Merricks; (03) 5989 9011; sculpture park and cellar door open Mon–Sun 11am–5pm; restaurant open Mon–Sun for lunch, Thurs–Sat for dinner; ptleoestate.com.au).

If you have a sweet tooth, call into Mornington Peninsula Chocolaterie and Ice Creamery. Almost too beautiful to eat, these handmade chocolates have won a swag of awards and gold medals, and tasting sessions are held throughout the day. (45 Cook St, Flinders; (03) 5989 0040; open Mon–Sun 9am–5pm; mpchoc.com.au.)

Alternatively, head into the centre of the peninsula on the Mornington-Flinders Road and drop in for a wine-tasting at one of the peninsula's 50 cellar doors. Another good spot to stop at is the cheese room at Red Hill Cheese. Made from local organic milk, from both cows and goats, the product range depends on the season and the type of milk available, but at any given time you can expect to find around ten or so varieties on sale. (81 William Rd, Red Hill; (03) 5989 2035; open Fri–Sun 11am–5pm; redhillcheese.com.au.)

SIDETRACK

Accessible by a 15-minute passenger ferry ride from Stony Point (about 5km south of Hastings), French Island is home to Victoria's largest population of koalas. Other inhabitants include a large population of long-nosed potoroos and diverse waterbirds including sea eagles and waders, which can be seen in and around the wetlands, mangroves and salt marshes. You can't take your car across, but bus tours are available and there are walks and bicycle trails (hire bikes at the general store) starting at Tankerton Foreshore Reserve, next to the jetty. For ferry information, see westernportferries.com.au.

😊 **KIDS' SPOT**

Kids like to pick their own strawberries, and Sunny Ridge Strawberry Farm is the largest strawberry producer in Australia. Take a farm tour, sample the fruit wines or succumb to the lure of rich strawberry jam, thick freshly whipped cream and homemade scones with a Devonshire tea in the farm's cafe. The homemade ice-cream is a must. Cnr Flinders and Shands rds, Main Ridge; (03) 5989 4500; open Mon–Sun 9am–5pm Nov–Apr (U-Pick season), Fri–Sun and public holidays 11am–4pm May–Oct; sunnyridge.com.au.

Opposite Relax with a warm soak in the natural thermal pools at the Peninsula Hot Springs *Above* The lure of fresh strawberries, Sunny Ridge Strawberry Farm

BEST EATS

- **Peninsula Hot Springs** Eat your heart out guilt free at one of three cafes at Peninsula Hot Springs – natural thermal-heated mineral pools – where the food is both healthy and delicious. Springs La, Fingal; (03) 5950 8777; open Sun–Mon for brunch, lunch and early dinner; peninsulahotsprings.com.
- **Ten Minutes by Tractor** The fine dining restaurant at this winery is very French and very good. 1333 Mornington Flinders Rd, Main Ridge; (03) 5989 6080; open Wed–Sun for lunch, Thurs–Sat for dinner (Mon–Sun in Jan); plan well ahead as reservations are essential and weekends can be booked out up to two months in advance; tenminutesbytractor.com.au.
- **Montalto Vineyard and Olive Grove** It's worth eating here for the view across the vines alone, through which winds a 1km long sculpture trail. Much of the food is grown in the kitchen garden. You can also order gourmet picnic hampers and wine to enjoy at one of six special private picnic locations on the property. 33 Shoreham Rd, Red Hill South; (03) 5989 8412; open Mon–Sun for lunch, Fri–Sun for dinner; montalto.com.au.
- **Merricks General Wine Store** Don't be deceived by the name or the rustic exterior: this place does seriously good food and also has a cellar door. 3458–3460 Frankston Flinders Rd, Merricks; (03) 5989 8088; open Mon–Sun for breakfast and lunch.

BEST SLEEPS

- **Arthurs Views** The panoramic views of Port Phillip are truly breathtaking in all of the four suites at this adults-only retreat just below the summit of Arthurs Seat. 10 Nestle Ct, Arthurs Seat; (03) 5981 8400; arthursviews.com.au.
- **Moonah Links Resort** Situated at Fingal, on the tip of the peninsula, this resort has two 18-hole golf courses and was home to the 2003 and 2005 Australian Open. Peter Thomson Dr, Fingal; (03) 5988 2000; moonahlinks.com.au.
- **Lindenderry Boutique Hotel** This Red Hill hotel is a great base if your main aim is to sample lots of local food and wine, and it has the Dining Room restuarant. 142 Arthurs Seat Rd, Red Hill; (03) 5989 2933; lancemore.com.au/lindenderry.
- **RACV Cape Schanck Resort** Enjoy long walks along the dramatic southern coastline at this modern hotel-style resort. Facilities include a restaurant with great views, championship golf course, day spa, indoor heated swimming pool and great facilities for kids. Trent Jones Dr, Cape Schanck; (03) 5950 8000; racv.com.au/travel-leisure/racv-resorts.html.
- **Caravanning and camping** No camping is allowed in Mornington Peninsula National Park, although you can pitch a tent on one of the many foreshore reserves at Dromana, Rosebud, Rye, Sorrento, Balnarring, Point Leo and Shoreham. You can also camp at Fairhaven on the west coast of French Island. There are several caravan parks on the peninsula too: see visitmorningtonpeninsula.org for details.

Coastal road trips

You don't have to get wet to enjoy a day beside the sea. Australia has some of the most scenic coastal driving routes in the world.

Beautiful rural scenery and one of the best coastal drives in Australia – all in one trip down the edge of New South Wales.

Southern Highlands and Grand Pacific Drive, NSW

Since going to print, some of the areas featured in this trip were affected by flooding. Some of the information, particularly about roads in and around Fitzroy Falls, Kangaroo Valley and Budderoo National Park, may have since changed – contact local visitor information centres for updates before travelling.

HOW LONG?

It's an easy day drive from Sydney, or you can make a weekend of it driving through forgotten hinterland valleys and exploring the back roads of the Southern Highlands. For a shorter trip, drive straight to Wollongong via the Sea Cliff Bridge.

WHEN TO GO

Any time of the year is a good time to do this drive, although the Southern Highlands can be cold in winter. During spring and autumn the Southern Highlands' parks and gardens are simply beautiful.

NEED TO KNOW

Several sections of this drive are narrow and winding, particularly the drive down Barrengarry Mountain to Kangaroo Valley; if you suffer from travel sickness, take some medication before you set off.

 Drive rating
Easy. Sealed roads with some winding sections

 Distances
Total distance, return loop from Sydney to Berry via Moss Vale: 276km
- Sydney to Moss Vale: 65km
- Moss Vale to Berry: 55km
- Berry to Wollongong: 60km
- Wollongong to Sydney: 96km

 Temperatures
January: 16–31°C
July: 9–16°C

 More information
- Kiama Information Centre, Blowhole Point Rd, Kiama; 1300 654 262; kiama.com.au
- Southern Gateway Centre, Princes Hwy, Bulli Tops; (02) 4267 5910; visitwollongong.com.au
- Southern Highlands Visitor Information Centre, 62–70 Main St, Mittagong; (02) 4871 2888; southern-highlands.com.au
- grandpacificdrive.com.au

Snapshot
Combine mountain and coastal scenery on this drive through the Southern Highlands south-west of Sydney and along the Grand Pacific Drive, a cliff-hugging, breathtakingly scenic coastal route. A highlight is the cantilevered Sea Cliff Bridge that curves around the cliffs. Most people do the cliff section of the drive heading south, but in the spirit of saving the best to last, and because the views are better heading north, we've approached the bridge from the opposite direction.

Previous Whalers Way, near Port Lincoln on the Eyre Peninsula *Opposite* Sunset over Garie Beach National Park

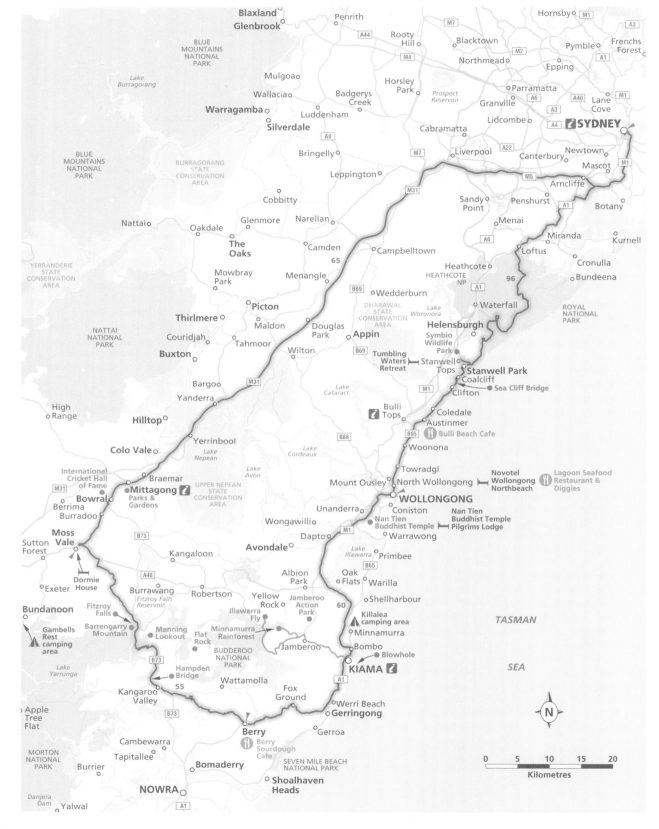

😊 KIDS' SPOT

Ready to ride the Perfect Storm? Jamberoo Action Park is the largest water-based theme park in New South Wales and offers activities for all ages. Teenagers love the Funnel Web, a monster-sized, cone-shaped ride, and the Perfect Storm, a thrilling vortex water ride. Banjo's Billabong has water slides, cannons, sprays and buckets. Other attractions include a wave pool and a 'rapid river' ride, as well as bobsleds, racing cars and a chairlift. 1215 Jamberoo Rd, Jamberoo; (02) 4236 0114; open Mon–Sun 10am–5pm, mid-Sept–Apr; jamberoo.net.

Above Fitzroy Falls in Morton National Park

SYDNEY TO BERRY VIA THE SOUTHERN HIGHLANDS

From Sydney, head south along the Hume Highway, turn off the freeway at Mittagong and wind your way through the highland towns of Bowral and Moss Vale, stopping to browse the galleries, bookshops and antiques stores. If you're a cricket fan, you'll want to spend a couple of hours at Bowral's International Cricket Hall of Fame (*see* p. 176). Gracious historic homes with well-established gardens and stately trees make this a great region to explore in autumn, when the turning leaves are ablaze with colour, and in spring, when the gardens are full of tulips and other blooms.

From Moss Vale take the Nowra Road up through the mountains to Fitzroy Falls in Morton National Park. Here you can stretch your legs on the short walk to the lookout above the dramatic waterfall that tumbles 82m to the floor of the ravine below.

Continuing south, follow the sign to Manning Lookout to enjoy spectacular views over Kangaroo Valley, one of the state's prettiest valleys. The road then descends through wild bushland, following a series of twists and turns down Barrengarry Mountain to reach the valley floor, before crossing historic Hampden Bridge. Built across the Kangaroo River in 1898, it is the oldest suspension bridge in Australia. Stop for a swim at Flat Rock at the end of Upper Kangaroo River Road or have a picnic on the riverbank near the old hall in the village centre.

It's not far from here to Berry, home to countless B&Bs, guesthouses, boutiques, antiques shops and cafes.

BERRY TO WOLLONGONG

Continue east to hit the coast at Kiama and check out the blowhole in the rocky point below the lighthouse. But be warned: if there's a fresh breeze blowing your way, you may end up getting soaked by the water whooshing through the tiny gap in the rocks.

SIDETRACK

The wheelchair-accessible boardwalk in Minnamurra Rainforest, which leads from the Rainforest Centre through subtropical and temperate rainforest to Minnamurra Falls, is great for little legs and strollers. The much steeper walk to the upper falls can be hard going, but the stunning view of Minnamurra Falls and the canyon at the end is worth it. There's a cafe on-site as well as nice picnic facilities, and you're almost guaranteed to see lyrebirds and wallabies. (345 Minnamurra Falls Rd (off Jamberoo Mountain Rd); (02) 4236 0469; open Mon–Sun 9am–5pm.)

SIDETRACK

If you have a head for heights, head up to the top of the Illawarra Fly, a 500m long, 25m high elevated tree-top walk. Climb the 45m high lookout (if you dare), get bouncy on the edge of the springboard cantilevers or fly through the canopy on the zipline tour. On a clear day you can see all the way to the coast, 35km away. (182 Knights Hill Rd, Knights Hill (10 minutes from Robertson); (02) 4885 1010; open Mon–Sun 9am–5pm; illawarrafly.com.)

Wollongong, the third largest city in New South Wales and a major coal, iron and steel producer, is, despite all that heavy industry, a very attractive place to spend a night. Explore the horseshoe-shaped cove of Wollongong Harbour, with its lighthouse, fishing fleet, fish markets and wonderful city beaches. Linger over coffee in one of the many cafes along the foreshore or stockpile some inner harmony at the eight-storey Nan Tien Buddhist Temple – the largest Buddhist temple in the Southern Hemisphere (180 Berkeley Rd, Berkeley; (02) 4272 0600; open Tues–Sun 9am–5pm; nantien.org.au).

WOLLONGONG TO SYDNEY

The Illawarra Escarpment tumbles into the sea just north of Wollongong and marks the beginning of the signposted section of the Grand Pacific Drive, as the road follows the coastline north through a succession of seaside suburbs and villages.

The Grand Pacific Drive crosses the famous Sea Cliff Bridge between Clifton and Coalcliff. This road (Lawrence Hargrave Drive) was originally built in the 1860s to service the coalmines that had already hollowed out the inside of the Illawarra Escarpment. Carved into the cliffs 40m above the surf, the road, although breathtakingly scenic, was at times breathtakingly dangerous. The cliffs, especially along the section between Coalcliff and Clifton, had a terrifying tendency to slide into the sea, sometimes taking sections of the road with them. Boulders would plummet downhill, narrowly missing school buses and cars on their way to the local shops. After dozens of such incidents, the road was finally closed in 2003 while a final solution was formulated: a multispan, balanced, cantilever bridge that curves around the cliffs 50m out to sea – out of the way of any errant rockfalls.

Beyond the bridge, the road climbs through ferny forest above the beach to Stanwell Tops, high on the edge of the escarpment. Paragliders and hang-gliders soar on the thermals rising from the ocean below, emulating aeronautical pioneer Lawrence Hargrave, who made aviation history here by rising 5m above the ground strapped to a huge box kite in 1894. On a clear day you can see as far south as Wollongong

and enjoy a great view of the route, over the Sea Cliff Bridge and the beaches beyond.

Soon after Stanwell Tops, Lawrence Hargrave Drive turns west to join the Princes Motorway, which leads north to Sydney, but you should veer off to the right along Lady Wakehurst Drive. This winding, narrow road will take you through the heart of Royal National Park, the world's second oldest national park, founded in 1879 (Yellowstone in the United States is seven years older). En route to Sydney's southern suburb of Waterfall, the road winds through eucalypt forests, over windswept heathland and across low-level river weirs. Sidetracks spear off to beaches and lookouts and there are dozens of great picnic and swimming spots along the way. Being so close to Sydney, the park is a popular place on sunny weekends, when traffic snarls can be frustrating, but if you time your drive for a weekday you'll pretty much have it to yourself.

☺ KIDS' SPOT

Symbio Wildlife Park is a down-to-earth zoo where you can unpack a picnic or fire up a barbecue, check out the crocodiles, koalas, meerkats or any of the other 1000 animals in the park, and cool off in the swimming pool. Lawrence Hargrave Dr, Helensburgh; (02) 4294 1244; open Mon–Sun 9.30am–5pm; symbiozoo.com.au.

BEST EATS

- **Berry Sourdough Cafe** People have been known to drive from afar to Berry just to pick up some bread from this cafe, which also does great lunches. 23 Prince Alfred St, Berry; (02) 4464 1617; open Wed–Sun for breakfast and lunch.
- **Lagoon Seafood Restaurant** Wollongong's best seafood restaurant sits right on the water's edge. Stuart Park North, Wollongong; (02) 4226 1677; open Mon–Sun for lunch and dinner; lagoonrestaurant.com.au.
- **Diggies** This is a perfect place for breakfast on the beach. 1 Cliff Rd, North Beach, North Wollongong; (02) 4226 2688; open Mon–Sun from 6.30am; diggies.com.au.
- **Bulli Beach Cafe** Here you'll find fish and chips, burgers and all-day breakfast with a beachfront view. 68 Trinity Row, Bulli; (02) 4284 8808; open Mon–Sun for breakfast and lunch, Fri–Sat for dinner; bullibeachcafe.com.au.

BEST SLEEPS

- **Dormie House** This elegant country house hotel overlooks Moss Vale Golf Course. Arthur St, Moss Vale; (02) 4868 1800; dormiehouse.com.au.
- **Pilgrims Lodge** Nan Tien Buddhist Temple offers peaceful accommodation in this motel-style retreat. 180 Berkeley Rd, Berkeley; (02) 4272 0500; nantien.org.au.
- **Novotel Wollongong Northbeach** The great rooms here have balconies overlooking the beach. 2–14 Cliff Rd, North Wollongong; (02) 4224 3111; novotelnorthbeach.com.au.
- **Tumbling Waters Retreat** Perched on the edge of the escarpment, this retreat offers superb ocean views. Stonehaven Rd, Stanwell Tops; (02) 4294 1888; tumblingwatersretreat.com.
- **Caravanning and camping** Gambells Rest campground in the Bundanoon section of Morton National Park has 10 sites (suitable for caravans and trailers), but you'll need to book first with the Fitzroy Falls Visitor Centre. Facilities include picnic tables, gas/electric barbecues, flush toilets, hot showers and drinking water. Killalea State Park near Shellharbour has some nice camping spots about a ten-minute walk from the beach; facilities include hot showers.

Opposite The magnificent Sea Cliff Bridge is a highlight of the Grand Pacific Drive *Above* Nan Tien Buddhist Temple, the biggest Buddhist temple in the Southern Hemisphere, also offers motel-style accommodation

Enjoy wildlife, wild surf and wild coastlines with spectacular cliff-top walking trails along Victoria's southern coastline.

Bass Coast, Vic.

HOW LONG?

It's a two-day drive, one way, from Melbourne, but allow another day for sightseeing at Wilsons Promontory. If you are pushed for time, a drive around Phillip Island makes a great daytrip on its own.

WHEN TO GO

During summer, from Melbourne Cup weekend through to Easter, is when most people head to Wilsons Promontory, which means that's when it is at its most crowded. Go in late spring for masses of wildflowers in full bloom and milder daytime temperatures that make for more pleasant bushwalking. Or go in winter and you'll have the place almost to yourself – just be sure to have lots of warm woollies for cold nights and for penguin-watching.

NEED TO KNOW

A Four Parks Pass provides entry to the Penguin Parade, Antarctic Journey,the Koala Conservation Centre and Churchill Island – see penguins.org.au. Campsites and accommodation at Wilsons Promontory are allocated on a ballot system during the peak summer holiday season (late Dec – 26 Jan), usually held in the preceding June. For details, call Parks Victoria on 1800 350 552 or visit parkweb.vic.gov.au.

 Drive rating
Easy. Sealed roads

 Distances
Total distance, Melbourne to Wilsons Promontory: 320km
- Melbourne to Penguin Parade, Phillip Island: 150km
- Phillip Island to Cape Paterson: 38km
- Cape Paterson to Wilsons Promontory: 105km

 Temperatures
January: 14–24°C
July: 5–15°C

 More information
- Phillip Island Information Centre, 895 Phillip Island Rd, Newhaven (1km over the bridge onto Phillip Island); 1300 366 422; visitbasscoast.com.au
- visitphillipisland.com
- visitpromcountry.com.au

 Snapshot
The Bass Coast drive from Melbourne to Wilsons Promontory might not be as well known as its more famous relative, the Great Ocean Road, but that means it's also less busy, which makes it a great ocean drive indeed. One beach after another opens up before you as you wind your way along the coast, past rugged cliff-top lookouts. Add to the mix the family-friendly attractions of Phillip Island – including the world famous Penguin Parade – and one of the state's most popular national parks, Wilsons Promontory, and you have all the ingredients for a great family road trip.

Opposite top left Boardwalk path through the mangroves at Rhyll Inlet *Top right* Lunchtime for Pelicans at San Remo *Bottom left* Wilsons Promontory Lighthouse *Bottom right* Pyramid Rocks, Phillip Island

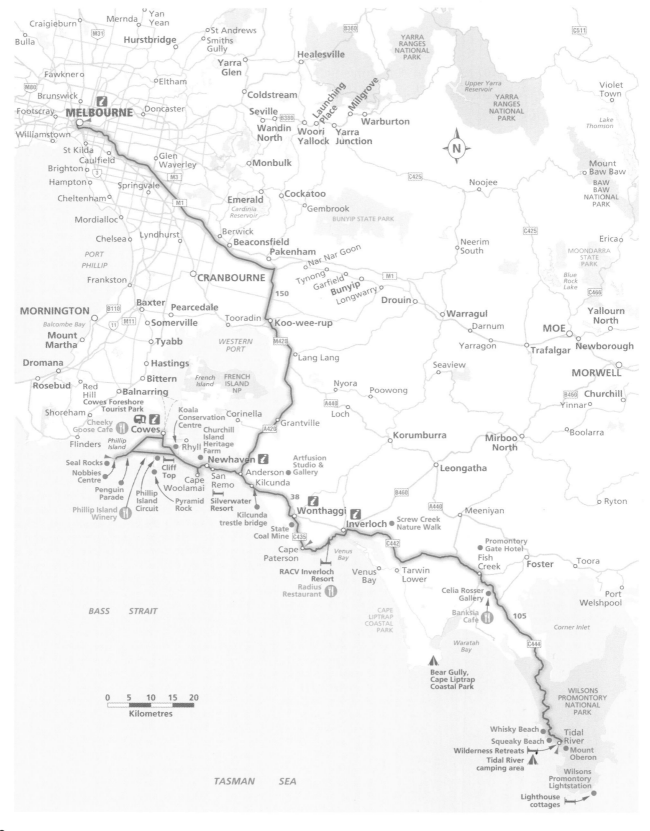

Bass Coast, Vic.

MELBOURNE TO PHILLIP ISLAND

Connected to the mainland by a bridge at San Remo, Phillip Island is about 120km south-east of Melbourne via the Monash Freeway (M1) and the South Gippsland and Bass highways, and will take about 90 minutes to reach. Call into Artfusion Studio and Gallery on the way, a sculpture and glass studio and art gallery where you can watch the artists at work and buy their wares at half the price that you'd find them for in Melbourne galleries. You'll find it at the roundabout at Anderson, before you get to San Remo. (9 Andersons Rise, Anderson; 0439 368 538; open Thurs–Sat and Mon 10.30am–5pm; artfusionstudioandgallery.com.)

From San Remo it's about 20 minutes to Cowes, the main town on the island, and a further 15 minutes or so to get to the Penguin Parade at the western tip of the island – but take your time, as there's plenty to see and do along the way.

Rhyll Inlet is a haven for birdlife, with thousands of pelicans, black swans, gulls and migratory waders. The walking track and boardwalk – which is also suitable for bicycles – provide a great way to explore the inlet and mangroves without getting your feet wet. Follow the track and boardwalk all the way from Conservation Hill to the seaside village of Rhyll (allow 90 minutes return) or just do the half-hour mangrove boardwalk.

About halfway between Rhyll and Cowes you can see koalas in the wild at the Koala Conservation Centre, where two elevated boardwalks let you get close to the koalas precariously perched in the treetops (1810 Phillip Island Tourist Rd; (03) 5951 2800; open Mon–Sun 10am–5pm, 6pm during summer holidays).

Next, visit the Nobbies Centre, a five-minute drive beyond the turn-off to the Penguin Parade. Inside, you'll find the Antarctic Journey attraction where you can get a taste for what life is like in the frozen south (kids will love the 'chill zone') and there's a display on the local marine life, including penguins and seals – Australia's largest fur-seal colony lives at Seal Rocks, just beyond the headland. Head out to the boardwalk outside: it's a fantastic cliff-top walk along the headland and if you have binoculars you'll get a great view of the seals. During big southern swells, the blowhole at the end of the walk puts on an impressive display. Note that the centre – and the road to it – closes one hour before sunset to protect the wildlife.

The Penguin Parade – when hundreds of little penguins (that's their official name, although they used to be called fairy penguins) come out of the sea at Summerlands Beach at dusk and waddle up the hill to their burrows – attracts thousands of visitors each night and is one of Victoria's most popular attractions. There are two

Frolicking fur-seals at Seal Rock near Phillip Island

viewing platforms and a number of tours, but the best is the Penguin Plus – it ensures a prime viewing position and you'll only have to share the experience with 150 others, rather than the bigger crowds at the main platform. The penguins start arriving at sunset, which in summer is about 9pm, and the lights are turned out 50 minutes after the first penguin arrives, so it can be a late night for little kids. It also gets cold, even in summer, so bring warm clothes and a cushion or blanket to sit on – those bench seats get hard after an hour or so! Make sure you book your tickets ahead of time (penguins.org.au) and arrive at least an hour before sunset, or you may find yourself without a seat. That said, some positions on the boardwalk leading down to the viewing platforms can give you a better view of the penguins as they head up the hill to their burrows. When you leave, don't forget to check under your car for penguins and keep an eye out for wildlife on the drive home.

Another don't-miss spot is Pyramid Rock, about halfway along the southern coast, off Back Beach Road. It's an easy 10-minute walk – much of it along wooden boardwalks – to the lookout platform, which provides great views not only over the triangular pile of rocks that gives this scenic point its name, but also north and south along the coast. The rocks are the remnant of a lava flow that once formed a land bridge to the point. You can also follow a cliff-top trail to Berry Beach; go early in the morning and you're almost guaranteed to see wallabies on the track.

Home to the Australian Motorbike Grand Prix each October, as well as the World Superbike Championship and the V8 Supercar Series, the Phillip Island Circuit (about halfway between the Penguin Parade and San Remo) is one of the most scenic racetracks in the world, although it's unlikely that the racers have much time to admire the panoramic ocean views; it's also one of the fastest tracks in the world. There's a display on the history of motor sport at the track, and you can also take a guided circuit tour, experience a racing simulator, ride a go-kart or buckle up for a few hot laps with a racing driver. (381 Back Beach Rd, Phillip Island; (03) 5952 9400; opening hours vary subject to race days and circuit hire; phillipislandcircuit.com.au.)

Penguins aren't the only birds to call Phillip Island home. Each year 23 million short-tailed shearwaters (also known as muttonbirds) migrate to southern Australia from the Bering Sea near Alaska, an epic 15,000km journey. About a million of them arrive on Phillip Island in late September to mate, then stay until April raising their chicks. Watching them arrive en masse at sunset is quite a spectacle. The best place to see them is Cape Woolamai, just south of San Remo.

☺ KIDS' SPOT

Explore Churchill Island Heritage Farm with the kids, where they can watch cows being milked and sheep being shorn, take a wagon ride and watch a blacksmith at work. The historic houses, which date from the 1850s, are fully furnished and open for self-guided tours. 246 Samuel Amess Dr, Churchill Island; (03) 5951 2800; open Mon–Sun 10am–5pm.

SAN REMO TO INVERLOCH

Back on the mainland, follow the Bass Highway to Wonthaggi, stopping along the way to admire the impressive Kilcunda trestle bridge. It's now part of the 16km Bass Coast Rail Trail between Anderson and Wonthaggi, Victoria's only coastal rail trail.

Take a trip back in time on an underground mine tour of the State Coal Mine in Wonthaggi. Established in 1909 when a miners' strike in New South Wales left the Victorian railways and Melbourne short of coal, the State Coal Mine soon had 1800 men working eight-hour shifts in almost 4822km of underground tunnels, hauling more than 660,000 tonnes of coal out of the ground each year. The mine began to decline after the Great Depression and was eventually closed in 1968, but it reopened a couple of years ago for guided tours. Each tour begins with a safety briefing and the donning of the obligatory hard hat, followed by a careful walk down the steep entrance to the mine, which is more than 60m below ground. It's a fascinating look at how the miners worked, and not much has changed since the last workers downed tools. Thankfully you don't have to slug it back uphill at the end: an old coal skip has been converted into a carriage that is winched to the surface. Above ground, you can visit several historic houses, including the winder house and museum, and there are barbecue facilities on-site. (State Coal Mine Heritage Area, Garden St, Wonthaggi; 13 1963; open Mon–Sun 10am–4.30pm, 90-minute underground tours at 11.30am and 2pm, bookings essential; parkweb.vic.gov.au.)

In theory it should only take about 15 minutes to drive the 14km between Cape Paterson and Inverloch, but it will almost certainly take you much longer, simply because it's impossible not to keep pulling over to admire the spectacular views along the way. Known as the Bunurong Coastal Drive, it's one of the most scenic short drives in Victoria, hugging the cliff-edged coastline the whole way, and there are lookouts, deserted beaches and short walking trails along the route. The road is well signposted from both Wonthaggi (it starts/ends 8km from the centre of the town) and Inverloch, and if you're looking for it on maps it will be marked as the C435.

Opposite Little penguins are one of Phillip Island's big attractions *Above top* The fascinating underground world of the State Coal Mine in Wonthaggi *Above bottom* No coastal drive is complete without a stop at the beach - here it's Inverloch Beach

INVERLOCH TO WILSONS PROMONTORY

Take a seaside stroll along the Screw Creek Nature Walk in Inverloch and then head to Wilsons Promontory (known as 'the Prom' to locals), stopping at Fish Creek on the way, where there's definitely something fishy going on. The Promontory Gate Hotel has a giant mullet perched on the corner of its roof, and most of the businesses in town have a piscatorial theme. There are several good galleries too, but don't miss the Celia Rosser Gallery. One of Australia's great botanical artists, Celia has painted all 78 known species of banksia – she even has a banksia named after her, *Banksia rosserae*; the only other woman who has a banksia named after her is Queen Victoria. (1791 Meeniyan–Promontory Rd, Fish Creek; 0455 777 334; open Fri–Sun 10am–4pm or by appointment; celiarossergallery.com.au.)

The seaside views continue as you head to the Prom, a wild and rugged knob of land hanging like a fishhook-shaped pendant off the southernmost tip of mainland Australia and bounded by sea on three sides. Its granite headlands, undeveloped beaches, rivers, walking trails and abundant wildlife make it one of Victoria's most loved national parks. The headland is crisscrossed by a network of trails, ranging from short 300m tracks leading to beautiful beaches to long overnight hikes. Must-see spots include Squeaky Beach, a beautiful arc of white sand flanked by large granite boulders that is famous for its squeaky sand; picturesque Whisky Beach; the panoramic views from the summit of Mount Oberon; and the historic 1859 lighthouse.

BEST EATS

- **Cheeky Goose Cafe** The truffled wild mushroom ragu and the raspberry and almond buttermilk pancakes are just two of the many delicious choices on the all-day breakfast menu that keep the crowds coming to this converted old church in Cowes. The Mediterranean-styled lunches and seafood dinners are also popular. 4/72 Chapel St, Cowes; (03) 5907 6900; open Mon–Sun for breakfast, lunch and dinner, may close during winter; cheekygoosecafe.com.au.
- **Phillip Island Winery** Delicious Gippsland cheese and antipasto platters are available with the wines and there's live acoustic music in the afternoons. 414 Berrys Beach Rd, Ventnor; (03) 8595 2155; open Thurs–Mon 11.30am–5.30pm; phillipislandwinery.com.au.
- **Radius Restaurant** At this bistro, part of the RACV Inverloch Resort, you'll enjoy fantastic sea views through the floor-to-ceiling windows along with fine local seafood, the house speciality. 70 Cape Paterson–Inverloch Rd, Inverloch; (03) 5674 0000; open Mon–Sun for lunch and dinner; racv.com.au/inverloch.
- **Banksia Cafe** Located at the Celia Rosser Gallery in Fish Creek, this is a good place for a coffee or light lunch. It has a sunny courtyard, surrounded by banksia plants. 1791 Meeniyan–Promontory Rd, Fish Creek; (03) 5683 2628; open Fri–Sun 10am–4pm; celiarossergallery.com.au.

BEST SLEEPS

- **Silverwater Resort** Although the resort isn't technically on Phillip Island (San Remo is on the mainland side of the bridge), it's still a great option for families, offering a mix of one-, two- and three-bedroom apartments – and your view is all Phillip Island. Facilities include two swimming pools; tennis, basketball and volleyball courts; and a playground with jumping pillows. 17 Potters Hill Rd, San Remo; (03) 5671 9300; silverwaterresort.com.au.
- **Clifftop** This rambling beach house B&B overlooking Smiths Beach on Phillip Island is a 15-minute drive from the Penguin Parade. The rooms are very large and most have knockout ocean views. 1 Marlin St, Smiths Beach; (03) 5952 1033; clifftop.com.au.
- **RACV Inverloch Resort** Choose from a wide range of accommodation here, from campsites and cabins to ocean-view hotel rooms and luxurious villas. Situated 5km from Inverloch, the resort is adjacent to the beach and offers plenty of facilities, including a bistro (see Best eats), tennis courts, a heated pool and walking and cycling tracks. 70 Cape Paterson–Inverloch Rd, Inverloch; (03) 5674 0000; racv.com.au/inverloch.
- **Tidal River** Accommodation options at the main settlement in Wilsons Promontory National Park include huts that sleep between four and six, ensuite cabins sleeping up to six people, and luxury wilderness retreats, each with ensuite and private deck (wildernessretreats.com.au). You can also stay in cottages at the lighthouse, but you'll need to be able to carry all your food and gear on the 19km hike in, and carry all your rubbish out. Wilsons Promontory Rd, Tidal River; (03) 5680 9555; parkweb.vic.gov.au.
- **Caravanning and camping** Nowhere is very far from anywhere on Phillip Island, but Cowes – the biggest town on the island – is right in the middle of things and the Cowes Foreshore Tourist Park is beside the beach, in the middle of Cowes (cowesforeshoretouristpark.com.au). Tidal River Campground at Wilsons Promontory National Park has 484 camping and caravan sites, including some powered caravan sites; facilities include toilets, hot showers, laundry facilities and some gas barbecues, as well as a general store and cafe. You can also camp at Cape Liptrap Coastal Park, on the opposite side of the bay from Wilsons Prom.

Opposite top Enormous boulders line the white sands of Squeaky Beach *Opposite bottom* Fish Creek Hotel sports its mullet with pride

Explore South Australia's Fleurieu Peninsula on this circular drive that follows the dramatic coastline, where grassy hills spill into the sea over sheer rocky cliffs.

Fleurieu Peninsula, SA

HOW LONG?

Allow two or three days to do the tour and return to Adelaide. Or make it a daytrip by heading back to Adelaide from Victor Harbor on the A13.

WHEN TO GO

The Fleurieu Peninsula is relatively mild during both summer and winter. It's at its most dramatic during the winter months, when wild seas pound against towering cliffs, and at its most beautiful during spring, when the grassy hills and coastal heathlands are blanketed with wildflowers. May through to October is whale-watching time.

NEED TO KNOW

The two-month Holiday Pass is great value if you intend to spend any time at all in South Australia's national parks. You can also buy a camping option so you never have to worry about paying camping fees, although you may still need to book your site online before you go. Buy passes at Department of Environment and Heritage (DEH) and National Parks offices throughout the state, or online at parks.sa.gov.au.

 Drive rating
Easy. Mostly sealed roads

 Distances
Total distance, Adelaide to Cape Jervis and return: 284km
- Adelaide to McLaren Vale: 40km
- McLaren Vale to Victor Harbor via Cape Jervis: 135km
- Victor Harbor to Adelaide via Strathalbyn: 109km

 Temperatures
January: 14–24°C
July: 9–15°C

 More information
- Victor Harbor Visitor Information Centre, the Causeway Building, 1 Esplanade, Victor Harbor; (08) 8551 0776; encountervictorharbor.com.au
- fleurieupeninsula.com.au

 Snapshot
Located practically on the outskirts of Adelaide, the Fleurieu Peninsula is famous for its wine, scenic coastline and gourmet produce. The heart of the wine-producing area is McLaren Vale, where olive and almond groves are scattered among the vineyards. Pretty Strathalbyn was settled by Scottish immigrants in the 1830s and is now a heritage town with 30 or so historic buildings and a popular place to shop for antiques and crafts. Victor Harbor, on the southern side of the peninsula, is the most popular seaside resort with lots of family attractions.

Opposite The jetty at sleepy Normanville

Fleurieu Peninsula, SA

B88

Wool Bay

YORKE PENINSULA

Coobowie

Edithburgh

TROUBRIDGE
ISLAND
CP
*Troubridge
Island*

GULF

ST VINCENT

N

0   3   6   9   12
Kilometres

Lonsdale

Port
Noarlunga

Old Noarlunga

A15

Maslin Beach

B23

Star of
Greece   Port Willunga

Aldinga

**Aldinga
Beach**

**Sellicks
Beach**

B23

Myponga
Beach

75

Myponga

*Myponga
Reservoir*

Carrickalinga

B23

Normanville

Yankalilla

HMAS
Hobart
wreck   Second
Valley

**Rapid Bay
camping area**

Rapid Bay

Colonel William Light
boulder

*FLEURIEU
PENINSULA*

Delamere

B37

60

Stringybark
camping area

Cape Jervis
Lighthouse

Kangaroo Island
SeaLink Ferry   B23

Cape
Jervis

Parsons
Beach

BACKSTAIRS

Cobbler Hill
camping area

Tapanappa
camping area

DEEP CREEK
CONSERVATION
PARK

Blowhole
Beach   Trig
camping
area

Waitpinga
Beach

PASSAGE

130

ADELAIDE TO MCLAREN VALE

Start your journey at McLaren Vale, a quick 45-minute drive from Adelaide via the Southern Expressway and Main South Road. It's a pretty area, a patchwork of vineyards dotted with historic wineries in a snug valley wedged between the tail end of the Mount Lofty Ranges and the coast.

McLaren Vale is one of the few wine regions in South Australia close to the sea, and the cool ocean breezes and sandy soils produce great shiraz, cabernet sauvignon and chardonnay wines. It's also one of the oldest wine-producing regions in Australia – the first vines were planted in 1841 – and many of the wineries feature beautiful stone-and-timber cellar-door tasting areas. You could easily spend a couple of days here tasting the wines at more than 60 cellar doors. For more information, see mclarenvale.info.

For a wine-tasting with a view, head to the tasting rooms at the top of the d'Arenberg Cube, a five-storey complex that looks like a giant Rubik's Cube floating above the grapevines and is a bit like Disneyland for wine lovers. Entry includes a self-guided tour of the Alternate Realities Museum, which features a wine aroma room, a virtual fermenter, an art gallery and wine-making displays. Wine-tasting masterclasses and blending sessions are also available and there is an excellent restaurant as well (see Best eats). (58 Osborn Rd, McLaren Vale; (08) 8329 4888; open Mon–Sun 10am–5pm; darenberg.com.au.)

But it's not just the fabulous wines that make this area so popular with foodies – there's also the almonds and olives planted by immigrant farmers from Greece and Italy in the late 1800s, and newer farming ventures that focus on venison, handmade cheeses, berries, beef, lamb, organic vegetables, trout and marron. All of these, plus freshly baked breads and tempting pies and pastries, homemade jams and preserves and delicious cakes, are piled high upon tables and trestles at the weekly Saturday morning farmers' markets in Willunga. On the second Saturday of each month the stalls spill over into the Quarry Markets across the road; enjoy browsing through the bric-a-brac, second-hand books and handmade jewellery and clothes.

MCLAREN VALE TO CAPE JERVIS

From McLaren Vale, head towards Port Willunga on the coast, following the tourist route signposted as the Fleurieu Way, where you'll enjoy the first of the many expansive coastal views that are a highlight of this drive. Take a break at Maslin Beach, South Australia's first official nudist beach, and enjoy a walk along the edge of the multicoloured cliffs that flank the beach (the clothing-optional end is at the far southern tip).

Continue south to Myponga and then take Reservoir Road, drive across the dam wall and wind your way down the steep hills to Myponga Beach, a cluster of small houses and shacks tucked away on a tiny beach. The views as you head down to the shore are fantastic. The seaside community of Carrickalinga is just down the road and you can follow a terrific coastal drive and walkway that leads from Carrickalinga to Normanville, yet another sleepy beachside town.

From here all the way to Cape Jervis, on the tip of the peninsula, the views are simply amazing, and you'll find yourself pulling over to the side of the road again and again to take photographs of the mostly treeless green hills dropping abruptly into the sea.

At Second Valley follow a short walk along the bottom of the dramatic cliffs, past the jetty, to a collection of very photogenic, very rusty boatsheds cobbled together with bits of scrap iron. This is a popular snorkelling and diving spot: the former Navy ship HMAS *Hobart* was scuttled off the coast here in November 2002, creating one of the best dive sites in Australia. As part of the preparation, many holes and hatches were cut into the wreck to facilitate access and navigation. Many of the ship's original fittings – including filing cabinets, sinks, toilets and tools – are still in place and can be viewed up close.

Opposite Be careful where you lay the picnic blanket on Maslin Beach; the southern end is reserved for nude bathing

SIDETRACK

Take a side trip to Rapid Bay for more stunning cliff-line views and to find the boulder that marks the spot where Colonel William Light first stepped ashore on his way to establish the colony of South Australia back in 1836. He recorded the event by carving his initials and the date into the boulder, now part of a grassy foreshore park and camping area.

There's not much to Cape Jervis – an angular lighthouse, the terminal for ferries to Kangaroo Island and that's about it, but the lookout over the point has great views across Backstairs Passage to Kangaroo Island (*see* p. 69) and is an excellent whale-watching vantage point during winter.

CAPE JERVIS TO VICTOR HARBOR

Heading east, Range Road follows a high ridge through the rural heartland of the peninsula, snaking its way towards Victor Harbor on the shores of Encounter Bay. Here, in 1802, Matthew Flinders, sailing around Australia, met the French explorer Nicholas Baudin, who was also circumnavigating the continent. Although England and France were at war at the time, their meeting was friendly and Flinders marked it with the name he gave the bay.

SIDETRACK

If you want to explore this coast in greater depth, there is a long-distance walking track that follows the shoreline from Cape Jervis to Goolwa via Victor Harbor. It's part of the 1200km long Heysen Trail, which continues up to Parachilna Gorge in the Flinders Ranges. Even if you are short of time or energy, you can still walk parts of the trail, at Parsons Beach and Waitpinga Beach in Newland Head Conservation Park or at the Bluff on the outskirts of Victor Harbor, and simply wander along the cliffs for as long and as far as you please.

In Victor Harbor learn about whales at the South Australian Whale Centre (2 Railway Tce, Victor Harbor; (08) 8551 0750; open Mon–Sun 10.30am–5pm; sawhalecentre.com), and about local history and the meeting of Flinders and Baudin at the Encounter Coast Discovery Centre (2 Flinders Pde, Victor Harbor; (08) 8552 5388; open Mon–Sun 1–4pm). You can also ride the country's only horse-drawn tram out to Granite Island, where you can walk around the island (allow 40 minutes) and visit a little penguin colony at dusk (penguin watching by guided tour only, book at the visitor centre or call (08) 8551 0776). The tramway is on the Esplanade, Victor Harbor (for information call (08) 8551 0720; trams run every 40 minutes from the mainland Mon–Sun 10am–4pm; horsedrawntram.com.au).

VICTOR HARBOR TO ADELAIDE VIA STRATHALBYN

Just a few minutes' drive from Victor Harbor, pretty Port Elliot is full of historic stone buildings and a fantastic seaside restaurant, Flying Fish Cafe (*see* Best eats). Goolwa, at the mouth of the Murray River, is another historic centre full of beautiful sandstone buildings, many of them now art galleries and restaurants. Take a walk along the river's edge, past historic boatsheds and slipways, where paddlesteamers once docked, or follow the boardwalk over the sand dunes for great coastal views.

SIDETRACK

The Murray River, Australia's longest waterway, seeps rather than spills into the sea at the Murray Mouth on Hindmarsh Island. There is a lookout platform and you can usually walk along the beach unless the area has been recently dredged, which occasionally happens during times of low water flows to prevent its closure.

☺ KIDS' SPOT

Most kids get excited at the sight of an old steam train and here they can even ride one. The historic Cockle Train – Australia's first railway – operates between Victor Harbor, Port Elliot and Goolwa. The train usually runs on weekends and Wednesdays, and daily during school holidays or long weekends (steamrangerheritagerailway.org). An enjoyable alternative is the 30km Encounter Bikeway, a dedicated bike path between the Bluff and Signal Point at Goolwa Wharf. The sealed path is suitable for all riders wanting a gentle seaside cycle, including escorted toddlers on trikes, and between May and October you may even spot whales as you ride.

From Goolwa, head inland back towards Adelaide via the Currency Creek wine region and Strathalbyn, keeping an eye out for the canoe tree along the way. This ancient red gum still carries the trace of the bark that was cut away by Aboriginal people to make a canoe long ago.

Strathalbyn is an attractive heritage town with about 30 historic buildings and a popular place to shop for antiques – there are dozens of antiques stores on High Street – and the Soldiers' Memorial Garden is a great place for a stroll or a picnic.

Head back to the city via the beautiful Adelaide Hills (*see* p. 85), a run that will take about an hour – that is, unless you get waylaid at one of the wineries or galleries along the way.

Opposite McLaren Vale's d'Arenburg Cube
Right Reflections at Birk's Harbour

BEST EATS

- **d'Arenberg Cube Restaurant** Settle in for a culinary adventure at this degustation-only fine diner inside the eye-catching d'Arenberg Cube offering a set menu of 11 courses matched with wines. Sister restaurant d'Arry's Verandah, in the adjacent 19th-century homestead, offers à la carte dining as well as a six-course degustation menu and is open for lunch daily. Book well ahead for the Cube restaurant. 58 Osborn Rd, McLaren Vale; (08) 8329 4888; open Thurs–Sun for lunch; darenberg.com.au.
- **Russell's Pizza** This quirky gourmet wood-fired pizzeria is housed in an eclectically decorated 1800s stone cottage. It's only open on Friday and Saturday nights, so competition for tables can be fierce. 13 High St, Willunga; (08) 8556 2571.
- **Star of Greece** Don't be misled by the name: it's not a Greek restaurant, but it was named after a ship that wrecked itself on the beach below in 1888. Perched high on the cliff-top overlooking the sea, the Star of Greece has multimillion-dollar views and offers a choice of dining experiences: upmarket fare in the restaurant and simpler snacks at the kiosk. 1 Esplanade, Port Willunga; (08) 8557 7420; open Wed–Sun for lunch, Fri–Sat for dinner; starofgreece.com.au.
- **Flying Fish** This seaside eatery is as famous for its views as it is for its fantastic food – it's right on the beach at Horseshoe Bay. 1 The Foreshore, Horseshoe Bay, Port Elliot; (08) 8554 3504; open Mon–Sun for lunch, Fri–Sat for dinner; flyingfishcafe.com.au.

BEST SLEEPS

- **Mulberry Lodge** This luxury country retreat surrounded by lovely gardens on the edge of Willunga township is a great base for exploring the vineyards and cellar doors of McLaren Vale. 202 Main Rd, Willunga; 0424 825 965; mulberrylodgewillunga.com.
- **Anchorage Seafront Hotel** This atmospheric old stone pub on the seafront in Victor Harbor offers a range of rooms from ensuite spa suites with balconies to budget rooms with shared bathrooms to self-contained cottages. 21 Flinders Pde, Victor Harbor; (08) 8552 5970; anchoragehotel.com.au.
- **Beach Huts Middleton** They're not actually on the beach, but these colourful candy-striped cabins certainly look like they should be and are named after some of the country's most famous stretches of sand. The real beach is only a few blocks away. 1 Charles St, Middleton; (08) 8554 3933; beachhuts.com.au.
- **The Boathouse** Beautifully restored, this riverfront boathouse at Birks Harbour has its own private wharf. 138 Liverpool Rd, Goolwa; (08) 8555 0338; birksharbour.com.au.
- **Caravanning and camping** In Deep Creek National Park, the Stringybark camping area is in a sheltered forest setting and has 16 sites, hot showers, toilets and rain water, as well as unpowered caravan sites. Central to the main walking trails, Trig has open grassy areas with 25 well-sheltered and shady sites suitable for caravans and camp trailers. There are 18 sites at Tapanappa with spectacular coastal views and ten at Cobbler Hill, close to Blowhole Beach. You can also camp at Rapid Bay and there are several commercial caravan parks in Victor Harbor.

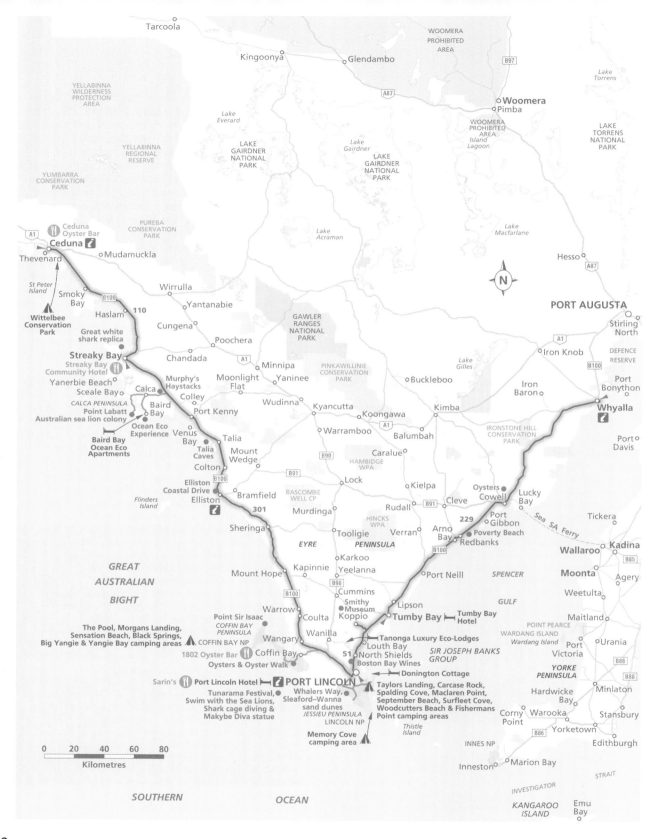

The Eyre Peninsula, the triangle of land jutting into the sea between Adelaide and the Great Australian Bight, is the outback gone coastal, where vast, undulating wheat fields tumble towards the sea over towering, knife-edged limestone cliffs.

Eyre Peninsula, SA

HOW LONG?

You'll need three to four days to explore the peninsula, more if you want to take a 4WD into the two national parks, and allow at least a day each way to get to (and from) Adelaide. A new car ferry service is currently under construction; when complete it will operate between Wallaroo on the Yorke Peninsula to Lucky Bay on the Eyre Peninsula; check for schedule updates at seasa.com.au.

WHEN TO GO

Temperatures are moderate most of the year. Summer is usually much drier than the winter months. The ocean is too cold for swimming during winter unless you have a good wetsuit.

NEED TO KNOW

If you intend to drive a 4WD in Lincoln or Coffin Bay national parks, you'll need to plan ahead. Access to Memory Cove in Lincoln National Park is restricted to just 15 vehicles per day, and you'll need to obtain a permit and key from the visitor centre in Port Lincoln. Access to the northern end of Coffin Bay National Park is at low tide only and you'll need a compressor to reinflate your tyres after driving on the sand.

 Drive rating
Easy. Mostly sealed roads, with some optional – but challenging – 4WD sections

 Distances
Total distance (without detours): 690km. The starting point, Whyalla, is 76km south of Port Augusta and 320km north-west of Adelaide. The finishing point, Ceduna, is 773km from Adelaide.
- Whyalla to Tumby Bay: 229km
- Tumby Bay to Port Lincoln: 51km
- Port Lincoln to Streaky Bay: 301km
- Streaky Bay to Ceduna: 110km

 Temperatures
January: 15–25°C
July: 8–16°C

 More information
- Ceduna Visitor Information Centre, 58 Poynton St, Ceduna; (08) 8625 3343; cedunatourism.com.au
- Port Lincoln Visitor Information Centre, 3 Adelaide Pl, Port Lincoln; 1300 788 378; visitportlincoln.net.au
- Whyalla Visitor Information Centre, Lincoln Hwy (at the northern entrance to Whyalla); 1800 088 589; whyalla.com/visitor-guide
- eyrepeninsula.com

 Snapshot
On this beautiful coastal drive you'll find beach after beach, visited only by the occasional angler, screeching seagulls and very few of the holiday crowds you'd find along the rest of the Australian coast. Campsites are right on the edge of the beach and you'll often be the only ones there. The distances between towns are not vast, so you could easily drive around the peninsula in three days, but take some extra time around Port Lincoln to explore Port Lincoln and Coffin Bay national parks.

☺ KIDS' SPOT

Take the kids to a treasure trove of history at the Smithy Museum in Koppio (a quick detour inland on the Bratten Way). This well-organised and fascinating museum focuses on farming prior to the late 1940s, and the complex includes a pine-log, thatched-roof shepherd's hut, a school house, a blacksmith's shop, lots of old rural machinery and tractors, and a women pioneers' room. Believe it or not, it's worth visiting just for the Bob Dobbins barbed wire collection alone. 1951 Koppio Rd, Koppio; (08) 8684 4243; open Tues–Sun 10am–5pm; nationaltrust.org.au/places/koppio-smithy-museum.

WHYALLA TO TUMBY BAY

If you're coming from Adelaide, the Eyre Peninsula officially begins at the shipping and iron ore–mining town of Whyalla, but the best bits of the peninsula are to be found further south along the Lincoln Highway, in places like Cowell. The pristine waters of the Eyre Peninsula produce some of the finest oysters in the world, and this sleepy town is home to some of the best. You can buy them almost anywhere in town – direct from the oyster farmers along Oyster Drive, from the bakery or the cafe, on the jetty or cooked and covered in sauces at one of the hotels. If oysters aren't your favourite food, try the whiting, another Eyre Peninsula specialty. While in Cowell, drop by the jade showroom at the Jade Motel (179 Lincoln Hwy). The local nephrite jade is one of the oldest and largest deposits in the world.

Continue south to Tumby Bay, through the villages of Arno Bay and Port Neill and past magnificent beaches such as Poverty Beach and Redbanks. Almost every town on the peninsula has a wooden jetty. Most were originally built to service the ships that would visit the small coastal towns to load up the annual wheat crop, which, apart from fishing and aquaculture, is still the region's main industry – in fact, the peninsula yields more than 45 per cent of South Australia's wheat crop. Most of the time, though, you'll find these jetties lined with locals fishing, who'll give you the run down on what fish are biting where and often try to give you the fish they caught as well!

Tumby Bay's main street follows the curve of the bay, and the best food in town (fresh local seafood, of course) is at the two hotels. Alternatively, buy some wine and takeaway from one of the seafood shops in town and eat at one of the picnic tables along the shoreline.

Opposite Port Lincoln Marina *Left* Tumby Bay sunset

TUMBY BAY TO PORT LINCOLN

Tumby Bay to Port Lincoln, on the tip of the peninsula, is an easy half-hour drive. Just before you get to Port Lincoln, drop into Boston Bay Wines for a wine-tasting and one of the best cellar-door views in the country (Lincoln Hwy, 6km north of Port Lincoln; (08) 8684 3600; open Mon–Sun 12–4pm).

Port Lincoln is home to the largest commercial fishing fleet in the Southern Hemisphere and is famous for its tuna. The annual Tunarama Festival is held on the Australia Day long weekend at the end of January. The headline event is the World Championship Tuna Toss, when crowds gather to see who can throw a 10kg tuna the furthest (the world record is more than 37m). Ask at the visitor centre for details of fishing charters, behind-the-scenes tours of fish-processing plants and aquaculture cruises.

Port Lincoln is also the place to come face to face with a great white shark on a cage dive. You don't have to be a certified diver to do it – but you may have to be certifiably crazy. There are several companies that offer shark-cage dive tours out of Port Lincoln – see

adventurebaycharters.com.au and sharkcagediving.com.au. A less scary alternative – if you can forget for a moment that these waters are home to great white sharks – is swimming with sea lions. Known as the puppy dogs of the sea, they are insatiably curious, love to play and will often mimic your actions, circling when you do and diving and surfacing with you; the same companies that run the shark dives also run half-day swim with sea lion tours.

But it's not just the fish that are fast and furious in Port Lincoln. Makybe Diva, the first horse to win the Melbourne Cup three times in a row (2003, 2004 and 2005), is owned by South Australian tuna fisherman Tony Santic, who named her by using the first two letters in five of his employees' names (Maureen, Kylie, Belinda, Diana and Vanessa). There is a life-size bronze sculpture of the great racehorse on the Port Lincoln waterfront.

Port Lincoln is the largest town on the peninsula and has plenty of quality restaurants, cafes, galleries and shops. However, the best part of this bit of the world is the scenery, and the nearby national park is a must, although you will need a 4WD to see the best of it.

SIDETRACK

South-east of Port Lincoln, Lincoln National Park has a number of scenic drives – the 4WD-only one to the rugged southern section of the park is largely along the cliff edges to the Sleaford–Wanna sand dunes, an endless expanse of towering white sand dunes bordering beaches pounded by enormous waves. The more sheltered, northern section of the park (2WD accessible) has a string of pretty bays and calm beaches – most with camping and picnic sites. Pick of the crop is Memory Cove, but you will need a gate key from the visitor centre in Port Lincoln before you go and a 4WD is recommended.

SIDETRACK

South-west of Port Lincoln, the Whalers Way is a 14km cliff-edged drive through private property, and it is worth the $30 it costs to get a key from the visitor centre in Port Lincoln. It's sublimely scenic, tracing the coastline the entire way, with several lovely picnic spots. Camp behind the dunes at Redbanks Beach near the end of the drive, a magic spot that never gets crowded out. It has sensational views (but no facilities) and a ladder to climb down to the rockpools on the beach. Get a camping permit when you pick up the key.

PORT LINCOLN TO CEDUNA

From Port Lincoln, head north along the western edge of the peninsula in the direction of Streaky Bay.

SIDETRACK

Coffin Bay National Park is about 40km from Port Lincoln and is great for 4WDs. You can drive the length of the peninsula to Point Sir Isaac but, be warned, the sand can trap even the most experienced off-roader. Lower your tyre pressure and carry a compressor to reinflate the tyres – you will need to do this several times during the trip. It's only 55km from the ranger station, but it will take about three hours each way. Much of the road is actually on the beach, so you need to check the tide chart before you set off. There are good camping spots along the way at Black Springs and the Pool at Point Sir Isaac – both sites are practically on the beach and the fishing is great. If you're in a conventional car there are also plenty of great beaches and lookouts to visit – and a campground at Yangie Bay – although you will not be able to get deep inside the park.

In Coffin Bay, ask one of the locals for directions to where you can buy some freshly shucked oysters (many local oyster growers sell them from backyard sheds for just a few dollars) and find a shady spot on the Oyster Walk that skirts the edge of the bay for a five-star picnic.

Further north, Elliston is home to a very scenic cliff-top drive, the Elliston Coastal Trail, with cliffs as sensational as those you'll see on the Great Australian Bight – and some quirky sculptures. A highlight of the next section is Talia Caves, which were hollowed out of the granite and limestone cliffs by the sea. There are steps down to a large cavern in the cliff base and a ladder to the Tub, a large, craterlike hole around 30m deep and 50m wide.

SIDETRACK

Follow the signs to Baird Bay and the Point Labatt Australian sea lion colony, the only permanent breeding colony on mainland Australia – all other colonies occur on offshore islands. There is a viewing platform on the cliff-top where you can watch mothers teaching their pups to swim (you'll need binoculars if you want a really good view), or you can get up close and personal on a swimming with sea lions and dolphin tour (Baird Bay Ocean Eco Experience, Baird Bay; (08) 8626 5017; best Sept–May; bairdbay.com).

Back on the highway, a local landmark, Murphy's Haystacks, is not far from the turn-off to Baird Bay. The 'haystacks' are actually a hilltop outcrop of large granite boulders with walkways between them. Local legend has it that a traveller mistook the rocks – which were on a farm owned by a Murphy – for hay, and the name stuck. It's a nice spot for a picnic.

In Streaky Bay, pop into the Shell Roadhouse to take a look at a replica of the biggest great white shark ever caught by rod and reel – a very scary 5m long and weighing in at a whopping 1520kg. It was caught in the waters off Streaky Bay in 1990 and is enough to put you off swimming in the Southern Ocean for life.

From Streaky Bay continue north to Ceduna (via Smoky Bay) and link up with the Eyre Highway, where you can either head west across the Nullarbor (see p. 27) or back east to Adelaide on Highway 1.

Eyre Peninsula, SA

BEST EATS

- **Sarin's** The Port Lincoln Hotel's restaurant is a good place to enjoy some local tuna or the southern rock lobster (crayfish), in season Dec–May (you'll need to pre-order it a day or so ahead). 1 Lincoln Hwy, Port Lincoln; (08) 8621 2026; open Mon–Sun for lunch and dinner.
- **1802 Oyster Bar** This is one of the best restaurants on the peninsula. The menu changes daily according to what's fresh and best, but expect lots of local seafood, including the delectable Coffin Bay oysters done more than a dozen ways. 61 Esplanade, Coffin Bay; (08) 8685 4626; open Tues–Sun for lunch and afternoon oysters and snacks, Thurs–Sun for dinner; 1802oysterbar.com.au.
- **Streaky Bay Community Hotel** Set right on the water's edge, this historic hotel has sensational views and a menu full of local seafood, including King George whiting. 33 Alfred Tce, Streaky Bay; (08) 8626 1008; open Mon–Sun for lunch and dinner.
- **Ceduna Oyster Bar** Stop here for a mid-afternoon snack of freshly shucked oysters, sushi or fish and chips while enjoying the sun and bay views from the oyster shed rooftop. Lot 20 Eyre Hwy; 0497 085 549; open Tues–Sun 10am–6.30pm.

BEST SLEEPS

- **Tumby Bay Hotel** This lovely old pub, built in 1904, is cheap, cheerful and comfortable and the views from the wide verandah look clear across the bay. There are also self-contained seafront apartments available. 1 North Tce, Tumby Bay; (08) 8688 2005; tumbybaypub.com.
- **Port Lincoln Hotel** The hotel is already in a great location, in the heart of town opposite Boston Bay, but it's worth paying extra for an ocean-view room with a balcony – otherwise all you'll enjoy is a view of the carpark. 1 Lincoln Hwy, Port Lincoln; (08) 8621 2000; portlincolnhotel.com.au.
- **Tanonga Luxury Eco-Lodges** The two cabins here have knockout views of the surrounding 200ha property. 83 Pope Dr, Charlton Gully, 35 minutes' drive from Port Lincoln; 0427 277 417; tanonga.com.au.
- **Donington Cottage** If you really want to enjoy Lincoln National Park but camping is not your thing, stay at this historic lighthouse keeper's house, which sleeps six people. You will need to bring your own linen and food, but it's worth it for the views alone. Spalding Cove, Lincoln National Park; bookings via the Port Lincoln Visitor Information Centre.
- **Baird Bay Ocean Eco Apartments** The apartments have absolute waterfront views and lots of luxury touches, including a coffee machine. 33 Baird Bay Rd, Baird Bay; (08) 8626 5017; bairdbayoceanecoapartments.com.
- **Caravanning and camping** There are caravan parks in most coastal towns. Beachside camping is available in both Lincoln and Coffin Bay national parks. The most popular site in Lincoln National Park is Memory Cove (4WD only; book at Port Lincoln Visitor Information Centre), but other good spots include Fishermans Point, Surfleet Cove, Taylors Landing and September Beach (each with toilet facilities) and the beachside bush camps at Carcase Rock, MacLaren Point, Spalding Cove and Woodcutters Beach. The best campgrounds for caravans are at September Beach or Surfleet Cove, although neither has power. In Coffin Bay the most popular campground is at Yangie Bay, a sheltered bay surrounded by dense shrub. All other campsites in the park are 4WD only and most have no facilities. Sensation Beach is quite exposed, while Big Yangie, Black Springs, Morgans Landing and the Pool near Point Sir Isaac all offer more sheltered beachside campsites. You can also camp overlooking the beach at Wittelbee Conservation Park, 10km south of Ceduna via Decres Bay Rd.

Opposite Sculpture trail at Elliston *Left* Beachside camping

Reefs, gorges, cliffs, desert dunes, turquoise waters, sandy beaches, wild dolphins and whale sharks – you'll find it all on this drive along the Western Australian coast from Perth to Exmouth.

Coral Coast, WA

Since going to print, some of the areas featured in this trip were affected by cyclones, particularly around the township of Kalbarri. Rebuilding is well underway, but you may experience a shortage of accommodation and other services. Contact local visitor information centres for updates before travelling.

HOW LONG?

Allow at least a week, one way. If you don't have time to do the whole trip, just do the Indian Ocean Drive from Perth to Geraldton for beautiful coastal scenery.

WHEN TO GO

Exmouth is dry and warm virtually all year – perfect beach weather. Almost all the region's scarce rain falls during the winter months. Whale shark season peaks between April and early July. Wildflower season is July to November.

NEED TO KNOW

Between early July and late November the coastal plains burst into bloom with more than 800 species of native flowers and flowering shrubs. Get the latest wildflower news from the locals at australiascoralcoast.com, which has a regularly updated wildflower hot spot page.

 Drive rating
Easy. Sealed roads but some long distances and remote sections

 Distances
Total distance, Perth to Exmouth: 1389km
- Perth to Cervantes: 200km
- Cervantes to Geraldton: 223km
- Geraldton to Kalbarri: 155km
- Kalbarri to Carnarvon: 446km
- Carnarvon to Exmouth: 365km

 Temperatures
January: 21–36°C
July: 12–30°C

 More information
- Geraldton Visitor Centre, 246 Marine Tce, Geraldton; (08) 9956 6670; visitgeraldton.com.au
- Kalbarri Visitor Centre, 70 Grey St, Kalbarri; (80) 9937 1104; kalbarri.org.au
- Ningaloo Visitor Centre, 2 Truscott Cres, Exmouth; (08) 9949 3070; visitningaloo.com.au
- Shark Bay World Heritage Discovery and Visitor Centre, 53 Knight Tce, Denham; 1300 367 072; sharkbayvisit.com.au
- australiascoralcoast.com

 Snapshot
Outback red-desert dunes meet astonishingly turquoise sea on this long stretch of coastline between Perth and Exmouth, an ancient landscape of reefs, gorges, cliffs and startling rock formations. Ningaloo Reef is every bit as magnificent as Queensland's Great Barrier Reef, with the added advantage that it is one of the few places in the world where you can actually walk straight from the beach to the coral, as well as being home (between April and early July) to amazing whale sharks.

Opposite Red Bluff, Kalbarri

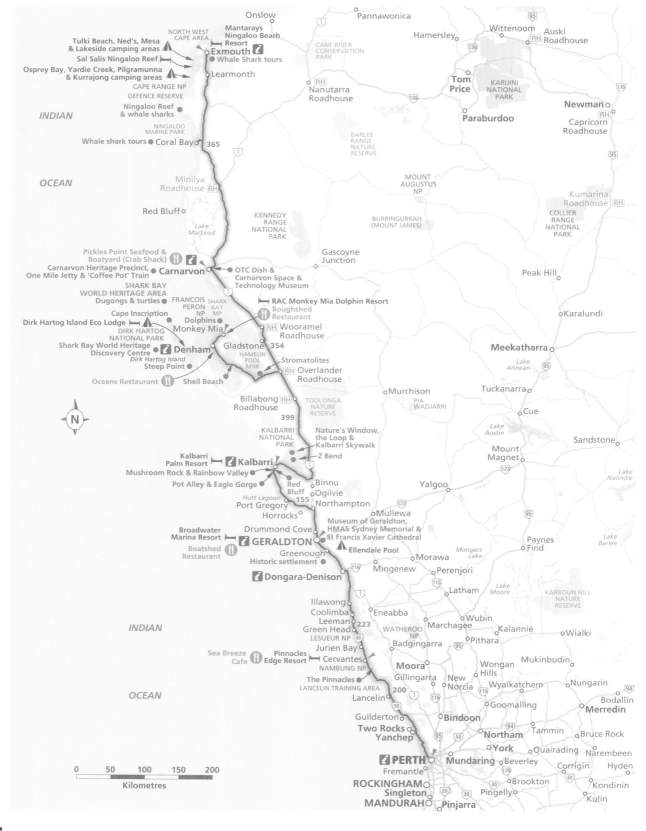

Coral Coast, WA

Onslow
Pannawonica
Hamersley
Wittenoom
Auski
Roadhouse

NORTH WEST
CAPE AREA
Tulki Beach, Ned's, Mesa
& Lakeside camping areas
Sal Salis Ningaloo Reef
Osprey Bay, Yardie Creek, Pilgramunna
& Kurrajong camping areas

Mantarays
Ningaloo Beach
Resort
Exmouth
Whale Shark tours
Learmonth

CANE RIVER
CONSERVATION
PARK

Nanutarra
Roadhouse

**Tom
Price**

KARIJINI
NATIONAL
PARK

Newman

CAPE RANGE NP
DEFENCE RESERVE

INDIAN

Ningaloo Reef
& whale sharks

Paraburdoo

Capricorn
Roadhouse

NINGALOO
MARINE PARK

OCEAN

Whale shark tours ● Coral Bay
365

Minilya
Roadhouse

BARLEE
RANGE
NATURE
RESERVE

MOUNT
AUGUSTUS
NP

Kumarina
Roadhouse

Red Bluff

Lake
MacLeod

KENNEDY
RANGE
NATIONAL
PARK

Gascoyne
Junction

BURRINGURRAH
(MOUNT JAMES)

COLLIER
RANGE
NATIONAL
PARK

Peak Hill

Pickles Point Seafood &
Boatyard (Crab Shack)
Carnarvon Heritage Precinct,
One Mile Jetty & 'Coffee Pot' Train

Carnarvon
OTC Dish &
Carnarvon Space &
Technology Museum

Karalundi

SHARK BAY
WORLD HERITAGE AREA
Dugongs & turtles

FRANCOIS
PERON
NP

SHARK
BAY
MP

RAC Monkey Mia Dolphin Resort
Boughshed
Restaurant

Wooramel
Roadhouse

Meekatharra

Lake
Annean

Cape Inscription
Dirk Hartog Island Eco Lodge
DIRK HARTOG
NATIONAL PARK
Shark Bay World Heritage
Discovery Centre

Dolphins
Monkey Mia

Denham

Gladstone
354

HAMELIN
POOL
MNR

Dirk Hartog Island
Steep Point
Oceans Restaurant ● Shell Beach

Stromatolites
Overlander
Roadhouse

Murchison

Tuckanarra

Cue

Lake
Austin

Sandstone

Billabong
Roadhouse
399

TOOLONGA
NATURE
RESERVE

PIA
WADJARRI

Mount
Magnet

Lake
Noondie

KALBARRI
NATIONAL
PARK

Nature's Window,
the Loop &
Kalbarri Skywalk
Z Bend

Yalgoo

Kalbarri
Palm Resort
Kalbarri
Mushroom Rock & Rainbow Valley
Pot Alley & Eagle Gorge

Red
Bluff
155

Binnu
Ogilvie
Northampton

Lake
Barlee

Hutt Lagoon
Port Gregory
Horrocks

Mullewa
Museum of Geraldton,
HMAS Sydney Memorial &
St Francis Xavier Cathedral

Paynes
Find

Broadwater
Marina Resort
Boatshed
Restaurant

Drummond Cove
GERALDTON

Greenough
Historic settlement

Dongara-Denison

Ellendale Pool

Morawa

Mingenew

Perenjori

Mongers
Lake

KARROUN HILL
NATURE
RESERVE

INDIAN

Illawong
Coolimba
Leeman
223
Green Head
Jurien Bay

Eneabba
WATHEROO
NP
Marchagee

Latham

Lake
Moore

Wubin
Kalannie
Pithara

Wialki

OCEAN

Sea Breeze
Cafe
Pinnacles
Edge Resort
LESUEUR NP
Cervantes
NAMBUNG NP

Badgingarra

Moora
Gillingarra
New
Norcia

Wongan
Hills

Mukinbudin

Nungarin

The Pinnacles
LANCELIN TRAINING AREA
Lancelin
200

Wyalkatchem

Goomalling

Bodallin
Merredin

Guilderton
Two Rocks
Yanchep

Bindoon

Northam
York

Tammin

Bruce Rock

INDIAN

PERTH
Mundaring

Quairading

Naremberen

OCEAN

Fremantle
ROCKINGHAM
Singleton
MANDURAH
Pinjarra

Beverley

Brookton

Corrigin

Hyden

Pingelly

Kondinin

Kulin

0   50   100   150   200
Kilometres

PERTH TO GERALDTON

There aren't many places in Australia where you can see the sea from the middle of the desert, but the Pinnacles, near Cervantes, is one. Thousands of huge limestone pillars rise out of a stark landscape of yellow sand in Nambung National Park, approximately 245km (three hours' drive) north of Perth via the Indian Ocean Drive (State Route 60). In places they reach up to 3.5m tall. The towers were formed as the mineral-rich sands were compacted inside the surrounding dune system, which in turn eroded away leaving the crazy spikes that exist today.

The Pinnacles are 17km south of Cervantes, just one of several seaside towns on the Indian Ocean Drive, which runs north along this extraordinarily beautiful coastline through the townships of Lancelin, Cervantes and Jurien Bay. They all have seemingly endless white-sand beaches lapped by sparkling blue water, wooden jetties and local fish and chips shops selling just-caught and freshly cooked crayfish at bargain prices. You don't have to leave the coast until you get to Geraldton (223km north of Cervantes) and it's one of the best coastal road trips in the country.

Don't miss the National Trust–protected village of Greenough, 24km south of Geraldton, a collection of 11 restored buildings including a gaol, courthouse, police station, churches and a school in what was once a vibrant country community but is now just a ghost town – albeit a very solidly built one. And keep an eye out along the way for the surreal leaning trees, growing sideways thanks to the prevailing winds.

Above Limestone pinnacles of Nambung National Park

GERALDTON TO KALBARRI

Learn about one of the continent's first recorded atrocities at the Museum of Geraldton – the massacre of the survivors of the *Batavia* shipwreck, which took place some 80km off this coast, 150 or so years before the British arrived in Botany Bay on the other side of the continent. Apart from the riveting shipwreck story, there is also a large gallery focusing on another equally famous maritime mystery, the disappearance of HMAS *Sydney* in 1941 after a battle with the German warship HSK *Kormoran*. (1 Museum Pl, Batavia Coast Marina, Geraldton; (08) 9431 8393; open Mon–Sun 9.30am–3pm; museum.wa.gov.au/museums/museum-geraldton.) The wreck of the *Sydney* was finally discovered off Dirk Hartog Island in 2008. A memorial to the crew has been built on Mount Scott overlooking Geraldton. The silver dome of seagulls represents the 645 lost sailors, and a southern wall displays ghostly photographs of the ship and the names of the crew, while a bronze statue of a woman gazes desperately out to sea as if awaiting news. Visit at sunset or in the early morning and you can't help but be moved by this striking piece of art.

Another remarkable work of art is the St Francis Xavier Cathedral, with its Californian Mission–style twin towers, a Brunelleschi-esque cupola like the one in Florence and a mix of Romanesque, French Renaissance, Eastern Orthodox and even Islamic architectural elements inside. It was designed in 1915 by the famous architect-priest Monsignor John Cyril Hawes, who also built other remarkable chapels and churches in places such as Mullewa, Morawa and Perenjori as well as in the Bahamas. Completed in 1938, it's one of the most original and unusual cathedrals in Australia and worth a look even if churches aren't your usual thing.

It will take about two hours to get to Kalbarri, but spear off Highway 1 at Northampton and follow the coastal route via Port Gregory and Hutt Lagoon, a pink salt lake. If you're arriving in Kalbarri at sunset you're in for a treat. Along the coast, wind and wave erosion have exposed layers of coastal cliffs that rise more than 100m above the ocean. From Red Bluff, on the southern outskirts of town, the extensive views encompass colourful coastal limestone and sandstone ledges, which are at their best in the late afternoon when they glow in the setting sun. There are scenic lookouts signposted off the main road at Mushroom Rock, Rainbow Valley, Pot Alley and Eagle Gorge and you can walk between them on the Mushroom Rock Nature Trail, a leisurely two-hour-return walk.

Kalbarri, a fishing settlement at the mouth of the Murchison River, was only formally settled in the 1950s. It's an ideal place to spend a few days in the sun, splashing in the shallows on the town's river beach, but it's the gorges and cliffs of Kalbarri National Park, which surrounds the town, that are the main attraction.

If you have a head for heights step out onto Kalbarri Skywalk, two glass-floored lookout platforms cantilevered 17 and 25 metres beyond the rim of a gorge above the Murchison River, 100 metres below (at the West Loop site in the national park).

Less vertigo-inducing but just as insta-worthy is Nature's Window, about 26km north-east of the town. It's part of a wider area of the park known as the Loop, where a short cliff-top walking trail runs above a loop of the Murchison River, leading to several lookouts along the way. Nature's Window is a natural rock arch that perfectly frames the upstream view and has become a must-have photo for travellers to the area. About 11km down the road, another star attraction is the Z Bend, a Z-shaped gorge cut deep into the rock by the river.

KALBARRI TO MONKEY MIA

Heading north from Kalbarri, it will take about three hours to get to Hamelin Pool Marine Nature Reserve, one of only two places in the world where you will find marine stromatolites – ancient 'living fossils'. Much more interesting than they look, these rocky lumps, seemingly strewn untidily around the beach, are actually constructed by microscopic living organisms – up to 3 billion of them per square metre – using sediment and other organic material. The stromatolites may be up to 1.5m high. Because they grow very slowly, a 1m high stromatolite could be about 2000 years old. They are able to survive here because Hamelin Pool's water is twice as saline as seawater.

A few kilometres down the road is remarkable Shell Beach, which is made up of millions of tiny coquina shells and is one of only two such beaches in the world. It stretches for approximately 110km and is up to 10m deep. When the first European settlers arrived in the area building materials were scarce, but they soon found that compacted coquina shells could be made into blocks. Several buildings still standing in Denham are built from these blocks. The most westerly town in Australia, Denham began life as a pearling port (locals tell stories of streets kerbed with pearl shell, though that could be an urban myth) but is now better known for its prawn and crayfish industry.

Denham is opposite Dirk Hartog Island, the first place that Europeans visited so close to the mainland. Captain Dirk Hartog arrived on the *Eendracht* on 25 October 1616, announcing his arrival by nailing an inscribed pewter plate to a wooden post at the site now known as Cape Inscription. The island is accessible by barge from Steep Point (the westernmost point on the Australian mainland) and only 20 vehicles are allowed on the island at any one time. All tracks on the island are sandy and 4WD only, but tours and boat transfers are available from Denham (dirkhartogisland.com or sharkbaydive.com.au).

Learn all about the early exploration of the area, and the World Heritage status of the bay, at the Shark Bay World Heritage Discovery Centre. It's a fascinating museum, with interactive displays and a replica of Hartog's Plate. (53 Knight Tce, Denham; 1300 367 072; open Mon–Fri 9am–4.30pm, Sat–Sun 9am–1pm, 10am–4.30pm Apr–Oct.)

About 400 bottlenose dolphins live in the waters of Shark Bay near Monkey Mia, and most mornings several dolphins drift into the shallows to be hand-fed by scores of eager tourists, as they have been since 1964, when a woman from

one of the nearby fishing camps befriended the dolphins and began regularly feeding them. It is one of the few places in Australia where dolphins visit daily, not seasonally, and, unlike most dolphin encounters, this one costs nothing.

But the dolphins are not the only attraction of this World Heritage–listed marine park. Turtles are frequently seen in the bay and it is also home to about 10,000 dugongs (around 10 per cent of the world's dugong population), who feed on Shark Bay's massive meadows of seagrass. Monkey Mia Dolphin Resort (*see* Best sleeps, p. 149) runs afternoon sailing cruises to see them, as well as a range of other sailing trips, including sunset sails. Nearby Francois Peron National Park is also worth exploring. Here red pindan dunes spill into the sea and the colours are extraordinary. It's also a great place to see sharks, rays, turtles, whales, dolphins, birds and other wildlife. Tracks are 4WD only, but day tours are available from Monkey Mia (monkeymiawildsights.com.au or wulagura.com.au).

Opposite Z bend at Kalbarri National Park *Above* Stromatolites at Hamelin Pool

MONKEY MIA TO EXMOUTH

It's a long haul from Monkey Mia to Exmouth, approximately 700km, so break the journey at Carnarvon. Australia's first live satellite television broadcast was transmitted from Carnarvon in 1966. The massive OTC (Overseas Telecommunications Commission) dish on the edge of town was Australia's first Earth station for satellite tracking and communications, and one of just eight in the world.

The Carnarvon Heritage Precinct is a collection of historic buildings and museums near the One Mile Jetty (no prizes for guessing how long it is). Built in 1897, the jetty is a major tourist attraction and popular fishing spot. If you don't feel like walking its length, take the cute 'Coffee Pot' train, named for its unusually shaped smoke stack.

In Coral Bay, 238km further north, you can walk straight from the beach to Ningaloo Reef, which is great for novice snorkellers (but be aware of boats in the water). You can also take a glass-bottom boat tour over the coral. Ningaloo Reef is one of the few places in the world where whale sharks routinely gather in large numbers close to the coast, coming here each year between April and early July to feed on the abundant plankton. Despite their name, these massive but harmless fish are truly the gentle giants of the deep – they can measure up to 18m in length, with an adult whale shark weighing in at more than 15 tonnes and having a mouth more than 1m wide.

 KIDS' SPOT

Astronaut Buzz Aldrin (the second person to ever set foot on the moon) opened the Carnarvon Space and Technology Museum at the OTC Satellite Earth Station in 2012. Kids (and space geeks) will enjoy its interactive exhibits, spacecraft equipment, displays telling the story of Carnarvon's role in the space race, historic satellite broadcast footage and a full-size replica of the *Gemini* capsule. Mahoney Ave, Carnarvon; (08) 9941 2223; open Mon–Sun 10am–3pm, 10am–2pm Oct–Mar; carnarvonmuseum.org.au.

Whale shark tours operate from both Coral Bay and Exmouth, and all employ spotter planes to help locate the huge fish. Because whale sharks swim near the surface, you don't have to scuba dive to see them, just snorkel. But you do have to be pretty fit. Despite their massive bulk, whale sharks are fast swimmers and a tour involves lots of clambering in and out of the boat and sprint-like swims to keep up with the mighty sharks. It's worth it, though: as you swim above or beside them, all else disappears and, even though there are a dozen or so other swimmers in the water with you, it feels like it's just you and the whale shark. Forget all those other '100 things to do before you die' lists: this is a special, awe-inspiring experience that everybody really should try to do at least once in their life.

BEST EATS

- **Sea Breeze Cafe** Cervantes is a rock-lobster fishing town, so even the local fish and chip shop sells freshly caught and cooked crayfish at the market (or beach) price. 10 Cadiz St, Cervantes; (08) 9652 7233; open Mon–Sun for lunch and dinner.
- **Boatshed Restaurant** Come here for great seafood chowder and other fishy dishes. 359 Marine Tce, Geraldton; (08) 9921 5500; open Mon–Sat for dinner.
- **Oceans Restaurant** Watch sharks, rays and dolphins from the deck as you eat at this licensed restaurant overlooking Shark Bay. Shark Bay Rd, 8km south of Denham; (08) 9948 1765; open Mon–Sun for breakfast and lunch Apr–Oct; oceanpark.com.au.
- **Boughshed Restaurant** This restaurant at the RAC Monkey Mia Dolphin Resort (see Best sleeps) has great views and a menu that focuses on local seafood – try the tuna takaki or the linguine with Shark Bay blue swimmer crab and Exmouth prawns. It's popular, so you'll need to book ahead for dinner. 1 Monkey Mia Rd, Monkey Mia; (08) 9948 1171; open Mon–Sun for breakfast, lunch and dinner; parksandresorts.rac.com.au/monkey-mia.
- **Pickles Point Seafood & Boatyard** Also known as the Crab Shack, this place does great steamed blue crabs and prawns and ready-to-cook filleted fish – all straight from the fishing boats. 143 Harbour Rd, Carnarvon; (08) 9941 4078; open Mon–Fri 10am–4.30pm, Sat 10am–1pm.

BEST SLEEPS

- **Pinnacles Edge Resort** If you plan on seeing the Pinnacles at sunset or sunrise – the best times for photography – this low-key resort with a pool, modern rooms and self-catering apartments in the centre of town makes a good base. 7 Aragon St, Cervantes; (08) 9652 7788; pinnaclesedgeresort.com.au.
- **Broadwater Marina Resort** These stylish and quite spacious apartments overlook the Indian Ocean and are just a few minutes' walk from the restaurants and shops in the city centre. 298 Chapman Rd, Geraldton; (08) 9965 9100; mariner.broadwaters.com.au.
- **Kalbarri Palm Resort** The resort has comfortable motel-style rooms just a couple of blocks back from the river mouth and beach. 8 Porter St, Kalbarri; (08) 9937 2333; palmresort.com.au.

- **Dirk Hartog Island Eco Lodge** Enjoy beautiful ocean views from your room in the historic shearers' quarters at this family-run lodge. The owners, who used to farm sheep on the island, are the third generation to live there, and they also run 4WD and fishing tours in the surrounding national park. The family-style meals around the firepit are a highlight. 62 Dirk Hartog Island Dr, Dirk Hartog Island; (08) 9948 1211; dirkhartogisland.com.
- **RAC Monkey Mia Dolphin Resort** All overnight visitors to Monkey Mia must stay here. Fortunately the resort has a range of accommodation, from beachfront villas and family studios to backpacker dorms and powered caravan and tent sites (some also beachfront). The facilities include a swimming pool, hot tub, tennis court, internet cafe, barbecues, mini-mart and laundry. 1 Monkey Mia Rd, Monkey Mia; 1800 871 570; parksandresorts.rac.com.au/monkey-mia.
- **Sal Salis Ningaloo Reef** This is one of the coast's top 'glamping' spots, where you can enjoy the outdoors in style. The main camp building where you eat and drink has great views across the dunes to the sea beyond, and each of the five 'tents' has a supremely comfortable bed, a ceiling fan, solar-powered lights and an ensuite bathroom. Cape Range National Park; (08) 9949 1776; salsalis.com.au.
- **Mantarays Ningaloo Beach Resort** Right on the beach in Exmouth's new marina development, this resort offers a range of rooms, from one-bedroom studios to three-bedroom beachfront bungalows. 900 Madaffari Dr, Exmouth; (08) 9949 0000; mantaraysningalooresort.com.au.
- **Caravanning and camping** Camp beside Ellendale Pool, a beautiful deep freshwater swimming pool on the Greenough River encircled by tall sandstone cliffs near the ghost town of Greenough, about 47km east of Geraldton via Ellendale Road. There are beachside bush-camping spots in Cape Range National Park near Exmouth and powered sites at RAC Monkey Mia Dolphin Resort (see above). On Dirk Hartog Island you can camp overlooking the sea near the historic homestead or at one of the national park campgrounds (dirkhartogisland.com). But elsewhere, aside from roadside rest areas, you'll be restricted to caravan parks, which you'll find in almost every town along this route.

Opposite Swimming with whale sharks at Ningaloo Reef

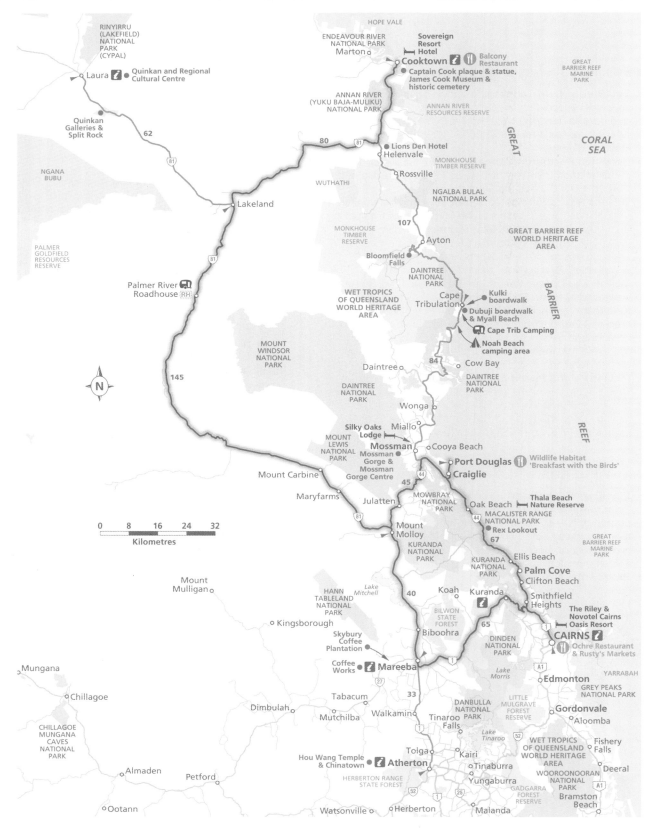

RINYIRRU
(LAKEFIELD)
NATIONAL
PARK
(CYPAL)

Laura ⓘ ● Quinkan and Regional
Cultural Centre

Quinkan
Galleries &
Split Rock

NGANA
BUBU

62

81

PALMER
GOLDFIELD
RESOURCES
RESERVE

Lakeland

81

Palmer River
Roadhouse RH

145

MOUNT
WINDSOR
NATIONAL
PARK

N

HOPE VALE

ENDEAVOUR RIVER
NATIONAL PARK
Marton

Sovereign
Resort
Hotel

Cooktown ⓘ 🍴 ● Balcony
Restaurant
● Captain Cook plaque & statue,
James Cook Museum &
historic cemetery

ANNAN RIVER
(YUKU BAJA-MULIKU)
NATIONAL PARK

ANNAN RIVER
RESOURCES RESERVE

80   81

● Lions Den Hotel
Helenvale
○ Rossville

MONKHOUSE
TIMBER RESERVE

GREAT
BARRIER REEF
MARINE
PARK

CORAL
SEA

WUTHATHI

NGALBA BULAL
NATIONAL PARK

107

MONKHOUSE
TIMBER
RESERVE

○ Ayton

Bloomfield
Falls ●

DAINTREE
NATIONAL
PARK

GREAT BARRIER REEF
WORLD HERITAGE
AREA

GREAT

BARRIER

WET TROPICS
OF QUEENSLAND
WORLD HERITAGE
AREA

Cape
Tribulation

● Kulki
boardwalk
● Dubuji boardwalk
& Myall Beach
🏕 ● Cape Trib Camping
▲ ● Noah Beach
camping area

84

● Cow Bay

REEF

MOUNT
WINDSOR
NATIONAL
PARK

○ Daintree

DAINTREE
NATIONAL
PARK

Wonga ○

Miallo ○

Silky Oaks
Lodge ●

MOUNT
LEWIS
NATIONAL
PARK

Mossman ●
Mossman
Gorge &
Mossman
Gorge Centre

Cooya Beach ○

● Port Douglas 🍴 Wildlife Habitat
'Breakfast with the Birds'
● Craiglie

Mount Carbine ○

Maryfarms ○

81

Julatten ○

45   44

MOWBRAY
NATIONAL
PARK

Oak Beach ○

Thala Beach
Nature Reserve

44   MACALISTER RANGE
NATIONAL PARK
● Rex Lookout

67

GREAT
BARRIER REEF
MARINE
PARK

0   8   16   24   32
Kilometres

Mount
Mulligan ○

Mount
Molloy ▽

KURANDA
NATIONAL
PARK

40

HANN
TABLELAND
NATIONAL
PARK

Lake
Mitchell

Koah ○

BILWON
STATE
FOREST

KURANDA
NATIONAL
PARK

Kuranda
ⓘ

Ellis Beach ○

● Palm Cove
● Clifton Beach
Smithfield
Heights

The Riley &
Novotel Cairns
Oasis Resort

Kingsborough ○

Skybury
Coffee
Plantation

Coffee
Works ⓘ ● Mareeba

27

Mungana ○

○ Chillagoe

CHILLAGOE
MUNGANA
CAVES
NATIONAL
PARK

Biboohra ○

65

DINDEN
NATIONAL
PARK

Lake
Morris

CAIRNS ⓘ
🍴 Ochre Restaurant
& Rusty's Markets

A1

YARRABAH

● Edmonton

GREY PEAKS
NATIONAL PARK

Tabacum ○

Dimbulah ○

Mutchilba ○

Walkamin ○

33

Tinaroo
Falls ○

DANBULLA
NATIONAL
PARK

LITTLE
MULGRAVE
FOREST
RESERVE

Lake
Tinaroo

52

WET TROPICS
OF QUEENSLAND
WORLD HERITAGE
AREA

● Gordonvale
○ Aloomba

Fishery
Falls ○

○ Deeral

Almaden ○

○ Petford

○ Ootann

Hou Wang Temple
& Chinatown

ⓘ ● Atherton

HERBERTON RANGE
STATE FOREST

Tolga ○

Kairi ○

○ Tinaburra

○ Yungaburra

52   25

Herberton ○

1

Watsonville ○

Malanda ○

WOOROONOORAN
NATIONAL
PARK

GADGARRA
FOREST
RESERVE

A1

Bramston
Beach ○

Explore the magnificent Wet Tropics and the beautiful Queensland coastline between Cairns and Cooktown, the only place on the planet where two World Heritage-listed areas (the Wet Tropics and the Great Barrier Reef) converge.

Tropical Way, Qld

HOW LONG?

If you just drive straight to Cooktown, it will take less than a day, but the sidetracks on this road trip offer some of the best scenery in the country, so take your time and allow a couple of days.

WHEN TO GO

Summer is very wet and humid and some minor roads may be affected by flooding. Cyclones may also occur during the summer wet season. Winter is warm and sunny with little rain.

NEED TO KNOW

Most of the unsealed roads in Far North Queensland become impassable after rain. Check road conditions before travelling at qldtraffic.qld.gov.au or call 13 1940.

 Drive rating
Easy. Sealed roads with optional 4WD route

 Distances
Total distance, Cairns to Cooktown via Port Douglas (without detours): approximately 325km
- Cairns to Mareeba: 65km
- Cairns to Port Douglas: 67km
- Port Douglas to Cape Tribulation: 84km
- Mount Molloy to Cooktown: 225km
- Lakeland to Laura: 62km
- Bloomfield Track 4WD option, Cooktown to Cape Tribulation: 33km

 Temperatures
January: 23–37°C
July: 16–30°C

More information
- Atherton Visitor Information Centre, cnr Main St and Silo Rd, Atherton; 1300 366 361
- Cooktown Visitor Information Centre, Botanic Gardens, 1 Walker St, Cooktown; (07) 4069 5763; cooktownandcapeyork.com
- Kuranda Visitor Information Centre, Centenary Park, Therwine St, Kuranda; (07) 4093 9311; kuranda.org
- Mareeba Visitor Information Centre, 345 Byrnes St, Mareeba; (07) 4092 5674; mareebaheritagecentre.com.au
- tropicalnorthqueensland.org.au

 Snapshot
There are two main reasons that thousands of visitors head to Tropical North Queensland each year: the rainforest and the Great Barrier Reef. Explore them both – with or without a 4WD – on this scenic coastal drive from Cairns to Cooktown.

CAIRNS TO MOUNT MOLLOY VIA THE COAST

This trip starts with a choice. There are two ways to head north from Cairns to hook up with the Mulligan Highway: by the sea or through the hinterland. The coastal way, the Captain Cook Highway (recently rebranded the Great Barrier Reef Drive), is one of the most picturesque roads in the country. The first section to Port Douglas hugs the coast, one eye-stretching sea view unfurling after another, and there are plenty of places to pull over and admire the scenery along the way, including Rex Lookout, approximately 56km north of Cairns, which looks out over Trinity Bay.

Head west just before Port Douglas and wind your way up into the highlands and Mount Molloy.

😀 KIDS' SPOT

A must-see spot in the Wet Tropics is Mossman Gorge, a beautiful boulder-strewn river gorge in dense rainforest 20km north of Port Douglas. The Mossman Gorge Centre offers easy access to the gorge, with shuttles departing every 10 minutes, as well as a cafe, Indigenous art gallery and gift shop. Kids will love the two Dreamtime Gorge Walks on Kuku Yalanji land, run by Indigenous guides. The walks start with a traditional 'smoking' ceremony that cleanses and wards off bad spirits, then meander through the rainforest, taking in traditional huts or humpies, a swim in a waterhole and, at the end, bush tea and damper. 212 Mossman Gorge Rd, Mossman; (07) 4099 7000; open Mon–Sun 8am–6pm; mossmangorge.com.au.

SIDETRACK

The rainforest meets the sea at Cape Tribulation in the Daintree rainforest, 64km north of Mossman. The road to the cape is sealed, but you'll need to take the ferry across the Daintree River. There are four wheelchair-accessible boardwalks through the rainforest and mangroves, all of which include interpretive boards; these are a great way to explore the wet forests and swamps without getting your feet wet. The Dubuji and Kulki boardwalks lead out to beautiful Myall Beach. Swimming is not recommended, however, as estuarine crocodiles live in the park's creeks and nearby coastal waters; also beware of marine stingers from October to May. The roads are narrow and winding, are not recommended for caravans and may be closed after heavy rain.

Top Boyd's Forest Dragon in the Daintree Rainforest *Bottom* Cairns Esplanade

CAIRNS TO MOUNT MOLLOY VIA THE TABLELAND

The alternative, slightly more direct way north is to climb straight into the mountains from Cairns via a series of tight, twisting switchback turns through the World Heritage–listed rainforest up to Kuranda and Mareeba, where the country opens out into fields of sugarcane, paddocks of macadamia and mango trees, and exotic orchards laden with strange-looking fruit.

This is also coffee country: almost all of Australia's coffee is grown in the Mareeba area. Skybury Coffee Plantation runs guided tours and also has a terrific cafe – taste some of their delicious own-grown coffee on the deck, which has views that seem to stretch forever (136 Ivicevic Rd, Paddys Green; (07) 4093 2190; open Mon–Sun 10am–4pm; skybury.com.au). Or learn about how the coffee is roasted at Coffee Works in Mareeba (136 Mason St, Mareeba; 1800 355 526; open Mon–Sun 9am–2pm).

SIDETRACK

The township of Atherton is 33km south of Mareeba. One hundred years ago, this sleepy little town had a flourishing Chinatown that had sprung up during the 19th-century gold rushes. Today the only sign of this once thriving community of more than 1100 is the small timber-and-iron Hou Wang Temple, built in 1903, that somehow managed to survive while all around it buildings were demolished and carted away for scrap. It's now protected by the National Trust and houses a fascinating museum crammed with innovative, interactive displays and artefacts. Free guided tours run on demand and are well worth the hour or so it takes to explore the old Chinatown area and the interior of the temple, which is still fitted out with the original elaborate carvings, bell and metal vessels brought from China last century. (86 Herberton Rd, Atherton; (07) 4091 6945; open Wed–Fri 9am–4pm, Sat 10am–2pm; nationaltrust.org.au/places/hou-wang-temple.)

MOUNT MOLLOY TO COOKTOWN

Head north through the township of Mount Molloy and on towards the Palmer River Roadhouse, where prospector James Venture Mulligan found 102 ounces of gold in 1872, sparking a ten-year gold rush that eventually led to permanent settlement in the area and, 133 years later, the naming of a new highway. If you need sustenance, the roadhouse serves a killer hamburger, or keep going the extra 48km to Lakeland, which also brews up its own, very good locally grown coffee.

SIDETRACK

One of Australia's – and the world's – best collections of prehistoric rock paintings is also one of the least known. Located near the tiny township of Laura, about 60km north-west of Lakeland, the Quinkan Galleries include artworks painted between 30,000 and 35,000 years ago, listed by UNESCO as being among the top ten rock-art sites in the world. One of the most accessible sites is at Split Rock, just a few kilometres east of town. There are three galleries here, connected by a boardwalk, that encompass paintings of flying foxes and the bizarre, spiteful, tall spirits with knobbly knees and bent limbs, the Quinkans. There's not a lot of interpretive information at the site, so it helps if you call into the Quinkan and Regional Cultural Centre just down the road before climbing the hill to the site. It's an excellent information centre and museum, with all sorts of displays on the art and local Aboriginal culture and history, including storyboards, artefacts, films and recorded oral histories. The road to Laura is sealed. (Lot 2, Peninsula Development Rd, Laura; (07) 4060 3457; opening hours vary so call first to check; quinkancc.com.au.)

It's about 80km to Cooktown from Lakeland, but take a small 4km detour off the Mulligan Highway down the coast road to drop into the Lions Den Hotel (look out for the signs for the Bloomfield Track about 25km south of Cooktown; although the track is 4WD, this first section is fine for 2WD and caravans). You can't miss it, as it's the only thing there! Built in 1875 at the height of the rush, this historic hotel, knocked together with scraps of wood and iron, is full of quirky decorations and walls adorned with visitors' signatures. (398 Shiptons Flat Rd, Helenvale; (07) 4060 3911; open Mon–Sun from 9am.)

COOKTOWN

A sleepy, half-forgotten type of place set to burst onto the tourist trail, Cooktown still has a last-frontier feel to it, all wide, white-verandahed pubs and swaying palm trees, laconic locals and steamy rainforests. It's also one of Queensland's oldest historic towns and the only place in Australia where James Cook and his crew spent an extended period of time ashore. Back in 1770, Cook's ship, the *Endeavour*, ran afoul of the Great Barrier Reef, seriously damaging its hull. It was sink or swim, and Cook needed to find safe waters fast, so he sailed his damaged vessel into the closest river he could find and set up camp at what is now known as Cooktown for seven weeks while he repaired his ship.

Cook's landing site on the banks of the Endeavour River in the centre of town is now marked with a plaque and statue commemorating the great navigator, and the excellent James Cook Museum is worth a few hours of your time (50 Helen St, Cooktown; (07) 4069 5386; open Mon–Sun 9am–4pm May–Sept, Tues–Sat 10am–1pm Oct–Apr).

Take a stroll through the beautiful Botanic Gardens in Walker Street – established in 1878 it's one of the oldest gardens in the state. The historic cemetery on Boundary Street is also good for a wander: informative plaques recount the history and stories of some of the people buried here, such as the Normanby Woman, a mysterious European woman found living with the local Aboriginal people, who died before anyone could find out who she was, and Mary Watson, who escaped an attack on nearby Lizard Island by taking to the open seas in a big pot (like a small tank) used for boiling down bêche-de-mer. There is also a large shrine to the many Chinese who died here during the Palmer River gold rush of the 1870s.

Take the wild way home

If you have a 4WD and want to get off the beaten track, take the Bloomfield Track back to Port Douglas. This is the controversial road that was blazed through the Daintree rainforest back in the 1980s. A highlight is Wujal Wujal (Bloomfield) Falls, which are at their best after rain or very early in the dry season, when a thundering torrent spills over a basin-like cliff into the river. It's a sacred site and not signposted, but tours with Traditional Owners can be arranged through the Shire Council in the nearby community of Wujal Wujal; call (07) 4083 9100. You also have a good chance of seeing cassowaries foraging beside the road or darting into the rainforest as you drive past.

Opposite Stock up on tropical produce at Rusty Markets in Cairns *Left* Endeavour River, Cooktown

BEST EATS

- **Ochre Restaurant** This famous waterfront Cairns restaurant serves creative native Australian cuisine – 'wild food' with a strong Asian twist – but it's not all bush tucker. And despite being popular with international tourists keen to try wallaby and crocodile, it's still one of the best places to eat in town. 6/1 Marlin Pde, Cairns; (07) 4051 0100; open Mon–Sat for lunch, Mon–Sun for dinner; ochrerestaurant.com.au.
- **Rusty's Markets** This is the place to pick up fresh fruit and local produce. 57–89 Grafton St, Cairns; (07) 4040 2705; open Friday 7am–9.30pm, Sat–Sun 7am–1.30pm.
- **Wildlife Habitat** Port Douglas has plenty of eating choices on its main thoroughfare, Macrossan Street, but its best breakfast is served on the southern edge of town: it's the daily 'Breakfast with the Birds' at this well-known wildlife centre, where you can also 'Lunch with the Lorikeets'. Port Douglas Rd, Port Douglas; (07) 4099 3235; open Mon–Sun for breakfast and lunch.
- **Balcony Restaurant** This restaurant at the Sovereign Resort Hotel (*see* Best sleeps) overlooks the Endeavour River and serves up a surprisingly innovative menu, given the remoteness of the location. 128 Charlotte St, Cooktown; (07) 4043 0500; open Mon–Sun for dinner April–Oct.

BEST SLEEPS

- **Novotel Cairns Oasis Resort** In a great location close to the centre of Cairns, this resort has one of the largest swimming pools in town. 122 Lake St, Cairns; (07) 4080 1888; novotelcairnsresort.com.au.
- **Thala Beach Nature Reserve** Perched atop a privately owned headland near Oak Beach on the only beachfront nature reserve between Cairns and Port Douglas, this eco-friendly lodge has its own 2km stretch of secluded beach exclusive for the use of Thala guests and is flanked by the Wet Tropics rainforest. 5078 Captain Cook Hwy, Oak Beach; (07) 4098 5700; thalabeach.com.au.
- **Silky Oaks Lodge** The lodge offers luxury treehouse or riverside accommodation at the edge of Mossman Gorge in the Daintree Rainforest. All lodges features spa baths and verandah hammocks and the complex includes the Healing Waters Spa. Finlayvale Rd, Mossman; (07) 4098 1666; silkyoakslodge.com.au.
- **Sovereign Resort Hotel** The best place to stay in Cooktown is this hotel in the middle of the main street, which has large airconditioned rooms and a resort-style swimming pool set in tropical gardens. 128 Charlotte St, Cooktown; (07) 4043 0500; sovereignresort.com.au.
- **The Riley** At the northern end of the Cairns Esplanade the eye-catching 12-storey elliptical glass tower of the Riley overlooks the Coral Sea and boasts the highest rooftop bar in Cairns, a huge lagoon pool with an artificial beach, two restaurants and a day spa. 131–141 Esplanade, Cairns; (07) 4252 7777; crystalbrookcollection.com/riley.
- **Caravanning and camping** You can camp at Noah Beach, about 8km south of Cape Tribulation. The small sites are unsuitable for caravans or larger campervans, however. The camping area is closed in the wet season and after heavy rains. Cape Trib Camping offers lots of room with powered and unpowered sites in a big grassy area beside Myall Beach surrounded by rainforest and coconut trees – facilities include a handy coconut spike to husk the unlimited supply of free coconuts (capetribcamping.com.au). Caravanners can choose from a range of caravan parks in and around Cairns, Port Douglas and Cooktown and you can also camp at Palmer River Roadhouse.

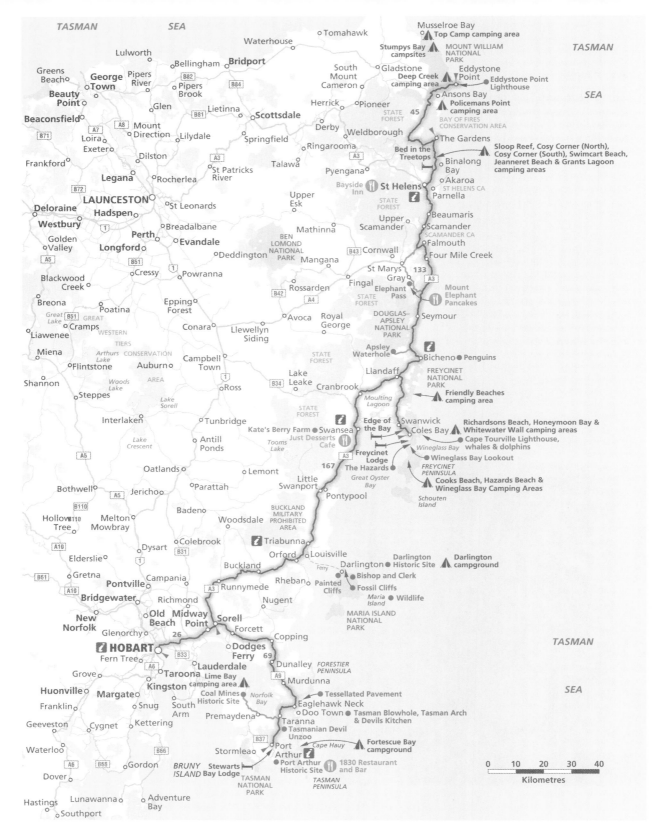

Tasmania's east coast is home to some of the most beautiful coastal scenery in the state.

East Coast, Tas.

HOW LONG?

Three to four days is ideal, including a full day in Port Arthur on the Tasman Peninsula. But if you only have one or two days to spare, follow the east coast as far north as Coles Bay, before either returning to Hobart or heading inland on the Heritage Highway (Highway 1) to Launceston and Devonport.

WHEN TO GO

Spring to autumn is the best time, as most rain falls during the winter months. The roads can be icy during winter.

NEED TO KNOW

No dogs are allowed in national parks, including the carpark at the beginning of the Wineglass Bay walk. If you are planning on spending more than one or two days in national parks, a National Parks Pass will save you money: for most travellers the eight-week Holiday Pass, which covers all parks, offers the best value. Buy a park pass at national park visitor centres and most Tasmanian visitor centres, or online at parks.tas. gov.au. For information on ferries to Tasmania, *see* p. 163.

 Drive rating
Easy. Sealed roads with some winding sections

 Distances
Total distance, Hobart to Bay of Fires via Port Arthur: 468km
- Hobart to Port Arthur: 95km
- Port Arthur to Wineglass Bay (Freycinet National Park): 237km
- Wineglass Bay to Bay of Fires: 136km

 Temperatures
January: 10–23°C
July: 2–11°C

 More information
- Hobart Visitor Information Centre, 20 Davey St, Hobart; (03) 6238 4222; hobarttravelcentre.com.au
- Port Arthur Information Centre, 6973 Arthur Hwy, Port Arthur; (03) 6251 2310; portarthur.org.au
- discovertasmania.com.au

 Snapshot
Tasmania's eastern seaboard is a spectacularly scenic coastline: a long, ragged strip of peninsulas, islands, channels and windswept beaches, flanked by rugged mountains enclosing gorges, waterfalls and forests. One minute you are driving through open paddocks and farmlands and quaint historic villages full of convict-built stone houses, along the course of a twisting, shallow river, then the next you find yourself in dense, lush rainforest. This three- or four-day drive meanders up the east coast with stops at the convict ruins at Port Arthur and dramatic Freycinet National Park.

HOBART TO PORT ARTHUR

From Hobart, head north-east out past the airport to Sorell and then cut across to Dunalley and wind down to Eaglehawk Neck. This narrow isthmus of land, only a few hundred metres wide, is the reason Port Arthur was chosen as the site for a prison in 1830: the tiny strip of land was easily patrolled, few people could swim, the surrounding bush was dense and inhospitable and, if all else failed, a line of snarling dogs roused the soldiers if anyone tried to get by.

The coastline of the Tasman Peninsula is riddled with dramatic rock formations and extraordinary rock pillars and sea stacks. The Tessellated Pavement, an expanse of rock resembling giant tiles, is on the northern side of Eaglehawk Neck; the Tasman Blowhole and the ruins of once-huge sea caves at Tasman Arch and the Devils Kitchen are on the southern side. The Cape Hauy walking trail, which starts at the Fortescue Bay camping area in Tasman National Park, is a sensational four-hour-return walk that delivers wonderful views of cliffs and rock formations (although, be warned, there are hundreds of steps).

 KIDS' SPOT

Love Me Doo, Doodle Doo, Much-A-Doo, Gunnadoo, Doo Come In, Just Doo It … Kids will enjoy reading out the names of all the cottages in Doo Town, just past Eaglehawk Neck, all of which end (or start) with 'doo'. Legend has it that the tradition began in 1935, although the reason why has been lost in the mists of time.

The ruins of the convict settlement at Port Arthur are among Australia's most significant historical sites and were added to the World Heritage list in 2010. More than just a gaol, Port Arthur was an industrial village, complete with shipworks, flour mill, timber mill, and shoemaking, smithing and brick-making operations. More than 12,500 convicts called the settlement home between 1830 and 1877, and it became known as 'Hell on Earth', thanks largely to a cruel experiment in penal reform whereby silence and solitary confinement replaced physical punishment as a means of rehabilitation; in reality it just sent the prisoners mad. There are more than 30 buildings on the 40ha site, a mixture of furnished houses, atmospheric ruins and re-created gardens. Take the time to visit the Interpretation Centre to gain a deeper understanding of convict life and join a guided walking tour for an overview of the site before exploring on your own. Buildings worth seeing include the ruined penitentiary and church, both gutted by fire in 1897, the cruciform-shaped separate prison and the furnished museum houses. Tickets are valid for two days and include guided walking tours and harbour cruises. Evening ghost tours are also available. (Arthur Hwy, Tasman Peninsula; 1800 659 101; open Mon–Sun 8.30am–dusk; portarthur.org.au.)

SIDETRACK

Most people head straight to the Port Arthur historic site, but there's another World Heritage convict site a half-hour drive away on the shores of Norfolk Bay near Lime Bay (35km via the B37 and Saltwater River Road). Port Arthur's bad boys were sent to the coal mines here as punishment, where they were forced to work, and live, underground. You can no longer see the underground workings of the mines, but the houses, barracks, offices and punishment cells are still there, now mostly roofless ruins. It's free to enter, and, more often than not, you'll be the only person there. (Coal Mines Historic Site, Lime Bay; 1800 659 101; open Mon–Sun during daylight hours; portarthur.org.au.)

From the Tasman Peninsula, head back to Taranna and head north, reconnecting with the Tasman Highway (A3) at Sorell.

 KIDS' SPOT

Many older kids will be fascinated by the (gruesome) sight of a group of Tasmanian devils tearing apart a dead wallaby in a feeding frenzy (staff collect roadkill for the animals) at the Tasmanian Devil Unzoo. The wild population of devils has been decimated in recent years by a mysterious facial cancer; entry fees help fund much needed research. 5990 Arthur Hwy, Taranna; (03) 6250 3230; open Mon–Sun 9am–5pm, later in summer; tasmaniandevilunzoo.com.au.

Opposite If you have the time, Maria Island makes for a memorable sidetrip

SORELL TO FREYCINET NATIONAL PARK

It's a pretty drive north on the A3 – along descriptively named sections of road, such as the climb up Break-Me-Gall Hill and the descent of Break-Me-Neck Hill – and across the valley floor, following the river, to Orford, from where the road, carved into the mountainside above the Prosser River, winds its way to the coast. Stretch your legs at Triabunna and watch the anglers unload their catch or carry out their deckside chores.

SIDETRACK

You'll need to leave your car at Triabunna, but if you have time to spare take the 20-minute ferry out to Maria Island. Ferries depart regularly throughout the day in summer, less frequently during winter (Triabunna Wharf; (03) 6256 4772; encountermaria.com.au). Just 20km long and 13km wide, Maria Island was originally settled by whalers and sealers before it became a penal colony in 1825. The colony was soon infamous for the high number of escapes – one unlucky group drifted across the channel on a raft only to walk ashore into the arms of two lost policemen – and it was known among convicts as a place of relative comfort. By 1832 the convict settlement had been abandoned in favour of Port Arthur and, after a second incarnation as a convict probation station between 1842 and 1850, it was eventually taken over by a flamboyant Italian entrepreneur, Diego Bernacchi, who planted grapes, cultivated silkworms and established a cement works. But none of these enterprises survived the Great Depression and by the 1930s the island was home to just a handful of farmers, though many of the original convict buildings still stand to this day.

Steep and mountainous in the interior, the island is ringed by stretches of white sandy beaches and limestone cliffs. The entire island is now national park and home to a staggering amount of wildlife, including possums, wallabies, pademelons, echidnas, kangaroos, wombats, Cape Barren geese, little penguins, muttonbirds and the endangered forty-spotted pardalote, one of the smallest and rarest birds in Australia.

The Painted Cliffs – beautifully patterned sandstone cliffs – are an easy 90-minute-return walk from the convict buildings at Darlington (where the ferry wharf is). Alternatively, head off in the other direction to some spectacular cliffs along the northern shore of the island, which contain thousands of marine fossils. If you're up for a challenge, there's a strenuous four-to-five-hour-return climb to the summit of the mountain known as Bishop and Clerk. It entails lots of rockhopping and scrambling over large boulders but provides amazing views from the top.

Between Triabunna and Swansea, the cliff-hugging road meanders beside deserted beaches and offers magnificent coastal views across Great Oyster Bay to the rocky peaks of the Freycinet Peninsula. From Swansea, continue north to Cranbrook then take the turn-off to Coles Bay and Freycinet National Park, one of Tasmania's most popular parks. The distinctive pink granite peaks of the Hazards dominate the scenery as you drive along the edge of the bay to the tiny town of Coles Bay, a collection of holiday houses clinging to the shoreline.

There are many secluded beaches in the park, but the one everyone wants to see is Wineglass Bay, a perfect semicircle of white sand washed by teal blue waters, instantly recognisable from hundreds of postcards, posters and tourist brochures. The one-hour walk up to the lookout over Wineglass Bay is worth the steep climb. What's more, while you'll see a few people on the trek, if you continue down to the beach (two hours return), you're just as likely to have it to yourself, as the walk deters most daytrippers. Before you leave the park, take a drive up to the lighthouse at Cape Tourville for stunning sunset views as well as whale- and dolphin-spotting in season.

FREYCINET NATIONAL PARK TO BAY OF FIRES

Retrace your steps back to the A3 and head for Bicheno, a great place to see penguins as they waddle ashore to their burrows at dusk, and then on to St Helens, a pretty fishing town on the edge of narrow Georges Bay.

SIDETRACK

For a change of scenery head inland to Douglas–Apsley National Park, just north of Bicheno. Apsley Waterhole is just a ten-minute walk from the carpark off Rosedale Road, and if you explore further you'll find deep river gorges, waterfalls, swimming holes and a dolerite-capped plateau crisscrossed by walking tracks.

SIDETRACK

The very pretty but steep and winding road up the range through the rainforest to St Marys via Elephant Pass is popular with motorcyclists – and caravanners, so the going can be slow sometimes. The Pancake Barn at the top of the pass is a local institution and popular with tour groups (see Best eats).

North of St Helens in Bay of Fires Conservation Park is an area known as the Gardens, named by Lady Jane Franklin, the wife of Governor John Franklin, who spent some time in the region in the 1840s. It offers sweeping views of the coastline north, good (though unpatrolled) swimming beaches, lots of rockpools to explore and very photogenic and rather ubiquitous orange-lichen-covered boulders to climb over and around and paddle between. Because it's a conservation park, rather than a national park, you can even bring your dog.

The park stretches north to Ansons Bay, about 15km away, but to get there you either have to walk along the beaches or take the unsealed 52km inland road. It continues to Mount William National Park, which boasts exactly the same type of scenery but has more established campgrounds and toilet facilities, although you have to pay the normal national park entry and camping fees. At the southern end of the national park is historic Eddystone Point Lighthouse, a striking pink granite tower on a point that juts out into the sea. From the northern end of the park at Musselroe Bay, you can see across to the Bass Strait islands.

Opposite Freycinet Lodge *Below* Distinctive orange rocks of Bay of Fires

BEST EATS

- **1830 Restaurant and Bar** Most restaurants at major tourist attractions are usually pretty ordinary, but this licensed bistro in the grounds of Port Arthur Historic Site is a stand-out. The menu features local produce including salmon, Tasmanian scallops, Cape Grim beef, venison and even wallaby. Port Arthur Historic Site; 1800 659 101; open Mon–Sun for dinner. There are also two cafes on-site open for lunch.
- **Just Desserts Cafe** This rustic cafe at Kate's Berry Farm is the spot to stop for an ice-cream or a Devonshire tea accompanied by one of Kate's thick homemade jams – strawberry, raspberry, Himalayan wildberry, youngberry or wild blackberry are all on offer. 12 Addison St, Swansea; (03) 6257 8428; open Mon–Sun 9.30am–4.30pm.
- **Mount Elephant Pancakes** The pancakes here are famous – the sign out the front says so – and just about anything and everything you can ever imagine in or on a pancake features on the menu. 824 Elephant Pass, St Marys; (03) 6372 2263; open Mon–Sun 9am–5pm.
- **Bayside Inn** St Helens is known as the 'game-fishing capital of Tasmania', but you don't have to catch your own – the Bayside Inn does great seafood, along with good steaks and crayfish in season. The large dining room may lack some style but has million-dollar views over Georges Bay. 2 Cecilia St, St Helens; (03) 6376 1466; open Mon–Sun for lunch and dinner.

BEST SLEEPS

- **Stewarts Bay Lodge** These bayfront cabins are just a 15-minute walk from the Port Arthur ruins. All of the 40 cabins have well-equipped kitchens but there is also a restaurant on-site. 6955 Arthur Hwy, Port Arthur; (03) 6250 2888; stewartsbaylodge.com.au.
- **Edge of the Bay** The luxury suites set on the beachfront have dazzling views across the bay to the pink granite peaks of the Hazards on the Freycinet Peninsula. There's a licensed restaurant, and the Coles Bay cafes are just a 20-minute walk up the beach. 2308 Coles Bay Rd, Coles Bay; (03) 6257 0102; edgeofthebay.com.au.
- **Freycinet Lodge** You're right in the middle of the national park here, and many of the cabins have water views. There are a range of tours on offer as well as special packages. Coles Bay Rd, Freycinet National Park, Coles Bay; (03) 6256 7222; freycinetlodge.com.au.
- **Bed in the Treetops** This B&B hideaway high on a hill has spectacular views. 701 Binalong Bay Rd, Binalong Bay, just north of St Helens near the Bay of Fires; (03) 6376 1318; bedinthetreetops.com.au.

- **Caravanning and camping** One of the best-kept beachside camping secrets in Australia is at beautiful Lime Bay near the Coal Mines Historic Site on the Tasman Peninsula – shady campsites with million-dollar water views. There are also basic camping facilities and unpowered caravan sites at Fortescue Bay in Tasman National Park, and there is a large open camping area close to the creek at Darlington on Maria Island. Camping at Freycinet is also by the beach with beautiful views and there are plenty of shady sites to choose from, including powered sites for campervans and caravans; the park is very popular, however, so it's best to book ahead (parks. tas.gov.au). There is also good camping at the Friendly Beaches close to the border of the park. In the southern section of Bay of Fires Conservation Park there are six free camping areas, most overlooking the beach; facilities are basic and include pit toilets but no water or firewood. In Mount William National Park there are several sheltered camping areas at Stumpys Bay in the north of the park; there are also campsites at the far northern end of the park, just before Musselroe Bay, and at the end of the beachside road from Eddystone Point to Deep Creek, in the southern section of the park. As with all national parks, no dogs are allowed.

Drive across the top of Tasmania, coast to coast, east to west, through pretty wine regions, along beautiful stretches of coastline and into fascinating historic towns.

North Coast, Tas.

HOW LONG?

Allow at least a week, one way, including a day or two in Launceston.

WHEN TO GO

Summer is mild and winter tends to be the wettest season, but any time is a good time to do this road trip. To see the lavender at its best, go in January; for tulips, go in spring.

NEED TO KNOW

Spirit of Tasmania has two car ferries that cross Bass Strait between Station Pier in Port Melbourne and Devonport, in both directions. The journey takes about ten hours and departs from both ports at 7.30pm, arriving at 6am the following morning. During peak holiday time (mid-Dec–mid-Mar and during Easter) there is also a daytime sailing, departing at 9am and arriving at 6.30pm, and overnight sailings, departing about 9pm and arriving at 6.30am. Onboard accommodation ranges from airline-style reclining seats to private cabins, including two-berth and four-berth cabins, which you can book for exclusive use or opt to share with other passengers. (Spirit of Tasmania, 1 Waterfront Pl, Port Melbourne; (03) 6419 9320; spiritoftasmania.com.au.)

Drive rating
Easy. Sealed roads

Distances
Total distance, St Helens to Arthur River (without detours): 508km
- St Helens to George Town: 182km
- George Town to Devonport: 118km
- Devonport to Stanley: 126km
- Stanley to Arthur River: 82km

Temperatures
January: 10–23°C
July: 2–11°C

More information
- Devonport Information Centre, 145 Rooke St, Devonport; (03) 6420 2900; visitcradlecoast.com.au
- Launceston Visitor Information Centre, 68–72 Cameron St, Launceston; 1800 651 827; northerntasmania.com.au
- Stanley Information Centre, 45 Main Rd, Stanley; (03) 6458 1330; stanleyandtarkine.com.au
- Tasmanian Travel Centre; (03) 6238 4222; discovertasmania.com.au

Snapshot
Tasmania's north coast is one of its best-kept secrets. It is a place of rugged beauty, where fertile farmlands edge the wild waters of Bass Strait. From the boulder-strewn, white-sand beaches of the north-east, the main route across the top of the island travels through beautiful rainforest, some of the state's best wine-producing areas and along the spectacular coastal Bass Highway past pretty fishing villages to finally reach the wilderness of the west coast at the aptly named Edge of the World lookout.

Opposite top left Piper's Brook Vineyard *Top right* Rainforest fungi at Dismal Swamp *Bottom left* Crayfish traps *Bottom right* St Columba Falls is one of the tallest in Tasmania

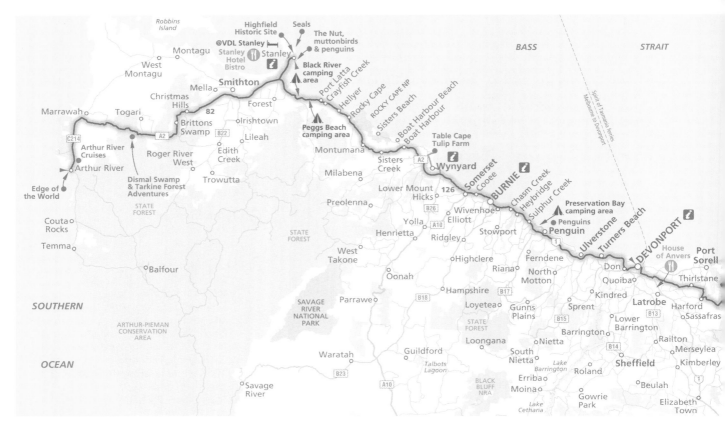

ST HELENS TO GEORGE TOWN

Start in St Helens, a fishing town on the edge of narrow Georges Bay, and head west over the rolling hills and into the rainforest-clad mountains. Stop at Pyengana Dairy Factory for a taste of their fabulous cheddar (St Columba Falls Rd, Pyengana; (03) 6373 6157; open Mon–Sun 9am–5pm Oct–Mar, 10am–4pm Apr–Sept; pyenganadairy.com.au) and then take a short detour to walk out to beautiful 90m high St Columba Falls, surrounded by myrtle forest.

Stop for a break at the historic tin-mining town of Derby and, if you like golf, head north up to Bridport on the coast and play a round at Australia's top-ranked public golf course, Barnbougle Dunes Golf Links, which often features in various 'top 100 courses in the world' lists. It's a beautiful – and challenging – links course above the dunes and even non-golfers will appreciate the view from the clubhouse. (425 Waterhouse Rd, Bridport; (03) 6356 0094; barnbougle.com.au.)

Spend a few hours visiting some of the cellar doors around Pipers Brook to taste some of Tassie's famous sparkling wines – the Wine Room at Jansz has an interpretive centre where you'll learn all about why Tassie is so good

at putting the bubbles into wine (1216B Pipers Brook Rd; (03) 6382 7066), while Pipers Brook, practically next door, does a great lunchtime antipasto platter (1216 Pipers Brook Rd; (03) 6382 7555; open Mon–Sun 10am–5pm, closed Tues–Wed during winter).

SIDETRACK

Take a short side trip to Bridestowe Lavender Estate, about a 20-minute drive south of the Pipers Brook wine region. It is at its most colourful and fragrant in December and January; whatever you do, don't leave without trying the lavender biscuits. (296 Gillespies Rd, Nabowla; (03) 6352 8182; open Mon–Sun 9am–5pm; bridestowelavender.com.au.) Thrill-seekers can enjoy a range of adventure tours at nearby Hollybank Wilderness Adventures. As well as segway tours and a tree-top obstacle course, it offers a continuous-cable zipline tour, which includes a ride on a 700m flying fox; the tour takes three hours. (66 Hollybank Rd, Underwood; (03) 6395 1390; hollybankadventures.com.au.)

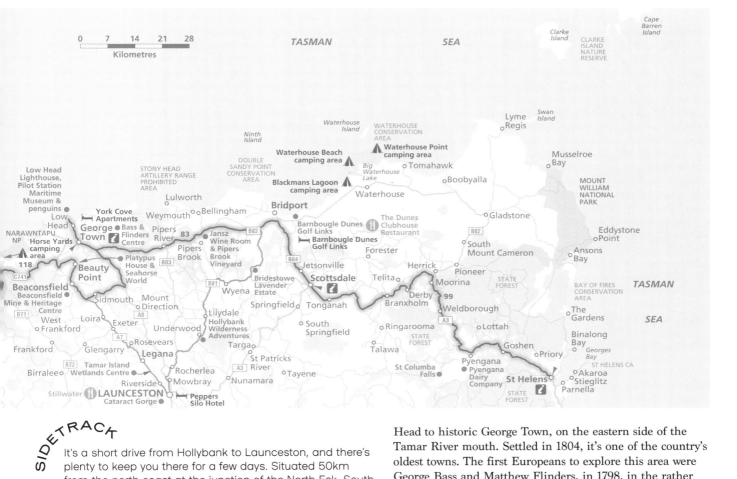

It's a short drive from Hollybank to Launceston, and there's plenty to keep you there for a few days. Situated 50km from the north coast at the junction of the North Esk, South Esk and Tamar rivers, Launceston is Tasmania's second largest city, and the third oldest city in Australia (after Sydney and Hobart). Its mix of Victorian and Georgian architecture and its abundance of parks and gardens make it one of the country's prettiest places too. Cataract Gorge, ten minutes' walk from the city centre, is a piece of wilderness in the heart of the city. The chairlift crossing the gorge is the longest single-span chairlift in the world, and the adjacent reserve is the site of a restaurant and kiosk. Head north through the outskirts of the city, past rambling, sometimes crumbling, hillside manor houses and across the river flats to the Tamar Island Wetlands Centre, where you can stroll the boardwalk watching for birdlife – it's less than ten minutes from the city centre. The blink-and-you'll-miss-it riverside village of Rosevears is just a few minutes up the road and home to several wineries (northerntasmania.com.au).

Head to historic George Town, on the eastern side of the Tamar River mouth. Settled in 1804, it's one of the country's oldest towns. The first Europeans to explore this area were George Bass and Matthew Flinders, in 1798, in the rather tiny sloop, the *Norfolk*. There's a beautiful huon-pine replica of the boat at the Bass and Flinders Centre, which you can board and explore. It's quite astounding that they managed to cross Bass Strait and circumnavigate Tasmania in it for three months. (8 Elizabeth St, George Town; (03) 6382 3792; open most days Mon–Fri 10am–4pm, Sat–Sun 11am–2pm; bassandflinders.org.au.)

Drive north out to Low Head on the edge of Bass Strait, to the red-and-white lighthouse. The old Pilot Station, built by convicts in 1835, is now a maritime museum with 12 rooms of historical displays and, if you time your visit right, you can hear the fog horn sound on Sundays at noon. Even if you don't visit the museum, it's worth the 5km drive just to admire the views and to try to spot one of the little penguins that burrow in the coastal scrub, although they mostly sleep during the day. If you want to make sure you see them, join an evening tour (Low Head Coastal Reserve; 0418 361 860; penguintourstasmania.com.au).

BEACONSFIELD TO STANLEY

Cross the river on the Batman Bridge (named after the co-founder of Melbourne, not the Caped Crusader) and head north to Beaconsfield, where you can relive the tragedy and triumph of the 2006 mine collapse in the Beaconsfield Mine and Heritage Centre. Miners Brant Webb and Todd Russell were trapped almost 1km underground for 14 days, while rescue teams achieved what many thought was impossible, burrowing deep into the rock to bring the two men back to the surface, alive (tragically, their workmate Larry Knight was killed in the initial rockfall). The rescue display includes the torn overalls the miners were wearing at the time and fascinating details about how they survived and what the rescuers were faced with as they tried to reach them. It's both harrowing and inspiring in equal measure. When you're done with the rescue, there are rooms of mining and local history exhibits and you can climb up to an elevated walkway to look down on the mine yard, which remains as it was when workers walked off the job for the last time in 2012. (West St, Beaconsfield; (03) 6383 1473; open Mon–Sun 9.30am–4.30pm; beaconsfieldheritage.com.au.)

Wiggle your way west on the C741 towards Devonport, the terminal for the Bass Strait ferry service to Melbourne, and follow the coastline through places like the village of Penguin, home to a large colony of – you guessed it! – penguins, and then on to Wynyard.

 KIDS' SPOT

With seahorses and platypus to see, it's worth taking the kids to Beauty Point, a pretty little hamlet at the mouth of the Tamar River. It's just up the road from Beaconsfield, so most people combine their visit to the Mine and Heritage Centre with a visit to the Platypus House (200 Flinders St, Beauty Point; (03) 6383 4884; platypushouse.com.au) and Seahorse World (200 Flinders St, Beauty Point; (03) 6383 4111; seahorseworld.com.au), next door to each other on Inspection Head Wharf. Both are open Mon–Sun 9.30am–4pm and combined tickets are available.

SIDETRACK

If you're here in spring (Sept–Oct) drive out to Table Cape and visit Table Cape Tulip Farm to wander through rows and rows of stunning blooms, all the by-product of the farm's main business, growing the bulbs (363 Table Cape Rd, Wynyard; (03) 6442 2012; best viewing is late Sept to mid-Oct). The farm covers most of the flat-topped circular headland; if you're lucky enough to be flying over it (Wynyard is the region's main airport), the patchwork of brilliant red, yellow, pink and purple flowers is a breathtaking sight.

Boat Harbour, a tiny collection of beach houses that march up the dune behind a white, sandy beach, is just 15km down the road. It's the type of place where you can easily lose yourself for a week of sun, sand and sea, even if the water tends to be a little on the cold (read freezing!) side.

It's a lovely half-hour drive to your next port of call, Stanley. Best known for the distinctive 152m high, flat-topped, circular headland called the Nut that looms above the town, Stanley is a pretty fishing community. The Nut is actually the stump of a volcano, and it's a steep climb to the top (though you can also take a chairlift) where there's a 40-minute circular walking track with great coastal and ocean views.

Ten thousand muttonbirds nest on the Nut and when they all take off to go out to sea at once, it's an amazing sight. You can also see penguins at dusk; there's a viewing platform at Godfreys Beach in the Nut State Reserve. Or take a cruise aboard the *Sylvia C* to check out the colony of about 600 or so Australian fur seals that haul out on a tiny speck of an island called Bull Rock, around 600m offshore (6 Wharf Rd, Stanley; (03) 6458 1294; stanleysealcruises.com.au).

Take a drive up the hill to tour Highfield Historic Site, a beautiful Regency-era home that was originally built for Edward Curr, chief agent of the Van Diemen's Land Company, not long after the company first established Stanley as the base for their sheep-raising enterprise, in 1826. The sensational views across to the Nut and Bass Strait are worth it, even if historic houses aren't quite your thing. (143 Greenhills Rd, Stanley; (03) 6458 1100; open Mon–Sun 9.30am–4.30pm Sept–May, Mon–Fri 9.30am–4.30pm June–Aug; historic-highfield.com.au.)

Opposite Colourful countryside at Table Cape Tulip Farm *Top* Australian fur seals at Bull Rock *Middle* Highfield Historic Site *Bottom* The chairlift up the Nut in Stanley

STANLEY TO THE EDGE OF THE WORLD

From Stanley it's a beautiful drive up and over endless
windswept and heath-covered dunes, past picturesque
stone cottages with streamers of thick kelp drying on their
clotheslines and through impossibly green paddocks of grass
to the tiny township of Arthur River on the west coast.

Stop along the way to drop into Dismal Swamp – literally.
A rather magical place that doesn't deserve its harsh name,
Dismal Swamp is a giant sinkhole, filled with ancient
blackwood trees and other trees, and is part of Tarkine Forest
Adventures, a strange mix of theme park, art gallery and
nature park that somehow manages to meld together. From
the top, follow the walkway, take the buggy or slip down a
curvy 110m slide to the swamp floor 40m below (that's the
theme-park bit). At the bottom, four meandering boardwalks
make it easy to check out life in a swamp without getting
your feet wet (the nature park part). Local artists display
artwork and extraordinary sculptures throughout the site and
it's all a bit Alice in Wonderland-ish as you wander through
the forest, stumbling across trees with eyes, pop-up crayfish
and alien-looking swamp creatures – but well worth seeing
(the art part). The cafe also serves great coffee. (Tarkine
Forest Adventures, 26059 Bass Hwy, Togari; (03) 6456 7138;
open Mon–Sun 9am–5pm Dec–Jan, 10am–4pm Feb–Nov;
dismalswamptasmania.com.au.)

At Arthur River take a 14km cruise up the river into the
heart of the Tarkine Wilderness for a barbecue lunch in a
clearing amid old-growth forest (arthurrivercruises.com).
Or head out to the Edge of the World, a wild and desolate
place where the river pours into the sea, monstrous waves
crash onto a rocky shore and the wind is so strong it almost
blows you off your feet. They have a saying in these parts:
'If the wind stopped blowing the cows would fall over.'
It's easy to believe.

Opposite Chocolate making at House of Anvers *Above* Walking
through Dismal Swamp

BEST EATS

- **Barnbougle Dunes** You don't have to be a golfer to enjoy the views from the clubhouse restaurant. It's perched high upon a sand dune between the 9th and 18th greens and overlooks the beach. The menu features a great range of Tasmanian produce and local wines. 425 Waterhouse Rd, Bridport; (03) 6356 0094; open Mon–Sun for lunch and dinner; barnbougle.com.au.
- **Stillwater** Don't miss this restored riverside mill if you take the sidetrack to Launceston. It's one of the best places to eat in Launceston and is well worth the splurge. 2 Bridge Rd, Launceston; (03) 6331 4153; open Mon–Sun for breakfast and lunch, Tues–Sat for dinner.
- **House of Anvers** You haven't lived until you've had breakfast in a chocolate factory! The brioche with choc-hazelnut spread and a thick hot-chocolate with Aztec chilli and spice are the perfect way to start the day, although there's plenty of savoury options as well. You can also watch chocolate being made, indulge in a chocolate platter or buy some produce to take away. 9025 Bass Hwy, Latrobe, near the turn-off to Devonport airport; (03) 6426 2958; open Mon–Sun 7am–5pm, hot meals served until 3pm; anvers-chocolate.com.au.
- **Stanley Hotel Bistro** The good-value lunches and dinners here feature local produce and Tasmanian wines prominently. Try the octopus, caught fresh at Stanley Wharf. 19–21 Church St, Stanley; (03) 6458 1161; open Mon–Sun for lunch and dinner; stanleytasmania.com.au.

BEST SLEEPS

- **Barnbougle Dunes** Motel-style cabins overlook the first tee of the beautiful golf course, luxury two-bedroom ocean villas have waterfront decks and four-bedroom bunker villas have sweeping views of the course. There are also suites at the Lost Farm Lodge at sister course Barnbougle Lost Farm, which is just across the river from the Dunes. 425 Waterhouse Rd, Bridport; (03) 6356 0094; barnbougle.com.au.
- **Peppers Silo Hotel** Spend a night or two inside the barrel of a silo at Launceston. The abandoned 35m high grain silos on Kings Wharf were recently transformed into a state-of-the-art nine-storey hotel, complete with cornerless rooms. 89–91 Lindsay St, Launceston; (03) 6700 0600; peppers.com.au/silo.
- **York Cove Apartments** The one- and two-bedroom apartments at this riverfront hotel are huge, but it's the mesmerising water views from the floor-to-ceiling glass windows that really take the breath away. Spacious hotel rooms are also available but lack the drop-dead gorgeous views. 2 Ferry Blvd, George Town; (03) 6382 9900; yorkcove.com.au.
- **@VDL Stanley** This comfortable B&B occupies the beautifully renovated 1843 bluestone VDL Store on the waterfront beneath the Nut. 16 Wharf Rd, Stanley; (03) 6458 2032; atvdlstanley.com.au.
- **Caravanning and camping** Waterhouse Conservation Area, 50km east of Bridport, has a number of waterfront campgrounds that are very popular in summer, particularly Waterhouse Point. You can also camp at Horse Yards in Narawntapu National Park, north-west of Beaconsfield, and at Preservation Bay near Penguin, and there are two campgrounds in Peggs Beach Conservation Area, east of Stanley. See parks.tas.gov.au for camping information. Most of the towns along this route have caravan parks.

Capital city to capital city

Getting from A to B doesn't have to be a chore. Put the fun back into the journey with these beaut commutes.

Take the kids to Canberra and introduce them to sporting legends, Australian icons, dinosaurs, astronauts, rock art and wild kangaroos.

Sydney to Canberra

HOW LONG?

You'll need a full day to get there – though you can do the journey in three hours if you stick to the highway and don't stop – then at least one or two full days exploring Canberra and surrounds.

WHEN TO GO

Any time of the year is a good time to do this drive, although Canberra can be very cold in winter, when snow is not uncommon in the Brindabella Ranges. The famous Floriade (Canberra) and Tulip Time (Bowral) annual flower festivals take place during mid-September to mid-October.

NEED TO KNOW

Watch out for kangaroos in rural areas, particularly when driving in the early morning or late afternoon.

Drive rating
Easy. Sealed roads

Distances
Total distance, Sydney to Canberra: 289km
• Sydney to Bowral: 118km
• Bowral to Goulburn: 80km
• Goulburn to Canberra: 91km

Temperatures
January: 12–26°C
July: 0–10°C

More information
• Canberra and Region Visitor Information Centre, Regatta Point, Barrine Dr, Parkes, Canberra; 1300 554 114; visitcanberra.com.au
• Goulburn Visitor Centre, 201 Sloane St, Goulburn; 1800 353 646; goulburnaustralia.com.au
• Southern Highlands Visitor Information Centre, 62–70 Main St, Mittagong; (02) 4871 2888; southern-highlands.com.au

Snapshot
A holiday in Canberra visiting its amazing range of museums and family-friendly attractions is a great thing to do with kids. And even though three hours on a highway can seem like forever when you're bored in the backseat, the good news is that there are also plenty of kid-friendly – and adult-friendly – things to see and do on the way there.

Previous Driving across the Sydney Harbour Bridge
Opposite Parliament House in Canberra

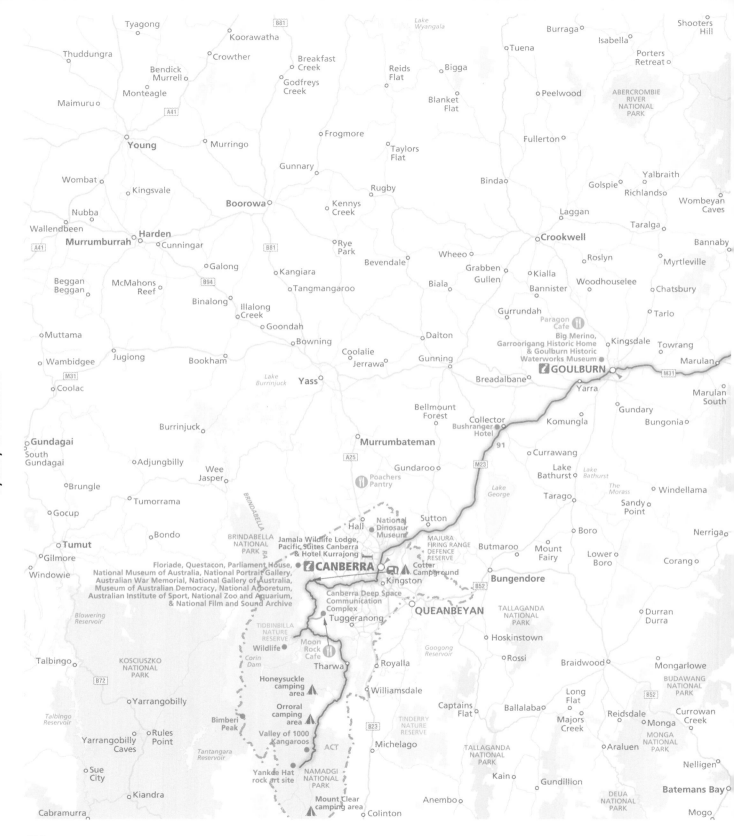

Tyagong

Thuddungra

Koorawatha

Crowther

Breakfast
Creek

B81

Lake
Wyangala

Burraga

Tuena

Isabella

Shooters
Hill

Porters
Retreat

Bendick
Murrell

Godfreys
Creek

Reids
Flat

Bigga

Peelwood

ABERCROMBIE
RIVER
NATIONAL
PARK

Monteagle

Maimuru

A41

Frogmore

Taylors
Flat

Blanket
Flat

Fullerton

Yalbraith

Wombat

Young

Murringo

Gunnary

Rugby

Binda

Golspie

Richlandso

Wombeyan
Caves

Kingsvale

Nubba

Boorowa

Kennys
Creek

Laggan

Taralga

Wallendbeen

Harden

Crookwell

Bannaby

Murrumburrah

Cunningar

B81

Rye
Park

Bevendale

Wheeo

Grabben
Gullen

Kialla

Roslyn

Woodhouselee

Myrtleville

Chatsbury

A41

Galong

Kangiara

Biala

Bannister

Tarlo

Beggan
Beggan

McMahons
Reef

B94

Tangmangaroo

Dalton

Gurrundah

Paragon
Cafe

Big Merino,
Garroorigang Historic Home
& Goulburn Historic
Waterworks Museum

Kingsdale

Towrang

Binalong

Illalong
Creek

Goondah

Muttama

Bowning

Bowning

Coolalie
Jerrawa

Gunning

Breadalbane

GOULBURN

Marulan

Wambidgee

Jugiong

Bookham

Lake
Burrinjuck

Yass

Yarra

M31

Marulan
South

M31

Coolac

Bellmount
Forest

Collector
Bushranger
Hotel

Komungla

Gundary

Bungonia

Gundagai

Burrinjuck

Murrumbateman

A25

91

Currawang

South
Gundagai

Adjungbilly

Poachers
Pantry

Gundaroo

M23

Lake
Bathurst

Lake
Bathurst

Brungle

Wee
Jasper

Tarago

The
Morass

Windellama

Gocup

Tumorrama

BRINDABELLA
NATIONAL
PARK

National
Dinosaur
Museum

Sutton

MAJURA
FIRING RANGE
DEFENCE
RESERVE

Butmaroo

Boro

Nerriga

Bondo

Hall

Jamala Wildlife Lodge,
Pacific Suites Canberra
& Hotel Kurrajong

Mount
Fairy

Lower
Boro

Corang

Tumut

BRINDABELLA
NATIONAL
PARK

Cotter
Campground

Gilmore

Floriade, Questacon, Parliament House,
National Museum of Australia, National Portrait Gallery,
Australian War Memorial, National Gallery of Australia,
Museum of Australian Democracy, National Arboretum,
Australian Institute of Sport, National Zoo and Aquarium,
& National Film and Sound Archive

CANBERRA

Kingston

Bungendore

B52

Windowie

Canberra Deep Space
Communication
Complex

QUEANBEYAN

TALLAGANDA
NATIONAL
PARK

Durran
Durra

Blowering
Reservoir

TIDBINBILLA
NATURE
RESERVE

Tuggeranong

Googong
Reservoir

Hoskinstown

Talbingo

KOSCIUSZKO
NATIONAL
PARK

Wildlife

Corin
Dam

Moon
Rock
Cafe

Tharwa

Royalla

Rossi

Braidwood

Mongarlowe

B72

Yarrangobilly

Honeysuckle
camping
area

Williamsdale

Long
Flat

BUDAWANG
NATIONAL
PARK

B52

Talbingo
Reservoir

Rules
Point

Bimberi
Peak

Orroral
camping
area

Captains
Flat

Ballalaba

Reidsdale

Monga

Currowan
Creek

Yarrangobilly
Caves

Valley of 1000
Kangaroos

ACT

Michelago

TINDERRY
NATURE
RESERVE

B23

Majors
Creek

MONGA
NATIONAL
PARK

Araluen

Sue
City

Tantangara
Reservoir

Yankee Hat
rock art site

NAMADGI
NATIONAL
PARK

TALLAGANDA
NATIONAL
PARK

Nelligen

Kiandra

Kain

Gundillion

DEUA
NATIONAL
PARK

Batemans
Bay

Cabramurra

Mount Clear
camping area

Colinton

Anembo

Mogo

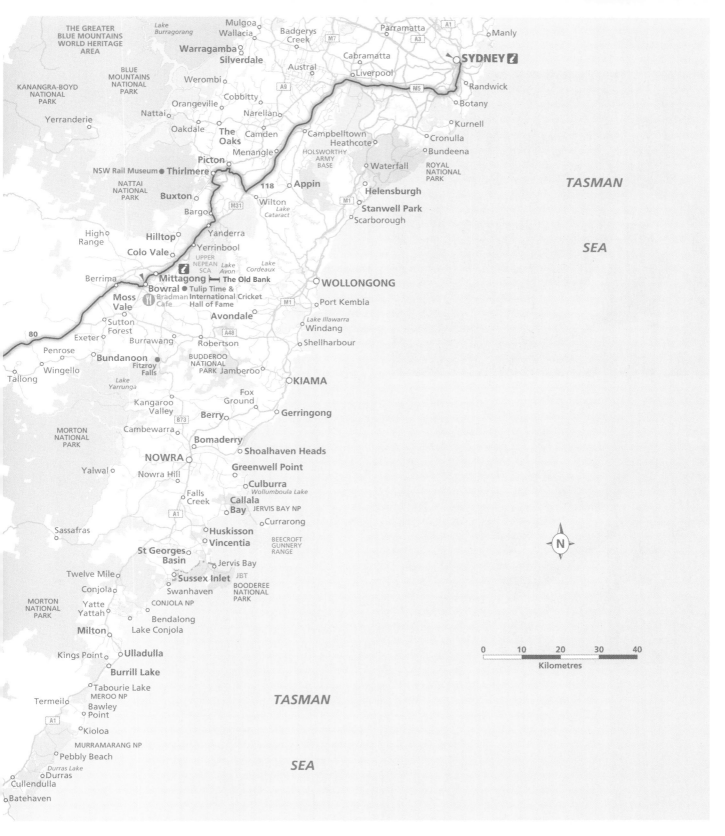

Top Dressing room exhibit at the International Cricket Hall of Fame in Bowral *Bottom* The 15.2m tall Big Merino in Goulburn

SYDNEY TO BOWRAL

Head out of Sydney on the M5 Motorway. The collection of trains at the New South Wales Rail Museum, near Thirlmere, just an hour south of Sydney, is the biggest collection of heritage rolling stock in Australia and star exhibits include several steam locomotives, a prison van, a mail van and the opulent Governor General's Carriage, described as a 'Palace on Wheels'. Steam-train rides take place most Sundays, heading from Thirlmere to the little village of Buxton and back. (10 Barbour Rd, Thirlmere; (02) 4681 8001; open Mon–Fri 10am–4pm, Sat–Sun 9am–5pm; nswrailmuseum.com.au.)

The Southern Highlands villages of Mittagong, Bowral, Berrima and Moss Vale are just off the motorway, about half an hour or so further south, and are ideal places to take a break. There are lots of parks and gardens where adults and kids can work off some excess energy, as well as many lovely riverside picnic spots.

If you're a cricket fan, don't miss the International Cricket Hall of Fame in Bowral. It's actually just as interesting for those who know nothing about the game as it is for cricket tragics – after all, there are few sporting heroes who capture the imagination of Australians more than Sir Donald Bradman, the greatest batsman of all time. The story of the young Bradman honing his cricketing skills by using a cricket stump to hit a golf ball against the curved brick stand of a water tank has become a modern fable, demonstrating to countless sporting hopefuls across the country that practice can indeed make perfect. Bradman grew up in Bowral and the Hall of Fame is at Bradman Oval, just metres away from where the cricketing legend hit his first century in a schoolboy match against Mittagong, back in the summer of 1920–21. A highlight of the collection is the Bradman Gallery, which recounts the great man's life and cricketing career through exhibits that not only cover his 'wizardry with the willow' but also examine the social reasons why he became a national icon. It's an outstanding collection of memorabilia, bats, balls, blazers, hand-written letters, photographs and slides. There's a replica dressing room and even a water tank where you can have a go at hitting a golf ball with a stump. (St Jude St, Bowral; (02) 4862 1247; open Mon–Sun 10am–5pm; internationalcrickethall.com.)

Fitzroy Falls is another worthwhile 15-minute detour from Moss Vale (*see* p. 115).

BOWRAL TO GOULBURN

Goulburn is about an hour's drive from Bowral. Of course, no visit to Goulburn is complete without a stop at the iconic Big Merino, a massive three-storey-high, 100-tonne concrete sheep near the southern motorway exit to the town. The bakery opposite does tasty pies.

If you're interested in history call ahead to arrange a tour of Garroorigang Historic Home on the southern edge of town. Originally a bullockies pub built in 1857, it became a school for gentlemen's sons in 1868 and has stayed in the same family's hands since – it is the home of the Hume family, descendants of explorer Hamilton Hume. Still a private residence, almost all of the furniture and artefacts are original and the house is packed full of antiques and family memorabilia – much of it priceless and some of it very rare. (209 Braidwood Rd, Goulburn; (02) 4822 1912; call ahead before visiting; garroorigang.com.au.)

Another fascinating historic site in Goulburn is the Historic Waterworks Museum at Marsden Weir, which houses one of the world's few fully operational 19th-century beam engines (a type of steam engine). Built in 1883 on the banks of the Wollondilly River, the pump house provided a reticulated water supply to the growing city. The museum is open for 'steaming days', when the engine can be seen in operation, four times a year – contact Goulburn visitor centre for details. Even if the pump house is closed, the weir-side park is a great place for a picnic. (Fitzroy St, Goulburn; (02) 4823 4448; open Mon–Tues 10am–2pm, Sun and public holidays 10am–4pm; goulburnwaterworks.com.au.)

SIDETRACK

Canberra's just down the road, but detour off the Federal Highway to the tiny town of Collector. The Bushranger Hotel was built in the 1850s (it was originally called Kimberley's Inn) and is known for the infamous shooting of Constable Samuel Nelson by bushrangers Ben Hall, Johnny Dunn and John Gilbert in 1865. Locals tell the story of Hall staying in the pub overnight and taunting the police from his bedroom window before the shooting. The hotel has a display of memorabilia from the era, plus sketches and a portrait of Ben Hall. (24 Church St, Collector; (02) 4848 0071; open Mon–Sun 11am–late, although Mon and Tues opening times may vary.)

CAPITAL ATTRACTIONS

You could easily spend two or three days touring the many museums and galleries in the capital – many of them are even free.

Don't miss Parliament House, where you can see parliament in action during Question Time at 2pm each sitting day and free guided tours of the house depart regularly throughout the day (Capital Hill; (02) 6277 5399; open Mon–Sun 9am–5pm, later when Parliament sits; aph.gov.au). Also worth seeing are the National Gallery of Australia (Parkes Pl, Parkes; (02) 6240 6411; open Sun–Mon 10am–5pm; nga.gov.au); the National Portrait Gallery (King Edward Tce, Parkes; (02) 6102 7000; open Mon–Sun 10am–5pm; portrait.gov.au); and the National Film and Sound Archive, which holds 100 years of Australian film, radio, and television history. There is a range of changing exhibitions, but the best reason to come here is for one of the regular movie screenings: catch an Australian classic or an international cult film on the big screen. (McCoy Cct, Acton; (02) 6248 2000; open Mon–Sun 10am–4pm; nfsa.gov.au.)

☺ KIDS' SPOT

The nation's capital offers wonderful family-friendly things to see and do right in the heart of the city. Questacon, the National Science and Technology Centre, makes science fun through more than 200 hands-on exhibits that will keep you (and your kids) entertained for hours. The full-motion roller-coaster simulator and the artificial earthquake are always big hits. (King Edward Tce, Parkes; (02) 6270 2800; open Mon–Sun 9am–5pm; questacon.edu.au.) The National Museum of Australia has exhibitions specifically geared to younger visitors (Lawson Cres, Acton; (02) 6208 5000; open Mon–Sun 9am–5pm; nma.gov.au), while bigger kids and parents will appreciate the Australian War Memorial (Treloar Cres, top of ANZAC Pde; (02) 6243 4211; open Mon–Sun 10am–5pm; awm. gov.au). Many of the displays at the Museum of Australian Democracy in Old Parliament House are also aimed at school-age kids (18 King George Tce, Parkes; (02) 6270 8222; open Mon–Sun 9am–5pm; moadoph.gov.au).

AROUND CANBERRA

Head north from the city centre on Northbourne Avenue and the Barton Highway out towards Hall to visit the National Dinosaur Museum, home to 23 complete skeletons, hundreds of fossils, a dozen or so animatronic dinosaurs and a dinosaur garden (cnr Gold Creek Rd and Barton Hwy; 1800 356 000 or (02) 6230 2357; open Mon–Sun 10am–5pm; nationaldinosaurmuseum.com.au).

Circle back towards the city. If you ever were (or have with you) a budding sports star, head to the Australian Institute of Sport (AIS): go behind the scenes on a 90-minute guided tour, watch champions train and learn what it takes to win a gold medal (Leverrier Cres, Bruce; (02) 6214 1010; tours Mon–Sun at 10am, 11.30am, 1pm and 2.30pm; experienceais.com/visit-ais).

Follow Tourist Drive 5 (Cotter Road/Paddys River Road) to the excellent Tidbinbilla Nature Reserve, a great place to see some Australian wildlife. There are walking trails, ranger-guided activities, great picnic facilities and prolific wildlife, including koalas and the endangered brush-tailed rock wallaby.

SIDETRACK

Explore the universe at Canberra Deep Space Communication Complex. This information centre, which stands beside the huge dishes that track spacecraft currently in orbit, is a must for anyone interested in space. Displays include a space suit, space food and archival film footage of the *Apollo* moon landings. (421 Discovery Dr, Tidbinbilla; (02) 6201 7880; open Mon–Sun 9am–5pm, free entry; cdscc.nasa.gov.)

Continue south past Tharwa on the Naas Road to Namadgi National Park. Namadgi is the Aboriginal name for the rugged mountains south-west of Canberra, and the park covers 105,900ha, making up more than half of the Australian Capital Territory. Bimberi Peak (1913m) is the park's highest feature and is only 315m lower than Mount Kosciuszko. The park's unsealed roads are narrow and can be slippery when wet or frosty, but they are worth the trouble, as much of Namadgi's beauty lies beyond its main roads and picnic areas.

One of the park's best (and most accessible) rock-art sites is at Yankee Hat, named after a nearby mountain that is supposed to look like a colonial American hat. Great for families with kids or grandparents in tow, the 6km trail meanders through open grasslands past mobs of eastern grey kangaroos and along boardwalks skirting the edge of Bogong Swamp. The rock-art gallery is in the overhang of a huge weathered granite boulder, its lower sides covered in vibrant white and ochre paintings of human figures, kangaroos, wombats, koalas, dingos and birds. The wide open grasslands of Namadgi are one of the best places to see wild kangaroos – they are so plentiful that the locals have nicknamed the area around Gudgenby the 'Valley of 1000 Kangaroos'.

😊 KIDS' SPOT

Take the kids tiger-spotting at the National Zoo and Aquarium, which has Australia's largest collection of big cats. The two-hour Zooventure Tour is a great way to get up close and personal to tigers, lions, bears and other creatures (the zoo looks after 28 endangered species). (Lady Denman Dr, next to Scrivener Dam; (02) 6287 8400; open Mon–Sun 9.30am–5pm; nationalzoo.com.au.) Nearby is the National Arboretum, a 250ha forest park that features more than 44,000 trees from 100 countries along with walking trails, picnic facilities, forest sculptures and a free adventure park called the Pod Playground, with giant acorn cubbies on stilts, net tunnels, climbing frames, spiral slides and nest swings that kids will love (Forest Dr, off Tuggeranong Pkwy, Weston Creek; (02) 6207 8484; nationalarboretum.act.gov.au).

BEST EATS

- **Bradman Cafe** Stop for a coffee or enjoy a light lunch at this bright and airy cafe inside the International Cricket Hall of Fame. St Jude St, Bowral; (02) 4861 2039; open Mon–Sun 8am–4pm; internationalcrickethall.com.
- **Paragon Cafe** This Art Deco gem has a menu as old-fashioned as the decor, which is half its charm (just don't expect fine dining). It's kid friendly and the milkshakes are great. 174 Auburn St, Goulburn; (02) 4821 3566; open Mon–Sun for breakfast and lunch.
- **Moon Rock Cafe** The cafe at the Canberra Deep Space Communication Complex serves snacks and light meals throughout the day, and there is a playground for kids. 421 Discovery Dr, Tidbinbilla; (02) 6281 2190; open Mon–Sun 9.30am–4pm; cdscc.nasa.gov.
- **Poachers Pantry** Stock up on smoked meats for picnics, try some wine at the cellar door or enjoy a long lunch at the Smokehouse Restaurant. 431 Nanima Rd, Hall; (02) 6230 2487; open Fri–Sun for lunch, platters available Mon–Thurs 11.30am–3pm; poacherspantry.com.au.

BEST SLEEPS

- **The Old Bank** Built in 1892, Mittagong's former CBC Bank, which closed in the 1970s and languished as a dilapidated pigeon coop for years, has been remade into a charming boutique hotel with five suites, a studio, a cottage and a cosy library with a log fire. 83 Main St, Mittagong; 0419 982 191; oldbankhotel.com.au.
- **Hotel Kurrajong** Designed by the same architect who designed Old Parliament House, this gracious Art Deco hotel in Canberra was the home of former prime minister Ben Chifley, who preferred living in the hotel rather than at the Lodge, throughout his parliamentary career up until his death in 1951. 8 National Cct, Barton; (02) 6234 4444; hotelkurrajong.com.au.
- **Jamala Wildlife Lodge** Enjoy close encounters with exotic animals – giraffes, lemurs, bears and big cats – without leaving your room at this luxury lodge at the National Zoo and Aquarium. Rooms feature glass walls that front animal enclosures – you can even feed a giraffe from your balcony. Stays include two private tours of the zoo. 999 Lady Denman Dr, Canberra; (02) 6287 8444; jamalawildlifelodge.com.au.
- **Pacific Suites Canberra** This apartment hotel is close to the city centre. The apartments have plenty of room to move, a fully equipped kitchen, cable TV and laundry facilities. Other facilities include a pool and free parking. It's mainly a business hotel, which means you can often get a good weekend rate. 100 Northbourne Ave, Braddon; (02) 6262 6266; pacificsuitescanberra.com.au.
- **Caravanning and camping** The Cotter Campground beside the Cotter River, about 14km from Canberra's city centre, is suitable for caravans and camper trailers and has hot showers, flush toilets and electric barbecues. There are three designated campsites within Namadgi National Park: Ororral Valley, Honeysuckle Creek and Mount Clear, though all have a three-night limit and you'll need to pre-book at environment.act.gov.au. The basic facilities include pit toilets, picnic tables and fireplaces. There are no designated caravan sites, although small campervans are allowed at Honeysuckle. For details of caravan parks in and around Canberra see visitcanberra.com.au.

Opposite Lookout over the National Arboretum *Left* Go back in time at Goulburn's Paragon Cafe

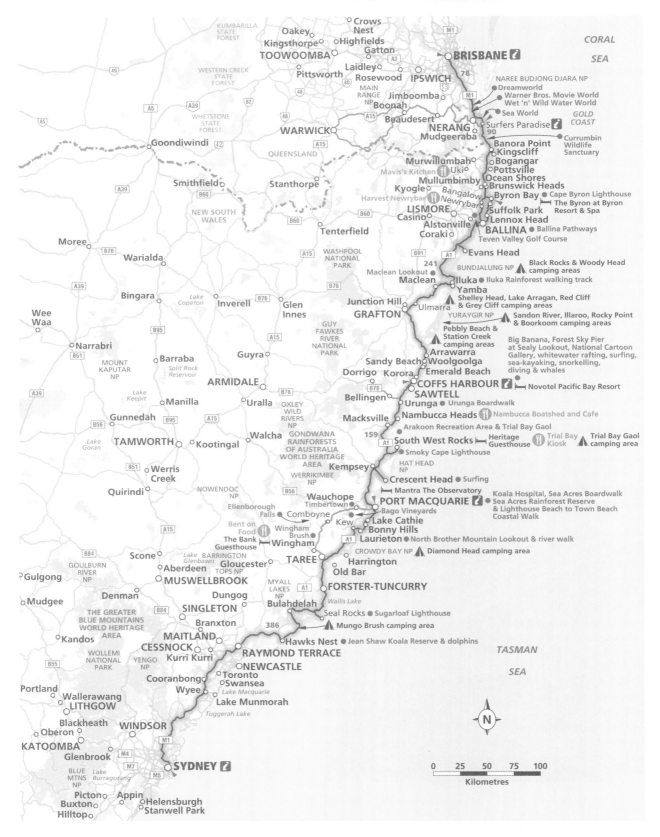

Take your time and explore the New South Wales north coast and hinterland on this holiday road trip between Sydney and Brisbane.

Sydney to Brisbane via the coast

Since going to print, some of the areas featured in this trip were affected by bushfires and flooding. Some of the information, particularly about roads in national parks and camping areas, may have since changed – contact local visitor information centres for updates before travelling.

HOW LONG?

As long as you like, but allow at least two or three days. If you avoid the detours and stick to the Pacific Highway, you could, however, do the drive in ten hours.

WHEN TO GO

Any time of the year is a great time to do this drive, although summer is the best time to go if you plan to swim – generally, the water in the lakes and ocean is warm enough for swimming between September and April. If you want to see whales, go between June and November.

NEED TO KNOW

Most of the coastal towns along this route are busy during school holidays, so book accommodation or campsites ahead at those times, especially in summer.

 Drive rating
Easy. Sealed roads

 Distances
Total distance, Sydney to Brisbane (without detours): 954km
- Sydney to Port Macquarie: 386km
- Port Macquarie to Coffs Harbour: 159km
- Coffs Harbour to Byron Bay: 241km
- Byron Bay to Surfers Paradise: 90km
- Gold Coast to Brisbane: 78km

 Temperatures
January: 18–27°C
July: 7–19°C

 More information
- Coffs Harbour Visitor Information Centre, 35–61 Harbour Dr, Coffs Harbour; (02) 5622 8900; coffscoast.com.au
- Port Macquarie Visitor Information Centre, cnr Clarence and Hay sts, Port Macquarie; 1300 303 155; portmacquarieinfo.com.au
- pacificcoast.com.au

 Snapshot
For many of us, a drive along the New South Wales north coast is a blur lost in the holiday rush of getting from A to B. But get off the highway and on to the back roads and you'll soon find there's much more than roadhouses and petrol stations to see along the way. Think beautiful beaches; wild World Heritage–listed national parks and rainforest; lush, fertile farmland valleys laced with wide, fish-filled rivers; and an array of interesting villages and regional towns hiding some of the state's best-kept holiday secrets.

SYDNEY TO PORT MACQUARIE

From Sydney, head north on the Pacific Motorway and Pacific Highway. After three hours of cut-and-thrust traffic, you'll be ready for a break, so take the turn-off to the twin towns of Tea Gardens and Hawks Nest, just north of Newcastle and the Hexham Bridge. This is the home of the Jean Shaw Koala Reserve and you'll often see koalas around the village streets, while from the beaches you may spot the resident pod of dolphins.

Take the coast road to Mungo Brush, deep inside Myall Lakes National Park. This shady, lakeside clearing beneath the tea trees is one of the most popular spots in the park and a great place to stretch your legs, unpack a gourmet picnic or go for a paddle.

The road rejoins the highway near Bulahdelah, but don't stay on it for long; instead, take the Lakes Way, which winds through Bulahdelah State Forest and along the shores of Myall Lake to Forster–Tuncurry. Along the way, turn off to Seal Rocks, a sleepy fishing village where anglers sell shells outside their boathouses and the pace of life is about as relaxed as you can get. Walk up to Sugarloaf Lighthouse on the point overlooking the beach.

Take the 'back way' to Port Macquarie along the coast road from Kew through Laurieton. In Laurieton, the lookout at North Brother Mountain has great views over Camden Haven River and its expanse of waterways and beaches. Follow the walk along the Camden Haven River and watch the pelicans swoop down to steal fishy scraps from the fisher folk cleaning their catches.

From Laurieton, the coast road cuts through heath-covered sand dunes, over headlands with views along endless stretches of beach, and skirts the shores of Lake Cathie (pronounced 'cat-eye'). In spring, the bushland beside the road is carpeted with Christmas bells and flannel flowers.

SIDETRACK

The other 'back way' to Port Macquarie is via Tourist Drive 8 (which has some unsealed sections), from Taree via Wingham and Wauchope. Take a walk through Wingham Brush with its resident flying foxes and visit Ellenborough Falls, one of the largest single-drop waterfalls in the Southern Hemisphere. The village of Comboyne is perched high on an open plateau and from there the road winds its way back down the mountain rainforest towards Wauchope.

Time your drive into Port Macquarie to coincide with the afternoon feeding (usually about 3pm) at the Koala Hospital in the grounds of Roto House in Lord Street. Walk along the boardwalk at nearby Sea Acres, the second largest coastal rainforest reserve in New South Wales, or take the three-hour coastal walk from Lighthouse Beach to Town Beach, which has elevated timber boardwalks to help you get across the rocky headlands that separate five beautiful beaches.

Opposite top Jacaranda in bloom on Comboyne Road in Port Macquarie's hinterland *Right* Port Macquarie's iconic breakwall

 KIDS' SPOT

Go back in time *and* get lost in Wauchope! Timbertown is a re-creation of a 19th-century timber-getting village, complete with steam-train rides, horse-and-carriage rides, timber-cutting displays and whip-cracking lessons (Oxley Hwy, Wauchope; (02) 6586 1940; open Mon–Sun 9.30am–4pm during New South Wales school holidays, closed Tues–Wed outside of school holidays; timbertown.com.au). Bago Vineyards has the largest hedge maze in New South Wales, and kids love searching for the giant musical chimes, recycled bells (made from gas cylinders) and marimba (a cross between a piano and a xylophone) hidden deep in the maze (Milligans Rd, off Bago Rd, Wauchope; (02) 6585 7099; maze open Mon–Sun 9am–5pm, last admission 4pm; bago.com.au).

PORT MACQUARIE TO COFFS HARBOUR

Head back to the Pacific Highway and head north. Once in Kempsey, turn off the highway again to visit the village of Crescent Head, home to one of the best right-hand surf breaks in the country and a favourite with longboard riders from all over the world. You can also take Tourist Drive 12 to South West Rocks along the banks of the Belmore and Macleay rivers and drive up to Smoky Cape Lighthouse and Arakoon Recreation Area to wander around the ruins of historic Trial Bay Gaol. Built in 1877, closed in 1903, and reopened in 1915 to hold people of German descent thought to be enemy sympathisers during World War I – they were allowed out onto the beaches during the day but locked up at night – this is a gaol with a view. It's now a museum and you can walk through the old cells. (Trial Bay Gaol Access Rd, Arakoon; (02) 6566 6168; open Mon–Sun 9am–4.30pm.)

Back on the highway, take a break at Urunga and go for a wander on the over-water boardwalk, which runs along the river and across the dunes to the beach. A second boardwalk leads off into the mangroves of the Urunga Lagoon.

SIDETRACK

About 5km north of Urunga, turn left and drive west to Bellingen and up into the mountain-top rainforest at Dorrigo (see p. 45).

From the Bellingen turn-off, it's 25km to Coffs Harbour. The locals insist their bananas can't be beaten, although blueberries are rapidly replacing bananas as the main crop in the district. Drive through the fruit farms in the hills on the way to Sealy Lookout in Bruxner Park, where the impressive Forest Sky Pier is cantilevered more than 20m out over the edge of the Great Dividing Range and provides great views of Coffs Harbour and the coast.

Beyond lazing around on the beaches, there is plenty to do in and around Coffs, including whitewater rafting on the nearby Nymboida River, sea-kayaking tours and learn-to-surf classes, whale-watching (May–Nov) and snorkelling and diving in Solitary Islands Marine Park, where you can see hard corals and grey nurse sharks. One thing you shouldn't miss is the National Cartoon Gallery. Housed in an old World War II bunker, it's home to a staggering collection of 16,000 cartoons and caricatures (mainly of the political and satirical persuasion), and exhibitions change monthly. (John Champion Way, near Hogbin Dr–Albany St roundabout; (02) 6651 7343; open Mon–Sun 10am–4pm; mgnsw.org.au/organisations/bunker-cartoon-gallery.)

☺ KIDS' SPOT

You can't drive through Coffs without a visit to the famous Big Banana, the 'big thing' that started the craze of building monster-sized roadside attractions across the country. The Big Banana theme park offers ice-skating, toboggan rides, puppets and a three-storey-high inflatable water slide, but it's worth stopping for a chocolate-coated frozen banana on a stick if nothing else. 351 Pacific Hwy, just north of Coffs; (02) 6652 4355; open Mon–Sun 9am–4.30pm; bigbanana.com.

COFFS HARBOUR TO BRISBANE

From Coffs, it will take you about an hour to get to Grafton, where the first things you'll notice are the magnificent trees. The most famous are the jacarandas, celebrated each October in the annual Jacaranda Festival, but if you take the time to drive through the residential streets you'll also find avenues of figs, Illawarra flame trees and a host of others.

From Grafton, head north-east along the banks of the Clarence River to hit the coast at Yamba. You'll pass through lovely little villages, including the historic 19th-century river port of Ulmarra, once a thriving centre of river traffic and now home to a collection of galleries, antiques shops and craft stores. Maclean, 28km further on, calls itself 'the Scottish town in Australia' – many of the stores and street signs highlight its Scottish heritage. Take a drive up to the lookout for great views of the township, river and valleys.

North of Maclean the countryside is predominantly sugarcane, and the road follows the river to Yamba. The 30-minute ferry trip across the bay to Iluka is one of the best-value cruises around (see clarenceriverferries.com.au for timetables) and there is a terrific 2.5km easy walk that takes you right through the centre of World Heritage rainforest.

For some great picnic sites, head north to Evans Head, a sleepy little village at the mouth of the Evans River, where there are dozens of shaded sites along the riverbank. From here it's about a 30-minute drive to Ballina, on the mouth of the Richmond River. Again, the beaches here are wonderful. Explore them on the walking and cycling track that hugs the coastline and follows the river wall.

☺ KIDS' SPOT

Ask any Australian kid where they would like to go on their next holiday and it's likely that the Gold Coast will feature near the top of their list. There's just so much to do! Kids can get up close and personal to some of Australia's cutest animals at Currumbin Wildlife Sanctuary, and theme parks like Dreamworld offer adrenalin-rush action rides. Wet 'n' Wild Water Park has epic water slides and a wave pool, and there's plenty of Hollywood thrills at Warner Bros. Movie World – see destinationgoldcoast.com for details of these parks, as well as the wax museum, trampoline park, learn-to-surf schools, indoor skydiving and AquaSplash Inflatable Water Park, full of water slides and blow-up toys. Not everything has to cost a bomb either: Broadwater Parklands has several fun-filled free playgrounds, including splash parks, a calm-water beach and a jumping bouncy pillow.

Head inland from Ballina to play a round of golf in the rainforest at Teven Valley Golf Course (1684 Eltham Rd, Teven; (02) 6687 8386; tevenvalleygolfcourse.com.au), stop for lunch and a spot of window-shopping at Bangalow, or wind your way along the coast via the beachside communities of Lennox Head and Suffolk Park. Before you know it, the iconic Cape Byron Lighthouse on Australia's most easterly mainland point will be shimmering on the horizon. About an hour to the north are the Gold Coast and the beautiful hinterland of the Scenic Rim (see p. 75). From there, it's just another 80km to Brisbane via the Pacific Motorway.

BEST EATS

- **Bent on Food** Good coffee and cakes are served here, as well as lots of other pantry goodies and light lunches made with local produce. 95 Isabella St, Wingham; (02) 6557 0727; open Mon–Sun for breakfast and lunch; bentonfood.com.au.
- **Trial Bay Kiosk** Located near the sandstone gaol at Arakoon, this licensed restaurant has fantastic water views. Arakoon National Park, Cardwell St, South West Rocks; (02) 6566 7100; open Tues–Sun for breakfast and lunch, Fri–Sat for dinner; trialbaykiosk.com.au.
- **Nambucca Boatshed and Cafe** Drop in for excellent coffee or a light lunch overlooking the river. Nambucca Boatshed, Riverside Dr, Nambucca Heads; (02) 6568 6511; open Mon–Sun for breakfast and lunch; nambuccaboatshed.com.au.
- **Mavis's Kitchen** The menu may be simple but the food is exceptionally good, and what can't be grown in the biodynamic organic vegetable garden is sourced locally, so food miles are low. 64 Mount Warning Rd, Uki, via Murwillumbah; (02) 6679 5664; open Wed–Sun for breakfast and lunch, Fri–Sat for dinner; maviseskitchen.com.au.
- **Harvest Newrybar** It's worth seeking out this deli, bakery and restaurant in the tiny hamlet of Newrybar, in the hills behind Byron Bay, as the food is fabulous, whether you go for breakfast or brunch, or fine dining at night. 18 Old Pacific Hwy, Newrybar; (02) 6687 2644; open Mon–Sun for lunch and dinner, Sat–Sun for breakfast; harvestnewrybar.com.au.

BEST SLEEPS

- **The Bank Guesthouse** This beautifully restored guesthouse occupies the former Bank of New South Wales building in the centre of Wingham. 48 Bent St, Wingham; (02) 6553 5068; thebankguesthouse.com.au.
- **Mantra The Observatory** The spacious apartments, which all have a private balcony, overlook Port Macquarie's Town Beach. 40 William St, Port Macquarie; (02) 6586 8000; mantratheobservatory.com.au.
- **Heritage Guesthouse** Located in the heart of South West Rocks, the guesthouse has nine large ensuite rooms, with two rooms (rooms 5 and 6) opening out onto the sun-soaked balcony. 21–23 Livingstone St, South West Rocks; (02) 6566 6625; heritageguesthouse.com.au.
- **Novotel Pacific Bay Resort** There's a string of beachside resorts just north of Coffs Harbour, and this is the pick of the bunch, offering beach access, pool, day spa and restaurant. Cnr Pacific Hwy and Bay Dr, Coffs Harbour; (02) 6659 7000; pacificbayresort.com.au.
- **The Byron at Byron Resort and Spa** Set within a beautiful 18ha patch of coastal rainforest, the 92 one-bedroom suites all have views over the rainforest canopy and two enclosed balconies. It's just five minutes from Byron Bay, behind Tallow Beach 77–97 Broken Head Rd, Byron Bay; (02) 6639 2000; thebyronatbyron.com.au.
- **Caravanning and camping** Mungo Brush in Myall Lakes National Park is very popular with campers and caravanners, so you'll need to book ahead (call (02) 4984 8200). Caravan camping is available at Diamond Head in Crowdy Bay National Park near Laurieton and there are also waterfront caravan and camping sites at Trial Bay Gaol campground at Arakoon near South West Rocks. Yuraygir National Park between Coffs Harbour and Grafton is another popular camping spot, especially in summer, with six campgrounds. There's also great beachside camping in Bundjalung National Park near Iluka – Woody Head has hot showers, a kiosk and room for 103 tents and caravans but no power (bookings essential (02) 6646 6134). The Black Rocks campground, roughly midway between Evans Head and Iluka, is behind the dunes of Ten Mile Beach. Caravanners are spoilt for choice: there are caravan parks in almost every town in the region, and many are right on the beach, but you will need to book ahead in the summer holiday season. Contact local visitor centres for details.

Opposite top Lennox Head is a popular surf destination
Opposite bottom Ballina's Big Prawn

Turn the Sydney–Melbourne commute into a fun trip and enjoy great beaches, lakes, rivers and lots of wildlife, including penguins, seals, whales and even tigers.

Sydney to Melbourne via the coast

Since going to print, some of the areas featured in this trip were affected by the 2020 bushfires. Some of the information, particularly about national park camping areas, may have since changed – contact local visitor information centres for updates before travelling.

HOW LONG?

Take as long as you like, but allow at least three days. If you are in a hurry, you might manage it in two days, stopping overnight at Mallacoota.

WHEN TO GO

This drive is great year-round, although summer is the best time if you plan to swim. If you want to see whales, travel between June and November.

NEED TO KNOW

Most of the coastal towns along this route are busy during school holidays, so book accommodation or campsites ahead at these times, especially in summer. Dogs are not allowed in the national parks along the way, even if you are only dropping in for half an hour or so to visit a lookout or unpack a picnic.

 Drive rating
Easy. Sealed roads

 Distances
Total distance, Sydney to Melbourne: 1037km
- Sydney to Batemans Bay: 278km
- Batemans Bay to Eden: 200km
- Eden to Lakes Entrance: 241km
- Lakes Entrance to Melbourne: 318km

 Temperatures
January: 16–24°C
July: 5–17°C

 More information
- Batemans Bay Visitor Information Centre, Princes Hwy, Batemans Bay; 1800 802 528; eurobodalla.com.au
- Eden Information Centre, Princes Hwy, Eden; (02) 6496 1953; sapphirecoast.com.au
- Lakes Entrance Visitor Information Centre, cnr Marine Pde and Princes Hwy, Lakes Entrance; 1800 637 060; visiteastgippsland.com.au
- Narooma Visitor Information Centre, Princes Hwy, Narooma; (02) 4476 2881
- sydneymelbournetouring.com

 Snapshot
You can drive between Sydney and Melbourne in less than nine hours if you stick to the mostly dual-carriageway Hume Highway, but it's not much fun. If you take the Princes Highway instead and meander your way along the coast, it becomes a driving holiday rather than just an interstate commute. The beaches are beautiful, there is lots to see and do to keep kids amused, and foodies are spoiled for choice in the pretty seaside villages along the way.

Opposite top left **Koalas on Raymond Island** *Top right* **Lakes Entrance harbour** *Bottom left* **Ride the Discovery Trail** *Bottom right* **Rural landscape of Gippsland**

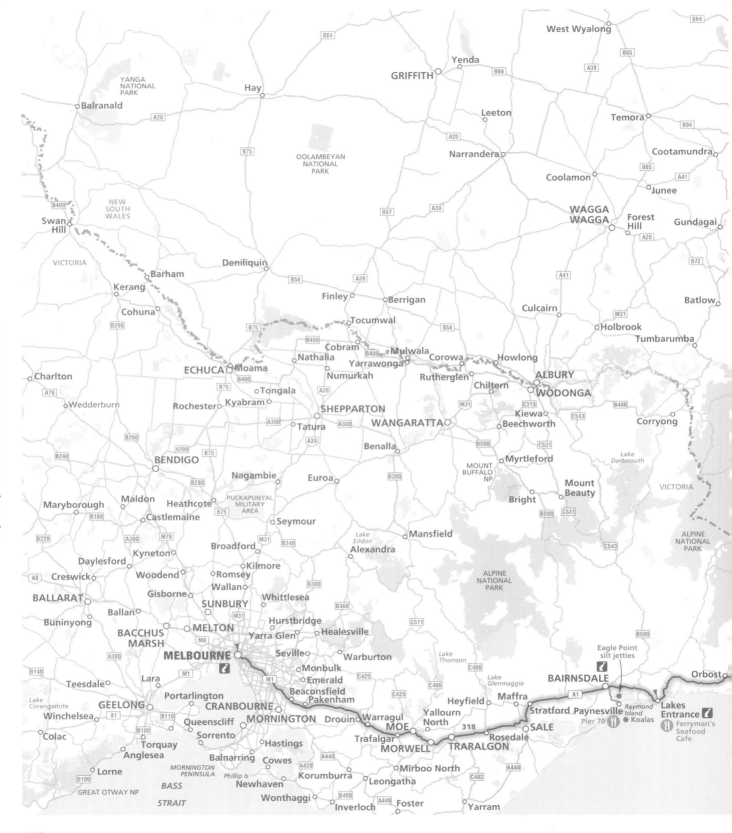

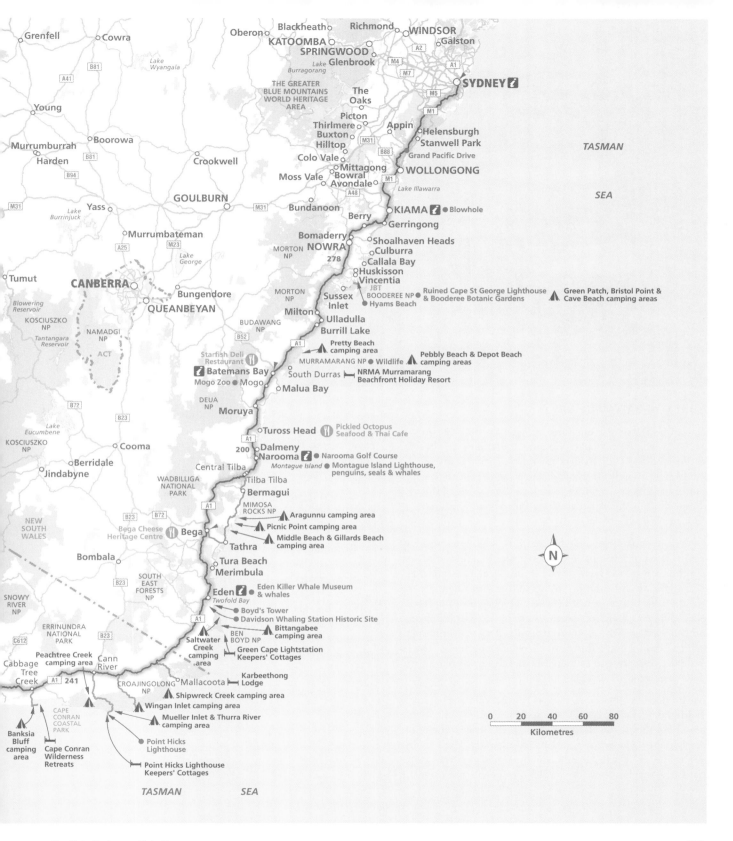

SYDNEY TO BATEMANS BAY

The fun begins on the outskirts of Sydney on the Grand Pacific Drive, which snakes along the cliff edges on the cantilevered Sea Cliff Bridge (*see* p. 115). Catch a wave whooshing through the Blowhole at Kiama, browse the boutiques in Berry and then take a walk on some of the whitest sand in the world at Jervis Bay, about 30 minutes south of Nowra.

There's no actual town called Jervis Bay, so follow the signs to Huskisson or Vincentia. Whatever you do, make sure you take the turn-off to Hyams Beach on the way. It's reputed to have the whitest sand in the world. Activities here are all either on, beside or in the water. The bay offers beaches, rocky platforms and reefs, extensive seagrass beds, estuaries and deep-water cliffs, so naturally scuba diving, swimming, surfing, boating and fishing are all popular pastimes. The bay also has a resident pod of dolphins and is a great place to go whale-watching.

Nearby Booderee National Park is worth exploring. Highlights include coastal walks with fantastic views, a ruined lighthouse and Booderee Botanic Gardens, the only Aboriginal-owned botanic gardens in Australia. Here you'll find a number of self-guided trails lined with interpretive boards that explain how the local Koori people use the plants for food and medicine. There's a lovely rainforest boardwalk and you'll almost always see kangaroos grazing on the grassy picnic areas. Koori-led tours and other tours are available during the school holidays.

If you want to see Australian animals close up in the wild, head to Murramarang National Park, where you'll often see kangaroos on the beaches and around the picnic areas, particularly at Pebbly Beach.

At the mouth of the Clyde River, Batemans Bay is the largest town on the Eurobodalla Coast – Eurobodalla means 'land of many waters', and there are plenty of ways to get wet, with boat ramps, wharves and jetties in almost every coastal village. Batemans Bay is a great place to throw in a fishing line or head out to sea on a fishing charter. You can also go kayaking, stand-up paddleboarding and sailing or just laze around on a stunning beach.

BATEMANS BAY TO EDEN

In 1851 gold was discovered just south of Batemans Bay, near the present-day village of Mogo, and by the 1860s more than 30,000 diggers were working the goldfields. Today Mogo is a popular pit stop, with a string of shops selling everything from new-age crystals and handmade jewellery to antiques.

In Narooma take a penguin-watching or snorkel-with-seals tour out to Montague Island, which has a historic lighthouse and is home to about 10,000 pairs of little penguins as well as colonies of Australian and New Zealand fur seals. It's a great spot for whale-watching too, between September and November (montagueisland.com.au). Narooma is also home to one of the most scenic golf courses in the country, where even non-golfers will enjoy the 'sea-forever' views on the cliff-edge top six (Ballingalla St, Narooma; (02) 4476 0500; open Mon–Sun; naroomagolf.com.au).

The section of the coast between Narooma and Bega is great for shopping. There are lots of quirky galleries and boutiques, particularly in the twin villages of Central Tilba and Tilba Tilba. Both are heritage listed, and the vibrantly painted wooden houses and shopfronts look much the same as they would have at the end of the 19th century.

SIDETRACK

A scenic alternative between Tilba and Tathra is Tourist Road 9, which follows the coast and travels through lush dairy-farming country, the fishing village of Bermagui and the forests of Mimosa National Park.

Eden, on the shores of Twofold Bay, is one of the best places to see whales and was once one of the most important whaling centres in the country. The Eden Killer Whale Museum examines the role whales have played in the town's fortunes. One of the most interesting stories is that of Old Tom, leader of a pack of killer whales (orcas), who, in exchange for whale scraps, would help the whalers hunt and kill the huge baleen whales in the harbour by rounding them up and directing them towards the boats. (184 Imlay St, Eden; (02) 6496 2094; open Mon–Sat 9.15am–3.45pm, Sun 11.15am–3.45pm; killerwhalemuseum.com.au.)

Opposite Grand Pacific Drive, near Clifton *Right* Kids love exploring the bushland around Mogo

:) KIDS' SPOT

Make a stop in Mogo to visit some furry (and scaly) friends. Animals at Mogo Zoo include Nepalese red pandas, white lions, snow leopards, bears and tigers. Enjoy a range of animal encounters with meerkats, snakes and lemurs, hand-feed the big cats and go behind the scenes to become a keeper for a day. (222 Tomakin Rd, Mogo; (02) 4474 4930; open Mon–Sun 9am–5pm, keeper talks and feeding sessions held regularly throughout the day; mogozoo.com.au.)

EDEN TO MELBOURNE

Just south of Eden, Ben Boyd National Park – named after mid-1800s entrepreneur Benjamin Boyd – contains two other prominent legacies of the whaling era. At Davidson Whaling Station Historic Site, inspect the former whaling station buildings. Further east, Boyd's Tower is a huge square tower. Boyd built it in 1846 as a lighthouse, but the government would not give permission for the privately owned structure to be used that way, so it became a lookout for spotting whales.

SIDETRACK

The highway cuts inland between Eden and Lakes Entrance, but take the time to explore the beaches and waterways around Mallacoota, Croajingolong National Park and Cape Conran Coastal Park, two wilderness parks in the area that feature heathlands, rivers, wild ocean beaches and banksia woodlands brimming with nectar-feeding birds. Pick a beach, any beach, and you can walk for hours. Point Hicks (in Croajingolong) is said to be the first part of Australia's east coast sighted by James Cook in 1770 and was named after his lieutenant aboard the *Endeavour*. Join a free guided tour of the historic lighthouse at the point (Point Hicks Rd; 13 1963; tours Fri–Mon 1pm).

Opposite The staircase of Point Hicks Lighthouse
Below Melbourne's Degraves Street

Lakes Entrance is at the northern end of the Gippsland Lakes, the largest inland waterway in Australia – a network of lakes and lagoons covering more than 60,000ha. The Mitchell River silt jetties at Eagle Point, about a 15-minute drive from Paynesville, are the second longest silt jetties in the world (the longest are on the Mississippi). Silt jetties are long, thin strips of land that have been built up over millions of years; these ones are more than 8km long. You can drive out to the end and get great views all the way with the river on one side and the lake on the other.

SIDETRACK

Raymond Island is home to one of the largest koala colonies in Victoria. There's a marked koala trail to follow – the koalas rest in the trees in people's front gardens, and you'll sometimes see them prowling along fences and ambling along footpaths. Watch where you are walking though, as it's easy to trip over when your eyes are focused on the tree-tops. The Raymond Island ferry departs every half-hour from Paynesville and the crossing takes roughly three minutes. The ferry is free for pedestrians and cyclists, and you'll see your first koalas only a block or so from the wharf, so you don't need to drive.

From Bairnsdale (which is also the terminus of the Great Alpine Road, *see* p. 219) it will take about three hours to get to Melbourne via the Princes Highway, although a more scenic alternative is to continue following the coast south from Sale along the South Gippsland Highway instead and visit Wilsons Promontory, Phillip Island and the Bass Coast (*see* p. 121).

BEST EATS

- **Starfish Deli Restaurant** Pizza, pasta, seafood and lots of local oysters, all served with water views overlooking the Clyde River. Promenade Plaza, Clyde St, Batemans Bay; (02) 4472 4880; open Mon–Sun for brunch, lunch and dinner.
- **Pickled Octopus Seafood & Thai Cafe** The large deck overlooking Tuross Lake is a nice place to soak up some sun as you feast on local oysters, prawns, fish and Thai street food. 93D Trafalgar Rd, Tuross Heads; (02) 4473 6084; open Wed–Sun for lunch and dinner.
- **Bega Cheese Heritage Centre** The cafe here has a shady verandah, a great spot to enjoy a ploughman's lunch of Bega cheese and pickles, afternoon tea or a milkshake. 11–13 Lagoon St, Bega; (02) 6491 7762; open Mon–Sun 9am–5pm for cheese tastings, snacks and light lunches.
- **Ferryman's Seafood Cafe** Watch the fishing trawlers unload their catch while you eat some of it in the floating restaurant that was once a car ferry. Middle Boat Harbour, The Esplanade, Lakes Entrance; (03) 5155 3000; open Thurs–Mon for lunch and dinner; ferrymans.com.au.
- **Pier 70** The deck here is a great place for brunch, a casual lunch or dinner on the waterfront, right beside the Raymond Island ferry wharf. There's live music on Sunday afternoons. 70 The Esplanade, Paynesville; (03) 5156 1199; open Tues–Sun for lunch and dinner; pier70.com.au.

BEST SLEEPS

- **NRMA Murramarang Beachfront Holiday Resort** The one- and two-bedroom villas sit right on the edge of the sand, and there are also powered caravan sites, a licensed restaurant, a playground and a swimming pool. An added attraction is the resident mob of kangaroos, and the sheltered beach is ideal for kids. Mill Beach, Banyandah St, South Durras; 1300 795 813; nrmaparksandresorts.com.au.
- **Green Cape Lightstation** The lighthouse keepers' cottages, built in 1880, have been restored and are available for accommodation. The three cottages – one three-bedroom and two two-bedroom – have fully equipped kitchens. Linen is provided but bring your own food, and a book or boardgame as there is no TV. Green Cape Rd, Ben Boyd National Park; 1300 072 757; nationalparks.nsw.gov.au.
- **Karbeethong Lodge** Built in 1903, the lodge overlooks the serene expanse of water that surrounds Mallacoota. The 12 ensuite bedrooms all open out onto the verandah for great views. 16 Schnapper Point Dr, Mallacoota; (03) 5158 0411; karbeethonglodge.com.au.

- **Point Hicks Lighthouse** The three lighthouse keepers' cottages here are available for rent. Linen is supplied (for a small fee), but you'll need to bring your own food. Croajingolong National Park; 13 1963; parkstay.vic.gov.au/point-hicks-lighthouse.
- **Cape Conran Wilderness Retreats** Glamp it up in these handsome hard-floored safari-style tents. Each has a double bed, small fridge, reading lights and a deck. Cape Conran Coastal Park; 13 1963; wildernessretreats.com.au.
- **Caravanning and camping** You'll find good caravan parks at most towns and there are lots of camping options in the national parks as well, but you'll need to book well ahead during summer, when all these places are very popular. In Booderee National Park near Jervis Bay, top spots include Green Patch, Bristol Point and Cave Beach. In Murramarang National Park, the largest campground, Pretty Beach, has 70 sites (including powered caravan sites) and facilities include hot showers. Pebbly Beach is the best place to go to see kangaroos on the beach and has 20 sites, cold showers and gas barbecues, but it's not suitable for caravans. Depot Beach is another lovely spot and also has powered caravan sites and hot showers. At Mimosa Rocks National Park near Bermagui, you can park your caravan at Gillards Beach; Aragunnu and Picnic Point campgrounds are not suitable for caravans but camper trailers are okay. In Ben Boyd National Park near Eden you can camp at Bittangabee Bay and Saltwater Creek. Further south, Croajingolong National Park has several waterfront campgrounds, and you can camp beside the beach at Banksia Bluff Camp and East Cape Beach at Cape Conran.

Take the long way round from Melbourne to Adelaide and enjoy some of southern Australia's most scenic coastline.

Melbourne to Adelaide via the coast

HOW LONG?

Allow three or four days. If you are short of time and have driven the Great Ocean Road before, head straight to Mount Gambier on the Hamilton and Princes highways.

WHEN TO GO

If you want to see whales, go between June and November. The Blue Lake at Mount Gambier is at its bluest during summer. Lobster season is October through to May.

NEED TO KNOW

The Great Ocean Road is busy during school holidays and on weekends. Some sections of the beach in Coorong National Park are closed during the bird-breeding season (24 Oct – 24 Dec) – see environment.sa.gov.au for more details.

 Drive rating
Easy. Sealed roads

 Distances
Total distance, Melbourne to Adelaide via the coast: 990km
- Melbourne to Mount Gambier via Great Ocean Road: 533km
- Melbourne to Mount Gambier via Princes Hwy: 446km
- Mount Gambier to Kingston SE via Robe: 168km
- Kingston SE to Adelaide: 294km

 Temperatures
January: 14–21°C
July: 4–13°C

 More information
- Great Ocean Road Visitor Information Centre, 100 Great Ocean Rd, Apollo Bay; 1300 689 297; visitgreatoceanroad.org.au
- Lady Nelson Visitor Centre, Jubilee Hwy East, Mount Gambier; 1800 087 187; discovermountgambier.com.au
- Lorne Visitor Centre, 15 Mountjoy Pde, Lorne; (03) 5289 1152
- Penola Coonawarra Visitor Information Centre, 27 Arthur St, Penola; (08) 8737 2855
- Robe Visitor Information Centre, 1 Mundy Tce, Robe; 1300 367 144; robe.com.au
- Warrnambool Visitor Information Centre, 89 Merri St, Warrnambool; 1800 637 725
- southaustralia.com/places-to-go/limestone-coast

 Snapshot
Following the coast between Melbourne and Adelaide is not the quickest way to travel between the two cities, but it's certainly the most spectacular route. The numerous highlights include the Great Ocean Road, a mysterious blue lake, arguably the best red wine in Australia and the beautiful beaches of the Limestone Coast.

Opposite Bowman Scenic Drive, Beachport

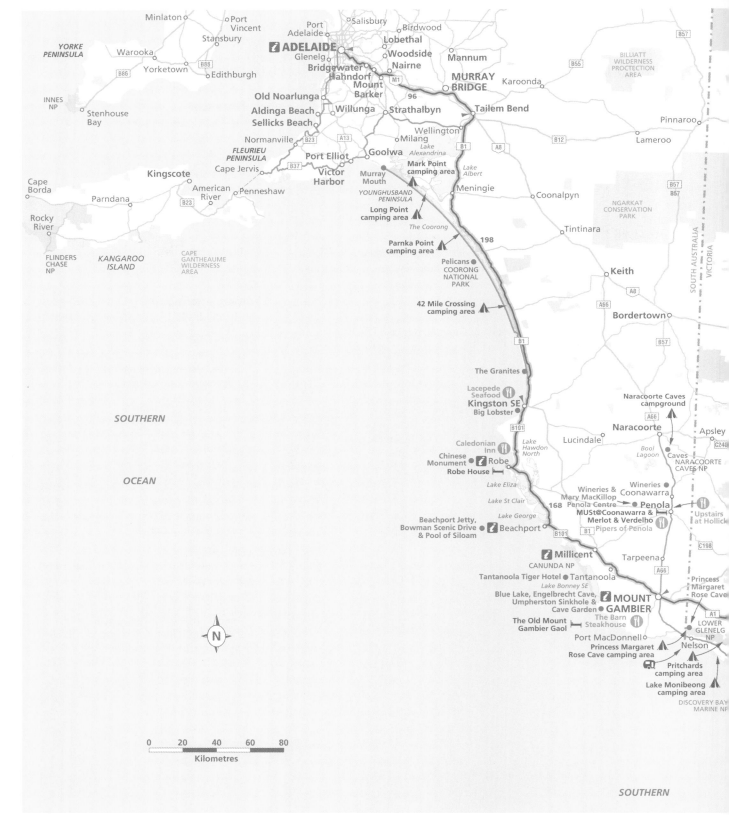

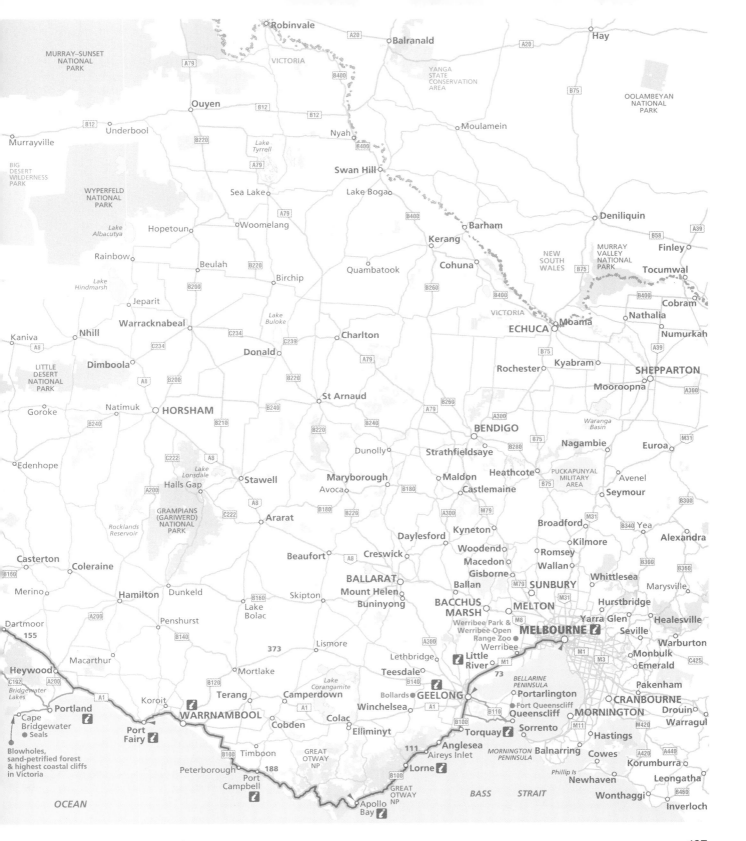

MELBOURNE TO MOUNT GAMBIER

From Melbourne, head west on the M1 Monash Freeway and Princes Highway towards Werribee and Geelong. Stop at Werribee Park to explore its 10ha of exquisite formal gardens, Victoria State Rose Garden and magnificent 60-room Chirnside Mansion, built between 1874 and 1877 by Scottish brothers Thomas and Andrew Chirnside. Armed with little more than determination and a few hundred pounds, and motivated by their family motto 'Do or Die', the brothers set about creating a vast pastoral empire of more than 38,000ha. Today the mansion, with its blacksmith, farmyards and manicured gardens, is the ideal of a British country estate, and a rare glimpse into the extravagant opulence of a bygone era. Behind the mansion, trailing down towards the Werribee River is an extraordinary outdoor exhibition, the Werribee Park Sculpture Walk.

☺ KIDS' SPOT

If you can't get to Africa, Werribee Open Range Zoo might well be the next best thing. Explore the zoo on your own or take part in a number of adventure tours, such as the Open Vehicle Adventure, during which you come face to face with the wildlife from the back of an open vehicle, just as you do on safari in Africa. You can also do a behind-the-scenes tour. Princes Hwy; 1300 966 784; open Mon–Sun 9am–5pm; zoo.org.au/werribee.

Winning works from the annual Helen Lempriere National Sculpture Award, held every March and April in the mansion's formal gardens, form the basis of the permanent exhibition. (K Road, Werribee South; 13 1963; open Mon–Sun 10am–5pm.)

Take a walk along the waterfront in Geelong and check out the 104 brightly painted bollards – each one represents a historic or well-known Geelong character, ranging from lifesavers to footballers and ladies in neck-to-knee bathing costumes. They are the work of artist Jan Mitchell, who transformed the old timber piles from a demolished pier into much photographed works of art. Learn the stories behind the characters at geelongaustralia.com.au/bollards.

SIDETRACK

Half an hour to the east of Geelong is the Bellarine Peninsula, full of stately Victorian-era mansions that have been transformed into restaurants and guesthouses. Take a 75-minute tour of Fort Queenscliff, which has been guarding the entrance to Port Phillip since the 1860s and has one of just three of the world's black lighthouses (Kings St, Queenscliff; (03) 5258 1488; tours Mon–Fri 11am, Sat–Sun and school holidays 11am and 1pm; fortqueenscliff.com.au).

Follow the coast from Geelong to Port Fairy along the Great Ocean Road (*see* p. 3) then continue across the border to Mount Gambier.

SIDETRACK

Discovery Bay Marine National Park encompasses a dramatic 50km long sweep of ocean beach backed by huge dunes and coastal lakes. There's so much fabulous nature to see here: mainland Australia's largest breeding colony of fur seals at Cape Bridgewater, blowholes, a sand-petrified forest and the highest coastal cliffs in Victoria, rising 130m above sea level. The Bridgewater Lakes, 16km west of Portland, are great for picnics, swimming, boating, waterskiing and surf-fishing. The park is adjacent to Lower Glenelg National Park, where the Glenelg River has carved a 15km long and, in places, 50m deep gorge through the limestone, as well as some extraordinary caves including the richly decorated Princess Margaret Rose Cave.

Umpherston Sinkhole at Mount Gambier

MOUNT GAMBIER TO KINGSTON SE

Located just west of the Victoria–South Australia border, Mount Gambier is roughly halfway between Melbourne and Adelaide. South Australia's second largest city is also home to some of Australia's youngest volcanoes and lots of crater lakes, caves and sinkholes, but is best known for its Blue Lake, a 75m deep lake inside an extinct volcanic crater on the edge of town. Actually there are three lakes here, but only one changes colour each year: in winter, the lake is a steely grey, but over the course of a few days in November the water changes to a brilliant cyan blue and stays that way until March. Though there are lots of theories, no one is quite sure why this happens. You can drive (or walk) around the rim of the volcano, and there are several lookouts that enable you to peer down into it. You can also take a glass-panelled lift down into the crater for a close-up view during a 45-minute Aquifer Tour. (John Watson Dr, Mount Gambier; (08) 8723 1199; open Mon–Sun, tours on the hour 9am–5pm Nov–Jan, 9am–12pm Jun–Aug, 9am–2pm rest of the year; aquifertours.com.)

The ground beneath the city of Mount Gambier is a labyrinth of flooded limestone caves. The most accessible is the Engelbrecht Cave, which extends under seven city streets. Once used as a dump by one of the city's whisky distilleries, it's now open for tours. (26 Chute St, Mount Gambier; (08) 8723 5552; open Mon–Sun 9am–4pm, tours on the hour.)

Other must-see spots around town include two sunken sinkhole gardens: the Cave Garden – a State Heritage Area – is in the middle of town and has a free 15-minute sound-and-light show every night at about 8pm (Watson Dr, Mount Gambier); and Umpherston Sinkhole, about 2km from the town centre, is also worth visiting at night, when possums descend en masse to feed – BYO torch (Jubilee Hwy East, Mount Gambier). Both are open 24 hours and are free to enter.

SIDETRACK

Known as Australia's answer to Bordeaux, the Coonawarra is famous for its red wines, particularly cabernet sauvignon, thanks to a legendary 12km long, 2km wide cigar-shaped strip of rich terra-rossa soil. According to the experts, this soil, which sits atop a white limestone base that was once the ocean floor, is one of the most productive *terroirs* outside Europe. More than 20 Coonawarra wineries have cellar-door sales outlets and most are open seven days a week.

The heart of the Coonawarra is the tiny township of Penola, which is full of antiques stores, galleries and boutiques. Petticoat Lane, the oldest residential part of Penola, retains red-gum kerbing and is lined with original timber-and-stone cottages. The township's most famous past resident though is undoubtedly Mary MacKillop, Australia's first saint. Together with Father Julian Tenison Woods, Mary MacKillop founded the religious order of the Sisters of St Joseph in Penola in 1866. Learn all about Mary MacKillop's life and her good work in the Mary MacKillop Penola Centre, which is full of historic displays as well as a Mary MacKillop shrine, an old schoolhouse and a gift shop packed full of every type of Mary MacKillop memento you can imagine. (Cnr Portland St and Petticoat La, Penola; (08) 8737 2092; open Mon–Sun 10am–4pm; mackilloppenola.org.au.)

SIDETRACK

Naracoorte Caves is South Australia's only World Heritage site. The 26 caves have acted as pitfall traps, collecting animals for at least 500,000 years, and consequently preserving the bones of a range of prehistoric megafauna such as the *Thylacoleo carnifex* (a marsupial lion), thylacine, *Zygomaturus* (a giant wombat-like creature) and sthenurine kangaroos. (Hynam–Caves Rd, 10 km south of Naracoorte; (08) 8760 1210; open Mon–Sun 9am–5pm, tours available; naracoortecaves.sa.gov.au.)

From Mount Gambier head towards the coast via Millicent. Keep an eye out on the way for the prowling tiger on the roof of the Tantanoola Tiger Hotel. In the 1880s, after the discovery of a number of mauled sheep, locals became convinced that a Bengal tiger had escaped from a travelling circus. In 1895, 4000 missing sheep and a lot of hysteria later, a beast was shot by bushman Tom Donovan. It turned out, though, that it was not a tiger but an Assyrian wolf, thought to have stowed away on a boat that was shipwrecked off the coast – and that the culprit responsible for the missing sheep was actually a local called Charlie Edmondson. The wolf-tiger was stuffed and is still on display inside the hotel.

Beachport has one of the longest jetties in South Australia and some great fresh lobster shops. Don't miss the Bowman Scenic Drive, a short but stunning coastal drive that sweeps around the beaches and dunes south of the town centre, taking in lookouts along the way. It skirts the edge of the Pool of Siloam, a salt lake seven times saltier than the sea, which is reputed to cure all matter of aches and pains, particularly those of an arthritic or rheumatic kind. The high salt content makes the water very buoyant, and on a hot day it's a great place for a soak and a float.

Home to around 1200 or so people, Robe is today a pretty sleepy sort of place, but in the 1850s it was South Australia's second busiest international port. There are more than 80 historic buildings and sites around town; pick up a heritage walking trail map at the visitor centre near the beach. Robe's popularity in the late 19th century was partly the result of a £10 landing tax imposed on all gold seekers arriving in Victoria during the gold rush. For many, particularly the Chinese gold seekers, that was more than the cost of their voyage to Australia, so they chose to arrive in Robe instead and head overland to the diggings on foot. There's a monument to the 16,000 Chinese who walked the 200 miles (320km) to Ballarat and Bendigo near the Customs House.

SIDETRACK

A favourite with 4WD fans, the beach run between Beachport and Robe via Nora Creina is a challenging drive, with soft sand, sharp rocks and some wickedly steep dunes, but it is also great fun. It's less than 60km but will take you half a day. You need to check the tides carefully before you go, air down your tyres to about 15–20 psi and be prepared to get stuck at least once or twice. It's also easy to lose the track, so ask at the visitor centre in Robe or Beachport for the 4WD trip notes.

The Limestone Coast, as this section of South Australia is called, is famous for its southern rock lobster, and the Big Lobster, a 17m high spiny red crustacean, is just half an hour up the road at Kingston SE. Legend has it that the original lobster was only meant to be 17 feet tall, but the builder misread the plans and used metres instead. There are plenty of places to buy real lobster, as well as fish and chips, in town. The lobster season is from October through to May.

KINGSTON SE TO ADELAIDE

For most of the way, the three-hour drive from Kingston SE to Adelaide skirts the edge of Coorong National Park, a place of wild natural beauty. Home to an enormous variety of birds, the area was made famous by the 1976 movie based on Colin Thiele's children's novel *Storm Boy*, about a young boy who befriends a pelican – the area is home to one of the largest breeding colonies of the Australian pelican.

SIDETRACK

If you have a 4WD, drive along the stunning narrow ribbon of sand called the Younghusband Peninsula for 150km, from the Granites just north of Kingston SE to the mouth of the Murray River. Separated from the mainland by a chain of saltwater lagoons, the peninsula has huge flocks of waterbirds, gorgeous beaches and tall dunes, but you need to be wary of wind and tide conditions and the route should not be attempted in winter.

SIDETRACK

Take the car ferry across the Murray River at Wellington and explore the Fleurieu Peninsula (see p. 129).

Follow the A1 to Adelaide via the lovely Adelaide Hills (see p. 85).

BEST EATS

- **The Barn Steakhouse** You'll find the best steaks in Mount Gambier here. Local grass-fed beef is aged on the premises for eight weeks then cooked over mallee coals. It's the perfect match for a local Coonawarra cab sav. 747 Glenelg River Rd, Mount Gambier; (08) 8726 9999; open Mon–Sun for dinner.
- **Upstairs at Hollicks** Floor-to-ceiling windows offer views across the vineyard and beyond to the broader Coonawarra region. The superb seasonally inspired menu features a high proportion of local produce. Ravenswood La, Coonawarra; (08) 8737 2752; open Mon–Sun for lunch, Sat for dinner; hollick.com.
- **Pipers of Penola** An elegant French-inspired establishment in a converted church, this is one of South Australia's most highly awarded regional restaurants. 58 Riddoch St, Penola; (08) 8737 3999; open Tues–Sat for dinner, bookings essential; pipersofpenola.com.au.
- **Caledonian Inn** The 'Cally' offers a fine range of quality pub food with good seafood. 1 Victoria St, Robe; (08) 8768 2029; open Mon–Sun for lunch and dinner.
- **Lacepede Seafood** If you fancy a lunch of fresh lobster (or fish and chips), head to this place down by the jetty in Kingston SE. Eat in the shady waterfront park opposite – although you'll have to fend off the hungry seagulls. Marine Pde, Kingston SE; (08) 8767 2549; open Mon–Sun 10.30am–5pm Oct–May.

BEST SLEEPS

- **The Old Mount Gambier Gaol** Home to outlaws and the condemned from 1866 until 1995, the gaol has been refurbished and made into a boutique budget hotel, with the old bars and razor-wire fences still in place. Rooms range from dormitories to self-contained family units and, while the guards' peepholes in the doors have been covered over for privacy and cells now include a toilet and basin, almost all the original gaolhouse fittings and fixtures are still in place. The difference of course these days is that all prison guests get a key. 25 Margaret St, Mount Gambier; (08) 8723 0032; theoldmountgambiergaol.com.au.
- **MUSt@Coonawarra** Stylish motel-type rooms are available here in the heart of Penola. 126 Church St, Penola; (08) 8737 3444; mustatcoonawarra.com.au.
- **Merlot Verdelho** These two contemporary townhouses in Penola sleep up to 12 people. Arthur St, Penola; 0413 512 559; merlotverdelho.com.au.
- **Robe House** Built in 1847, this was one of the first houses to be built in Robe, as the home of the Government Resident. There are four self-contained apartments in the historic sandstone house, each with queen-sized brass beds and ensuites – two rooms have log fires. 1 Hagen St, Robe; (08) 8768 2770; robehouse.com.au.
- **Caravanning and camping** For camping and caravanning options along the Great Ocean Road, *see* p. 9. You can camp at Lake Monibeong in Discovery Bay, and there are several camping sites spread out along the river, as well as caravan sites at Princess Margaret Rose Cave and Pritchards, in Lower Glenelg National Park. Kywong Caravan Park in Nelson has a large bush-camping area as well as powered caravan sites (kywongcaravanpark.com.au). The lakeside campsites at Three Mile Bend in Beachport Conservation Park are just a few kilometres from Beachport town centre. Naracoorte Caves Campground has powered caravan sites and in the Coorong there are a number of beachside campsites – 42 Mile Crossing, Parnka Point, Long Point and Mark Point are suitable for caravans but do not have power.

Tackle the dunes on the 4WD track between Beachport and Robe

Country drives

Leave the traffic snarls behind and get back to nature.

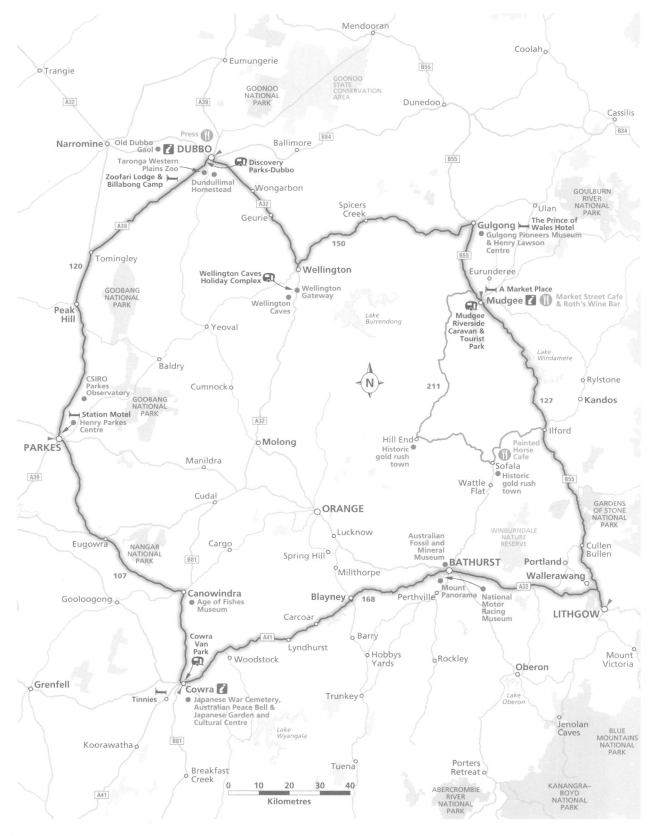

Historic gold-rush towns, fascinating museums, parks, gardens, caves and an amazing zoo make this drive through the central west of New South Wales great to do with kids, while the award-winning food and wine make it just as enticing for adults.

Central West, NSW

HOW LONG?

There are plenty of things to see and do on this road trip, so don't try to rush it – five days to a week would be ideal. You can, however, cut the loop short by heading back to Lithgow from Parkes via Orange. Even though it only saves around 50km or so, it will cut a day or two off the trip.

WHEN TO GO

Any time of the year is a good time to do this drive, although the central west, particularly around Bathurst, gets quite cold in winter. Summer is usually dry but can be hot.

NEED TO KNOW

Most roads on this trip are sealed, apart from some sections around Hill End and Sofala. All roads are suitable for caravans.

 Drive rating
Easy. Mostly sealed roads

 Distances
Total distance, starting and ending at Lithgow (with detours): approximately 750km. Lithgow is 152km west of Sydney.
- Lithgow to Mudgee: 127km (via Sofala and Hill End: 211km)
- Mudgee to Dubbo via Wellington: 150km
- Dubbo to Parkes: 120km
- Parkes to Cowra via Canowindra: 107km
- Cowra to Lithgow: 168km

 Temperatures
January: 16–31°C
July: 1–14°C

 More information
- Cowra Visitor Information Centre, Olympic Park, Mid Western Hwy, Cowra; (02) 6342 4333; visitcowra.com.au
- Dubbo Visitor Centre, cnr Newell Hwy and Macquarie St, Dubbo; (02) 6801 4450; dubbo.com.au
- Mudgee Visitor Information Centre, 84 Market St, Mudgee; 1800 816 304 or (02) 6372 1020; visitmudgeeregion.com.au

 Snapshot
West of Sydney, beyond the sandstone curtain of the Blue Mountains, is a region of subtle beauty, a place of wide open landscapes and clear skies, endless paddocks dotted with grazing sheep and cattle, parched hills and dry river beds in summer, and cool, crisp days in winter. The central west hides a wealth of Australian history and some great attractions; there is lots to see and do, and the distances between towns are reasonably short – all of which makes this a great drive to do with children.

Previous Peaceful rural landscape of Parkes, New South Wales

LITHGOW TO MUDGEE

From Lithgow, drive 7km north-west along the Great Western Highway then take the turn-off to Mudgee and follow this road over the range towards Ilford.

SIDETRACK

Take the signposted turn-off to Sofala, 27km down an unsealed road that is dusty but usually in pretty good condition and easy to drive. Sofala claims to be the oldest surviving gold town in Australia, dating from the beginnings of the gold rush in May 1851. The main street once stretched for 16km and the population numbered tens of thousands. Today Sofala is a sleepy little village on the banks of the Turon River, which is still a good place to fossick for gold.

Like Sofala, Hill End, 38km west on another unsealed road, is a ghost of its former grandeur – it was once one of the largest inland towns in New South Wales. In 1872 Beyers and Holtermann discovered the largest single mass of gold found in Australia, and Hill End became a place where fortunes were made overnight. By 1874 the settlement had a mile of shops, 28 hotels, five banks, several opium dens, an oyster bar, two newspapers and a brewery. Soon the population climbed to more than 8000. It is now a national historic site, managed by the National Parks and Wildlife Service, and most of the buildings date back to the 1870s, when the gold rush was at its height. From Hill End a pretty one-hour's drive along an unsealed road through tiny gold-rush towns leads to Mudgee.

Mudgee was first settled in the 1830s and, even though it is in the heart of gold-rush territory, it has always been a centre for farming. Wool and, more recently, wine are the town's major industries. There are about 40 wineries in the district and many are small boutique operations, so you'll find labels you haven't seen before in retail bottle shops. The region is best known for its reds and ports but was actually one of the first in Australia to grow chardonnay. It's also a hotspot for tree-changers who specialise in growing and making artisan and gourmet food products – you'll find everything from olives, venison, fish, honey and cheese to condiments and, of course, lots of wine.

MUDGEE TO DUBBO VIA WELLINGTON

With its crooked, narrow streets overhung with wooden verandahs trimmed with iron lace, Gulgong, 25km north of Mudgee, is instantly recognisable (for those old enough to remember) as the town portrayed on the old paper $10 note. The town's major claim to fame, though, is its close association with poet and storyteller Henry Lawson, who went to school in nearby Eurunderee, about midway between Mudgee and Gulgong along Henry Lawson Drive – although there is nothing left of the old bark school these days except for a commemorative plaque. Nearby is a picnic-area memorial to the writer at the site of his old home (the only relics that remain are the fireplace and chimney).

The Henry Lawson Centre in Gulgong tells the history of Lawson, his career and his family, and has the largest collection of Lawson material outside the Mitchell Library in Sydney (147 Mayne St, Gulgong; (02) 6374 2049; open Mon–Fri 10am–3.30pm, Sat–Sun 10am–1pm; henrylawsongulgong.org.au).

Opposite Wellington Gateway and its unusual chime *Left* Henry Lawson Centre in Gulong

Gulgong was established during the gold rush when Tom Saunders discovered gold lying on the ground at nearby Red Hill in 1870. The town's life and times have been preserved not only in the many old buildings along the main street, but also in the photographs of Charles Bayliss and Beaufoy Merlin. These photographs, known as the Holtermann Collection, consist of more than 500 original negatives taken in Gulgong and Hill End, and accurately portray life in these two boomtowns at the height of the gold rush in 1872. View some of the photographs at the huge Gulgong Pioneers Museum, which displays tools and firearms, needlework and clothing, gold-mining equipment, an old hotel bar, old shops, vehicles and coaches, war memorabilia, a school house and a settler's cottage. It's well worth spending a few hours ferreting among the displays. (73 Herbert St, Gulgong; (02) 6374 1513; open Mon–Sun 9am–5pm; mgnsw.org.au/organisations/gulgong-pioneer-museum-historical-society.)

From Gulgong head west to Wellington to visit Wellington Caves. The turn-off on the Mitchell Highway is hard to miss, as it is marked by the Wellington Gateway, a huge, fantastic and unusual wind chime. It was made from the girders of the old Wellington Bridge, which fell down in 1989, leaving the town isolated until a new one could be built. The controversial sculpture is described as 'echoing the image of a cave with metallic stalactites' and is constructed in the shape of a giant seed pod, 'representing the fertility of the valley'.

The caves reserve includes two show caves, Cathedral and Gaden caves, with wonderful displays of stalagmites and stalactites, including what is reputed to be the world's largest stalagmite, the Altar. There are regular guided tours of these caves, but they involve lots of steps, which can make it tricky for toddlers. Also in the reserve is a restored phosphate mine, which has been barely touched, except by a few palaeontologists looking for fossils, in the past 80 years. The walls of Bone Cave in the eastern loop of the mine are embedded with thousands of fragments and fossils. The 350m long mine is accessible for wheelchairs and strollers. Most tours take about an hour and a half. (Caves Rd, Wellington; (02) 6845 2970; open Mon–Sun 9am–4.30pm; wellingtoncaves.com.au.)

From Wellington head north-west to Dubbo.

DUBBO TO PARKES

One of Dubbo's most fascinating attractions is Old Dubbo Gaol, on the main street. Last used as a prison in 1966, this sandstone gaol built in the 1870s housed – and hanged – many of the central west's most notorious outlaws and has the largest collection of hangman's ropes in New South Wales. Despite these grisly statistics, it's quite kid-friendly, with characters in costume performing various skits (during school holidays) as well as some quaint animatronic models and good holographic displays. (90 Macquarie St, Dubbo; (02) 6801 4460; open Mon–Sun 9am–4pm; olddubbogaol.com.au.)

Two kilometres past the Taronga Western Plains Zoo is Dundullimal Homestead, the oldest standing slab homestead in Australia. Built in 1841, the homestead and stable buildings provide a glimpse into what life must have been like for wealthy settlers and squatters. (23L Obley Rd, Dubbo; (02) 6884 9984; open Tues–Sat 11am–3pm; nationaltrust.org.au/places/dundullimal-homestead.)

It will take a little more than an hour to get to Parkes via the Newell Highway.

KIDS' SPOT

Go wild at Taronga Western Plains Zoo, on the outskirts of Dubbo. See black rhinos, hippos, lions, tigers, giraffes and elephants – just some of the 700 animals spread out across 300ha of bushland. Explore the zoo in a golf cart or hire a bike instead. Fascinating talks and feeding sessions are held at various animal enclosures throughout the day, or take a behind-the-scenes tour to get face to face with incredible African animals. Obley Rd, Dubbo; (02) 6881 1400; open Mon–Sun 8.30am–4pm, tickets valid for two days; taronga.org.au/dubbo-zoo.

PARKES TO COWRA VIA CANOWINDRA

Parkes is most famous for its giant radio telescope, which relayed *Apollo 11* television pictures from the Moon in 1969 and was made famous once again in the 2000 movie of that story, *The Dish*. Unlike in the movie, you aren't allowed into or onto the Dish – either to play cricket or just to have a look – but the visitor centre has an informative display and a number of interesting exhibits; it also has a great view of the Dish and free barbecue facilities. (CSIRO Parkes Observatory, Newell Hwy, 20km north of Parkes; (02) 6861 1777; open Mon–Sun 8.30am–4.15pm; parkes.atnf.csiro.au.)

Even though it looks like a pretty normal country town, Parkes is actually the 'Elvis Capital of Australia'. Here, during the second week of January, thousands of Elvis impersonators arrive for the annual five-day Elvis Festival and the town explodes in a hip-wiggling swirl of sequined jumpsuits, gold lamé, black leather and blue suede shoes. Real sequins, gold lamé and black leather suits once worn by the King – more than 100 items in all, including some serious diamond-encrusted bling, movie and stage clothing, books, documents and memorabilia – are on display at the King's Castle museum. Owned by Greg Page (the original yellow Wiggle), it's said to be the fourth biggest collection of Elvis memorabilia in the world (the largest is at Graceland, Presley's US mansion). The King's Castle is one of four museums that make up the Henry Parkes Centre, along with the Antique Machinery Museum, the Motor Museum and the Henry Parkes Museum of local history. (Pioneer Park, 66/78 Newell Hwy; 1800 624 365 or (02) 6862 6000; open Mon–Fri 9am–5pm, Sat–Sun 10am–3pm; entry fee gives access to all four museums; mgnsw.org.au/organisations/henry-parkes-museums.)

From Parkes, head next to Cowra via Eugowra – scene of Australia's largest gold robbery by bushrangers Ben Hall and Frank Gardiner and their gang in 1862 – and Canowindra, where the dog-legged, verandah-fringed main street is lined with galleries and boutiques and is a good place to take a break. Three hundred and sixty million years ago the central west was home to bizarre fish with armour and lungs; Canowindra's Age of Fishes Museum has a large display of fossils of these fish, which were found nearby (cnr Gaskill and Ferguson sts; (02) 6344 1008; open Mon–Sun 10am–4pm; ageoffishes.org.au).

COWRA TO LITHGOW VIA BATHURST

Cowra's claim to fame is as the site of the largest prison breakout ever, which took place in 1944 when 1000 Japanese POWs tried to escape from a prison camp on the edge of town. Two hundred and thirty-one prisoners were killed, along with four Australian soldiers. After the war, in a spirit of forgiveness and international friendship, Japan established its only Australian war cemetery here. Further efforts towards reconciliation led to Cowra being chosen to host Australia's United Nations World Peace Bell, a privilege usually granted only to capital cities, and to the construction of the town's beautiful and very peaceful Japanese Garden and Cultural Centre. The largest Japanese garden in the Southern Hemisphere, it's designed to represent the landscape of Japan, with hills standing in for mountains, cascading streams symbolising rivers and ponds representing inland lakes. The garden's cultural centre has museum-quality examples of Japanese art and craft on show, including some exquisitely embroidered wedding kimonos, gorgeous ceramics and more than 400 beautifully crafted Japanese dolls. (Ken Nakajima Place, Cowra; (02) 6341 2233; open Mon–Sun 8.30am–5pm; cowragarden.com.au.)

Cowra is also home to more than 35 vineyards, and many have cellar doors open for tastings – although mostly on weekends. From Cowra, it's about a two-hour drive to Lithgow on the Mid Western Highway. Stop at Bathurst on the way to take a quick lap of Mount Panorama, home of motor racing since 1938. The National Motor Racing Museum is situated at the end of Conrod Straight (400 Panorama Ave, Bathurst; (02) 6332 1872; open Mon–Sun 9am–4.30pm; nmrm.com.au). For most of the year the track is a public road and it's great fun to drive (slowly – normal speed limits apply) around all the famous landmarks.

☺ KIDS' SPOT

Most kids seem to have a favourite dinosaur, so visit the Australian Fossil and Mineral Museum, which displays more than 2000 fossil and minerals, including dinosaur skeletons and insects trapped in amber. 224 Howick St, Bathurst; (02) 6331 5511; open Mon–Sat 10am–4pm, Sun 10am–2pm; somervillecollection.com.au.

BEST EATS

- **Painted Horse Cafe** The food served in this little cafe in the heart of historic Sofala is very smart – seafood is delivered fresh from Sydney several times a week. 27 Denison St, Sofala; (02) 6337 7092; open Thurs–Sun for brunch and lunch.
- **Market Street Cafe** The food here is all made with fresh produce sourced from within 100 miles of Mudgee. 79 Market St, Mudgee; (02) 6372 0052; open Thurs–Sun for breakfast and lunch.
- **Roth's Wine Bar** A Mudgee institution since 1923, when it was a general store with a sly grog shop out the back, Roth's serves tapas and pizza and provides live music most weekends. 30 Market St, Mudgee; (02) 6372 1222; open Wed–Sat from 5pm; rothswinebar.com.au.
- **Press** Here you'll find the best coffee in Dubbo, as well a wide choice of salads and gluten-free lunches in a former newspaper office. 33 Bultje St, Dubbo; (02) 6885 0621; open Mon–Sun for brunch and lunch; pressdubbo.com.au.

Roth's Wine Bar in Mudgee was once a sly grog shop

BEST SLEEPS

- **A Market Place** This three-bedroom Californian bungalow in Mudgee is a good family option. 18 Market St, Mudgee; (02) 6372 2437; amarketplacemudgee.com.au.
- **The Prince of Wales Hotel** Built in the 1880s, this is one of Gulgong's oldest hotels, but has new motel-style units out the back. 97 Mayne St, Gulgong; (02) 6374 1166; princeofwalesgulgong.com.au.
- **Dubbo Zoo** The zoo has some great family options, with safari-style ensuite canvas lodges at Zoofari Lodge and tents at Billabong Camp, complete with stretcher beds. In both cases, the accommodation includes all meals and after-hours, behind-the-scenes tours led by rangers – the Zoofari Lodge tours focus on exotic animals, those at Billabong Camp on Australian animals. Obley Rd, Dubbo; (02) 6881 1488; taronga.org.au/dubbo-zoo.
- **Station Motel** The rooms here are decorated with abstract images of Elvis in concert. 82 Peak Hill Rd, Parkes; (02) 6862 8444; southerncrossmotelgroup.com.au.
- **Tinnies** A two-bedroom cottage, Tinnies is a lovely adults-only retreat in the middle of a vineyard. Chiverton Rd, Cowra; (02) 6342 9251; tinniesatbackcreekvineyard.com.au.
- **Caravanning and camping** There are not many bush-camping options in the central west, but every town has at least one caravan park and many are within walking distance of the town centre. Discovery Parks–Dubbo has lots of facilities for kids (discoveryholidayparks.com.au). Pet-friendly camps include Mudgee Riverside Caravan and Tourist Park, which has waterfront sites (mudgeeriverside. com.au); the Wellington Caves Holiday Complex beside Wellington Caves (call (02) 6845 2970); and Cowra Van Park beside the Lachlan River (cowravanpark.com.au). All allow dogs on a leash.

See the best of the Snowy Mountains on this loop drive from Cooma, tracing a figure eight across the roof of Australia.

Snowy Mountains, NSW

HOW LONG?

Three to four days would allow enough time to enjoy the drive and visit most things along the way, and leave time for some fishing or bushwalking. Cut the loop in half by heading west from Kiandra to Cabramurra.

WHEN TO GO

This is a drive to do in summertime, when the days are mild and dry (though the nights can still get very cold). It is also quite spectacular during autumn, when the deciduous trees in many of the towns are at their most colourful. The road from Khancoban to Cabramurra is closed in winter, when snowfalls are frequent.

NEED TO KNOW

The road is fully sealed and is fine for campervans and motorhomes, but the section between Thredbo and Khancoban is not recommended for caravans. All vehicles travelling through Kosciuszko National Park must have an entry permit, even if you do not intend to stop in the park. Permits are available at the national park entrance station on the Alpine Way 13km before Thredbo or the National Parks Visitor Centre in Khancoban.

Snow chains must be carried between 1 June and 10 October on the Alpine Way between Thredbo and Tom Groggin, the Kosciuszko Road beyond Sawpit Creek, and the Island Bend–Guthega Road for its full length. Four-wheel-drive vehicles are not required by law to carry snow chains, but it is recommended, particularly if you do not have a lot of experience driving on snow and ice. Chains can be hired at many service stations and ski-hire shops in the region, including Thredbo. For up-to-date road conditions, see livetraffic.rta.nsw.gov.au or call 13 2701.

Drive rating
Moderate. Sealed roads with some steep, winding sections

Distances
Total distance (with detours): approximately 570km. Cooma is 434km south-west of Sydney and 114km south of Canberra.
- Cooma to Tumut: 180km
- Tumut to Cabramurra via Tumbarumba: 142km
- Cabramurra to Thredbo: 140km
- Thredbo to Cooma: 96km

Temperatures
January: 10–25°C
July: –2–11°C

More information
- Cooma Visitor Centre, 119 Sharp St, Cooma; 1800 636 525; visitcooma.com.au
- Khancoban Visitor Centre, cnr Scammell St and Alpine Way, Khancoban; (02) 6076 9373
- Snowy Region Visitor Centre, Kosciuszko Rd, Jindabyne; (02) 6450 5600
- thredbo.com.au

Snapshot
Sheer mountainsides looming around almost every turn, alpine fields carpeted with wildflowers, pale-gold farming pastures studded with grazing sheep and cattle, and rumpled hillsides covered in orchards laden with fruit – you will see all of this and more on this drive through the Snowy Mountains in southern New South Wales. A loop of 570km along mostly alpine roads in and around Kosciuszko National Park, it begins and ends in Cooma, although you could start or finish the drive at any point along the way.

Opposite Taking a moment to enjoy the view from the summit of Australia's highest peak, Mount Kosciuszko

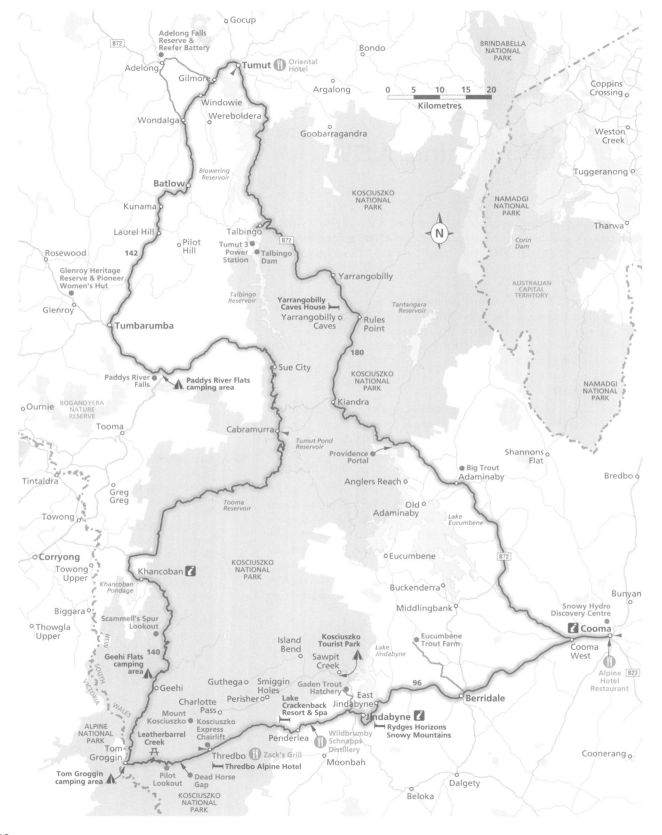

Snowy Mountains, NSW

COOMA TO TUMUT

Many of the roads along this drive were built between 1949 and 1974 by the Snowy Mountains Hydro-electric Authority (SMHEA) as access roads during the construction of the Snowy Mountains Scheme, still the largest engineering project ever undertaken in Australia. The Snowy Hydro Discovery Centre has displays that recount the history of the scheme, how it was built and how the massive dams and tunnels connect to feed the power stations and generators (1 Monaro Hwy, Cooma; (02) 6453 2888; open Mon–Fri 8am–5pm, Sat–Sun 8am–4pm).

From Cooma head north-west on the Snowy Mountains Highway towards Talbingo. Highlights of this section include the Big Trout, a huge fibreglass rainbow trout standing guard over the park in Adaminaby, and Providence Portal, where the water from Tantangara Dam, on the Murrumbidgee River, pours into Lake Eucumbene through a 14km tunnel (it's great for trout fishing).

Gold was discovered at Kiandra, near the junction of the highway and the Cabramurra Road, in 1859. Today all that remains are a few ruins covered by wildflowers and some display boards telling the story. (If you are looking to shorten the loop, head west to Cabramurra here.)

The next point of interest is Yarrangobilly Caves, 6.5km off the Snowy Mountains Highway in Kosciuszko National Park. These limestone caves are among the most richly decorated in Australia. Take a self-guided tour of South Glory Cave (open Mon–Sun 9.30am–4pm) or join a guided tour of one of the other caves. There is also a thermal pool with a water temperature of a constant 27°C, and there are bushwalks and picnic facilities.

The birthplace of Miles Franklin (author of *My Brilliant Career*), Talbingo is a pretty village beside Journama Dam in the shadow of the mountains. Drive to Talbingo Dam, where a lookout provides a view over the dam wall and mountains into the valley below, before touring Tumut 3 Power Station. This is the biggest power station in the scheme and you'll see pipes massive enough for a double-decker bus to drive through. The drive to Tumut, about 30 minutes away, follows the shoreline of Blowering Reservoir, and offers lovely views of the lake and mountains.

Scenic Tumut near Kosciuszko National Park

TUMUT TO CABRAMURRA VIA TUMBARUMBA

Famous for its autumn colours and annual Festival of the Falling Leaf, held in late April (see fallingleaffestival.com.au), Tumut is a thriving country town, set beside the Tumut River where there is a pleasant riverside walking track. The route continues on to Batlow, a 15–20-minute drive away through orchard country, where you can buy apples, pears, cherries and other stone fruit in season from many of the orchards.

SIDETRACK

An interesting detour that will only add about 15km to the trip is to the historic township of Adelong. A bustling town of 20,000 during a gold rush here in 1857, it is now a sleepy village of 900. Many of the buildings in the main street are listed by the National Trust, and there are quite a few galleries and craft stores to browse through. A kilometre out of town (following the Wagga Road through town until signposted) is the Adelong Falls Reserve. Adelong Creek flows by the ruins of the old Reefer Battery that served the gold mines until abandoned in 1910. The creek and hills here are said to have yielded more than 25 tonnes of gold; try your luck panning in the creek or take one of the pleasant short walks. There are picnic tables, barbecues and toilets.

Tumbarumba has some excellent antiques shops, and 8km from town along the Wagga Road is the Glenroy Heritage Reserve and the Pioneer Women's Hut, a fascinating museum dedicated to preserving the everyday objects of ordinary women (Wagga Rd, Tumbarumba; (02) 6948 3333; open Wed 11am–4pm, Sat, Sun and most public holidays 10am–4pm).

Land a trout

The Snowy Mountains is the premier trout fishery in New South Wales, with good numbers of both brown and rainbow trout in the fast-flowing rivers and streams, dams and lakes. The New South Wales Government's Gaden Trout Hatchery regularly releases rainbow and brown trout fry and fingerlings into the local waterways to maintain stock levels (10km north of Jindabyne on Gaden Rd; (02) 6451 3400; visitor centre open Mon–Sun 10am–4pm, guided tours at 10am and 2pm; dpi.nsw.gov.au/content/fisheries/info/gaden). Although some of the smaller streams can be affected by low summer flows, the Monaro and Thredbo rivers offer some of the best fly fishing in the world and you can catch good Atlantic salmon in Lake Jindabyne. A range of fly-fishing schools and guides caters for all levels of expertise, from absolute beginner to experienced angler. Contact local visitor centres for details.

Opposite top Dead Horse Gap *Opposite bottom* Kangaroos at Tom Groggin *Right* Driving the winding road to Tumbarumba

Continue south from Tumbarumba towards Khancoban. Paddys River Falls, just on the edge of town, has a pretty little waterfall with a nice picnic and barbecue area beside the river. Turn onto Elliott Way, signposted to Cabramurra. Part of Tourist Drive 5, this road is quite narrow and winding but very scenic. Built as a construction camp in 1951, Cabramurra is totally owned and operated by SMHEA, and is Australia's highest township, at 1488m. Petrol is available and a general store offers takeaways, but if you're planning to stop here for lunch your best bet is to bring a picnic and eat it at the lookout overlooking the village. Overnight accommodation is not available.

CABRAMURRA TO THREDBO

The road to Khancoban (closed in winter, between the June and October long weekends) crosses the wall of Tumut Pond Reservoir and passes Tooma Dam before descending through dry sclerophyll forest, crossing lush farmland on the valley floor and then climbing up to meet the Alpine Way. As it traverses the mountains, it reveals views of majestic peaks and alpine valleys. Rosellas flit through the tree-tops and if you're travelling in the morning or late afternoon you'll probably see a few kangaroos as well.

Stop at Scammell's Spur Lookout for panoramic views of the western face of the main range. From here the road descends to rest areas at Geehi, on the banks of the Swampy Plains River; Tom Groggin, near Tom Groggin station, home of Tom Riley, who was reputedly the original 'Man from Snowy River'; and Leatherbarrel Creek. All three rest stops have toilets, fireplaces and picnic and bush-camping areas.

Shortly after Pilot Lookout, which offers scenic views of the upper Murray River valley between the mountains, the road snakes its way through Dead Horse Gap, which, according to local legend, took its name from brumbies that were trapped here in severe snowstorms and died. The roadsides are lined with masses of white, lemon and pink wildflowers and even in mid-summer there are still patches of snow in the mountain crevices.

Ride the High Country

This is 'Man from Snowy River' country. Hard-riding pioneer mountain men were the inspiration for Banjo Paterson's famous poem and debate still rages today as to exactly who was the role model for the famous horseman. Horseriding has always been part of the Snowy Mountains way of life, and commercial horse treks through the mountains first began in the 1940s, so there are lots of places that offer trail rides and riding trips, ranging from one-hour easy treks across High-Country grazing lands to longer six-day camping trips in and around the back-country trails of Kosciuszko National Park. See cochranhorsetreks. com.au, reynellarides.com.au and snowywilderness.com.au or ask at a visitor centre.

Opposite Morning serenity at Lake Crackenback Resort & Spa *Above* Mountain-bike riding is very popular activity at Thredbo

THREDBO TO COOMA VIA JINDABYNE

Thredbo is a resort village that caters mainly for the winter skiing crowd but also offers a range of summer activities. Take the 15-minute ride on the Kosciuszko Express Chairlift (open Mon–Sun 9am–4.30pm) for spectacular valley views. From the top of the lift it's a fairly easy 6.5km walk to the top of Mount Kosciuszko, which at 2228m is Australia's highest peak. It was named in 1840 by the Polish explorer Count Paul de Strzelecki in honour of a Polish freedom fighter. The walk is easy enough to do on your own, but guided walks, including sunset and sunrise tours, are also available. If you have all day, combine this walk with the 10km Dead Horse Gap Walk, which takes you from the chairlift across the mountain and then back to the village through stands of snow gums and along the Thredbo River. Make sure you take water, warm clothing and sunscreen, as the weather can change suddenly and the sun can be severe, even when cool.

Mountain-bike riding is the other big summertime activity in Thredbo, which has regular championship racing events and an extensive network of trails, ranging from easy riding for novices and families to challenging terrain for the downhill demons. A highlight is the Thredbo Downhill, which involves riding a chairlift up the mountain then taking a white-knuckle bike ride down. Either bring your own bike and pick up a trail map in the village or hire one with helmet and map in Thredbo. For more details on bike trails, see thredbo.com.au/activities/biking. Other activities in Thredbo include golf, tennis, fly fishing, abseiling and bobsledding on a luge-style track.

Leaving Thredbo, the road slowly descends from the mountains to lakeside Jindabyne, which was one of two towns moved during the building of the snowy scheme (Adaminaby was the other).

SIDETRACK

Eucumbene Trout Farm is one place in the Snowies where you are guaranteed to catch a rainbow trout. Tour the trout hatchery or hire a rod and your catch will be cleaned and wrapped in foil with butter, crushed almonds and other goodies, ready to either take home or cook on the barbecues here. (Stoney Creek Rd, halfway between Jindabyne and Berridale; (02) 6456 8866; open Wed–Sun 10am–4pm; eucumbenetroutfarm.com.)

In the shadow of the mountains, the road traverses rolling countryside, passing grazing sheep and cattle on open pastures, towards Cooma – and the end of this Snowy Mountains loop.

BEST EATS

- **Alpine Hotel Restaurant** Drop in for good-value pub food. 170 Sharp St, Cooma; (02) 6452 1466; open Mon–Sun for lunch and dinner.
- **Oriental Hotel** If you haven't had any luck fly fishing, head here for some fresh local trout cooked in a variety of ways. 48 Fitzroy St, Tumut; (02) 6947 1627; open Mon–Sun for lunch and dinner.
- **Zack's Grill** This bistro at Bernti's Mountain Inn likes to boast it has the best steaks in the snow, but they also do seafood, or opt for tapas on the deck with great mountain views. 4 Mowamba Pl, Thredbo; (02) 6457 6332; open Mon–Sat 5pm–late in summer.
- **Wildbrumby Schnapps Distillery** This unique schnapps distillery has a cellar door, a sculpture garden and a great cafe for lunch. Drivers beware: the Wildbrumby Schnapps packs a punch! Alpine Way and Wollondibby Rd, halfway between Jindabyne and Thredbo; (02) 6457 1447; open Mon–Sun 10am–4pm in summer, 10am–5pm in winter; wildbrumby.com.

BEST SLEEPS

- **Yarrangobilly Caves House** This beautifully restored guesthouse near the caves and thermal pool in Kosciuszko National Park was built in 1917. Some rooms have ensuites and there are communal kitchens for self-catering – you'll need to bring your food with you. Minimum two-night stay. Yarrangobilly Caves Entrance Rd; (02) 6454 9597; nationalparks.nsw.gov.au.
- **Thredbo Alpine Hotel** Located in the centre of Thredbo village, this hotel has a range of motel-style rooms. Friday Dr, Thredbo; (02) 6459 4200; rydges.com.
- **Lake Crackenback Resort & Spa** Situated near the entrance to Kosciuszko National Park, this resort offers lake-view apartments and hill-top chalets, as well as a range of activities and services, including segway tours, kayaking, guided walks, night walks, mountain-bike hire and fly-fishing lessons. 1650 Alpine Way, Crackenback; 1800 020 524; lakecrackenback.com.au.
- **Rydges Horizons Snowy Mountains** The self-contained apartments here have balconies with lake views. Kosciusko Rd, Jindabyne; (02) 6456 2562; rydges.com.
- **Caravanning and camping** The best equipped camping for those who like all mod cons is at Kosciuszko Tourist Park, which has hot showers, powered caravan sites, wheelchair access, electric barbecues, picnic tables and fireplaces (14km north-west of Jindabyne at Sawpit Creek; kosipark.com.au). There are some nice summer camping spots at Tom Groggin on the banks of the Murray and beside Swampy Plain River at Geehi, 31km south of Khancoban. At the Paddys River camping area near Tumbarumba, dogs are permitted if on leads.

Snaking across the high peaks and upland plains of the Victorian High Country, this is one of the world's greatest alpine touring roads, offering sublime mountain scenery at almost every turn.

Great Alpine Road, Vic.

Since going to print, some of the areas featured in this trip were affected by the 2020 bushfires. Some of the information, particularly about national park camping areas, may have since changed – contact local visitor information centres for updates before travelling.

HOW LONG?

Four or five days would give you plenty of time to explore the alpine parks and historic towns along the route, although you could feasibly drive the full route in one long day. If you don't want to drive all the way to the coast, loop back to Bright from Omeo on the Bogong Alpine Way.

WHEN TO GO

The Great Alpine Road is fully sealed and is open year-round, but the Bogong Alpine Way closes between Falls Creek and Omeo during winter (access to the ski resort from Bright and Mount Beauty remains open). Unless you're keen on skiing, the best time to do this drive is in the warmer months or during autumn (April and early May) when the autumn colours, especially in Bright and Omeo, are stunning.

NEED TO KNOW

Snow chains must be carried during the snow season – from the Queen's Birthday weekend in June to the first weekend in October. They can be hired from outlets along the way. For road conditions, see traffic.vicroads. vic.gov.au. There is no fuel available at Falls Creek or Dinner Plain, so fill up at Omeo, Harrietville or Mount Beauty before heading up the mountain.

 Drive rating

Moderate. Sealed roads with extensive steep, winding sections. Larger caravans may have trouble negotiating some sections.

 Distances

Total distance, Wangaratta to Bairnsdale via Dinner Plain (without detours): 310km. Wangaratta is 67km south-west of Albury–Wodonga on the Hume Highway, or 245km north-east of Melbourne. Bairnsdale is 281km north-east of Melbourne.
- Wangaratta to Myrtleford: 48km
- Myrtleford to Bright via Mount Buffalo: 80km
- Bright to Omeo via Dinner Plain: 110km
- Bright to Omeo via Falls Creek: 137km
- Omeo to Bairnsdale: 121km

 Temperatures

January: 15–31°C
July: –2–14°C

 More information
- Alpine Visitor Information Centre, 119 Gavan St, Bright; 1800 111 885; visitbright.com.au
- Omeo Region Visitor Information Centre, 179 Day Ave, Omeo; (03) 5159 1455; omeoregion.com.au
- fallscreek.com.au
- mthotham.com.au
- victoriashighcountry.com.au

 Snapshot

The Great Alpine Road, stretching 300km or so from Wangaratta to Bairnsdale, is one of south-east Australia's classic touring routes. It begins in pastoral northern Victoria, not far from the Murray River, and takes you high into the ski fields of the Australian Alps and deep into the heart of two alpine national parks, before finally bringing you out, a stone's throw from the coast, in East Gippsland. On this great drive you'll also travel through gold-rush heritage towns, visit one of Victoria's best wine and gourmet food regions and enjoy spectacular alpine views.

Opposite top left Layers of mountains along the Great Alpine Road *Top right* The road is a bit more precarious in winter months; take your time *Bottom left* Great Alpine Road *Bottom right* The starkly beautiful snowgums

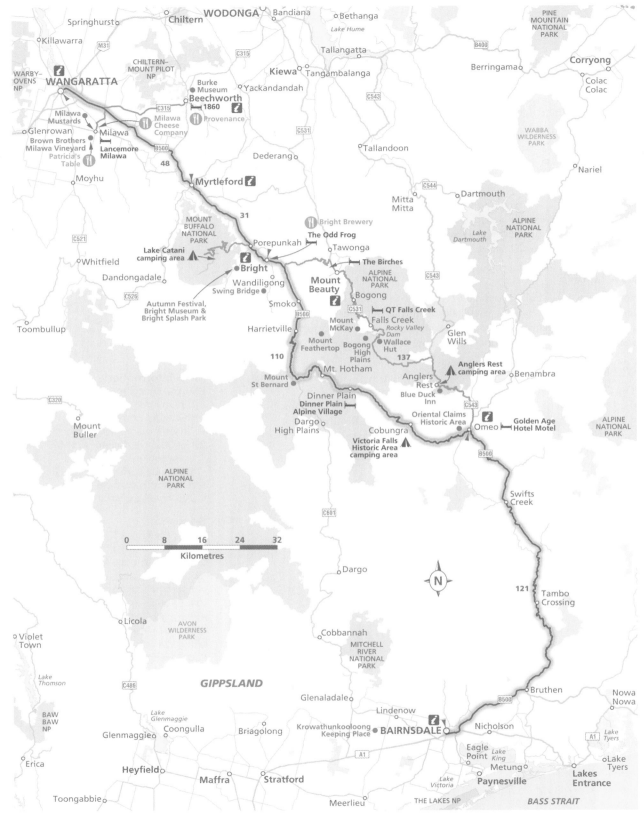

WANGARATTA TO BRIGHT

The Great Alpine Road begins in Wangaratta, 67km south-west of Albury–Wodonga on the Hume Highway. Take the Ovens Highway out of town towards Myrtleford and you're officially on the Great Alpine Road, but don't stay on it for long – two of the best side trips of this journey are just 10km down the road.

SIDETRACK

The road to the left leads you to Beechworth, Victoria's best preserved gold-rush town. The main street is lined with impressive buildings – a total of 32 buildings in Beechworth are classified by the National Trust. This is Ned Kelly country, and in his younger days Ned spent time at Beechworth Gaol. Visit his cell in the basement underneath the shire offices, where the information centre is today, as well as the courthouse, where Kelly was committed to trial. (Cnr Williams and Ford sts, Beechworth; 0408 054 327; guided tours Mon–Fri 11am, Sat–Sun 11am and 1pm; oldbeechworthgaol.com.au.) You'll also find more Ned Kelly memorabilia, including a replica of his armour, at the Burke Museum next to the Town Hall gardens. One of the oldest regional museums in Australia, it was founded in 1863 and named in honour of explorer Robert O'Hara Burke, of Burke and Wills fame, who was superintendent of police at Beechworth between 1854 and 1858, before he set off on his fateful expedition and died at Cooper Creek in 1861. It has an impressive collection of Aboriginal artefacts, exhibits on the goldfields and the Beechworth Chinese community, a natural history collection and a re-created street of 19th-century shops. (Loch St, Beechworth; (03)5728 8067; open Mon–Sun 10am–5pm.)

SIDETRACK

Take the turn-off to the right to Milawa, home to several wineries including Brown Brothers Milawa Vineyard, as well as the Milawa Cheese Company and a number of gourmet food stores. Most are open daily for tastings and sales and are great for stocking up on picnic supplies. (See milawagourmet.com.au.)

The Great Alpine Road travels on towards Myrtleford and Mount Buffalo, through hop fields and vineyards. Keep an eye out for the oddly shaped tobacco-curing sheds that still dot the countryside, a reminder of the days when tobacco was the main crop grown in the area – these days you're much more likely to find chestnuts, blueberries and grapevines.

SIDETRACK

Take the turn-off to Mount Buffalo National Park at Porepunkah. The park is a massive granite mountain, which was once three times its current size. Features include fantastically shaped granite boulders and cliffs, waterfalls, alpine lakes and snow-gum woodlands. In winter it is a popular tobogganing and downhill and cross-country skiing area. The road winds steeply up the mountain and there are a number of lookouts that offer sweeping views over the cliffs, across the mountains and all the way to Mount Kosciuszko.

Bright, 7km on from Porepunkah, is famous for its tree-lined avenues and autumn display, when the many stately trees in the parks, gardens and streets are ablaze with colour. Stop at one of the nice parks in town beside the Ovens River for a roadside rest or picnic. The annual ten-day Autumn Festival is held in late April and early May and includes a street parade, brass and highland bands, open gardens, a gymkhana and a ball, the Wandiligong Nut Festival – hazelnuts, walnuts and chestnuts are big around these parts – and farm tours (brightautumnfestival.org.au).

Everlasting daisies along the Great Alpine Drive

KIDS' SPOT

Need the kids to burn off some of their endless energy? The Bright Splash Park, with its four water-based play areas all themed around the gold rush, is the perfect place on a hot day. Best of all, it's free and there are plenty of nearby picnic tables for adults in the riverside parkland. Centenary Park, 125 Gavan St, Bright.

The hamlet of Wandiligong, 6km from Bright, was the site of a short-lived gold rush in the 1850s. There's not much gold left these days, but the village is classified by the National Trust. Follow the lovely walking trail along the river from Bright to Wandiligong; a highlight of the walk is a traditional Chinese swing bridge – it looks ancient but was actually built in 2003 as a tribute to the many Chinese who lived and worked on the diggings. There's also a re-created Chinese joss house in the Bright Museum (10 Railway Ave; 0429 127 444; open Sun 2–4pm, closed mid-June–early Sept).

BRIGHT TO OMEO

From Bright, the Great Alpine Road snakes its way through the valley via little villages such as Smoko, which was once surrounded by fields of tobacco. Mount Feathertop dominates the scenery and soon after Harrietville the road begins to

Great Alpine Road, Vic.

climb into the Alps. This is a spectacular part of the route: the road winds through forests of mountain ash and stringy bark that give way to stunning views of the valley below. After you enter Alpine National Park near Mount St Bernard, the road runs along the mountain ridge for about 30km, offering spectacular views on both sides; in winter, it can be icy, so care is needed.

The road passes through the ski villages of Mount Hotham and Dinner Plain before it begins to descend again to Omeo. About 40km from Dinner Plain the Victoria Falls Historic Area is signposted to the right. Victoria Falls was the site of Victoria's first hydro-electric scheme, built to provide electricity to a local mine. It's only a few minutes' drive off the main road and there's a great little picnic area beside the Victoria River.

SIDETRACK

An alternative route in summer is to travel from Bright to Omeo across the Bogong High Plains. From Bright the road cuts across beautiful farmland and gentle rolling hills to Mount Beauty, past wineries and groves of chestnut trees, before climbing up into the mountains to the ski resort of Falls Creek. It's a glorious stretch of road, skirting the edge of Rocky Valley Dam, winding among skeletal snow gums and with one sweeping view after another unfurling at each bend in the road – of which there are many. Much of the trip lies inside the boundaries of Alpine National Park, and there are plenty of places to pull off to snap photographs and admire the view or head off on a walk, such as the easy 750m stroll to Wallace Hut. Built by the Wallace brothers in 1889 from slabs of snow gum and old bits of kerosene tins, it's the oldest of the surviving High Country cattlemen's huts and is surrounded by beautiful gums. It is also, however, rickety and rustic, dark and lonely, and it's sobering to imagine the hard life these tough pioneers must have had as they spent months alone with their cattle on these windswept plains.

Take a detour to drive up to the top of Mount McKay, which at 1842m above sea level is the highest driveable point in Australia. From the grassy top gaze out over the treeless Bogong High Plains and see almost all of Victoria's highest peaks. As far as special views go, it's as good as it gets.

Once across the plains, the road descends beneath the snowline and follows babbling rivers past countless perfect picnic spots, before ending up at Anglers Rest, a popular trout-fishing spot at the convergence of three rivers, the Cobungra, Bundarra and Mitta Mitta. The historic Blue Duck Inn is just the spot to enjoy a cold drink while basking in the sunshine beside the river in the pub's front garden. The pub's name is actually a joke that stuck. Originally a butcher's shop that sold fresh meat to prospectors working the goldfields, the building was turned into a pub by a cashed-up miner in 1912, on the basis of a promise that the main road would later pass the site – which it never did. The despairing publican, Billy O'Connell, nailed a panning dish to the front of the hotel and wrote on it, in large letters and with irony, 'Blue Duck'. At the time this was a term used by miners to refer to a gold lease that produced no gold – a white elephant, in other words. (2855 Omeo Hwy, Anglers Rest; (03) 5159 7220; open Wed–Sun for lunch and dinner, Sept–May only.)

The tree-lined streets of Bright

Omeo, in the heart of rolling cattle-grazing land, is a small town that dates back to 1851. By the 1860s it was home to thousands of gold diggers and frontier cattlemen and was famous for its lawlessness. The original courthouse, where so many of the unruly diggers were once tried, is still standing, along with an 1890s post office, an 1858 log lockup, a blacksmith's shop, stables and a waterwheel – all in the historical park in the town centre. It's the country's most intact justice precinct (museum open Mon–Sun 10am–2pm).

Just out of town is the Oriental Claims Historic Area, one of the largest gold-sluicing operations in the world. It is unique in that its alluvial workings were mined for more than 50 years (from 1851) – usually alluvial gold is worked out first and quartz mines provide payable gold for longer periods. There is a 45-minute walk, called Ah Fongs Loop, through one of the richest sites in the area.

OMEO TO BAIRNSDALE AND THE COAST

The Great Alpine Road now winds its way through extensive forests, following various rivers and streams, almost all the way to Bruthen – a picturesque stretch of roughly 100km. From Bruthen it is another 24km to Bairnsdale.

Located on the banks of the Mitchell River, Bairnsdale is a sprawling town servicing the Gippsland and Lakes District. One of the most interesting places to visit here is the Krowathunkooloong Keeping Place, an Aboriginal cultural museum. Inside you'll find a collection of Aboriginal artefacts and modern art and crafts, as well as a very informative history of local Aboriginal communities. (37 Dalmahoy St, opposite the railway station; open Mon–Fri 9am–5pm.) From Bairnsdale follow the Princes Highway along the coast to Sydney or south-west to Melbourne.

BEST EATS

- **Patricia's Table** This restaurant is next to the cellar door at Brown Brothers Milawa Vineyard, and you can match the wines to delicious meals made with local produce. 239 Milawa–Bobinawarrah Rd, Milawa; (03) 5720 5540; open Mon–Sun for lunch, book ahead.
- **Milawa Cheese Factory** Here you'll find a tasting room and a licensed restaurant that's a great spot for a light lunch. 17 Factory Rd, Milawa; (03) 5727 3589; open Mon–Sun 9am–5pm.
- **Provenance** Enjoy fine dining in a grand old bank built in 1856. The menu is contemporary, a blend of French and Japanese with Australian bush flavours, and the restaurant offers exceptional service and a great local wine list. 86 Ford St, Beechworth; (03) 5728 1786; open Wed–Sun for dinner; theprovenance.com.au.
- **Bright Brewery** Overlooking the river in the heart of Bright, this brewery restaurant offers a surprisingly healthy range of meals (considering it's a brewery) as well as good-value gourmet pizzas and hand-brewed beers. 121 Great Alpine Rd, Bright; (03) 5755 1301; open Mon–Sun from 12pm until early evening; brightbrewery.com.au.

BEST SLEEPS

- **Lancemore Milawa** The spacious, elegantly furnished rooms here all have great views over vineyards towards the mountains. Opposite Brown Brothers Winery in Milawa, 223 Milawa–Bobinawarrah Rd, Milawa; (03) 5720 5777; lancemore.com.au/milawa.
- **1860** This beautifully restored 1860s cattleman's hut was relocated from the goldfields to Beechworth and has been transformed into luxury self-contained cabin accommodation. 4 Surry La, Beechworth; 0408 273 783; 1860luxuryaccommodation.com.
- **The Odd Frog** Don't let the name put you off: the pretty studios here have lovely bush views and are an easy walk from the centre of Bright. 3 McFadyens La, Bright; 0418 362 791; theoddfrog.com.au.
- **The Birches** These three spa chalets offer stunning views of Mount Beauty. Top of Ranch Rd, Mount Beauty; (03) 5754 1524; luxuryspachalets.com.au.
- **Dinner Plain Alpine Village** There are more than 200 private lodges here, ranging from cosy apartments to luxurious chalets. 1800 670 019; dinnerplainaccommodation.com.au.
- **QT Falls Creek** These five-star apartments in the heart of Falls Creek village are open year-round. 17 Bogong High Plains Rd, Falls Creek; (03) 5732 8000; qthotelsandresorts.com.
- **The Golden Age Hotel Motel** The ensuite rooms open out onto the wide verandah of this historic Art Deco pub in the centre of Omeo. 189 Day Ave, Omeo; (03) 51591344; goldenageomeo.com.au.
- **Caravanning and camping** During summer you can camp at Lake Catani in Mount Buffalo National Park, where you'll find unpowered sites suitable for car camping and small caravans or camper trailers, as well as hot showers. About 40km from Dinner Plain, the Victoria Falls Historic Area is a nice bush-camping area beside the Victoria River. The camping area at Anglers Rest near Omeo is a beautiful setting beside the Mitta Mitta River. There are also several good bush-camping spots just off the Bogong High Plains Road.

Opposite The green drive through Omeo *Left* A tasting flight of craft beer at Bright Brewery

A magical road trip through some of the best and wildest scenery Tassie has to offer.

Western Wilderness, Tas.

HOW LONG?

Take at least a week, one way, including a day or two in both Strahan and Cradle Mountain. To make the trip shorter, drive a loop from Launceston to Cradle Mountain and Strahan and cut up the middle of the state via the A5 beside the Great Lake.

WHEN TO GO

Summer is mild. Expect some snow in winter, particularly in and around Cradle Mountain. Rain is frequent on the west coast, year round. A lovely time to visit Cradle Mountain is autumn, when the deciduous beech cloaks the slopes in a deep rust red.

NEED TO KNOW

Bring your raincoat: the west coast is notoriously wet. If you are making your way around the island, you can drive the Western Explorer Road beyond Corinna up to Arthur River and Stanley: it's unsealed but fine for conventional cars and caravans (allow two to three hours). For information on ferries to Tasmania, *see* p. 163.

Drive rating
Moderate. Some unsealed roads and several steep, winding sections, but fine for conventional cars and caravans

Distances
Total distance, Hobart to Launceston via Cradle Mountain: 695km
- Hobart to Mount Field National Park: 73km
- Mount Field National Park to Strahan: 250km
- Strahan to Corinna: 93km
- Corinna to Cradle Mountain: 124km
- Cradle Mountain to Launceston: 155km

Temperatures
January: 12–21°C
July: 3–6°C

More information
- Cradle Mountain Visitor Centre, 4057 Cradle Mountain Rd, Cradle Mountain–Lake St Clair National Park; (03) 6492 1110; parks.tas.gov.au
- Hobart Visitor Information Centre, 20 Davey St, Hobart; (03) 6238 4222; hobarttravelcentre.com.au
- West Coast Visitor Information and Booking Centre, The Esplanade, Strahan; 1800 352 200; westcoasttas.com.au
- discovertasmania.com.au

Snapshot
Tasmania's rugged highlands and west coast constitute one of the world's wildest places, a sparsely inhabited region with craggy mountain ranges, 2000-year-old trees, wild rivers and great swaths of national parks. This week-long drive takes you deep into the wilderness. Be warned, though, there's a lot to see and do on this road trip: it may not look that far on a map, but it will take much more time than you think. Take it easy and enjoy the journey.

Opposite Tasmania's iconic Cradle Mountain

Temma

Balfour

West Takone

Henrietta

Highclere

Ulverstone   Turners Beach

Gawler   Riana   Northo Motton

DEVONPORT   Spreyton

Don

Latrobe

STATE FOREST

Oonah   Hampshire

SAVAGE RIVER NATIONAL PARK

Parrawe

ARTHUR–PIEMAN CONSERVATION AREA

Guildford

Loongana

Gunns Plains

South Nietta

STATE FOREST   Loyetea

Sprent

Topiary sculptures

Murals   Sheffield   Railton

Waratah

B23

Discovery Parks Cradle Mountain campground

Lake Barrington

Roland

Beulah

Gowrie Park

Mole Creek

Savage River

A10   124

Wilderness Gallery

Moina

Lake Cethana

Corinna Wilderness Experience & camping area

The Tarkine Hotel

Wilderness Retreats & Pete's Place

Peppers Cradle Mountain Lodge

Peppers Cradle Mountain Lodge cheese & wine tastings

Peppers Cradle Mountain Lodge

Pieman Heads

Corinna

Whyte River Walk & Pieman River Cruises

Overland Track

Crater Lake

Dove Lake Loop Track

Lake Rosebery

Lake Mackintosh

Marion's Lookout

Dove Lake

Lake Pieman

Cradle Mountain

Lake Plimsoll

Lake Rosebery   Tullah

GRANITE TOR CONSERVATION AREA

Roseberry

Renison Bell

Lake Murchison

Lake Rowallan

West Coast Heritage Centre

Zeehan

Remine (Trial Harbour)

93

A10

B27

CRADLE MOUNTAIN–LAKE ST CLAIR NATIONAL PARK

Mount Ossa

TASMANIAN WILDERNESS WORLD HERITAGE AREA

SOUTHERN

Ocean Beach

West Coast Wilderness Railway

Queenstown

Lake St Clair

Cynthia Bay Lake Walk

Cynthia Bay campground

View 42° Restaurant & Bar & Hamer's Hotel

Gordon River Cruises

Strahan Village Hotel

Strahan

B24

Overland Track

Lake St Clair Lodge

The Wall in the Wilderness

Penguins & short-tailed shearwaters

Bonnet Island

West Coast Wilderness Railway

Lake Burbury

Derwent Bridge

A10

Macquarie Heads

STATE FOREST

250

A10

OCEAN

Macquarie Harbour

Lake King William

Tarraleah

Sarah Island

FRANKLIN–GORDON WILD RIVERS NATIONAL PARK

Lake Catagunya

Warners Landing & Sir John Falls

SOUTHWEST CONSERVATION AREA

Lake Gordon

MOUNT FIELD NATIONAL PARK

Lake Dobson

SOUTHWEST CONSERVATION AREA

ADAMSFIELD CONSERVATION AREA

TASMANIAN WILDERNESS WORLD HERITAGE AREA

Strathgordon

B61

SOUTHWEST NATIONAL PARK

Lake Pedder

0   10   20   30   40
Kilometres

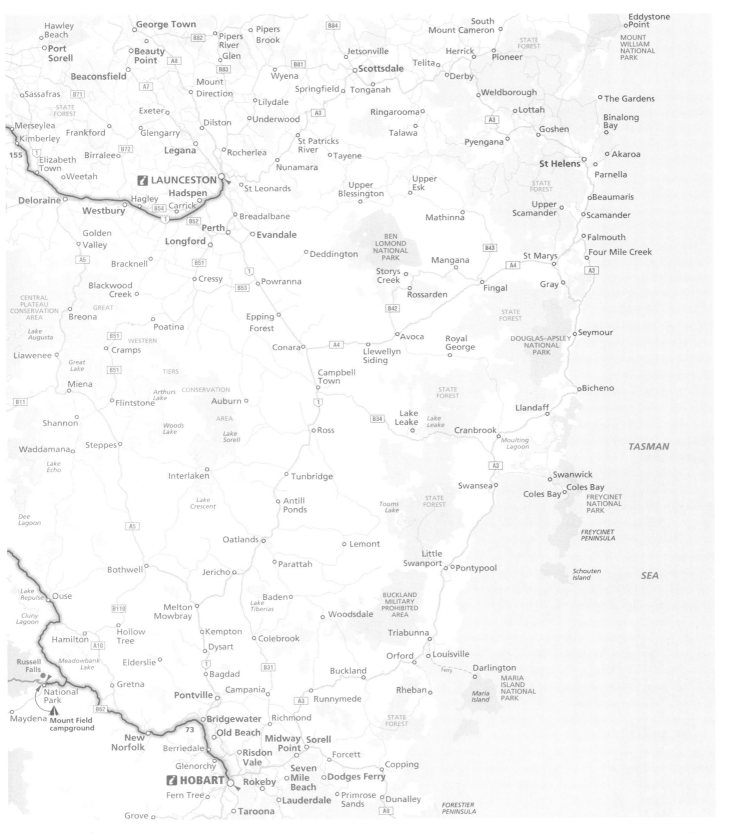

HOBART TO LAKE ST CLAIR

Begin in Hobart and follow the signs to Launceston before turning off to New Norfolk and Lake St Clair on the Lyell Highway. It's a pretty drive that will take about four hours, through the Derwent Valley, past farmlands, hop fields, forests and remnants of rainforest.

SIDETRACK

Take a short detour to Mount Field National Park. Tasmania's oldest national park and one of its most popular, it has a rich variety of vegetation, ranging from tall swamp-gum forests (some of the tallest trees in the world) and immense tree ferns to rainforest, pandani groves, sphagnum bogs and alpine tarns at the top of the mountain. Highlights include beautiful three-tiered Russell Falls, Lake Dobson and lots of wildlife.

Back on the road, make a quick stop at the Wall in the Wilderness in Derwent Bridge, just before the turn-off to Lake St Clair. It's still a work in progress, but when it's finished the wall will be a 100m long, 3m high sculpture in huon pine depicting the history of Tasmania's central highlands. (15352 Lyell Hwy, Derwent Bridge; (03) 6289 1134; open Mon–Sun 9am–5pm during summer daylight savings, Mon–Sun 9am–4pm for the rest of the year; thewalltasmania.com.au.)

Your next stop is Lake St Clair, just up the road. Carved out by glaciers over the last two million years, Lake St Clair is the deepest lake in Australia. Located at the southern end of Cradle Mountain–Lake St Clair National Park, it's the terminus of the six-day, 65km Overland Track, the island's major long-distance walk, but you don't have to slog it out on foot to get there: it's just a few minutes' drive from the township of Derwent Bridge. There's a lovely (short) walk you can do around the lakeshore at Cynthia Bay – if you're lucky you might even see an echidna or a platypus. If you want to see more, take the ferry to the northern end of the lake and take a short walk into the rainforest from there.

LAKE ST CLAIR TO STRAHAN

The drive from Lake St Clair to Strahan is simply spectacular. The first 80km section winds through the Franklin–Gordon Wild Rivers National Park, where it seems as if a new jagged-edged mountain rises up around every curve of the road. The contrast when you reach Queenstown is quite shocking. Here alpine wilderness has been transformed to a moonscape of treeless, eroded hills whose vegetation has been killed by almost 100 years of tree-felling, sulphurous pollution from smelters, and bushfires (although the vegetation has slowly started to make a comeback in recent years). Bizarre as it is, the landscape does have a certain kind of strange and unique beauty, and the steep drive down the mountain's hairpin turns is quite exciting.

It's 37km further to Strahan, situated beside the sea at the mouth of Macquarie Harbour, the second biggest natural harbour in Australia. This is the jumping-off place for Gordon River Cruises and, if you do only one thing in Strahan, do this. This serenely beautiful riverine wilderness is largely untouched and inaccessible except by air, on foot or via the river. It was preserved thanks to the efforts of conservationists in the early 1980s, who fought vigorously against a proposed hydro-electric dam on the Gordon River. Over three months about 6000 of them blockaded the river and construction roads, mostly at Warners Landing, 6km from the junction of the Franklin and Gordon rivers. The protest not only saved two of the world's most beautiful rivers, but effectively kick-started the Green Movement in Australia. Most cruises include a stop at the former convict settlement of Sarah Island. (Morning cruises depart Mon–Sun, additional afternoon cruises available in January; gordonrivercruises.com.au; worldheritagecruises.com.au.)

You can also take a twilight tour out to tiny Bonnet Island at the mouth of Macquarie Harbour and learn about what it's like to live in one of the wildest, wettest and stormiest places on Earth. A highlight is watching the little penguins and short-tailed shearwaters return to their burrows at dusk (gordonrivercruises.com.au).

SIDETRACK

Take a drive out to Ocean Beach. Stretching for more than 30km from Macquarie Heads in the south to Trial Harbour in the north, Ocean Beach is the longest beach in Tasmania. Thousands of shearwaters (muttonbirds) breed here during summer and provide an amazing wildlife spectacle each night at dusk as they return from their feeding forays over the ocean. Follow the walkway over the dunes to a viewing platform. To get to Ocean Beach, drive out of Strahan towards Zeehan and turn left at the first intersection past the caravan park. Follow this road for 4km and park behind the dunes.

😊 KIDS' SPOT

Ride into the wild on the thrilling West Coast Wilderness Railway, a historic Apt (rack and pinion) steam-train trip on a 35km railway of tight curves and spectacular bridges through the dense rainforest and steep gorges between Strahan and Queenstown. Trains run daily and a coach will take you back to Strahan at the end of the day. Over 18s can dress up in a pair of borrowed overalls and a cap and ride up front on the footplate, working with the driver as part of the half-day Footplate Experience. 1 Driffield St, Queenstown and/or 62 Esplanade, Strahan; (03) 6471 0100; wcwr.com.au.

Opposite A well-earned dip in Lake St Clair *Above* The picturesque lighthouse of Bonnet Island

STRAHAN TO CORINNA

Corinna, approximately 93km north of Strahan via mostly unsealed roads (allow two hours) and ferry, is one of those secret places that seems to have well and truly slipped beneath the tourist radar, despite being surrounded by some of the most beautiful, ethereal and enchanting rainforest on the planet. Even though the unsealed road is fine for normal cars, it's enough, it seems, to put most people off.

Stop en route at the West Coast Heritage Centre, in the small mining township of Zeehan, for an excellent look at local history, especially mining. The museum is larger than it looks, with 14 galleries in all. (114 Main St, Zeehan; (03) 6471 6225; open Mon–Sun 9.30am–4.30pm; wchczeehan.com.au.)

There are no shops in Corinna; in fact, there's not much at all, except a pub and some rustic-looking cabins. But it wasn't always this sleepy. When a gold nugget weighing almost 7kg (the biggest ever found in Tasmania) was discovered nearby in 1883, it sparked a huge gold rush, and Corinna boomed. The town boasted more than 30 buildings, including two pubs, one on either side of the Pieman River. The gold rush was short lived, however, and by the early 1900s the town was pretty much abandoned.

Today Corinna is the only surviving remote-area historic mining settlement in Tasmania. Only three of the original buildings remain: the old pub, the butcher's shop and a cottage, and all three are available as accommodation, along with 16 new cabins, called 'wilderness retreats'. A network of walking trails, of varying difficulty, passes just metres from these cabins. One of the best is the hour-long Whyte River Walk, which loops around from the cabins to the barge-crossing through a magical forest of myrtle, sassafras, huon pine and fairytale fungi. It's a beautiful way to start your day – the river is like glass, the trees are sheathed in tendrils of mist and fat pademelons are still too sleepy to get out of your way.

The Pieman River is every bit as beautiful as the Gordon River in Strahan and a half-day cruise on the huon-pine *Arcadia II* to Pieman Heads at the river mouth is well worth the splurge. A cheaper DIY alternative is to hire kayaks and head off on your own – the staff will even pick up your kayaks if you want to paddle down the river for a couple of hours then walk back through the rainforest.

CORINNA TO CRADLE MOUNTAIN

From Corinna, head north-east to Cradle Mountain. The drive takes about two hours or so, depending on conditions – beware of wildlife on the road and icy sections in winter.

The craggy peaks of Cradle Mountain are among the most photographed in the country and the valley is the starting point for the famous six-day Overland Track walk, which leads through the heart of some of Australia's finest mountain terrain. Ancient rainforests, alpine heath, buttongrass plains, stands of colourful deciduous beech, icy streams, rocky mountains – including Tassie's highest, Mount Ossa – and a wealth of wildlife are just some of the highlights. Fortunately there are also numerous day walks for all levels of fitness and enthusiasm. A favourite is the easy two-hour Dove Lake Loop Track, which takes you under the shadow of Cradle Mountain through the tranquil Ballroom Forest and back along the western shore of the lake. If you're keen for a climb, join the Overlanders on the chain-assisted trek to the top of Marion's Lookout (1223m) at the base of Cradle Mountain. The views from the top over Crater and Dove lakes are superb. Allow about four hours return.

Even if you don't want to walk, take the park shuttle bus from the visitor centre to Dove Lake for spectacular (depending on the weather) views of Cradle Mountain. And don't miss the Wilderness Gallery, next door to Cradle Mountain Hotel. With ten separate gallery rooms, it's the largest privately owned photographic gallery in Australia and all of the exhibits are inspirational – the type of photography that makes you long to step inside the frame and be part of the landscape within it. While many of the images focus on Tasmanian landscapes, there is also a program of changing exhibitions from around the world, a movie room with all-day screenings of Tasmanian films and a permanent display on the thylacine, or Tasmanian tiger, which includes recorded footage of the last known tiger and recordings of the stories of old trappers, played in a re-created trappers' hut. (3718 Cradle Mountain Rd, Cradle Mountain; (03) 6492 1404; open Mon–Sun 9am–5pm; wildernessgallery.com.au.)

From Cradle Mountain, it will take about two and a half hours to drive to Launceston (*see* p. 163). Good places to stop on the way include Sheffield, with its bright and colourful murals, and Railton, where many front yards have quirky topiary sculptures. In between the two towns you'll see vast fields of white poppies – Tasmania is the only state in Australia permitted to grow opium poppies as a crop.

BEST EATS

- **Hamer's Hotel** While away an afternoon just sitting by the fire here, enjoying a bowl of soup and watching the fishing boats laden with craypots dock at the wharf. 31 Esplanade, Strahan; (03) 6471 4335; open Mon–Sun for lunch and dinner.
- **View 42° Restaurant & Bar** It's a bit of a steep walk up to the top of the hill, but the view of Strahan and the harbour from the restaurant is worth it alone. In summer the seafood buffet is hard to resist. 1 Jolly St, Strahan; (03) 6471 4361; open Mon–Sun for dinner.
- **The Tarkine Hotel** As well as serving lunch and dinner, the hotel has a communal undercover barbecue area and often organises barbecue nights. Corinna; (03) 6446 1170; open Mon–Sun for lunch and dinner during summer.
- **Peppers Cradle Mountain Lodge** Each day the lodge holds a cheese- and wine-tasting, consisting of six handcrafted wines accompanied by three boutique cheeses, in the lodge lounge. The Highland Restaurant, also part of the lodge, serves dinner daily, but you'll need to book. 4038 Cradle Mountain Rd, Cradle Mountain; (03) 6492 2103; cradlemountainlodge.com.au.

BEST SLEEPS

- **Lake St Clair Lodge** The lodge has loft-style, two-bedroom cottages on the shoreline of Lake St Clair, each with a fireplace, and there is a restaurant on-site. Lake St Clair Rd, Derwent Bridge; (03) 6289 1137; lakestclairlodge.com.au.
- **Strahan Village Hotel** The spacious motel-style rooms high on the hill overlook the harbour. It's a bit of a steep walk up from the village centre (and reception, which is also at the bottom of the hill), but there is a carpark behind the hotel. And the views are fantastic. There are some renovated cottages on the waterfront if you don't fancy the hill-top. 41 Esplanade, Strahan; (03) 6471 4200; strahanvillage.com.au.
- **Corinna Wilderness Retreats** The cabins here have been built to blend in with the township's original buildings, so they have rusty tin roofs and rough-hewn timber exteriors. But inside they are much more comfortable than they look, each having a small kitchen, gas fireplace, ensuite and verandah that opens out onto the rainforest. You can also stay in Pete's Place, one of the settlement's three original buildings (it was the road patrolman's cottage until the 1960s). 1 Corrina Rd, Corrina; (03) 6446 1170; corinna.com.au.
- **Peppers Cradle Mountain Lodge** Upmarket accommodation is available here in tastefully decorated timber cabins that encircle the lodge, many of which have spas and most of which have great views. The lodge also offers a range of guided activities in and around the national park. 4038 Cradle Mountain Rd, Cradle Mountain; (03) 6492 2100; cradlemountainlodge.com.au.
- **Caravanning and camping** Camping and caravan sites are available near the entrance to Mount Field National Park, by the Tyena River; facilities include power, laundry and electric barbecues. At Lake St Clair you can camp at Cynthia Bay, where there are showers and laundry facilities. Strahan has a number of caravan parks, and you can park the van or camp at Corinna; the sites are unpowered but some have unimpeded river views. Camping is not permitted inside the day visitor area at Cradle Mountain, but there is a commercial campground 3km outside the park (Discovery Parks Cradle Mountain, Cradle Mountain Rd; (03) 6492 1395; discoveryholidayparks.com.au).

The rustic exteriors of Corinna Wilderness Retreats cabins hide a warm and cosy interior

Get back to nature on Western Australia's wild and wonderful southern coast between Perth and Esperance, where the tall forests meet the sea on one of the country's most scenic sections of coastline.

South-West, WA

HOW LONG?

Allow a week, one way; it will take about eight hours to drive back to Perth if you do it straight. For a scenic weekend road trip, drive cape to cape along Caves Road in the Margaret River region.

WHEN TO GO?

Summer is normally dry and warm, although tempered by sea breezes. Almost all the region's rain falls during the winter months, but winter is the best time to see whales. For wildflowers, visit in spring: the peak flowering time is August to November.

NEED TO KNOW

Fallen trees may sometimes block roads in the national parks of the South-West, so allow plenty of time for drives in case you find yourself needing to backtrack.

 Drive rating
Easy. Mostly sealed roads

 Distances
Total distance, return to Perth: 1901km
- Perth to Esperance via the coast: 1130km
- Perth to Margaret River: 268km
- Margaret River to Augusta: 43km
- Augusta to Albany: 364km
- Albany to Esperance: 474km
- Esperance to Perth (direct): 715km

 Temperatures
January: 14–25°C
July: 7–16°C

 More information
- Albany Visitor Centre, 221 York St, Albany; (08) 6820 3700; theamazingsouthcoast.com
- Esperance Visitor Centre, in the Historic Museum Village, cnr Dempster and Kemp sts, Esperance; 1300 664 455; visitesperance.com
- Margaret River Visitor Centre, 100 Bussell Hwy, Margaret River; (08) 9757 5911; margaretriver.com

 Snapshot
The south-western corner of Western Australia includes the Margaret River wine region, a stretch of rugged coastline where the Indian and Southern oceans meet, with towering old-growth jarrah and karri forests. To the east, the area known as the Great Southern region includes the beautiful Stirling Range, more wineries and the town of Albany, the oldest European settlement in Western Australia. Even further east, the beautiful turquoise coastline continues to Esperance.

Opposite top left Hiking towards Bluff Knoll *Top right* Cormorants at Wilson Inlet, near Denmark *Bottom left* Amazing wildflower of Dryandra Woodland *Bottom right* Wyadip Beach near Yallingup

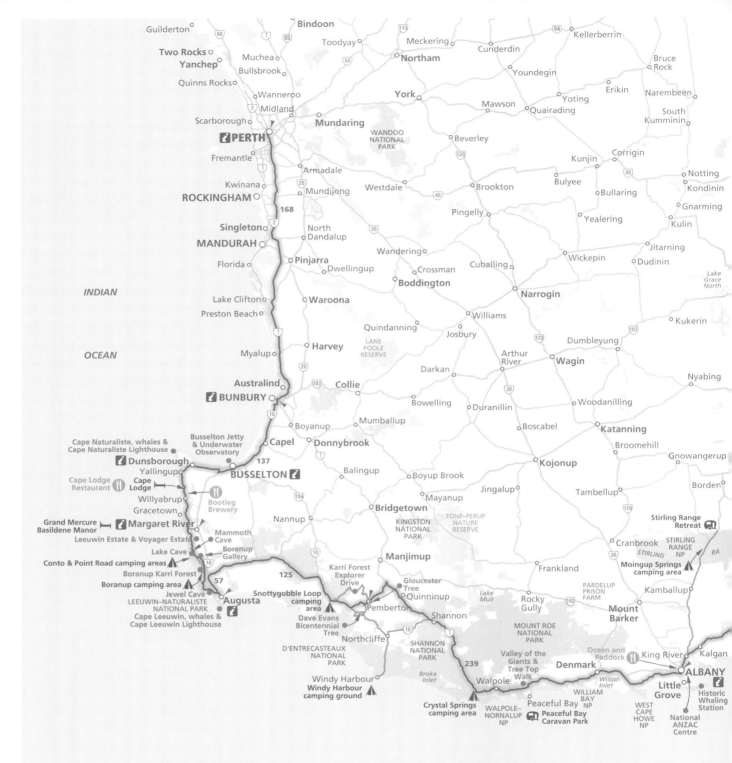

☺ KIDS' SPOT

Delve into a waterworld by visiting the underwater observatory at the end of Busselton Jetty. Take the guided tour and descend 8m below the surface to an observation chamber where you will see vividly coloured corals, sponges, fish and other sea creatures. Busselton beachfront; (08) 9754 0900; open Mon–Sun, tours depart on the hour 9am–4pm end Sept – end April, 10am–3pm May – end Sept; busseltonjetty.com.au.

PERTH TO MARGARET RIVER

Perth to Margaret River is about a three-hour drive. Stretch your legs at Busselton by walking the 2km heritage-listed wooden jetty – the longest in the Southern Hemisphere. If you don't feel like walking, there's a miniature train.

Say Margaret River and most people automatically think 'great wine'. And rightly so. The Margaret River region, a wild knob of land jutting into the sea off the bottom corner of Western Australia, bounded in the north by Cape Naturaliste and in the south by Cape Leeuwin, is home to some of the finest white wines produced in Australia (and plenty of terrific reds). But it also has some great art galleries, beautiful scenery, wildflowers, deserted beaches and fine food. And much of the coastline is protected as part of Leeuwin–Naturaliste National Park, which stretches 120km from Bunker Bay in the north to Augusta in the south.

The best way to explore the region is along Caves Road, a 110km scenic drive that stretches from cape to cape. The township of Margaret River is roughly in the middle and makes a good base. In the north, Caves Road begins at Cape Naturaliste. Take a tour of the lighthouse here or walk around the headland to enjoy views of the coastline and, depending on the time of year, possibly spot some migrating whales. Running south, the road cuts through the heart of the main wine-producing area. There are about 50 wineries clumped together in a stretch of around 15km.

Two of the most popular cellar doors are just a few minutes south of Margaret River township, on Stevens Road. Leeuwin Estate is set in bushland and its winery is constructed of natural timber, wrought iron and long sweeping curves of corrugated iron; like many of the wineries in Margaret River, it also has an art gallery (Stevens Rd; (08) 9759 0000; open Mon–Sun 10am–5pm; leeuwinestate.com.au). Practically next door is Voyager Estate, with its faux Cape Dutch architecture and extensive formal gardens (41 Stevens Rd; (08) 9757 6354; open Mon–Sun 10am–5pm; voyagerestate.com.au). Both wineries have excellent restaurants and offer tours and tastings at their cellar doors.

Opposite Cape Leeuwin, where two oceans meet *Left* Cape Naturaliste lighthouse

In Margaret River itself, wander through several rooms with handmade furniture, sculptures and paintings at Boranup Gallery (7981 Caves Rd, Margaret River; (08) 9757 7585; open Mon–Sun 10am–4pm; boranupgallery.com).

The limestone ridge of the Leeuwin–Naturaliste National Park hides a series of caves, many of which are open to the public. Explore Calgardup, Giants and Mammoth caves on your own (you'll need a torch) or join a tour – the most popular are Jewel Cave just north of Augusta, home to one of the longest straw stalactites to be found in any tourist cave; Lake Cave near Margaret River, which has some beautiful reflections; and the richly decorated Ngilgi Cave just north of Yallingup. Book tours at the visitor centre in Margaret River.

SIDETRACK

Take a detour off Caves Road, winding your way through the Boranup Karri Forest on Boranup Drive. Stop to enjoy a short walk through the tall trees.

Continue south past barely-there beachside communities as you head towards Cape Leeuwin, the most south-westerly tip of Australia. The lighthouse here has watched over the point where the Indian and Southern oceans meet since 1895. It's the perfect place to watch whales off the shore, and during spring masses of beautiful wildflowers dot the windswept headland.

AUGUSTA TO ALBANY

Head east to Pemberton. This is big-tree country, and the state's most famous tree, the Gloucester Tree, is 3km from Pemberton in Gloucester National Park. This 61m high giant karri made a great lookout to help spot forest fires in the 1930s and 1940s. Back then you had to get to the top the hard way, using special boots and a belt, but these days there's a spiral of iron spikes embedded in the trunk. Be warned though, it's harder (and scarier) than it looks, and less than a quarter of all those who try to climb the tree make it to the top.

There's an even bigger giant in Warren National Park, about 15 minutes' drive south-west of Pemberton: the Dave Evans Bicentennial Tree, another colossal karri, is a whopping 75m high, and you can climb it too, if you're game.

SIDETRACK

The two famous lookout trees are both part of the Karri Forest Explorer Drive, an 86km loop drive from Pemberton. It's largely unsealed, and there are some steep sections, like the descriptively named Heartbreak Trail (not suitable for caravans or motorhomes), a one-way side-trip loop above and beside the Warren River.

SIDETRACK

If you have a 4WD, spend some time exploring D'Entrecasteaux National Park. Pronounced don-truh-cast-oh, with the stress on the oh, it is named in honour of French explorer Bruni D'Entrecasteaux, who charted this coastline on a scientific expedition in 1792. The park is popular with anglers, who come here to fish from the rocks, beaches and riverbanks, and off-roaders, who like to tackle the sand dunes and sandy tracks. If you're looking for a rugged and remote coastal park where you can get away from it all, this is the one for you.

Follow the South Western Highway to Walpole and the Valley of the Giants in Walpole-Nornalup National Park – a forest of towering karri and tingle trees. Some, particularly the red tingle, are as high as 75m, with a base circumference of 20m. The best way to really get to grips with just how big these majestic trees are is to take the Tree Top Walk, which leads you along a 420m steel-truss tree-top walkway up and over a deep red tingle gully. Below, a boardwalk winds through a grove of tingle trees known as the Ancient Empire, some of which are 400 years old. One of the unique things about the red tingle trees is that, despite their towering height, they don't have a tap root; instead, they have a shallow root system that spreads as they grow older, causing the trees to buttress. Some are split or hollowed out at the base, forming huge woody arches and tunnels you can walk through. (Valley of the Giants Rd, Nornalup; (08) 9840 8263; open Mon–Sun 9am–5pm, last entry 4.15pm, with extended opening hours from 8am last entry 5.15pm, 26 Dec – 26 Jan; valleyofthegiants.com.au.)

From the Valley of the Giants it will take roughly 90 minutes to get to Albany – that is, if you don't get sidetracked by one of the numerous roads that branch off to stunning beaches in national parks like William Bay and West Cape Howe along the way.

Albany is a pretty town on King George Sound. Founded in 1827 by a party of 21 soldiers and 23 convicts who arrived on the *Amity*, it is the oldest town in Western Australia. It was also the last place to stop commercial whaling on mainland Australia, in November 1978. Join a guided tour of the Historic Whaling Station to learn about the history of whaling and conservation and climb aboard the last whalechaser boat in Australia (81 Whaling Station Rd, Frenchman Bay; (08) 9844 4021; open Mon–Sun 9am–5pm,

guided 40-minute tours run on the hour 10am–3pm and are included with ticket entry; discoverybay.com.au). Albany was also the final departure point for the first ANZAC troops on their way to the battlefields of World War I and the National ANZAC Centre is both a moving memorial and a fascinating museum that retells the story of the ANZACs and the conflict they fought in (67 Forts Rd, Albany; (08) 6820 3500; open Mon–Sun 9am–5pm, last entry 4pm; nationalanzaccentre.com.au).

ALBANY TO ESPERANCE

Follow the South Coast Highway towards Esperance.

SIDETRACK

One of few truly rugged mountain ranges in the west, the Stirling Range is also one of only a small number of areas in Western Australia that is high enough, and cold enough, to receive dustings of snow in winter – sometimes as much as 5cm on the highest peaks. About an hour's drive north-east of Albany, it's also one of the world's most important areas for wildflowers, with 1500 species (many of which grow nowhere else) packed within its boundaries. The 42km long Stirling Range Road is a very scenic unsealed road that cuts through the heart of the range, linking up with the sealed Chester Pass Road.

Opposite Karri Forest Explorer drive *Above* Valley of the Giants Tree Top Walk in Walpole-Nornalup National Park

SIDETRACK

Take a 60km detour off the South Coast Highway to Bremer Bay (or follow Borden–Bremer Bay Road from Chester Pass Road if you are approaching from the Stirling Range). This little seaside town is a gem of a place that the developers seem to have overlooked. Heaven knows why, as it's surrounded by stunning beaches with rolling surf, great expanses of sand dunes and views that stretch forever.

SIDETRACK

The highway skirts the edge of Fitzgerald River National Park, one of the most diverse botanical regions in the world. More than 1800 beautiful and bizarre species of flowering plants thrive here, nearly 20 per cent of the state's plant species. You can't miss the brightly coloured royal hakea, which towers above the surrounding plains, or the pretty qualup bell, which is not found anywhere else. Other highlights of this large tract of coastal wilderness include deserted beaches with 4WD access; inland lakes and rivers; cliffs full of sea-sponge fossils; and whale-watching at Point Ann, site of two whale-watching platforms, where southern right whales come to calve in large numbers in the bay's calm waters between June and October (the best access is from Bremer Bay but the road is not suitable for caravans or large motorhomes).

SIDETRACK

Hamersley Drive is a scenic unsealed drive bisecting the eastern section of Fitzgerald River National Park, which will bring you out at the coast not far from Hopetoun. Allow at least an hour for the 57km drive, longer if you like photographing wildflowers along the way. The road is fine for 2WD but not suitable for caravans or large motorhomes.

Once back on the highway near Ravensthorpe, it will take about two hours to get to Esperance. Take a drive around the aptly named Great Ocean Drive on the outskirts of town, which traces the sweeping curves of the coastline and offers views every bit as impressive as those on that other great ocean drive in Victoria, without the crumbling rock stacks of course – or the traffic. With dazzling white sand lapped by turquoise water, the beaches are so implausibly picture-perfect they look Photoshopped.

Head out to Cape Le Grand National Park, approximately 50km south-east of Esperance by sealed roads, to see whether Lucky Bay has really the whitest beach in Australia – similar claims are made for Whitehaven Beach in the Whitsundays and Hyams Beach in Jervis Bay in New South Wales, but the locals here say it has been 'scientifically proven'! There are some great bay-to-bay walking trails along the cliff-tops, where sea eagles soar above carpets of brightly coloured banksias and other wildflowers in full bloom during late winter and early spring.

From Esperance you can head north for 200km or so to Norseman. There you can hook up with the Eyre Highway, which runs east across the Nullarbor (*see* p. 27), or continue north to pick up the Great Eastern Highway and circle back to Perth.

Stirling Range Drive

BEST EATS

- **Cape Lodge** If you are serious about your food and wine, the chef's dinner here (Feb–Dec) is not to be missed – but it is only on Sundays. It's even better when you include a private cooking class with the chef. 3341 Caves Rd, Yallingup; (08) 9755 6311; open Mon–Sun for dinner, bookings essential; capelodge.com.au.
- **Bootleg Brewery** Try the gourmet venison burger or a beery beef hot-pot pie and a couple of glasses of light wheat beer in the grassy lakeside beer garden. Cnr Puzey and Johnson rds, Willyabrup, near Margaret River; (08) 9755 6300; open Mon–Sun for lunch and dinner; bootlegbrewery.com.au.
- **Ocean and Paddock** Two-time winner of the Best Fish and Chips in Western Australia, this restaurant serves seafood only from sustainable fisheries. 116 Middleton Ave, Albany; (08) 9842 6212; open Fri–Sun for lunch, Wed–Sun for dinner; oceanandpaddock.com.au.
- **Mount Barren Restaurant** Head here for just-caught local seafood and great steaks. Bremer Bay Resort, 1 Frantom Way, Bremer Bay; (08) 9837 4133; open Mon–Sun for lunch and dinner.
- **Taylor Street Quarters** This breezy waterside bistro offers classic pub meals in a former hospital that was relocated from Fremantle in the 1930s. 1 Taylor Street Jetty, Esperance; 0457 232 039; open Wed–Sun for lunch and dinner, Sat–Sun for breakfast.

BEST SLEEPS

- **Cape Lodge** It's the perfect combination of luxury accommodation and gourmet food, but it doesn't come cheap. 3341 Caves Rd, Yallingup; (08) 9755 6311; capelodge.com.au.
- **Grand Mercure Basildene Manor** This boutique manor house hotel with beautiful gardens is about five minutes' drive from Margaret River. 187 Wallcliffe Rd, Margaret River; (08) 9757 3140; basildenemanor.com.au.
- **Bremer Bay Beaches Resort and Tourist Park** This resort offers comfortable spa cabins (and caravan sites and campsites) and is within easy walking distance of beautiful beaches. Wellstead Rd, Bremer Bay; (08) 9837 4290; bremerbaybeaches.com.au.
- **The Jetty Resort** There's a range of room types at this family-run hotel, from motel rooms and family rooms to two-bedroom apartments. It's opposite the beach and some rooms have ocean views. 1 The Esplanade, Esperance; (08) 9071 3333; thejettyresort.com.au.

- **Caravanning and camping** The best campsites in Leeuwin–Naturaliste National Park are at Conto and Boranup campgrounds; both have toilets, barbecues, tables, water and individual sites in the bush. The Point Road campground at the northern end of Boranup Drive is 4WD only.

There are a number of campsites scattered throughout D'Entrecasteaux National Park, but you'll need a 4WD to access the coastal ones, apart from the camping ground at Windy Harbour (Windy Harbour Rd; (08) 9776 8398; unpowered sites only) and beneath the peppermints at Crystal Springs, both of which are accessible to 2WD vehicles. In neighbouring Hawke National Park there are campgrounds at Snottygobble Loop and Grass Tree Hollow.

Not far from the Valley of the Giants, there is a good, if a little rustic, caravan park at Peaceful Bay, which has large grassy powered sites just behind the beach (Peaceful Bay Rd; (08) 9840 8060).

In the Stirling Range you can camp at Moingup Springs, just off Chester Pass Road in the heart of the national park, where facilities include gas barbecues. Stirling Range Retreat, on the boundary of the park opposite the Bluff Knoll turn-off, has caravan sites and a camping area as well as self-contained cabins (Chester Pass Rd; (08) 9827 9229; stirlingrange.com.au).

In Fitzgerald River National Park, St Mary Inlet is a sheltered site behind the sand dunes near Point Ann, and Hamersley Inlet (also in the park) is a lovely lakeside camping spot. All the park's campgrounds have toilets and gas barbecues, but no drinking water.

In Cape Le Grand National Park near Esperance there are two beachside campgrounds, both with solar-powered hot showers: Lucky Bay has a boat ramp and large (unpowered) caravan sites with a great view overlooking the beach, while Le Grand Beach has small sites tucked behind a dune.

Follow the course of Australia's greatest river from its Snowy Mountains source to the sea off the coast of South Australia.

Murray River, NSW, Vic. and SA

HOW LONG?

Allow at least a week. If you want to cut it short, begin the trip at Albury: Lake Hume might not be the natural source of the river, but, given that it's the main storage reservoir and the water releases from here dictate the river levels and flows all the way downstream to the mouth 2225km away, it's close enough.

WHEN TO GO

Spring to autumn is best. Winter is generally wetter than summer and sees plentiful snow in the High Country.

NEED TO KNOW

All vehicles travelling through Kosciuszko National Park must have an entry permit, even if you do not intend to stop in the park. Permits are available at the national park entrance station on the Alpine Way, 13km before Thredbo, or the National Parks Visitor Centre in Khancoban. Snow chains must be carried between 1 June and 10 October on the Alpine Way between Thredbo and Tom Groggin. You cannot enter South Australia with fruit or vegetables of any type. For more details on fruit-fly exclusion zones, see murrayriver.com.au/fruit-fly-free-zone.

Opposite A quiet moment at Barmah Lakes

 Drive rating
Easy. Sealed roads

 Distances
Total distance, Jindabyne to Goolwa: 1450km
- Jindabyne to Echuca: 484km
- Echuca to Mildura: 377km
- Mildura to Goolwa via Mannum: 561km

 Temperatures
January: 18–32°C
July: 5–16°C

 More information
- Albury Visitor Information Centre, Railway Place, cnr Smollet and Young sts, Albury; 1300 252 879; visitalburywodonga.com
- Echuca Moama Visitor Information Centre, 2 Heygarth St, Echuca; 1800 804 446; echucamoama.com
- Khancoban Visitor Centre, cnr Scammell St and Alpine Way, Khancoban; (02) 6076 9373
- Mildura Visitor Information Centre, 180 Deakin Ave, Mildura; 1800 039 043; visitmildura.com.au
- Renmark Paringa Visitor Information Centre, 84 Murray Ave, Renmark; 1300 661 704
- Snowy Region Visitor Centre, 49 Kosciuszko Rd, Jindabyne; (02) 6450 5600
- visitthemurray.com.au
- murrayriver.com.au

 Snapshot
Before railways crisscrossed the land, the country's waterways were the only way to transport goods from remote inland settlements to the ports on the coast, and the Murray River was the country's greatest highway – Australia's Mississippi. And while it may be home to more houseboats than paddlesteamers these days, it is still a lifeline and focus of industry for a string of communities running from southern New South Wales to western South Australia. From its source in the Snowy Mountains in New South Wales, the Murray River flows more than 2500km west to seep into the sea near Goolwa in South Australia.

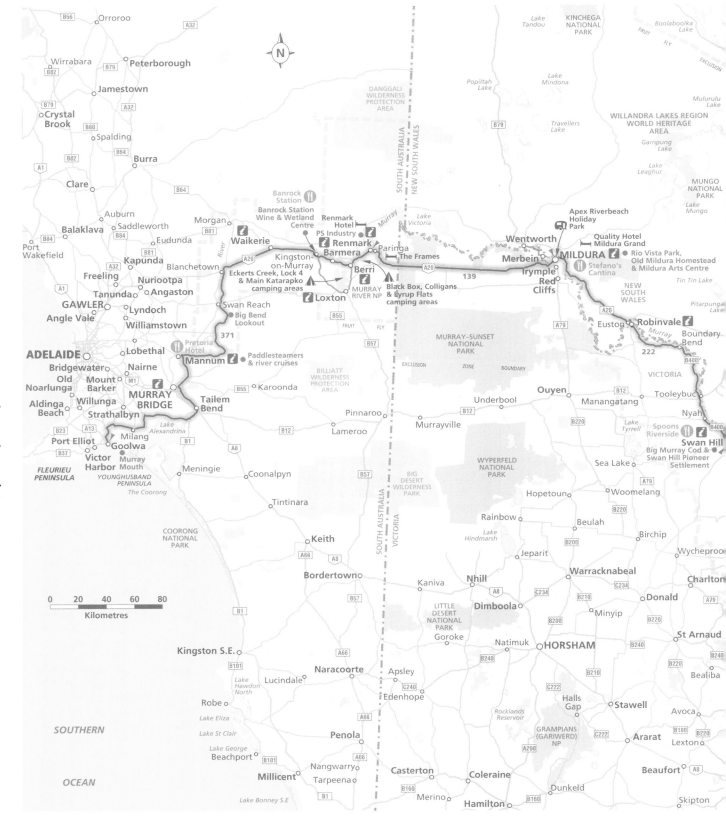

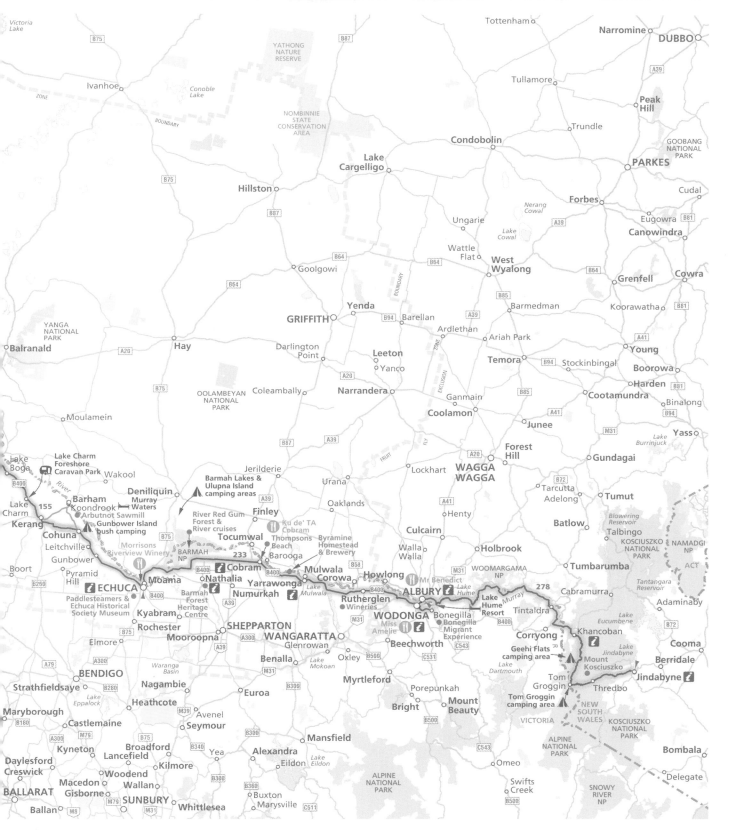

JINDABYNE TO ECHUCA

The source of the Murray is 40km south of Mount Kosciuszko in Victoria, but Jindabyne in the New South Wales Snowy Mountains makes a logical place to start this drive. Follow the Alpine Way through Kosciuszko National Park to Thredbo and Khancoban (*see* p. 211). Although the Tom Groggin camping area, 19km west of Thredbo, is on the Upper Murray, you won't really start to follow the river proper until you cross the state border into Victoria a few kilometres west of Khancoban on the Alpine Way. Follow the Murray River Road (C546) rather than the Murray Valley Highway alongside the Victorian side of the river to Albury. Enjoy some great views over the river and valley just before you get to Tintaldra.

You'll cross back into New South Wales briefly at Lake Hume. Built in the 1920s, this artificial lake – six times larger than Sydney Harbour – with its massive dam wall was a modern marvel at the time, although it's now somewhat overshadowed by the engineering feats of the Snowy Mountains Scheme, a few hours up the road. Nevertheless it is the main water-storage reservoir for the Murray and has a major influence on its flows.

Turn south along the lakeshore to Bonegilla and stop in at the Bonegilla Migrant Experience. Built as an army camp during World War II, this complex of unlined corrugated-iron huts became a staging place for refugees after the war and then, from the 1950s until 1971, a temporary home for some 300,000 assisted migrants from non-English speaking parts of Europe. Today it's a fascinating museum, where you can wander around the austere buildings listening to an audio tour that recounts the residents' stories. It's an intriguing look at Australia's immigration policies from the inside out. (82 Bonegilla Rd, Bonegilla; (02) 6020 6912; open Mon–Sun 10am–4pm; bonegilla.org.au.)

Continue west on the Murray Valley Highway through the Rutherglen wine area, famous for its unique rich, fortified tokays, ports and muscats. Call into Byramine Homestead and Brewery around halfway between Yarrawonga and Cobram. Built for Elizabeth Hume in 1842, after her husband was killed by bushrangers, it features a central octagonal 'fortress room' with trapdoors in the floor so that Elizabeth and her children could hide from any attackers in a secret underground cellar. The magnificent elms in the garden are thought to be the oldest in Victoria and the property is surrounded by one of the largest vegetable farms in the country. (1436 Murray Valley Hwy, Yarrawonga; (03) 5748 4321; open Sun–Thurs 10am–4pm; byraminehomestead.com.au.)

All along the length of the Murray, large sandbars form where the river bends, creating beautiful sandy beaches. The largest is Thompsons Beach at Cobram, and in summer it's one of the best places on the Murray for a swim. A further hour down the road is Barmah National Park, which together with parks on the New South Wales side of the river protects the largest river-red-gum forest in the world. Call into the Barmah Forest Heritage Centre in Nathalia (73 Blake St, Nathalia; (03) 5866 2289) before you visit, and then take the two-hour cruise along the narrowest and fastest-flowing section of the Murray through the wetlands and red-gum forests. Cruises depart from the day visitors' area in the park at 10.30am, several times a week. (See kingfishercruises.com.au for details.)

Above Driving through Barmah National Park

ECHUCA TO MILDURA

Echuca is the self-proclaimed paddlesteamer capital of the country and during this riverport's boom days in the 1880s hundreds of paddlesteamers loaded and unloaded their cargo at the historic wharf. Echuca still has the world's largest collection of working paddlesteamers, some more than a century old, including the PS *Adelaide* built in 1886, and the PS *Pevensey*, made famous in the 1980s TV series *All the Rivers Run*. A river cruise is the most popular thing to do in town and there are a number of cruise options. Head down to the wharf to check sailing times.

Before you go, drop into the Echuca Historical Society Museum to see the old river charts that the riverboat captains used to navigate the river. They're hand-drawn on long linen scrolls, and you wonder how they managed to work out where they were when sometimes all they had to go on was a picture of a tree on a bend! The museum is in the old police lock-up: go inside the old cells and browse through a huge collection of old photos and memorabilia from the riverboat era. (Cnr Dickson and Warren sts; (03) 5480 1325; open Mon–Sun 11am–3pm.) From Echuca it will take a little less than two hours to get to Swan Hill.

SIDETRACK

Take a 20-minute detour off the highway at Kerang to visit Koondrook. This cute little riverside town is a gem, with historic – sometimes ramshackle and crumbling – timber buildings dating from the 1880s, a steam-powered tramway and one of the oldest surviving lift bridges over the Murray. The town's fortunes have always been tied up with the timber industry and Arbutnot Sawmill has been milling the giant river red gums since 1889, producing railway sleepers and timber for wharves, as well as the paddleboats that once plied the river. Climb the walkway inside the historic mill to watch the giant saws at work on a guided tour. (12 Punt Rd, Koondrook; (03) 5453 2401; tours Mon–Fri 10.30am and 2pm.)

It's not a real Australian road trip without at least one big thing, and in Swan Hill that big thing is a big Murray Cod in the riverside park in the centre of town. This section of the river around Swan Hill is one of the most natural, and one of the best, places to catch one of the famed freshwater fish that grow to more than a metre in length and weigh in at more than 100kg.

KIDS' SPOT

An old-school lolly shop, free horse-and-cart rides, trips in a vintage car and a huge laser-light spectacular take you to the heart of Murray River history at Swan Hill Pioneer Settlement. This heritage park re-creates life on the river in the 19th century and is the oldest outdoor museum of its type in the country. Many of the buildings are originals relocated to this riverside site from across the district. The night-time laser light show, *Heartbeat of the Murray*, is said to be the first in the world to use a natural river environment as background. Monash Dr, Swan Hill; (03) 5036 2410; open Mon–Sun 9.30am–4pm; pioneersettlement.com.au.

As you head further west the river begins to widen, the river-red-gum forests give way to vast orchards, and farmgate stalls sell bags of oranges and other fruit and vegetables. The Murray is one of our most highly regulated rivers, with dams, weirs, locks and barrages along its length, and nowhere is that more apparent than in Mildura, which was set up in 1887 as an 'irrigation colony' and is now one of the country's biggest food producers.

Watch one of the locks in action at Rio Vista Park and learn about the two visionary Chaffey brothers from California who established this oasis – there are displays inside the old Mildura Homestead, which is a replica of the first homestead in the area, and in the much grander Rio Vista, home of W.B. Chaffey. The house is part of the Mildura Arts Centre, which includes the regional art gallery and its large collection of Australian art (199 Cureton Ave, Mildura; (03) 5018 8330; open Mon–Sun 10am–5pm).

SIDETRACK

Take a quick detour to Wentworth, about half an hour from Mildura via the Silver City Highway, to see where the Murray converges with our other great river, the Darling (*see* p. 255).

MILDURA TO GOOLWA

Head west from Mildura into South Australia. With the establishment of irrigation in the late 1890s, many of the riverside towns along the Murray, like Renmark, boomed in the first decades of the 20th century, in the process creating a rich legacy of classic Art Deco architecture and beautiful riverside parks and gardens. Call into the beautiful Art Deco Renmark Hotel. Established in 1897 it is the oldest community hotel in the British Empire – there's a museum inside the hotel (Murray Ave; (08) 8586 6755). The riverfront park opposite hosts a nightly possum parade, when local possums gather at dusk. You'll also see the PS *Industry* moored at the wharf here; it was built in 1911, decommissioned in 1968 and starred in the 1991 television series *The River Kings*. It's now a floating museum and open for inspection (Mon–Fri 9am–4.30pm, Sat–Sun 10am–2pm).

SIDETRACK

Detour off the Sturt Highway at Berri and loop through Loxton skirting the edge of Murray River National Park, a vast wetland brimming with swooping pelicans and other birdlife.

Banrock Station Wine and Wetland Centre, near Kingston-on-Murray, is one of the country's leading makers of table wine, producing more than 3.6 million litres per year. In 1925, when locks were being established along the Murray for irrigation, Lock 3 was built adjacent to Banrock Station, permanently flooding the lagoon and producing the wetland that is now listed as one of the 1200 most significant wetlands worldwide. Follow the three boardwalks that wind their way through and around the wetlands to birdwatching shelters along the way (the longest is 8km; allow three hours). When the wetlands are full, the lagoon is home to more than 160 species of birds. (Holmes Rd, Kingston-on-Murray; (08) 8583 0299; open Mon–Fri 9am–4pm, Sat–Sun 9am–5pm; banrockstation.com.au.)

Follow the highway west through the riverport town of Waikerie, then turn south at Blanchetown to follow the river to Swan Reach, where a cliff-top lookout provides views over the Big Bend, the river's longest single bend and also its tallest cliffs. Further south, Mannum was the birthplace of the Murray River paddlesteamer – pioneer William Randell launched the first one here in 1853 – and home port to the *Murray Princess* and *Proud Mary* paddlesteamers, both of which today operate multiday cruises along the sections of the river between Murray Bridge and Blanchetown (see murrayprincess.com.au and proudmary.com.au).

Follow the B45 around the shoreline of Lake Alexandrina, where the Murray River spreads out to become the largest freshwater lake in South Australia, wide and shallow, ringed with reeds and bursting with birdlife. From here, the Murray finally creeps towards the ocean, tracing one last great bend at Goolwa (*see* p. 129) before seeping into the sea at the Murray Mouth on Hindmarsh Island.

As you follow the twists and turns of the river on this source-to-sea road trip, you'll soon discover that life on the Murray tends to take on the rhythms of the river itself – slow and languid, relaxed and tranquil. If that doesn't make for a great driving holiday, nothing does.

Opposite Camping along the river near Kerang *Above* A paddleboat cruise near Mannum

BEST EATS

- **Mr Benedict** A top spot opposite the Albury Botanic Gardens, this cafe offers all-day breakfast, great coffee and lunch. 664 Dean St, Albury; (02) 6041 1840; open Wed–Sun for breakfast and lunch; mrbenedict.com.au.
- **Miss Amelie** Enjoy fine dining in the old Wodonga railway station. Station Building, 46 Elgin Blvd, Wodonga; (02) 6056 4170; open Fri for lunch, Tues–Sat for dinner; missamelie.com.au.
- **Ku de' TA Cobram** This cafe and bar sits right on the edge of the sand at Thompsons Beach in Cobram. The front wall, which is open to the beach in summer and covered in clear plastic in winter, offers fantastic views of the river and at night the river red gums that flank the beach are illuminated by strategically placed spotlights. There's usually live music on Friday and Saturday nights. Rockarama Rd, Cobram; (03) 5871 2929; open Wed–Sun for lunch, Wed–Sat for dinner; kudetacobram.com.
- **Morrisons Riverview Winery & Restaurant** Take a paddlesteamer from Echuca to the winery and enjoy the view of the billabong through the floor-to-ceiling glass windows as you feast. The innovative menu – more Melbourne than Moama – features tapas-sized dishes made to share. 2 Merool La, Moama; (03) 5480 0126; open Wed–Sun for lunch; morrisons.net.au.
- **Spoons Riverside** Located on the river beside the Swan Hill Pioneer Settlement, Spoons specialises in seasonal produce from the surrounding Murray–Mallee region. 125 Monash Dr, Swan Hill; (03) 5032 2601; open Mon–Sun for breakfast and lunch, Thurs–Sat for dinner; spoonsriverside.com.au.
- **Stefano's Cantina** Known locally as 'Feast Street', the stretch of Langtree Avenue between Seventh Street and Eighth Street in Mildura is lined with restaurants and cafes, and this Italian restaurant, in the cellars of the Mildura Grand Hotel, is the most famous of them all, belonging to celebrity chef Stefano de Pieri. The set menu changes according to what's fresh and the chef's whim of the day. Langtree Ave, Mildura; (03) 5022 0881; open Tues–Sat for dinner, bookings essential; stefano.com.au.
- **Banrock Station** Linger over a long lunch on the deck. Holmes Rd, Kingston-on-Murray; (08) 8583 0299; open Mon–Sun for breakfast and lunch; banrockstation.com.au.
- **Pretoria Hotel** Relax by the river in this waterside hotel, which serves delicious steak and seafood as well as all the classic pub bistro favourites. 50 Randall St, Mannum; (08) 8569 1109; open Mon–Sun for lunch and dinner; pretoriahotel.com.au.

BEST SLEEPS

- **Lake Hume Resort** Family friendly, the resort has a range of motel-style units and self-contained cottages and apartments. 1 Ray Welsh Dr, Lake Hume village; (02) 6026 4444; lakehumeresort.com.au.
- **Murray Waters** The stylish motel rooms overlook the river at Koondrook. 1 Keene St, Koondrook; (03) 5453 2300; murraywatersmotel.com.au.
- **Quality Hotel Mildura Grand** Stay at celebrity chef Stefano de Pieri's place, in the heart of Mildura's eating precinct. 129–137 Seventh St, Mildura; 1800 034 228; milduragrand.com.au.
- **The Frames** Perched above a bend of the Murray on the outskirts of Paringa, these three self-contained luxury retreats impress with the mix of water views, lavishly appointed interiors and private pools. Lot 7, Panorama Ct, Paringa; 0418 862 260; theframesluxuryaccommodation.com.au.
- **Caravanning and camping** For camping and caravanning options in the Snowy Mountains *see* p. 217. Lovely riverside camping spots can be found at Gunbower Island (east of Koondrook) and Barmah National Park. In Murray River National Park you can camp beside the river at Eckerts Creek, Lock 4, Main Katarapko, Black Box, Colligans and Lyrup Flats. Most of the towns along this route have riverside caravan parks: two favourites are Lake Charm Foreshore, between Kerang and Swan Hill, and the Apex Riverbeach Holiday Park in Mildura (apexriverbeach.com.au).

Outback adventures

Australia's outback is a place of endless surprises, and easier to get to than you might think.

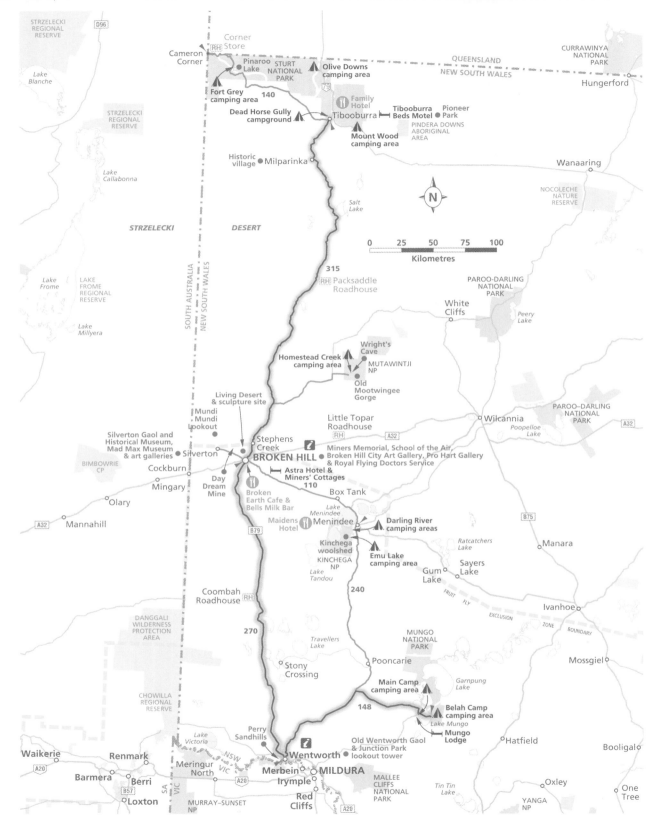

Enjoy spectacular outback scenery on this trip up the Silver City Highway in New South Wales, from Wentworth to Tibooburra.

Silver City Highway, NSW

HOW LONG?

Allow a week for this drive, as you'll want to spend a day or two exploring Broken Hill and the national parks along the way. You can cut the trip in half by choosing to drive only the Wentworth to Broken Hill or the Broken Hill to Tibooburra section.

WHEN TO GO

Summer can be very hot and the flies are extremely friendly. Winter is the most pleasant time to travel throughout the area (although nights can be cold).

NEED TO KNOW

Many of the roads in this area are unsealed. After rain, they may take up to 24 hours to dry out, sometimes even weeks. Travelling on roads that have a 'closed road' sign, even if you are in a 4WD, may incur a substantial fine. For up-to-date road-closure information see livetraffic.rta.nsw.gov.au or call 13 2701.

Drive rating
Easy. Mostly sealed roads with some unsealed sections suitable for 2WDs and caravans in dry weather.

Distances
Total distance (without detours to national parks): approximately 725km. The starting point, Wentworth, is 29km north-west of Mildura. Tibooburra is 1192km north-west of Sydney and Cameron Corner is 1328km from Sydney.
- Wentworth to Broken Hill: 270km
- Broken Hill to Menindee: 110km
- Broken Hill to Mutawintji National Park: 130km
- Broken Hill to Tibooburra: 315km
- Tibooburra to Cameron Corner, 4WD extension,: 140km

Temperatures
January: 14–32°C
July: 5–18°C

More information
- Broken Hill Visitor Information Centre, cnr Blende and Bromide sts, Broken Hill; (08) 8080 3560; destinationbrokenhill.com.au
- Wentworth Shire Visitor Information Centre, 66 Darling St, Wentworth; (03) 5027 5080; visitwentworth.com.au
- thecornercountry.com.au

Snapshot
The Silver City Highway, stretching from Wentworth at the confluence of the Darling and Murray rivers to Tibooburra and the Queensland border, cuts a straight line through the far west of New South Wales and offers a great taste of the outback. Along the way you'll travel through lush farming lands, vineyards and orchards; semi-arid mallee scrub; the 'Silver City' itself, Broken Hill; the frontier outback outpost of Tibooburra; and the red sand dunes and jump-ups – flat mesa-like mountains that rise dramatically from the surrounding plains – on the edge of the vast sandy deserts that form the centre of Australia.

Previous Enjoying the view on Arkaroola's open-top 4WD tour

WENTWORTH TO BROKEN HILL

A pretty river port with many heritage buildings, Wentworth has the distinction of being the town where Australia's two longest rivers, the Darling and the Murray, converge. From the lookout tower in Junction Park you can see the different-coloured waters eddy together beneath the cruising houseboats and the paddlesteamers that take passengers on lunch or tea-and-coffee river cruises.

One of the don't-miss attractions in town is Old Wentworth Gaol. Built in 1879, it was the first Australian-designed gaol to be built in Australia. The prison is now an interesting museum where you can wander through the old cells and grounds. There are some good displays on local history, notably one on Harry Nanya, an Aboriginal leader who resisted forsaking his traditional way of life long after European settlement in the area. (Beverley St, Wentworth; (03) 5027 3337; open Mon–Sun 10am–5pm.)

Leaving green, well-watered Wentworth, you will find the landscape quickly changes to dry mallee scrub. Your first taste of the outback is at Perry Sandhills, on the outskirts of town. These rolling, red sandhills are in stark contrast to the surrounding irrigated fields and are now a popular film and television backdrop, but they were once a favoured Aboriginal hunting and camping ground. The sandhills are constantly shifting as the wind picks up and redeposits the sand, uncovering the skeletal remains of giant prehistoric kangaroos and wombats. Ask at the visitor centre for directions.

Mungo National Park is signposted from Wentworth. Most of the 100km road is unsealed but in good condition when dry. Fifteen thousand years ago the vast, flat plain was a huge lake. Along the eastern shore of the ancient lakebed is a great crescent-shaped dune called a lunette – a huge 22km long wall of sand and clay eroded into weird and fantastic formations. Nicknamed the Walls of China by Chinese station workers in the 19th century, the lunette has been found to contain traces of ancient Aboriginal campfires and middens, countless early tools and the world's oldest cremated human remains, which are somewhere between 45,000 and 60,000 years old (the experts are still quibbling). When the first skeletal remains were discovered, back in 1968, the estimated date for the earliest human occupation of Australia was approximately 20,000 years ago. Mungo Woman, as the remains became known, along with another find made in 1974, named Mungo Man, redefined world prehistory and, in turn, helped ensure that the ancient lake system would become Australia's first World Heritage–listed national park.

Since then, more skeletal and fossil remains, both human and marsupial, have been found, including the skeleton of a buffalo-sized wombat, *Zygomaturus*, and, most recently, a set of 20,000-year-old human footprints. There is a short walk from the carpark to a viewing platform at the Walls of China, or take a 60km signposted drive tour through the park around the north-eastern shore of the lake. The park is particularly beautiful in the evening when the white-sand lunette changes colour and glows in the light of the setting sun.

Broken Hill is 270km north of Wentworth, along an almost dead straight, sealed road. Expensive petrol is available at Coombah Roadhouse about halfway along the road.

SIDETRACK

If you have a 4WD or an SUV, branch off the Silver City Highway to take the Darling River Road, which follows the course of the state's longest river to Menindee, about a two-hour drive (if you don't have a high-clearance vehicle, you can still visit Menindee and Kinchega, but you need to go via Broken Hill). In a good year, Menindee, which proudly proclaims itself the 'first' town on the Darling (meaning oldest), is a veritable desert oasis. It is here that the Darling River flows into the Menindee Lakes, forming three huge bodies of water, two of which are part of Kinchega National Park, although during times of extended drought when the Darling stops flowing the lakes may be dry. It's a beautiful spot to visit when there is water in the system and some of the best campsites in the state are strung out along the bank of the Darling River. When the lakes are full, birdlife is prolific, and the sunsets over the lakes are spectacular – although beware of kangaroos if driving after dark. Much of the park was originally Kinchega Station, and you can visit the original 62-stand woolshed, built in 1875, where more than six million sheep were shorn before the station became a national park in 1967. Back in Menindee, have a drink at Maidens Hotel. In 1860 Burke and Wills stayed here at the beginning of their ill-fated trip that ended at Cooper Creek. William Wright, the man who was blamed for a large part of the tragedy, was a station manager at Kinchega before he joined their party.

BROKEN HILL

Closer to Adelaide than Sydney (it runs on South Australian not New South Wales time), Broken Hill, nicknamed the Silver City, made its fortune from the wealth of silver and zinc lying underground here, which was first discovered in the 1880s. Since then, more than 800 miners have died in the mines under the city and one site you can't miss (you can see it from just about anywhere in town) is the Miners Memorial atop the 7km long Line of Lode, the original ore body.

For a greater understanding of what it is like to live in the outback, drop by the School of the Air, where you can listen to the children do their lessons and ask them about their lives on remote stations (cnr Lane and Brazil sts, Broken Hill; (02) 8087 3560; tourist sessions on school days 8.15am; schoolair-p.schools.nsw.gov.au). You can also tour the headquarters of the Royal Flying Doctor Service at Broken Hill airport (Airport Rd, Broken Hill; (08) 8080 3714; open Mon–Fri 9am–5pm, Sat–Sun 10am–3pm).

Broken Hill has become one of the state's most important arts centres. There are almost 30 galleries in town and at nearby Silverton (see Sidetrack left). If you only have time to visit three, make sure they are the Pro Hart Gallery (108 Wyman St; (08) 8087 2441; open Mon–Sat 9am–5pm, Sun 10am–5pm), the Broken Hill City Art Gallery (404 Argent St; (08) 8080 3444; open Tues–Sun 10am–3pm) and the sculpture site in the Living Desert Reserve on the outskirts of town, where 12 sandstone sculptures sit atop a hill overlooking the plains below – this is a great spot for a picnic and even has gas barbecues (take Kaolin St/Nine Mile Rd and follow the signs; open Mon–Sun 9am to half an hour after sunset Mar–Nov, 6am to half an hour after sunset Dec–Feb).

SIDETRACK

The tiny town of Silverton, 25km west of Broken Hill, is the most famous of all movie locations in New South Wales. It was pretty much a ghost town until it became the set for *Mad Max 2* back in 1981; since then dozens of movies and commercials have been filmed here. Drop in and have a cold drink at the Silverton Hotel and you'll hear all about them. The privately run Mad Max Museum, just down the road, likes to boast that it's Australia's first and only museum dedicated to *Mad Max 2*. It certainly blurs the line between collection and obsession at any rate! (Stirling St, Silverton; (08) 8088 6128; open Mon–Sun 9am–5pm in winter, 10am–4pm in summer.) Other attractions include underground tours of Day Dream Mine, showing how silver mining was done in the 1880s (signposted 12km off the Silverton Rd, around halfway between Broken Hill and Silverton; 0427 885 682; call ahead for opening hours); Silverton Gaol and Historical Museum (Burke St, Silverton; (08) 8088 5317; open Mon–Sun 9.30am–4.30pm); and other historical buildings and art galleries. Stop at the Mundi Mundi lookout (4km north of Silverton) for great views over the desert plains.

UNESCO World Heritage-listed
Mungo National Park

BROKEN HILL TO TIBOOBURRA

From Broken Hill it's a straight run north for 315km to Tibooburra along a mostly unsealed road that's dusty and sometimes a little corrugated but usually fine for 2WD cars and caravans.

SIDETRACK

Located 130km north-east of Broken Hill (you'll see the turn-off about 53km from Broken Hill), Mutawintji National Park is home to some spectacular gorge country and Aboriginal rock art that dates back more than 8000 years. Take a self-guided tour of Homestead Creek Gorge to Wright's Cave, where you can see engravings and stencils, or the longer walk to Old Mootwingee Gorge, a delightful swimming hole surrounded by towering red cliffs.

Stop at Milparinka, 39km south of Tibooburra, to stretch your legs and look at the historic courthouse and buildings around the now almost-deserted town, which testify to its past importance as an administrative centre. Then head on to Tibooburra, one of the last true frontier towns. The Family Hotel is famous for its rather saucy murals, painted by artist Clifton Ernest Pugh (three-time winner of the Archibald Prize, as well as a recipient of an Order of Australia medal in 1985) in the late 1960s. According to locals, Clifton became stranded at the pub during the wet season, got bored and started painting the walls. In Pioneer Park, on the edge of town, see a replica of the boat that the explorer Charles Sturt hoped to sail across the inland sea he was searching for (he established Fort Grey in what is now Sturt National Park in 1845). Tibooburra is a good base for daytrips into Sturt National Park with its dramatic jump-ups and beautiful Lake Pinaroo.

Corner Country

If you have a 4WD, head a further 140km north-west to Cameron Corner along a rough, unsealed road to the point where New South Wales, South Australia and Queensland meet among the red dunes of the Strzelecki Desert. There's not much at Cameron Corner – just the Corner Store on the Queensland side. But like all good corner shops it sells everything: fuel, basic mechanical gear, food supplies, snacks, cold beer and souvenirs. Stop and chat awhile with the owners, who can fill you in on local road conditions. Although conventional cars have been known to survive the trip, you really do need a vehicle with high clearance and caravans aren't recommended, although off-road camper trailers will be fine.

BEST EATS

- **Maidens Hotel** Enjoy classic country-style pub meals here in one of the state's most historic hotels. 59 Yartla St, Menindee; (08) 8091 4208; open Mon–Sun for lunch and dinner.
- **Broken Earth Cafe** The cafe sits atop the Line of Lode next to the Miners Memorial in Broken Hill and has great views of the city. Federation Way, Broken Hill; (08) 8087 1318; open Mon–Sun for lunch; brokenearthcafe.com.
- **Bells Milk Bar** Walk into a time capsule straight from the 1950s, before the old-fashioned milk bar morphed into just another fast-food takeaway. Beyond the shakes and spiders, the menu extends to ice-cream sundaes, hot waffles and apple pie. 160 Patton St, South Broken Hill; (08) 8087 5380; open Mon–Sun 10am–5.30pm; bellsmilkbar.com.au.
- **Family Hotel** Make sure you have a hearty appetite if you order a steak here because they are huge! They also do monster-sized schnitzels and a mean hamburger. 10 Briscoe St, Tibooburra; (08) 8091 3314; open Mon–Sun for dinner.

BEST SLEEPS

- **Mungo Lodge** Situated near the entrance to Mungo National Park, the lodge offers upmarket accommodation in stylish ensuite rooms with airconditioning and two verandahs – the perfect place to sit out the heat of the day or enjoy a bottle of local Mildura wine or a cold beer from the minibar. The lodge also has a licensed restaurant. 10142 Arumpo Rd, Buronga; (03) 5029 7297; mungolodge.com.au.
- **Astra Hotel** The Astra started life in the 1890s as the Commercial Hotel and was renamed in the 1950s, and it has recently been renovated and reinvented as a boutique hotel in a rather grand style. It has eight huge suites, each with ensuite, and most open out to the wide iron-lace balcony. 393 Argent St, Broken Hill; (08) 8087 5428.
- **Miners' cottages** Broken Hill also has a range of accommodation in historic miners' cottages, most made from corrugated iron, which cost about the same as a three-star motel unit. Some allow pets. Contact the Broken Hill Visitor Information Centre for details.

- **Tibooburra Beds Motel** This motel offers clean accommodation in a new house made from straw bales, so it's surprisingly cool in summer, and camping sites are also available. Cnr Briscoe and Brown sts, Tibooburra; (08) 8091 3333; tibooburrabeds.com.au.
- **Caravanning and camping** The campsites along the Darling River in Kinchega National Park are some of the prettiest in the state. The facilities are basic, but the campsites are nicely spread out along the bank. There is also good camping in Sturt and Mungo national parks. Homestead Creek camping ground in Mutawintji National Park has (unpowered) caravan sites and hot showers.

Opposite Dingo fence at Cameron Corner *Top right* Broken Earth Cafe

Explore the stark and ancient beauty of the Flinders Ranges in South Australia, where the roads through the weather-beaten ranges lead to rocky gorges covered in Aboriginal art. This is the outback at its most scenic and most accessible.

Flinders Ranges, SA

HOW LONG?

Allow at least three days from Quorn, and a day each way to get to and from Adelaide. If you are short of time, make Blinman the northernmost point of your loop.

WHEN TO GO

The best time to visit is in spring, when the ragged hills and valley floors are carpeted with wildflowers. The Flinders Ranges are fairly dry all year, with rain most likely during the summer months. Many businesses are closed during January and February, which can be uncomfortably hot.

NEED TO KNOW

While the Flinders Ranges are remote and rugged, the main roads are accessible to conventional vehicles and caravans; however, many sidetracks are 4WD only. Make sure you have a spare tyre (or two), as the rocky roads are very hard on tyres. Be aware that flash flooding can occur after rain. Leave your pets at home: most of this area is either protected by national park or is a private wildlife sanctuary.

Drive rating
Moderate. Some unsealed roads with optional 4WD sections, including some very challenging and remote tracks

Distances
Total distance, Quorn to Arkaroola loop: 676km
- Adelaide to Quorn: 326km
- Quorn to Wilpena Pound: 117km
- Wilpena Pound to Arkaroola: 207km
- Arkaroola to Leigh Creek: 133km
- Leigh Creek to Parachilna: 64km
- Parachilna to Quorn: 155km

Temperatures
January: 20–34°C
July: 3–16°C

More information
- Flinders Ranges Visitor Information Centre, 19 Railway Tce, Quorn; (08) 8620 0510; flindersandoutback.com.au
- Wadlata Outback Centre, 41 Flinders Tce, Port Augusta; 1800 633 060

Snapshot
The Flinders Ranges in central South Australia are an ancient landscape, full of weathered crags in primeval colours, mountains of rich purples and deep blues, cut through with red-rock gorges and surrounded by acres of white, yellow, red and purple wildflowers in spring. The countryside is one of the oldest on Earth: the mountains, once higher than the Himalayas, are more than 600 million years old and form one of Australia's richest geological areas. The Aboriginal Creation stories that are woven around the existence of these ancient landforms and gorges have been passed on for more than 40,000 years.

Opposite Elder Range, one of several ranges in the Flinders Ranges

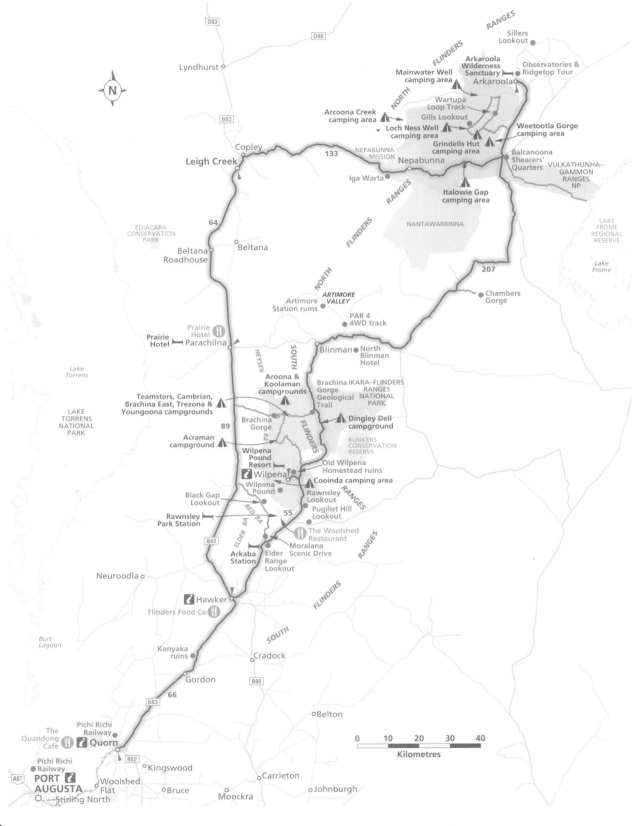

Flinders Ranges, SA

The Pichi Richi Railway is one of Australia's best known steam-train journeys. The rail line, originally known as the Port Augusta–Quorn Railway, opened in 1879; it closed 77 years later in 1956 and was restored in 1974 by the Pichi Richi Preservation Society. The line runs through deep rock cuttings, past stone-wall embankments and across spectacular iron bridges. Steam-train trips depart most weekends from Quorn and Port Augusta. 1800 777 245; pichirichirailway.org.au.

Old Wilpena Station

QUORN TO WILPENA

Start your Flinders loop at Quorn, a fascinating former railway hub, now home of the famous Pichi Richi Railway (*see* Kids' spot). The historic station buildings make for great photographs.

From Quorn, head north to Hawker, the last town of any size before the ranges, which provide a picturesque backdrop. Along the way, stop at the Kanyaka ruins. In 1856 the Kanyaka Station leases totalled 94,500ha and the property housed up to 70 workers and their families. Look for the grave of Hugh Proby, the third son of the Earl of Carysfort and past owner of the station, who was swept away by floodwaters while mustering sheep. His family shipped the huge, 1.5-tonne granite tablet from Scotland to mark the place of his burial.

SIDETRACK

Moralana Scenic Drive is a 28km unsealed road (fine for 2WDs) connecting the Wilpena and Leigh Creek roads, and is one of the best drives through the Flinders Ranges. It reveals stunning scenery including the southern wall of Wilpena Pound, the Black Gap Lookout, the Red Range and the Elder Range, and is especially colourful during spring and late afternoon. Signposted drive entrances are 24km north of Hawker on the Wilpena Road and 42km north of Hawker on the Leigh Creek Road.

The road is sealed all the way to Wilpena, in the heart of Flinders Ranges National Park. There are several lookouts signposted along the way giving great views of the Elder Range and the outer ramparts of Wilpena Pound, a crater-like pile of rock covering 8300ha that rises sharply from the surrounding flat plains – the rim is formed by the eroded stumps of massive mountains. The wooded interior – accessible through just one gorge – is 11km long and 8km across. The first settlers in the area were farmers who established sheep runs inside the pound in the 1850s. The word 'pound' was used because the farmers were struck by the resemblance of the formation to traditional enclosures for sheep, then known as pounds.

The visitor centre at Wilpena Pound Resort has maps of the many walking tracks, including the Hills Homestead track, a two-hour walk to the ruins of the old Wilpena Homestead. But the best way to really get a sense of what the pound looks like is from the air; 20- and 30-minute flights are available at the resort. (Wilpena Rd, Wilpena; 1800 805 802; wilpenapound.com.au.)

WILPENA TO ARKAROOLA

The road turns to gravel (still okay for 2WD and caravans) just past Wilpena and it is about three hours' drive to Arkaroola. Avoid driving at dawn or dusk, as collisions with wildlife, particularly kangaroos, are common.

SIDETRACKS

There are several tracks cutting across the national park and, while all roads in this area are scenic, the Brachina and Bunyeroo roads and the Blinman–Parachilna Road are especially so, as they follow dry creek beds and ancient gorge lines deep into the heart of the ranges. The Brachina Gorge Geological Trail is a 20km, self-guided driving trail that passes through 130 million years of Earth's history and is lined with interpretive signs explaining the area's geology; at Brachina Gorge, keep an eye out for rare yellow-footed rock wallabies. The trail is best travelled from east to west, from the Brachina Gorge–Blinman Road junction. Technically these unsealed roads are fine for 2WDs (especially if you have all-wheel-drive), but you'll be more comfortable in an SUV or 4WD. These rocky roads are also very hard on tyres.

The Flinders Ranges are famous for quandongs, an Australian native fruit that tastes a little like a tart peach or apricot, and the former copper-mining town of Blinman is home to the best quandong pies. You can (usually) get them at the general store to take away.

SIDETRACK

Chambers Gorge, off a 10km rough and rocky side road (fine for most vehicles except after rain, although once again you'll be more comfortable in an SUV or 4WD), has an extensive Aboriginal rock-engraving gallery. The best time to visit is late afternoon, when the setting sun turns the walls of the gorge a deep, dark red. In early spring, the area is often carpeted with masses of Sturt's desert peas.

Flinders Ranges, SA

If you have a 4WD, take the track out to Lake Frome in Vulkathunha–Gammon Ranges National Park (signposted at Balcanoona). Frome is the seventh largest lake in Australia, not that it ever has much water in it – like Lake Eyre, it's just one huge expanse of blinding white salt that only periodically fills with brackish water. The only public access is via the 4WD track through Vulkathunha, and even then it's off limits between 3pm and 5am, when it's reserved for traditional cultural use by the Indigenous owners. The road out is not particularly challenging, but the sense of loneliness once you've crossed the sand dunes and are out on the salt can be quite confronting.

SIDETRACK

Another great detour for those who like off-road adventures is the section of Vulkathunha–Gammon Ranges National Park on the western side of the main road. Being roughly halfway between the two resorts of Wilpena and Arkaroola, it tends to be ignored by most travellers to the area, which is a shame because it's home to one of the best 4WD tracks in the region and has some fantastic gorge-side camping spots. The Wortupa Loop Track is an 80km one-way loop through the centre of the park that takes roughly five hours and is definitely not for novices. It's quite difficult, with very steep sections that take you up to lookouts where it really does feel as if you can see forever, even if you can't actually see the track once it disappears over the edge of the crest.

Continue north to Arkaroola, a privately owned 61,000ha wilderness sanctuary at the far northern tip of the Flinders Ranges that features rugged mountains, soaring granite peaks, deep gorges and beautiful waterholes. It is also home to more than 160 species of birds and the yellow-footed rock wallaby. The four-hour Ridgetop Tour that travels along the spine of the mountains to stunning Sillers Lookout is a must, but you can also follow one of the many self-drive 4WD tracks – although, be warned: they are not for novices. Because there is no light pollution, this is also one of the best places to view the night sky and there are three observatories on the property. Scenic flights are also available. (Arkaroola Wilderness Sanctuary, Arkaroola village; (08) 8648 4848; arkaroola.com.au.)

ARKAROOLA TO QUORN VIA PARACHILNA

Head south from Arkaroola and join the Copley Road heading to the tiny modern mining community of Leigh Creek. Along the way, stop at Iga Warta, a few kilometres beyond the Aboriginal settlement of Nepabunna. Iga Warta, which means 'place of the native orange' in the local Adnyamathanha language, is an Aboriginal cultural centre and cafe that also runs bush-tucker walks, guided tours to rock-art sites and dreaming trails, and campfire story nights. (Via Copley; (08) 8648 3737; igawarta.com.)

At Leigh Creek, it's back on the bitumen for a quick run down to Parachilna. There's not much to Parachilna – a disused railway station and pub and that's about it – but a clever renovation and innovative menu has put the Prairie Hotel firmly on the map and it's a favourite with visiting movie stars and film crews, who often use the Flinders Ranges as a backdrop for films. The restaurant is best known for its 'feral' food – camel, kangaroo, emu and bush herbs and native spices. Keep an eye out for the distinctive road signs advertising the menu on the way into the town. (Cnr High St and West Tce, Parachilna; 1800 331 473; prairiehotel.com.au.)

From Parachilna, head back down the highway to Hawker, the purple walls of the Flinders Ranges a constant companion to the left, before finally finishing the loop at Quorn.

Opposite Walking along dry Lake Frome *Right* Parachilna Gorge Road

Public access routes

Crisscrossing the Flinders is a network of 4WD roads called public access routes, a series of little-advertised and rarely signposted tracks, mostly on private property, to areas of public interest and historical sites. They are poorly maintained, seldomly used and not for first-timers, but if you have a vehicle with low range and high clearance and a couple of spare tyres, and you're a confident off-roader, these tracks will lead you into the heart of the Flinders, where most people never venture.

A favourite is PAR 4 (as it's named on the few signposts that do exist). It's a gnarly, rocky and challenging track across the Artimore Valley, north of Blinman. Much of the track is actually a stony creek bed, and when it does head up over the hills or along ridgelines there are razor-sharp rocks, deep ruts and washaways and you need to think carefully about your approaches. It's only 26km long, but it takes about five hours to drive.

Most of the track is on what was once Artimore Station. Established in the mid-19th century, it was one of the biggest sheep runs in the colony, but by 1902, after years of drought, overstocking and plagues of rabbits, it was abandoned. All that's left now are the roofless ruins of the homestead, which make a great, if lonely, place to stop for lunch.

The scenery is dazzling, and if you're here in winter or spring (and it's been a good season), the gullies are full of red, purple, yellow, pink and white wildflowers and carpets of scarlet Sturt's desert peas. The track snakes its way through blood-red rock gorges and over the bald tops of hills, through the heart of Heysen country – artist Hans Heysen painted these landscapes again and again and the distant peaks are named the Heysen Range in his honour.

This really is a remote track and probably best done with a companion vehicle, just in case something does go wrong. Although it's not that far from the township of Blinman, there's no phone reception and you're unlikely to encounter other vehicles. If you get stuck in a rut or shred a tyre, you may have a very long wait for help, so let someone (like the local police or the folk at the hotel) know of your plans before you go, and make sure you check in again when you return.

For more information, visit environment.sa.gov.au and search for 'public access route', download a copy of '4WD Tracks and Repeater Towers of the Flinders Ranges and Outback South Australia' from flindersandoutback.com.au/outback/4wd/, or ask at one of the local visitor centres.

BEST EATS

- **The Quandong Cafe** You'll find good coffee and sandwiches in the oldest stone building in Quorn, as well as quandong pie. 31 First St, Quorn; (08) 8648 6155; open Wed–Mon for breakfast and lunch; quandongapartments.com.au.
- **The Woolshed Restaurant** The station-grown saltbush lamb at this restaurant inside a former woolshed is so tender you hardly need a knife; try the lamb tasting platter but leave room for the quandong cheesecake with quandong jam. Rawnsley Park Station, Flinders Ranges Way, Hawker (just south of Wilpena); (08) 8648 0700; open Wed–Sun for lunch and Mon–Sun dinner (summer lunchtime days vary, call first); rawnsleypark.com.au.
- **Flinders Food Co** This cafe is a nice place to stop for lunch with a nice selection of vegetarian and gluten-free options. 66 Elder Tce, Hawker; (08) 8648 4380; open Tues–Sun for breakfast and lunch.
- **Prairie Hotel** Don't let the colourful 'Road Kill: Eat Some Today' signs put you off. This authentic outback pub with an innovative menu is famous for its creative use of native foods. The feral mixed grill of emu, kangaroo, goat and camel is its signature dish. Cnr High St and West Tce, Parachilna; 1800 331 473; open Mon–Sun for lunch and dinner; prairiehotel.com.au.

BEST SLEEPS

- **Arkaba Station** The station's historic homestead is now a luxury lodge with quirky decorating touches by local wildlife artist Rosie Woodford Ganf, such as glass-topped wool bales for bedside tables, bed posts fashioned from old Myall fence posts and sheepskin rugs on the floor. Rates include accommodation, food, wine and guided tours. Wilpena Rd, between Hawker and Wilpena; 1300 790 561; arkabaconservancy.com.
- **Rawnsley Park Station** The owners of this working sheep farm on the southern face of Wilpena Pound have been welcoming travellers since 1968, first to simple cabins, then to a caravan park, and now to luxury eco-villas with stunning views of the surrounding ranges and a glass panel in the bedroom ceiling, so you can star gaze from under your doona. Flinders Ranges Way, Hawker; (08) 8648 0700; rawnsleypark.com.au.
- **Wilpena Pound Resort** The resort provides motel accommodation and permanent hard-floored safari tents, a pool, a licensed restaurant, fuel, a basic shop and tours. Wilpena Rd, Wilpena; 1800 805 802; wilpenapound.com.au.

- **Arkaroola Wilderness Sanctuary** Here you'll find comfortable motel-style units as well as budget rooms and self-contained cottages. Facilities include a licensed restaurant, pool, basic shop, fuel, mechanical repairs and a range of guided tours. Arkaroola village; (08) 8648 4848; arkaroola.com.au.
- **Prairie Hotel** Parachilna's historic hotel has a modern accommodation wing partly buried in earth to provide insulation from summer heat. Most rooms have beautiful views of the nearby ranges. Cnr High St and West Tce, Parachilna; 1800 331 473; prairiehotel.com.au.
- **Caravanning and camping** Rawnsley Park, Wilpena Pound Resort and Arkaroola Wilderness Sanctuary (see above) all have powered caravan sites and unpowered bush-camping sites. There are ten campgrounds scattered throughout Flinders Ranges National Park. The best are those spread along Brachina Gorge Road, where facilities include toilets and small water tanks, although you'll still need to carry your own water as the tanks may be empty if it has been dry. There are several camping areas within Vulkathunha–Gammon Ranges National Park (Weetootla Gorge is a great spot) and hot showers are available at Balcanoona Shearers' Quarters for just a few dollars.

Opposite 4WD driving across Arkaba Station *Above* Parachilna's historic Prairie Hotel

See the best of north-western Queensland, uncover the stories behind some of our outback legends and travel through some of the country's most iconic country towns on the Matilda Highway.

Matilda Highway, Qld

HOW LONG?

It's a *long* way – almost 2000km – and to really explore the region and its many museums and attractions you should allow two weeks. If you're pressed for time – or not sure your kids could cope with such a long road trip – consider flying to Longreach and hiring a car to explore the Winton–Hughenden–Richmond loop for a few days.

WHEN TO GO

The best time to travel is between April and September, when the roads in the Far North are open, temperatures are less extreme in outback areas and there are fewer flies. Daytime temperatures in winter are pleasant, but nights are very cold.

NEED TO KNOW

Most of the unsealed roads in the outback will quickly become impassable after rain. Check road conditions before travelling by calling 13 1940 or visiting qldtraffic.qld.gov.au and livetraffic.com.

Drive rating
Easy. Mostly sealed roads with some optional gravel roads; all roads suitable for caravans

Distances
Total distance, Bourke to Karumba: 1952km. Bourke is 764km north-west of Sydney, 924km south-west of Brisbane.
- Bourke to Cunnamulla: 257km
- Cunnamulla to Blackall: 501km
- Blackall to Longreach: 214km
- Longreach to Winton: 178km
- Winton to Cloncurry: 349km
- Cloncurry to Karumba: 453km

Temperatures
January: 23–37°C
July: 7–23°C

More information
- Bourke Visitor Information Centre, Kidman Way, Bourke; (02) 6872 1321; visitbourke.com.au
- Cunnamulla Fella Visitor Information Centre, Centenary Park, Jane St, Cunnamulla; (07) 4655 8470; paroo.qld.gov.au
- Longreach Visitor Information Centre, 99A Qantas Park Eagle St, Longreach; (07) 4658 4150; longreachtourism.com.au
- Winton Information Centre, Waltzing Matilda Centre, 50 Elderslie St, Winton; 1300 665 115; experiencewinton.com.au
- australiasdinosaurtrail.com
- queensland.com/Explore-Queensland/Outback-Queensland

Snapshot
The Matilda Highway is the name of a collection of sealed roads that spear through the heart of outback Queensland, from Bourke, south of the New South Wales–Queensland border, north to Karumba on the shores of the Gulf of Carpentaria. Along the way you'll travel through areas where dinosaurs once roamed; discover the inspiration for our unofficial national anthem, 'Waltzing Matilda'; and visit the birthplaces of Qantas, the Royal Flying Doctor Service and the Australian Labor Party.

Opposite Leave the traffic behind on the wide open roads of outback Queensland

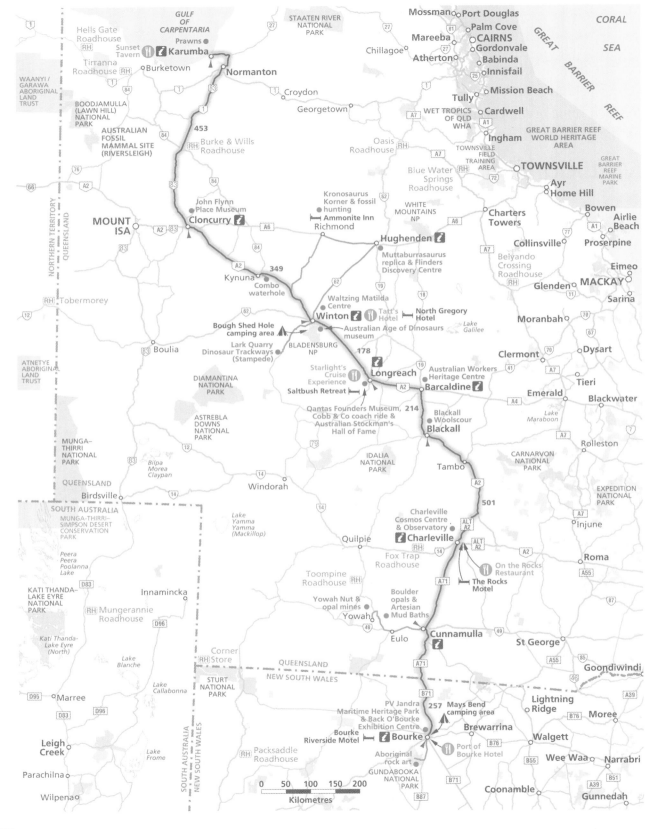

GULF
OF
CARPENTARIA

CORAL
SEA

Hells Gate
Roadhouse RH

Prawns
Sunset
Tavern
Karumba

Mossman
Port Douglas
Palm Cove
Mareeba
CAIRNS
Gordonvale
Babinda

Tirranna
Roadhouse RH
Burketown

Normanton

Chillagoe
Atherton

Innisfail

STAATEN RIVER
NATIONAL
PARK

Croydon

Georgetown

Tully
Mission Beach

WAANYI /
GARAWA
ABORIGINAL
LAND
TRUST

453

BOODJAMULLA
(LAWN HILL)
NATIONAL
PARK

Burke & Wills
Roadhouse RH

WET TROPICS
OF QLD
WHA

Cardwell

Ingham

GREAT BARRIER REEF
WORLD HERITAGE
AREA

AUSTRALIAN
FOSSIL MAMMAL
SITE
(RIVERSLEIGH)

Oasis
Roadhouse RH

TOWNSVILLE
FIELD
TRAINING
AREA

TOWNSVILLE

GREAT
BARRIER
REEF
MARINE
PARK

John Flynn
Place Museum
Cloncurry

Kronosaurus
Korner & fossil
hunting
Ammonite Inn
Richmond

Blue Water
Springs
Roadhouse RH

WHITE
MOUNTAINS
NP

Ayr
Home Hill

MOUNT
ISA

Hughenden

Charters
Towers

Bowen
Airlie
Beach

NORTHERN TERRITORY
QUEENSLAND

Tobermorey RH

349
Kynuna
Combo
waterhole

Muttaburrasaurus
replica & Flinders
Discovery Centre

Collinsville

Proserpine

Belyando
Crossing
Roadhouse RH

Eimeo
MACKAY

Glenden

Sarina

ATNETYE
ABORIGINAL
LAND TRUST

Boulia

Waltzing Matilda
Centre
Winton

Tatt's
Hotel

North Gregory
Hotel

Lake
Galilee

Moranbah

Bough Shed Hole
camping area

Lark Quarry
Dinosaur Trackways
(Stampede)

BLADENSBURG
NP

Australian Age of Dinosaurs
museum

178

Clermont

Dysart

DIAMANTINA
NATIONAL
PARK

Starlight's
Cruise
Experience

Longreach

Australian Workers
Heritage Centre

Barcaldine

Tieri

ASTREBLA
DOWNS
NATIONAL
PARK

Saltbush Retreat

Qantas Founders Museum,
Cobb & Co coach ride &
Australian Stockman's
Hall of Fame

214

Blackall
Woolscour

Blackall

Emerald

Blackwater

Lake
Maraboon

MUNGA-
THIRRI
NATIONAL
PARK

Bilpa
Morea
Claypan

Windorah

IDALIA
NATIONAL
PARK

Tambo

CARNARVON
NATIONAL
PARK

Rolleston

QUEENSLAND

Birdsville

501

EXPEDITION
NATIONAL
PARK

Injune

SOUTH AUSTRALIA

MUNGA-THIRRI–
SIMPSON DESERT
CONSERVATION
PARK

Lake
Yamma
Yamma
(Mackillop)

Quilpie

Charleville
Cosmos Centre
& Observatory

ALT
A2

Charleville

ALT
A2

Roma

Peera
Peera
Poolanna
Lake

KATI THANDA–
LAKE EYRE
NATIONAL
PARK

Mungerannie
Roadhouse RH

Fox Trap
Roadhouse RH

On the Rocks
Restaurant

The Rocks
Motel

Innamincka

Toompine
Roadhouse RH

Kati Thanda–
Lake Eyre
(North)

Yowah Nut &
opal mines
Yowah

Boulder
opals &
Artesian
Mud Baths

Cunnamulla

St George

Lake
Blanche

Corner
Store RH

Eulo

QUEENSLAND
NEW SOUTH WALES

Goondiwindi

Lake
Callabonna

STURT
NATIONAL
PARK

Lightning
Ridge

Moree

Marree

PV Jandra
Maritime Heritage Park
& Back O'Bourke
Exhibition Centre

257
Mays Bend
camping area

Brewarrina

Walgett

Wee Waa

Narrabri

Leigh
Creek

Lake
Frome

Packsaddle
Roadhouse RH

Bourke
Riverside Motel

Bourke

Aboriginal
rock art

Port of
Bourke Hotel

Parachilna

GUNDABOOKA
NATIONAL
PARK

Coonamble

Gunnedah

Wilpena

SOUTH AUSTRALIA
NEW SOUTH WALES

0   50   100 150 200
Kilometres

BOURKE TO CUNNAMULLA

You don't know Australia until you've been to Bourke, or at least so wrote writer and poet Henry Lawson, who was sent to Bourke by *The Bulletin* newspaper in the 1890s to sober up. Back then Bourke was a thriving river port. These days, however, Bourke is most famous for being just in front of the middle of nowhere: if you're 'back o' Bourke' then you're definitely in the outback.

In Lawson's day more than 100 paddlesteamers plied the river, ferrying at least 40,000 bales of wool down the Darling River to coastal seaports each year. There's just one paddlesteamer left on this section of the river these days, the tourist cruiser PV *Jandra*, but follow the track through the Maritime Heritage Park on the north side of the river and you'll pass by the rusting ruins of others, such as the PS *Wave*, left to decay high on the riverbank where it was stranded by floods back in 1929 after water levels dropped overnight. A 24km self-drive tour lined with interpretive boards – detailed in an excellent leaflet called Back O' Bourke Mud Map Tours, available free at the visitor centre – takes in this and other historic sites.

Also worth seeing is the Back O' Bourke Exhibition Centre. Less a collection of historical artefacts and more a gallery of stories and legends, it gives you a look at the town and outback through the eyes and words of writers such as Breaker Morant, Henry Lawson and Will Ogilvie, the poet who actually coined the phrase 'back o' Bourke'. (Kidman Way, Bourke; (02) 6872 1321; open Mon–Sun 9am–4.30pm in winter, 9am–3.30pm in summer; visitbourke.com.au.)

SIDETRACK

One of the best – and most accessible – Aboriginal rock-art sites in outback New South Wales lies 50km south of Bourke in Gundabooka National Park. Here, underneath the shelter of a rocky overhang near some waterholes in the Gunderbooka Ranges, painted in remarkably vivid white on a red rock wall, are depictions of boomerangs, spears, emus and dancing figures, and stencils of stone axes and hands.

Take the Mitchell Highway north out of town and allow about three hours to get to Cunnamulla.

Above Captain your own paddlesteamer at the Back O' Bourke Exhibition Centre

CUNNAMULLA TO LONGREACH

Cunnamulla, on the banks of the Warrego River, is in the heart of wool country and is typical of the down-to-earth country towns – with their two-storey, verandah-fringed pubs, grand post offices and imposing bank buildings – that you will pass through on this trip.

SIDETRACK

Fossickers keen to try their luck should detour 67km west to Eulo, home of the boulder opal. The Artesian Mud Baths are reason enough to make the trek. Rich in zinc, magnesium, potassium, calcium and iron, the mud is scooped up from the natural mud springs that bubble out of the ground, and the million-year-old thermally heated water is pumped up directly from the Great Artesian Basin into a brightly painted, claw-footed bath in a rustic open-air bathhouse. (7 Leo St, Eulo; (07) 4655 4890; treatments last an hour, bookings essential; artesianmudbaths.com.au.) In Yowah, a further 65km up the road, watch local miners cut and polish the unique Yowah Nuts – mini ironstone boulders that, if you're lucky, reveal a centre of solid opal when cut open; take a look at one of the mines; and ferret around the fossicking area.

Rejoin the highway at Charleville (which is about a two-hour drive from Cunnamulla). Here the clear night skies over the plains make for near perfect stargazing conditions and the Charleville Cosmos Centre and Observatory is well worth a visit (1 Milky Way Rd, Charleville; (07) 4654 7771; open Mon–Sun 12–9pm Apr–Sept, Mon–Fri 12–9pm Oct–Mar, night shows from 7.30pm, call or check website for show times in summer; cosmoscentre.com).

From Charleville continue north across the plains through Tambo to Blackall, where shearing legend Jack Howe set a world record in 1892 by shearing 321 sheep in seven hours and 40 minutes with blade shears. It took another 58 years before anyone could match his feat and that was with machine shears. Blackall Woolscour is the only steam-driven woolscour remaining out of the 52 that once operated across the country. Colourful local characters lead guided tours that explain each stage of wool processing. (302 Evora Rd, Blackall, signposted 4km outside of town; (07) 4657 6042; open Mon–Sun 9am–4pm, guided tours on the hour.)

From Blackall it's roughly an hour's drive to Barcaldine, where, just outside the railway station under a ghost gum (sadly killed a few years ago), striking shearers met in 1891 and the Australian Labor Party (ALP) was formed. Nearby, the Australian Workers Heritage Centre examines the roles of Australian workers of all kinds, from outback shearers to nurses and teachers (94 Ash St, Barcaldine; (07) 4651 2422; open Mon–Sun 10am–4pm; australianworkersheritagecentre.com.au).

LONGREACH TO WINTON

Longreach, the largest town along the Matilda Highway, is worth staying in for a day or two. You can easily spend half a day or more at the Australian Stockman's Hall of Fame, a huge museum depicting all aspects of outback life (not just the lives of stockmen – the name is a little misleading). There are three interconnecting levels, with exhibits on everything from explorers and bush sports to droving, transport and the Royal Flying Doctor Service. (Landsborough Hwy, Longreach; (07) 4658 2166; open Mon–Sun 9am–4pm; outbackheritage.com.au.)

Just across the road at the airport is the Qantas Founders Museum, where you can take a walk onto the wing of a Boeing 747 and tour a fully equipped jumbo jet and a 707 that once belonged to a sheik, complete with gold-plated seatbelt buckles. If you ever wanted to know what goes on behind the scenes while you're cruising at 30,000 feet, this is the place to find out. (1 Sir Hudson Fysh Dr, Longreach (07) 4658 3737; open Mon–Sun 9am–5pm; qfom.com.au.) And don't miss the unique chance to ride a replica Cobb & Co coach at full gallop (Outback Pioneers, 128 Eagle St, Longreach; (07) 4658 1776; outbackpioneers.com.au).

Winton is about two hours north-west via the sealed Landsborough Highway. The Australian Age of Dinosaurs Museum on the outskirts of town houses the skeletons and bones of three dinosaurs found in the area. The star attraction is *Australovenator wintonensis*, found on a local property in 2006. Nicknamed Banjo (Andrew 'Banjo' Paterson wrote 'Waltzing Matilda' while visiting friends near Winton in 1895), it's the largest carnivorous dinosaur and the most complete theropod skeleton yet found in Australia. Learn all about it on a guided tour of the museum and the adjacent fossil-preparation lab. Also on display are the bones of the 15m long plant-eating dinosaur Matilda (*Diamantinasaurus matildae*) and a recently unearthed titanosaur (*Savannasaurus elliottorum*, nicknamed Wade), which is thought to have been bigger still. (1 Dinosaur Dr, off Matilda/Landsborough Hwy, turn-off 12km east of Winton; (07) 4657 0078; open Mon–Sun 8.30am–5pm, three-hour guided tours on the hour 9am–2pm; australianageofdinosaurs.com.)

SIDETRACK

Dinosaur Trackways at Lark Quarry preserves the world's only known evidence of a dinosaur stampede: a set of hundreds of dinosaur footprints. About 95 million years ago, a large meat-eating dinosaur chased a horde of much smaller dinosaurs on the muddy shores of a lake. The resulting 3300 or so footprints made in the mud have been fossilised, and palaeontologists believe there were at least 150 dinosaurs involved, some the size of chickens, others the size of emus. The hunter was a large theropod, probably about 8 or 9m long, with sharp claws and even sharper teeth. You can view the footprints from a raised walkway. (Lark Quarry Conservation Park, 110km from Winton via Winton–Jundah Rd – about 65km is unsealed, but fine for 2WD; (07) 4657 0078; open Mon–Sun 8.30am–5pm, 45-minute guided tours at 9.30am, 11am and 2pm; dinosaurtrackways.com.au.)

Winton has long been celebrated as the birthplace of Australia's favourite song, 'Waltzing Matilda'. Its first public performance is believed to have taken place on 6 April 1895 at the North Gregory Hotel in Winton, and it is celebrated at the town's Waltzing Matilda Centre, which includes an indoor billabong where a holographic ghost tells the story behind the famous song, as well as an extensive museum on various aspects of outback life (50 Elderslie St; 1300 665 115; open Mon–Sun 9am–5pm Apr–Sept, Mon–Fri 9am–5pm and Sat–Sun 9am–3pm Oct–Mar; matildacentre.com.au).

Opposite top Woolshed in Cunnamulla *Opposite bottom* Star-gazing at Charleville Cosmos Centre *Right* Fossils and dinosaur footprints at Lark Quarry Conservation Park

The song was inspired by the suicide of a striking shearer in the Diamantina River in 1895. Banjo Paterson, picnicking at Combo waterhole with his fiancée, Sarah Riley, and Bob and Christina MacPherson from Dagworth Station, penned the words of a poem about a swagman camped by a billabong. Christina added some music, adapted from a Scottish marching song called 'The Bonnie Wood of Craiglea', and Australia's national song, 'Waltzing Matilda', was born.

SIDETRACK

Take a detour off the Matilda Highway and follow the 'Dinosaur Trail', a themed self-driving route from Winton to Richmond that takes in a number of dinosaur- and fossil-themed stops. There's a direct (dirt) road from Winton to Richmond that will take about three hours, but it's often in rough shape, so, unless you have a 4WD, take the Flinders Highway via Hughenden (allow around four hours if going this way). Stop to check out the 7m high model of the dinosaur *Muttaburrasaurus*, fondly known as Mutt, in Hughenden's main street and the replica skeleton in the Flinders Discovery Centre (37 Gray St, Hughenden; (07) 4741 2970; open Mon–Sun 9am–5pm, Mar–Oct).

In Richmond, visit Kronosaurus Korner, home of *Kronosaurus* and the Richmond pliosaur. Both were massive prehistoric marine reptiles rather than dinosaurs and the latter is the best preserved marine vertebrate skeleton in Australia. This whole area was once an inland sea, and the museum has one of the state's best collections of marine fossils. (91 Goldring St, Richmond; 1300 576 665; open Mon–Sun 8.30am–5pm Apr–Oct, Mon–Fri 8.30am–4pm, Sat–Sun 8.30am–3pm Nov–Mar; kronosauruskorner.com.au.) You can also try your hand at finding your own fossils at a free fossil-hunting site 12km outside Richmond (look for the fish-shaped 'fossil hunting' signs high on a pole beside the road). All you need is a small pick or a chisel and hammer, and if you don't have those you can buy them for a few dollars in the museum gift shop. Museum staff will identify any finds and you can take your fossils home.

SIDETRACK

Today Combo waterhole is little more than a large muddy puddle baking under a relentless sun, but a ring of coolibah trees, usually swarming with bright green budgerigars, provides welcome shade and makes a pleasant picnic spot. To get there, you follow a dirt road (4WD recommended) that branches off the Landsborough Highway near the pub-and-petrol-station town of Kynuna, about 150km north-west of Winton.

WINTON TO KARUMBA

Cloncurry, the birthplace of the Royal Flying Doctor Service, founded by John Flynn (the town is home to a museum in his name), marks the beginning of Gulf Savannah country. The next part of the Matilda Highway, which runs north to the coast, is also called the Burke Developmental Road, and is named after explorer Robert O'Hara Burke, who together with William John Wills, Charles Gray and John King passed through the rugged country to the west of here in 1861. The Burke and Wills Junction is a good rest stop before continuing on to Karumba on the Gulf of Carpentaria, the final town on the Matilda Highway.

Located at the mouth of the Norman River, Karumba is the centre of the gulf's prawning industry, and is surrounded by flat wetlands that extend inland for about 30km and encompass a series of meandering saltwater tidal estuaries – habitat for saltwater crocodiles and a vast array of birds, such as pelicans, cranes, brolgas and black swans. From Karumba link up with the trans-continental Savannah Way (*see* p. 287) and head east to Cairns, or west to Katherine and Darwin.

☺ KIDS' SPOT

Follow in the footsteps of dinosaurs on the fascinating Dinosaur Trail, which is great for kids, particularly those with a fascination for dinosaurs. Distances between attractions are vast though (by bored-kid-in-the-backseat standards), and there is quite a lot of driving with not much to see and do along the way (an average of two hours between towns). Pick up a free copy of the Dino Diary and Passport at the Flinders Discovery Centre (Hughenden), Kronosaurus Korner (Richmond) or Trackways Tour at Lark Quarry (near Winton). It's a dino-themed activity book filled with puzzles, car games, drawings to colour in, and dad-quality dinosaur jokes (Which dinosaur slept all day? The dino-snore!). Kids can get it stamped at each of the attractions along the way. Discover more at australiasdinosaurtrail.com.

BEST EATS

- **Port of Bourke Hotel** Mix with locals and enjoy some pub-style meals. 32 Mitchell St, Bourke; (02) 6872 2544; open Tues–Sun for lunch and dinner.
- **On the Rocks Restaurant** Enjoy contemporary dining on a breezy verandah here in the heart of Charleville – the menu is a mix of Aussie favourites with an Asian twist. 74 Wills St, Charleville; (07) 4654 2888; open Mon–Sat for dinner.
- **Starlight's Cruise Experience** For something a little different, join a sunset cruise along the Thomson River in Longreach and savour a camp-oven dinner on the riverbank. Bookings (07) 4658 1776; outbackpioneers.com.au.
- **Tatt's Hotel** This authentic outback pub serves good-value meals and great steaks. 78 Elderslie St, Winton; (07) 4657 1309; open Mon–Sun for lunch and dinner.

BEST SLEEPS

- **Bourke Riverside Motel** This place began life in 1875 as the Telegraph Hotel and the historic rooms have been made over into beautifully decorated, heritage-themed suites. The riverfront garden has more than 500 roses. 3–9 Mitchell St, Bourke; (02) 6872 2539; bourkeriversidemotel.com.au.
- **The Rocks Motel** Here you'll find modern motel-style units complete with coffee machine in the rooms and a swimming pool in the gardens. 74 Wills St, Charleville; (07) 4654 2888; rocksmotel.com.au.
- **Saltbush Retreat** The two-bedroom self-contained cottages are great for families. Facilities include a laundry and pool. 63–65 Ilfracombe Rd, Longreach; (07) 4658 3811; saltbushretreat.com.au.
- **North Gregory Hotel** This is the pub where 'Waltzing Matilda' was first performed. The rooms are basic, but most have ensuites. 67 Elderslie St, Winton; (07) 4657 0647; northgregoryhotel.com.
- **Ammonite Inn** The motel-style units are just across the road from the Kronosaurus Korner museum. 88 Goldring St, Richmond; (07) 4741 3932.
- **Caravanning and camping** There are caravan parks in most towns along the route. Top spots to bush camp include Mays Bend, beside the Darling River at Bourke, and Bough Shed Hole (a lovely swimming hole) in Bladensburg National Park, 24km from Winton. No water supplies are provided, and you must be self-sufficient at both campsites in Bladensburg.

Top Birthplace of 'Waltzing Matilda', North Gregory Hotel *Bottom* Camping in Bladensburg National Park, Winton

The waterfalls, billabongs and rock art of Kakadu are just some of the highlights of this Top End drive. Beyond Kakadu you'll find magical crocodile-free swimming holes in Litchfield National Park and magnificent gorge scenery near Katherine.

Top End, NT

HOW LONG?

How much time you spend in the Top End – and what you see and do – is limited only by the amount of time you have. Two days is the minimum just for Kakadu, allowing you to see only the highlights; five or six days will give you enough time to explore Kakadu and Katherine and take a quick look at Litchfield on the way back. If you don't have time to really explore Kakadu, just do Litchfield National Park, which is an easy daytrip from Darwin and where the waterfalls are just as spectacular.

WHEN TO GO

Kakadu is open all year and is most popular in the dry season (May to November). The ideal time to go is actually the tail end of the wet or early in the dry season (May or early June). While some of the 4WD tracks to the falls will be closed (if you really want to see them the best way is by scenic flight), all the sealed roads are open, the wetlands and billabongs are full and covered in lilies, and the countryside is lush and green. If you don't mind a bit of humidity the wet, or green, season has its own rewards – the waterfalls are spectacular during February and March, there are no crowds and hotel rooms are practically half price.

NEED TO KNOW

Dogs are not allowed in the national parks. The roads (apart from 4WD tracks) are suitable for caravans. Road conditions can change rapidly during the wet season – for up-to-date information on road closures see parksaustralia.gov.au/kakadu. And watch out for crocs: you see so many crocodile warning signs across the Top End that it's easy to become blasé, but *never* enter the water unless you know it's safe. Most fatal crocodile attacks in the Northern Territory in the past 20 years have occurred when people have entered the water outside of designated swimming areas.

 Drive rating
Easy. Mostly sealed roads with optional 4WD tracks

 Distances
Total distance, return to Darwin: approximately 1140km
- Darwin to Jabiru: 256km
- Jabiru to Cooinda: 57km
- Cooinda to Katherine: 253km
- Katherine to Darwin: 316km
- Darwin to Litchfield: 120km

 Temperatures
January: 24–33°C
July: 18–32°C

 More information
- Darwin Information Centre, 6 Bennett St, Darwin; 1300 138 886; tourismtopend.com.au
- parksaustralia.gov.au/kakadu
- kakadutourism.com
- northernterritory.com

 Snapshot
Despite its fearsome reputation as a 'last frontier', the Top End – including Kakadu – is surprisingly easy to get around, even without a 4WD, as the majority of roads are sealed. You can explore such iconic destinations as Kakadu, Katherine Gorge and Litchfield National Park in a conventional 2WD car, although there are some great 4WD adventures to be had as well. And once you are inside the national parks, none of the main attractions involve long walks to access them, although, once again, there are plenty of challenging treks if that is what you are after.

Opposite top left Twin Falls, Kakadu National Park *Top right* Jacana (aka Jesus birds) at Fogg Dam Conservation Area *Bottom left* Magnetic termite mounds in Litchfield National Park *Bottom right* Swimming in style at Gunlom Falls

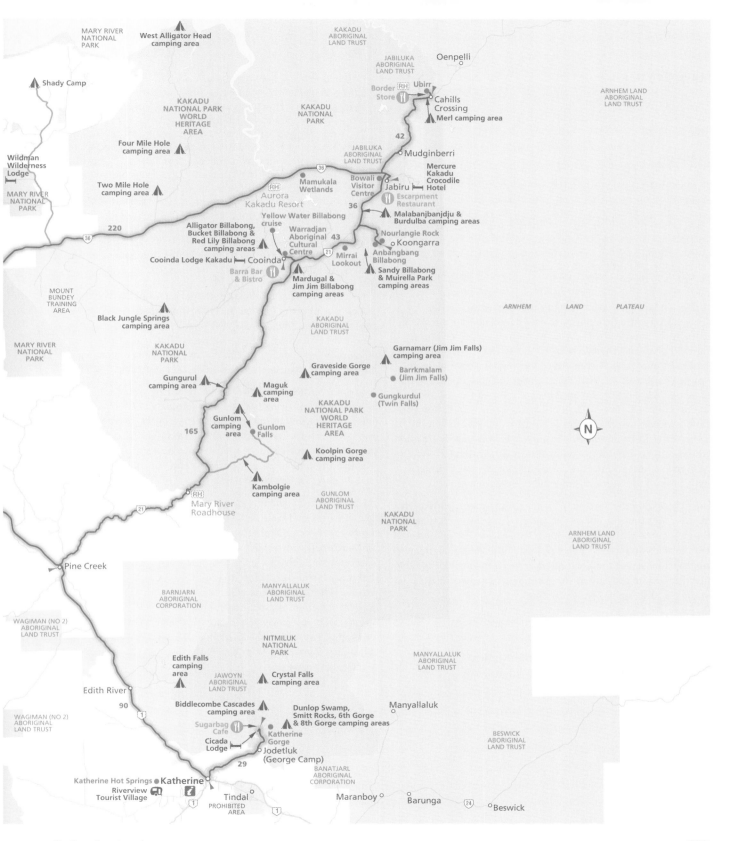

DARWIN TO JABIRU

Head south out of Darwin on the Stuart Highway and then left onto the Arnhem Highway past the tiny township of Humpty Doo.

SIDETRACK

If you are travelling during the wet season (or the very beginning of the dry season) take a side trip out to Fogg Dam. It's accessible all year but is at its very best in the Wet, when huge numbers of wading birds gather at the dam wall (which you can drive across) and the lily-covered wetlands spread out across the plains. (Don't bother going during the Dry, as there is no water then.) Unlike Kakadu, which has an entry fee, visiting Fogg Dam is free.

At the Adelaide River Bridge join a Jumping Crocodile Cruise. There are a couple of cruises available, but for sheer heart-in-the-mouth thrills opt for one of the smaller boats that will give you ringside seats to the action when the super-sized saltwater crocs spring out of the muddy water to snatch a piece of meat. It's a little bit touristy, but that doesn't mean it's not worth doing – the animals are wild and there are strict regulations around how much they can be fed, and the show of power when a 5m apex predator launches itself out of the water just metres away from you is both terrifying and exhilarating. (Adelaide River Bridge, 3220 Arnhem Hwy; most cruises are 90 minutes long and depart several times daily, year-round; jumpingcrocodilecruises.com.au.)

The Window on the Wetlands Visitor Centre atop Beatrice Hill provides an overview of the wetlands, with information and displays on their wildlife, seasonal changes and the problems of feral animals and weeds. The top floor of the centre commands superb views across the flood plains, especially during the early morning or late afternoon. (Arnhem Hwy, Beatrice Hill; (08) 8988 8188; open Mon–Sun 8am–5.30pm.)

☺ KIDS' SPOT

Kids will enjoy counting the turtles swimming in the water feature at the Bowali Visitor Centre. The adjacent Anmak An-me cafe is a great place for a snack or cup of coffee (or an ice-cream for the kids). Kakadu Hwy, Jabiru; (08) 8938 1120; open Mon–Sun 8am–5pm May–Oct, 9am–3pm Nov–Apr; parksaustralia.gov.au/kakadu/plan/visitor-centres.

SIDETRACK

Roughly halfway between Darwin and Kakadu, Shady Camp in Mary River National Park – where a tidal barrage across the river has fresh water one side, salt water the other – is famous for its barramundi fishing. Some of the Top End's biggest barramundi are caught here during the 'run off' when flood waters subside between February and May. It's also home to the densest population of saltwater crocodiles anywhere in the country and there are several crocodile-watching platforms set up on the riverbank. There's a campground here, and at night, when the tide is high, if you have a good torch you'll often see dozens of saltwater crocodiles – some up to 4m long – waiting to haul out and cross the barrage, which is about as wide as a single-lane road, into the fresh water, right where many folks fish during the day.

One of the most magnificent national parks in Australia, Kakadu is also the largest, covering more than 2 million ha and the entire catchment of the South Alligator River. The World Heritage area encompasses five main habitats: savannah woodlands; floodplains and billabongs; monsoon forest; rocky escarpments; and tidal flats and coast.

You could easily spend two weeks exploring – walking the hiking trails, floating in forest-fringed pools beneath waterfalls, gazing at ancient rock-art galleries, foraging for food on bush-tucker tours, cruising crocodile-filled rivers and bumping down rocky dirt tracks – and never get bored. But it's also the type of place where you can see much more than you'd expect in just three days.

At the very least spend a couple of hours watching magpie geese, egrets and countless other birds in the cool and breezy over-water shelter at Mamukala Wetlands (7km east of South Alligator River) and call into the Bowali Visitor Centre near Jabiru to learn about Kakadu's landscapes and habitats. It's also the place to check the latest information on road conditions, and the adjacent Marrawuddi Gallery has a great selection of art for sale; chances are you'll meet the artists, as many pieces are created by tour guides in the park. (Kakadu Hwy; (08) 8938 1120; open Mon–Sun 8am–5pm May–Oct, 9am–3pm Nov–Apr; parksaustralia.gov.au/kakadu/plan/visitor-centres.)

Time your trip to Ubirr – 20 minutes' drive north of Jabiru on the Oenpelli Road – for great sunset views over the Arnhem Land escarpment after viewing the ancient Aboriginal rock-art galleries. One of the major Aboriginal art sites of Kakadu, Ubirr was used as a shelter for thousands of years and its walls are adorned with paintings in an array of styles. Bring a torch for the short walk back down and watch out for wildlife on the road if driving back to your hotel or campsite after dark.

JABIRU TO KATHERINE

If the waterfalls are still flowing take an early morning scenic flight from Jabiru – well worth the splurge, particularly in the wet season – then do the one-hour walk around more rock-art galleries at Nourlangie Rock. During the Dry you can walk around the edge of Anbangbang Billabong at its base. Climb Mirrai Lookout for woodland views, before driving on to Cooinda, home of the Warradjan Aboriginal Cultural Centre, an excellent, free interactive museum telling the stories of the Traditional Owners (Kakadu Hwy; (08) 8979 1500; open Mon–Sun 9am–5pm). The turn-off to Jim Jim Falls and Twin Falls is just before you reach Cooinda, but its 4WD only and usually closed until early June.

At Cooinda, make sure you do the Yellow Water Billabong cruise, a two-hour tour of this breathtakingly beautiful landlocked billabong fringed by pandanus, paperbark swamps and monsoon rainforest. Take the sunset or sunrise cruise and you'll see thousands of birds and more than likely a few big crocodiles as well. (Yellow Water Cruises; (08) 8979 1500; cruises depart several times daily year-round, bookings essential; kakadutourism.com.)

SIDETRACK

It's about 82km from Cooinda to the boundary of the park. Along the way, take a detour (unsealed but fine for 2WD) to Gunlom Falls, one of the few you can see in the park without a 4WD. The 30m high falls featured in the classic Australian adventure comedy movie *Crocodile Dundee*. The falls are at their most dramatic at the end of the wet season, but they are most popular in the dry season, when you can climb up a steep rocky track and soak in the sensational views at the plunge pool at the top – crocodile free, it's surely one of the best wet-edge pools in the universe.

The Kakadu Highway and Nature's Way end at the Stuart Highway junction, 58km from the park boundary, a few kilometres south of Pine Creek. Continue south for 90km to Katherine and Nitmiluk National Park, where the Katherine River carves a series of deep gorges through towering red sandstone cliffs. During the dry season hire canoes or take one of several cruises to explore the gorges. Wear comfortable walking shoes, as all the cruise tours involve some walking between gorges. (Nitmiluk Tours; 1300 146 743; nitmiluktours.com.au.)

The natural thermal springs at Katherine Hot Springs are right on the bank of the Katherine River and signposted from the centre of town. It's a popular place to swim – the water is warm rather than hot and there are picnic grounds and walking tracks.

Above Water lily at Yellow Water Billabong

KATHERINE TO DARWIN

Katherine is 316km south-east of Darwin on the Stuart Highway, and a straight run back will take about three hours. But it's worth making a couple of stops along the way. The township of Adelaide River is the site of the largest war cemetery in Australia, the resting place of 54 civilians and 434 service men and women killed in the 1942 air raids on Darwin; also remembered are 287 service personnel, lost in Timor and other northern regions, who have no known grave.

The entrance to magnificent Litchfield National Park is 60km from Adelaide River via Batchelor. In the rivers, billabongs and waterholes of the Top End there is pretty much one simple rule: don't swim unless you want to become a crocodile snack. Thankfully, the waterfalls and river pools of Litchfield National Park are the exception to this rule. Here there are several major freshwater swimming holes fed by beautiful waterfalls, most of which are open for swimming, and almost all are accessible by conventional 2WD vehicles.

The first attraction after entering the park is a large group of magnetic termite mounds – 2m high thin towers, all aligned north–south to keep the inside of the mound cool against the heat of the sun. Buley Rockhole is the first turn-off, a chain of spa-like pools linked by small waterfalls and one of the most popular places to swim in the park. From here walk (90 minutes return) or drive to Florence Falls, where you can visit a platform that looks out over the twin falls and plunge pool, or descend the stairs to reach the base of the falls, returning to the carpark via the circuit track that winds through the monsoon forest if you don't fancy climbing the stairs.

SIDETRACK

A few kilometres on from the Buley Rockhole turn-off is the 4WD-only track to the Lost City, a group of fantastically shaped, eroded sandstone towers. The 10km track is fairly easy going, but narrow and one-way for the most part; you'll need to watch for oncoming vehicles and be prepared to pull off the track to let them pass.

Continue on to Tolmer Falls and then Wangi Falls, where two waterfalls cascade into a very large plunge pool amid rainforest. It is the most accessible of the swimming holes and includes wheelchair access to the water, although the swimming is sometimes closed during and after heavy rain due to powerful currents in the plunge pool. An interpretive nature trail leads from the camping and shady barbecue area to the top of the falls and back down to the carpark.

From Wangi Falls, head north-west back to Darwin. This road is unsealed, and may be inaccessible in the wet season, but is very pretty, with several shallow creek crossings. A good stop on the way back is the Territory Wildlife Park, a 400ha park that showcases the native plants and animals of the region and has a fabulous free-flying bird-of-prey demonstration (Cox Peninsula Rd, Berry Springs; (08) 8988 7200; open Mon–Sun 9am–5pm, demonstration times vary; territorywildlifepark.com.au).

BEST EATS

- **Escarpment Restaurant** Don't go home without trying the lemon-myrtle beer-battered local barramundi, dukkah-dusted kangaroo fillet and Gunbalanya beef – grown in west Arnhem Land it has a distinctive flavour thanks to the cattle's wetlands diet – at this restaurant in the Crocodile Hotel (*see* Best sleeps). Flinders St, Jabiru; (08) 8979 9000; open Mon–Sun for lunch and dinner.
- **Border Store** Locals swear that the curries, soups and stir-fries served in the garden outside this general store near the boundary of Arnhem Land are the best Thai food in the Territory. The store also does takeaway if you are camping. Oenpelli Rd, Ubirr; (08) 8979 2474; open Mon–Sun for lunch and dinner during the dry season.
- **Barra Bar & Bistro** Cooinda Lodge's bistro menu features crocodile, buffalo and other wild game, as well as hamburgers, barra and chips, and cook-your-own steak with buffet salad. Kakadu Hwy, Jim Jim; (08) 8979 1500; open Mon–Sun for breakfast, lunch and dinner.
- **Sugarbag Cafe** Find a table on the deck and enjoy the spectacular views over Katherine River at this licensed cafe inside the visitor centre in Nitmiluk National Park. 1300 146 743; open Mon–Sun for breakfast and lunch.
- **Adelaide River Inn** This hotel offers good-value steaks, barramundi and burgers, served with loads of friendly outback hospitality. Eat under the shady trees in the tropical beer garden. 106 Stuart Hwy, Adelaide River; (08) 8976 7047; open Mon–Sun for lunch and dinner.

BEST SLEEPS

- **Wildman Wilderness Lodge** Five-star ensuite safari tents and eco-style cabins nestle on the edge of the Mary River Wetlands. Guided tours are on offer, including an air-boat (like a hovercraft) tour. Signposted from Point Stuart Rd, off the Arnhem Hwy, roughly halfway between Darwin and Jabiru; (08) 8978 8955; wildmanwildernesslodge.com.au.
- **Mercure Kakadu Crocodile Hotel** This famous crocodile-shaped hotel, right in the middle of Jabiru, is a very comfortable four-star establishment with all mod cons. 1 Flinders St, Jabiru; (08) 8979 9000; kakadutourism.com.
- **Cooinda Lodge Kakadu** Here you'll find comfortable, family-friendly motel-style units set in resort gardens, along with a pool, bistro and licensed restaurant, just across the road from Yellow Water Billabong. Kakadu Hwy, Jim Jim; (08) 8979 1500; kakadutourism.com.
- **Cicada Lodge** A luxury, fully Indigenous-owned eco-resort in Nitmiluk National Park, Cicada Lodge also offers a range of cultural and sightseeing tours. Nitmiluk National Park; (08) 8971 0877; cicadalodge.com.au.

- **Caravanning and camping** You can camp at more than 25 designated camping areas in Kakadu. You can also camp in Mary River and Nitmiluk national parks, and there are a number of commercial caravan parks in and around Kakadu, Katherine, Pine Creek and Adelaide River. The Riverview Tourist Village in Katherine is a two-minute walk from the hot springs (440 Victoria Hwy, Katherine; (08) 8972 1011; riverviewtouristvillage.com.au). In Litchfield National Park, you can camp at Wangi Falls, which has unpowered caravan sites, and Florence Falls; there's also 4WD camping, during the dry season only, at Tjaynera Falls (Sandy Creek) and Surprise Creek Falls – all four spots offer great swimming.

Opposite Wangi Falls, Litchfield National Park *Above* The famous crocodile-shaped Mercure Kakadu Crocodile Hotel

Epic journeys

Find your spirit of adventure on one of these epic drives and coast-to-coast transcontinental road trips.

From sea to sea, this trip across the top of Australia from Cairns to Broome is one of the country's most beautiful outback journeys.

Savannah Way, Qld, NT and WA

HOW LONG?

You'll need at least three weeks to drive the whole route comfortably, but you can break it up into shorter one-week sections, such as from Katherine to Broome, if you are short of time.

WHEN TO GO

Some sections of this route are impassable between November and April, so this is a dry-season-only drive. The best time to go is between May and October.

NEED TO KNOW

Even though the road may be blacktop almost all the way these days, it's still a long drive through a remote landscape. You'll need to be willing to camp most nights, and carry your own supplies, including water, and spares.

Previous The Petermann Ranges run across the border of Western Australia and Northern Territory *Opposite top left* Historic boab tree *Top right* Sundowners at Karumba *Bottom left* Echidna Chasm, Purnululu National Park *Bottom right* Adels Grove near Boodjamulla National Park

Drive rating
Moderate. The main route (apart from a 700km section between Normanton and Borroloola) is sealed, but often only for the width of one lane, so you need to move onto the dirt shoulder to pass oncoming traffic; the route is, however, suitable for caravans. There are some 4WD-only detours.

Distances
Total distance, Cairns to Broome one way (without detours): 3700km
- Cairns to Undara: 264km
- Undara to Karumba: 517km
- Karumba to Burketown: 534km
- Burketown to Cape Crawford: 592km
- Cape Crawford to Katherine: 626km
- Katherine to Kununurra: 513km
- Kununurra to Halls Creek: 314km
- Halls Creek to Derby: 547km
- Derby to Broome: 224km
- Kununurra to Derby via Gibb River Rd: 650km

Temperatures
January: 24–37°C
July: 11–33°C

More information
- Halls Creek Visitor Information Centre, 2 Hall St, Halls Creek; (08) 9168 6262 or 1800 877 423; hallscreektourism.com.au
- Karumba Visitor Information Centre, 149 Yappar St, Karumba; (07) 4745 2211
- Katherine Visitor Information Centre, cnr Lindsay St and Katherine Tce, Katherine; 1800 653 142; visitkatherine.com.au
- Kununurra Visitor Centre, 75 Coolibah Dr, Kununurra; 1800 586 868 or (08) 9168 1177; visitkununurra.com
- savannahway.com.au

Snapshot
In the not-so-distant past, a trip across the top of Australia was an arduous journey, along rough tracks that were impassable to anything other than a heavy-duty 4WD. But with the upgrading of the transcontinental Savannah Way, the breathtaking landscape of the north is now open for all to enjoy. At almost 4000km, this is not a road trip to be taken lightly – or in a rush – but it is one of the most beautiful outback drives. Highlights include endless savannah plains, forests of boab trees, remote gorges and the spectacular Purnululu National Park.

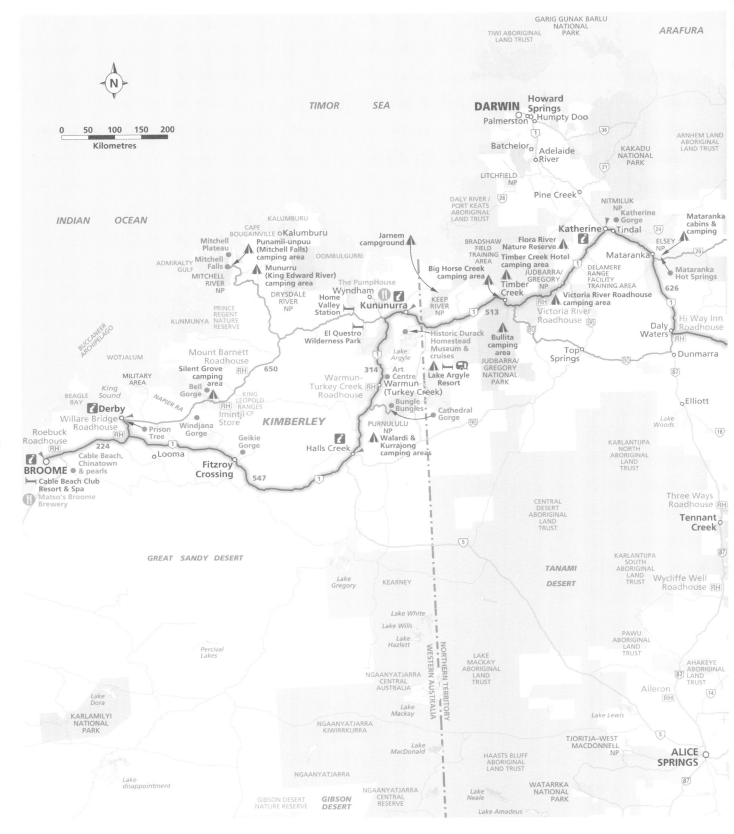

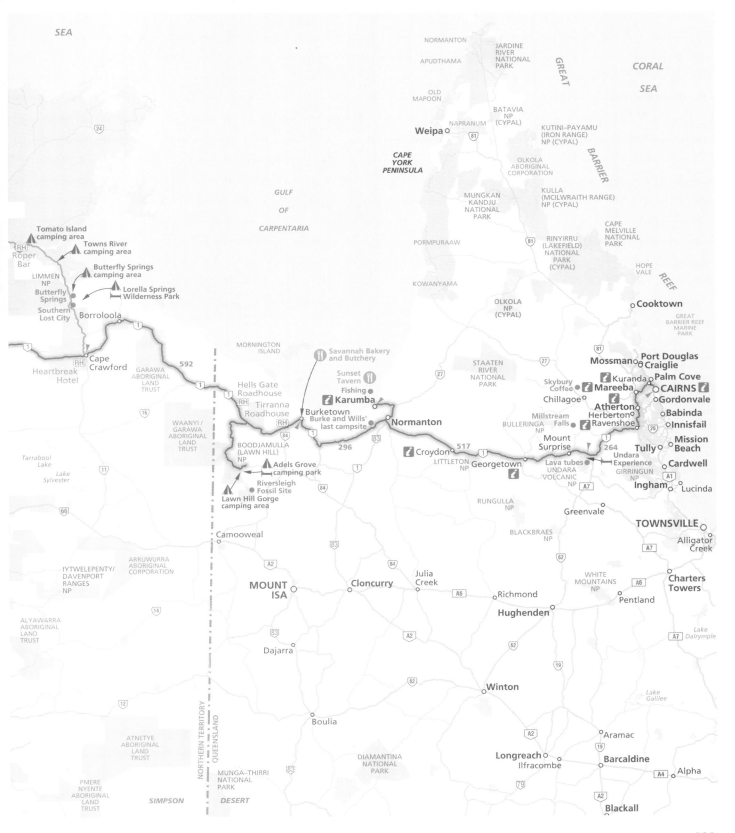

CAIRNS TO UNDARA

The journey begins at Cairns, from where you snake your way up through the rainforest to the Atherton Tablelands and the market town of Kuranda and on to Mareeba. This is coffee country – 80 per cent of Australian coffee is grown in the Mareeba area and it's your last chance for a decent cup for the next few weeks, so head to Skybury Coffee plantation (136 Ivicevic Rd, Paddys Green; (07) 4093 2190; open Mon–Sun 10am–4pm; skybury.com.au) or Coffee Works in Mareeba (136 Mason St, Mareeba; 1800 355 526; open Mon–Sun 9am–2pm). For more ideas on things to see and do in the Atherton Tablelands *see* p. 151.

Continue west through Ravenshoe (Queensland's highest town), stretch your legs at Millstream Falls (the widest in Australia) and spend a night or two at the Undara Experience, where you can explore some of the world's largest lava tubes on a guided tour. These lava tubes, which extend more than 160km, were formed approximately 190,000 years ago when a large volcano erupted violently, spewing molten lava over the surrounding landscape. The lava, estimated at 233 cubic kilometres or enough to fill Sydney Harbour in just six days, flowed rapidly down a dry riverbed. The top outer layer cooled and formed a crust while the molten lava below drained outwards leaving behind a series of hollow tubes. (Undara Volcanic National Park, Savannah Way; (07) 4097 1900; open Mon–Sun, some tours do not operate during the wet season, Dec–Apr; undara.com.au.)

UNDARA TO CAPE CRAWFORD

You'll spend the next few days travelling across the Gulf Savannah – golden, grass-covered plains, where great Brahman cattle roam the countryside in unfenced paddocks that stretch for miles. From here on, keep an eye out for road trains and be ready to move onto the dirt shoulder if you see one approaching; watch out too for flying stones hitting your windscreen. Take a break in the historic town of Croydon, so well preserved it feels frozen in time since the gold rush of the 1880s.

At Karumba, one of the few towns actually on the Gulf waters, you could spend a day or two fishing and make a nightly pilgrimage to the Sunset Tavern on the point to watch the sun sink into the sea while tucking into fresh barramundi and chips (*see* Best eats, p. 293). Seventy kilometres down the road, at Normanton, the bitumen peters out and it's a well-made but unsealed road to Borroloola, 700km away. There are a few river crossings, but in the middle of the dry season

these shouldn't be too dramatic. Stop at Burke and Wills' last campsite (Camp 119) and spend a few days exploring the lush oasis of Boodjamulla (Lawn Hill) National Park. Here Lawn Hill Creek cuts through the sandstone countryside to form spectacular gorges, best explored by canoe, which you can hire in the park. Take one of the several short bushwalks or explore nearby Riversleigh World Heritage Fossil Site, one of the world's richest fossil sites, although it does a take some imagination, peering at the fragments of bone embedded in the hillside, to picture the giant marsupials and other strange beasts of which they are the remains.

Cross the Northern Territory border and take a 15-minute helicopter ride from the carpark of the Heartbreak Hotel at Cape Crawford over the Lost City, a large expanse of tall sandstone columns only accessible by air (book at the Heartbreak Hotel; (08) 8975 9928; capecrawfordtourism.com.au).

CAPE CRAWFORD TO KUNUNURRA

If you've had enough of the dust by now, you can hit the blacktop at Cape Crawford and take the Carpentaria Highway to Daly Waters on the Stuart Highway.

SIDETRACK

Alternatively, keep to the dirt and head north-west to Mataranka via Roper Bar and Limmen National Park, a remote and rugged place with spectacular sandstone formations, numerous rivers and wetlands. It's a popular fishing destination and prime barramundi country. Butterfly Springs, in the middle section of the park, is a beautiful swimming hole that's home to thousands of common crow butterflies (and is also a great spot to camp). Most people come to Limmen, however, to see the towering rock pillars at the Southern Lost City; a 2km easy walking trail winds among the rock formations and often through clumps of prickly spinifex, so wear long pants.

From Daly Waters, head north on the Stuart Highway to Mataranka. Stop for a dip at Mataranka Hot Springs, before spending a night or two in Katherine. A highlight here is the sunset cruise through Katherine Gorge in Nitmiluk National Park (*see* p. 277). From Katherine take the Victoria Highway west to Timber Creek and the Western Australian border.

SIDETRACK

If you want to kick up more dust, head south on the Stuart Highway and turn west just before Dunmarra, onto the Buchanan Highway. This sometimes-rough track travels west through wide-open cattle country; highlights include stopping at Top Springs Hotel to wash away the grime and camping underneath the boab trees in Judbarra/ Gregory National Park. Although you can travel this route in a conventional 2WD vehicle, many of the roads inside the park are 4WD only, very rough and notoriously hard on tyres, so make sure you are prepared with a couple of spares and a puncture repair kit. Return to the bitumen at Timber Creek.

From Timber Creek, head west to Kununurra. If the banded domes of Purnululu National Park, aka the Bungle Bungles, in the Kimberley are on your bucket list (*see* p. 292) but you don't fancy negotiating your way across the wickedly rough 4WD track to get there, you're in luck: it's a bit of a well-kept secret but there's a national park on the Territory side of the Western Australian border – Keep River National Park – that has the same geological landforms as the Bungles but with sealed road access. The best way to see them is on the 7km Jarnem Loop walk that leaves from the Jarnem campground and loops around the rocky escarpment – highlights, aside from close up views of the banded domes, include spectacular views from the top of the range and a rock-art gallery.

The Kimberley's youngest town, Kununurra was built in the early 1960s to serve the Ord River Irrigation Project, which created Lake Argyle. The lake is a great place to watch the sun go down with a glass of wine on a sunset cruise (see lakeargyle.com). It is also the heart of Durack country, the land of the pioneering cattle-droving family who were among the first Europeans to explore and settle in this remote area. Their history is immortalised in the Australian classic *Kings in Grass Castles*, by Mary Durack, and you can visit the Historic Durack Homestead Museum, the reconstructed Durack family homestead, which was originally on Argyle Downs Station but was moved to its present site when the lake was proposed (Lake Argyle Rd, Lake Argyle; (08) 9168 1177; open Mon–Sun 8.30am–4.30pm Apr–Sept).

Opposite Kayaking through Lawn Hill Gorge, Boodjamulla National Park *Left* Locals lined up at Daly Waters pub

KUNUNURRA TO BROOME

Head west out of Kununurra along the Victoria Highway to the junction of the Great Northern Highway and turn south towards Halls Creek.

SIDETRACK

An exciting 4WD alternative to the blacktop is the Gibb River Road, which cuts through the heart of the Kimberley to meet the sea at Derby and is an incredible adventure in itself. To reach it, turn right onto the Great Northern Highway then turn left after 8km. *See* p. 11 for more details.

Walking into Cathedral Gorge, Purnululu National Park

Further south on the Great Northern Highway is Warmun (Turkey Creek), where you can visit the Warmun Art Centre, a studio and sales/exhibition space for local artists. Significant painters from this area include Rover Thomas and Queenie McKenzie, some of whose works now hang in the National Gallery in Canberra, and it's a great spot to see (and buy) work of emerging artists. (Great Northern Hwy; (08) 9168 7496; gallery usually open Mon–Fri 9am–4pm but call first to check before visiting; warmunart.com.au.)

SIDETRACK

One of the most impressive sights in outback Australia is the Bungle Bungle Range in Purnululu National Park, east of the highway about halfway between Kununurra and Halls Creek. The distinctive beehive-shaped towers of the Bungle Bungles are made up of sandstones and conglomerates, and their orange and black or grey banding is due to alternating layers of iron oxide and cyanobacteria. Although it is only 55km from the main road into the park, the route is 4WD only and takes a couple of hours. The most visited site is serene Cathedral Gorge, a fairly easy walk. However, the best way to see the domes is on a scenic flight, which you can do from Kununurra (see kingfishertours.net).

Continue south to Halls Creek and and west to Fitzroy Crossing. At Geikie Gorge (near Fitzroy Crossing) take a one-hour cruise with national park rangers and learn about the ecology, geology and history of the gorge. Try to time your trip for sunset, when the walls of the gorge glow a deep, vibrant red.

From Fitzroy Crossing it's an easy run into Derby and then on to Broome. The port of Derby is on vast King Island Sound; tides here are the largest in the Southern Hemisphere, up to 12 metres. Stroll along the unusual horseshoe-shaped jetty to see the tidal variation; it's also a popular place to fish for barramundi and a lovely spot to watch the sunset. Just outside of town is the Prison Tree, a big boab with a 2m high opening and a hollowed-out centre, which was once used to hold prisoners waiting to appear at the local courthouse. Derby is a good base for scenic flights and cruises to the magnificent Buccaneer Archipelago (see derbytourism.com.au for details of flights).

The popular resort town of Broome is 224km to the west along the Great Northern Highway. Take a sunset camel ride on beautiful Cable Beach, a 23km expanse of white sand washed by turquoise ocean, wander around historic Chinatown with its unique iron architecture, and, of course, check out the pearls that this former pearling port is famous for.

BEST EATS

- **Sunset Tavern** Have some great fresh-caught fish with chips and a glass of something cold as you watch the sun set over the Gulf. 2 Ward St, Karumba Point; (07) 4745 9183; open Mon–Sun for lunch and dinner.
- **Savannah Bakery and Butchery** Burketown is the self-proclaimed 'Barramundi Fishing Capital of the World', although it's the barra pies at this bakery that are really famous, along with the 'roadkill' pies and sausages with buffalo, crocodile, emu, kangaroo, camel and wild boar. 86 Beames St, Burketown; (07) 4745 5290; open Mon–Fri 8am–5pm, Sat 9am–1pm.
- **The Pumphouse** Situated in the old pump house on the Ord River, 3km from town, this is the best place to eat in Kununurra. Built in 1961, the pump station was decommissioned in 1972 when the Ord River Dam was built, but it has now been transformed into a stylish waterfront eatery without losing its heritage: get a table inside and you'll be sitting between the monster pumps and other assorted bits of machinery. The best place to sit, though, is out on the deck overlooking the lake. Lakeview Dr, Kununurra; (08) 9169 3222; open Sat–Sun for lunch, Tues–Sun for dinner.
- **Matso's Broome Brewery** Enjoy bar snacks, burgers, steaks or fish and chips on the verandah or in the beer garden overlooking Roebuck Bay. The brewery produces eight beers and a dangerously drinkable alcoholic ginger beer. 60 Hamersley St, Broome; (08) 9193 5811; open Mon–Sun 7am–10pm.

BEST SLEEPS

- **Undara Experience** Set on what was originally Rosella Plains Station, a cattle station owned and run by the Collins family (the first white settlers in the district) since 1862, this establishment offers a range of accommodation options, including huts, railway carriages, pre-erected tents and camp and caravan sites. Undara Volcanic Park, Savannah Way; (07) 4097 1900; open Mon–Sun; undara.com.au.
- **Adels Grove** Beside a spring-fed creek perfect for swimming, Adels Grove, which was once a botanical garden, is just 10km from the entrance of Boodjamulla (Lawn Hill) National Park. There are two unpowered campgrounds, as well as a range of accommodation options including permanent tents with made-up beds and river views and airconditioned donga-style cabins with ensuites. There's also a convivial bar and restaurant on a deck overlooking the creek. Cruises and walking tours of Lawn Hill Gorge and the nearby fossil fields at Riversleigh World Heritage Area are a highlight. Lawn Hill Rd, Lawn Hill; (07) 4748 5502; adelsgrove.com.au.

- **Lorella Springs Wilderness Park** You could easily spend a week exploring this family-owned 400,000ha wilderness park on the edge of the gulf, fishing, birdwatching and 4WD exploring. Lorella has several nice swimming spots, although the most popular are the hot springs, which flow between the campground and the rustic outdoor bar. Self-contained airconditioned cabins and motel-style ensuite rooms are also available. It's 200km south of Roper Bar, 140km north-west of Borroloola. The turn-off is signposted off the Savannah Way – the 29km road in to the station can be corrugated and dusty; (08) 8975 9917; lorellasprings.com.au.
- **Lake Argyle Resort & Caravan Park** Choose from luxury lakeview villas, studio cabins or a shady campsite, and have a swim in the infinity pool. 525 Lake Argyle Rd, Lake Argyle, via Kununurra; (08) 9168 7777; lakeargyle.com.
- **Cable Beach Club Resort & Spa** The only resort in Broome located on Cable Beach, this is still the best place in town to stay – and watch the sun go down with a cocktail in hand. 1 Cable Beach Rd, Broome; (08) 9192 0400; cablebeachclub.com.
- **Caravanning and camping** Undara Experience has powered caravan and camping sites and in Boodjamulla (Lawn Hill) National Park you can camp near Lawn Hill Gorge (not suitable for caravans) or at nearby Adels Grove – during June, July and August you'll need to book ahead (see individual entries left). In Limmen National Park there are boat ramps and basic campgrounds at Towns River and Tomato Island and you can also camp at Butterfly Springs and Lorella Springs Wilderness Park (see entry above). Elsey National Park near Mataranka has both tent and unpowered caravan sites and you can camp beside a waterfall (no swimming, it's croc country) in Flora River Nature Reserve 122km south-west of Katherine – facilities include hot showers. There are commercial campgrounds at Victoria River Roadhouse and Timber Creek or bush camp in Judbarra/Gregory National Park at Big Horse Creek, which is just off the sealed Victoria Highway; it has a boat ramp and is very popular with anglers, which means it can often be very crowded. Less crowded is the campground at Bullita Homestead on the banks of the East Baines River but it's not suitable for caravans. Jarnem campground in Keep River National Park offers great views of sandstone outcrops. Lake Argyle has possibly the best caravan park pool in the country – a wet-edge pool overlooking the lake (see entry above) – and if you have a 4WD you can camp at Purnululu National Park. Other towns with caravan parks include Karumba, Kununurra, Halls Creek, Fitzroy Crossing and Broome. See p. 11, for more camping options on Gibb River Road.

Take the coast road north through cities full of classic Queensland architecture to reach Cairns with detours along the way to beautiful beaches and lush national parks.

Brisbane to Cairns, Qld

Since going to print, some of the areas featured in this trip were affected by flooding. Some of the information, particularly about roads in about roads in national parks and camping areas in the southern section of this road trip, may have since changed – contact local visitor information centres for updates before travelling.

HOW LONG?

It's best to take your time and allow ten days, though it is feasible to do the trip in just three days, stopping overnight at Seventeen Seventy and Airlie Beach on the way.

WHEN TO GO

Any time of the year is a good time to do this drive, although the best swimming weather on the southern beaches is during the summer months. The Far North is best in winter, when the days are dry and the water is free of marine stingers – Irukandji and box jellyfish – which are very painful and can even be fatal. The best time to see whales in Hervey Bay is from August to October.

NEED TO KNOW

Much of this route follows the Bruce Highway, one of the country's main transport corridors, which means truck traffic can be heavy at certain times. Most of the coastal towns along this route are busy during school holidays, so book accommodation or campsites ahead at these times.

 Drive rating
Easy. Sealed roads

 Distances
Total distance, Brisbane to Cairns via the Bruce Highway: approximately 1700km
- Brisbane to Noosa: 140 km
- Noosa to Bundaberg: 263km
- Bundaberg to Seventeen Seventy: 130km
- Seventeen Seventy to Rockhampton: 240km
- Rockhampton to Mackay: 330km
- Mackay to Airlie Beach: 150km
- Airlie Beach to Townsville: 277km
- Townsville to Cairns: 348km

 Temperatures
January: 25–31°C
July: 18–22°C

Note: These temperatures are for the Whitsunday region. The far northern coast is much milder during winter, when average daytime temperatures are in the mid-20s, but is very humid in summer.

 More information
- Hervey Bay Visitor Information Centre, 227 Maryborough–Hervey Bay Rd, Hervey Bay; 1800 811 728; visitfrasercoast.com
- Noosa Visitor Information Centre, 61 Hastings St, Noosa Heads; 1300 066 672; visitnoosa.com.au
- Townsville Information Centre, Flinders Mall, Townsville; 1800 801 902; townsvillenorthqueensland.com.au
- tourismwhitsundays.com.au

Snapshot
A leisurely drive up the Queensland coast from Brisbane to Cairns, or the same trip in reverse, is a classic summertime holiday road trip that doesn't have to be done in summer – the further north you go, the warmer it gets! While the beaches are the main drawcard, there is also the Great Barrier Reef and its offshore islands to explore, along with some fantastic rainforest hinterland detours. Pack your sunscreen and swimmers and enjoy the best of the Sunshine State.

Opposite Sunshine Beach near Noosa Heads on the Sunshine Coast

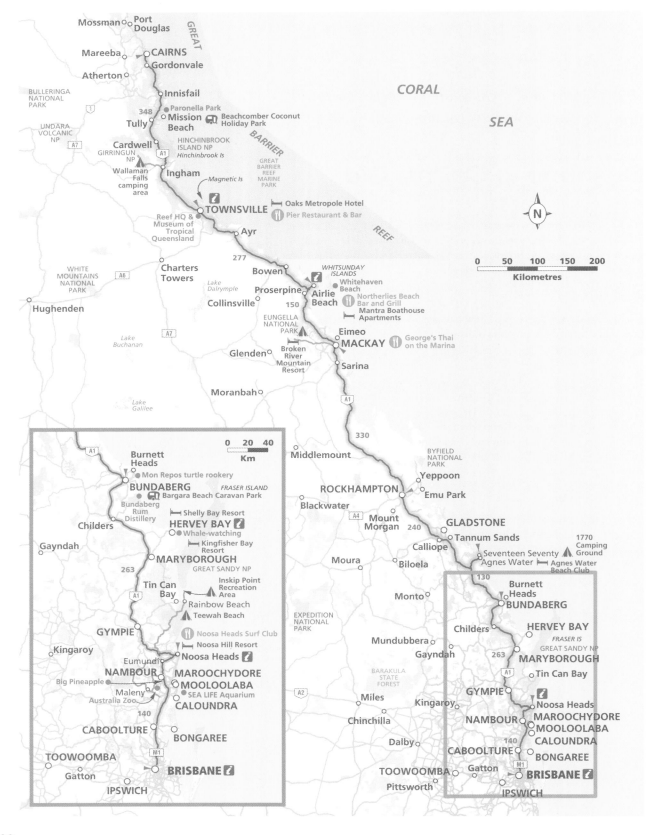

Mossman
Port Douglas
Mareeba
CAIRNS
Atherton
Gordonvale

BULLERINGA NATIONAL PARK
UNDARA VOLCANIC NP
Innisfail
CORAL
SEA

Paronella Park
Mission Beach
Beachcomber Coconut Holiday Park
Tully
348

Cardwell
GIRRINGUN NP
HINCHINBROOK ISLAND NP
Hinchinbrook Is
Wallaman Falls camping area
Ingham
Magnetic Is
GREAT BARRIER REEF MARINE PARK

TOWNSVILLE
Oaks Metropole Hotel
Pier Restaurant & Bar
Reef HQ & Museum of Tropical Queensland
Ayr

WHITE MOUNTAINS NATIONAL PARK
Charters Towers
Lake Dalrymple
277
Bowen
WHITSUNDAY ISLANDS
Whitehaven Beach

Hughenden
Collinsville
Proserpine
Airlie Beach
150
Northerlies Beach Bar and Grill
Mantra Boathouse Apartments

Lake Buchanan
EUNGELLA NATIONAL PARK
Eimeo
MACKAY
George's Thai on the Marina
Glenden
Broken River Mountain Resort
Lake Galilee
Moranbah
Sarina

Middlemount
BYFIELD NATIONAL PARK
Yeppoon
ROCKHAMPTON
Emu Park
330

Burnett Heads
Mon Repos turtle rookery
BUNDABERG
FRASER ISLAND
Bargara Beach Caravan Park
Bundaberg Rum Distillery
Childers
Shelly Bay Resort
HERVEY BAY
Whale-watching
Gayndah
Kingfisher Bay Resort
MARYBOROUGH
GREAT SANDY NP
263
Tin Can Bay
Inskip Point Recreation Area
Rainbow Beach
Teewah Beach
GYMPIE
Noosa Heads Surf Club
Kingaroy
Noosa Hill Resort
Eumundi
Noosa Heads
NAMBOUR
Big Pineapple
MAROOCHYDORE
Maleny
MOOLOOLABA
Australia Zoo
SEA LIFE Aquarium
CALOUNDRA
140
CABOOLTURE
TOOWOOMBA
BONGAREE
Gatton
BRISBANE
IPSWICH

Blackwater
GLADSTONE
Tannum Sands
Mount Morgan
240
Calliope
1770 Camping Ground
Seventeen Seventy
Agnes Water
Moura
Biloela
Agnes Water Beach Club
130
Burnett Heads
BUNDABERG
Monto
HERVEY BAY
Childers
FRASER IS
GREAT SANDY NP
Mundubbera
MARYBOROUGH
Gayndah
263
Tin Can Bay
BARAKULA STATE FOREST
Miles
GYMPIE
Noosa Heads
Kingaroy
NAMBOUR
MAROOCHYDORE
Chinchilla
MOOLOOLABA
CALOUNDRA
140
CABOOLTURE
BONGAREE
Dalby
TOOWOOMBA
Gatton
BRISBANE
Pittsworth
IPSWICH

EXPEDITION NATIONAL PARK

0 50 100 150 200
Kilometres

0 20 40
Km

KIDS' SPOT

Crikey! Take in the amazing crocodile shows, the giraffes, rhinos and zebras roaming through the open-range Africa exhibit, and the many species of Australian wildlife at the renowned Australia Zoo (1638 Steve Irwin Way, Beerwah; (07) 5436 2000; open Mon–Sun 9am–5pm; australiazoo.com.au). Or explore the wonders of the deep at Mooloolaba's SEA LIFE Sunshine Coast Aquarium, where the kids (or you) can be kissed by seals, handle sea stars and sea cucumbers, watch a variety of shows and presentations, learn about marine conservation, or walk through the shark-tunnel aquarium that houses more than eight species of shark. If you're game, you can even dive with the sharks, as well as swim with seals or become a seal trainer for the day. Parkyn Pde, Mooloolaba; (07) 5458 6280; open Mon–Sun 9am–3pm, 9am–5pm during Queensland school holidays; underwaterworld.com.au.

BRISBANE TO BUNDABERG

From Brisbane, head north to the Sunshine Coast, about 90 minutes' drive from the city centre via the Bruce Highway. Spend some time in Noosa browsing the boutiques or watching the passing parade from one of the cafes along Hastings Street (Noosa's main street), then take a walk through Noosa National Park (at the eastern end of Hastings Street) to the headland. If you're lucky, you may see koalas along the way. A great bargain is the all-day ticket on the wooden ferry that plies the waterways between Hastings Street, Noosaville and Tewantin. Take the 90-minute-return trip, or hop on and off as often as you like.

If you're not in a rush – and you shouldn't be on this trip because there are so many terrific things to see and do – spend a lazy day paddling the waterways around the Noosa area. Cooloola is considered one of the best canoeing spots in Australia and the tannin-stained water of the upper Noosa River is famous for its spectacular reflections. Other local attractions include taking a 4WD along Teewah Beach, which also has some fantastic beachside camping spots, or exploring the rainforest-clad hills of the Noosa hinterland on a day drive.

Head west out of Noosa to Eumundi, where every Saturday and Wednesday morning crowds flock to the famed markets to browse a huge array of local produce, art and crafts. If you are not in town on market day, there are several art galleries and craft studios to browse on the main street. From Eumundi drive south to Nambour and then cut west to Mapleton along the spine of the Blackall Range to Montville and Maleny for great views of the coast and hinterland and good shopping. Take the short loop drive out of Maleny along Mountain View Road for more views, a picnic and a boardwalk stroll through Mary Cairncross Scenic Reserve, a 55ha remnant rainforest reserve with an excellent Rainforest Discovery Centre. Wind your way down the mountains along the Maleny–Kenilworth Road via Conondale and cross the beautiful Obi Obi Valley to negotiate the steep, mountain-hugging ascent back up the range (not suitable for caravans) to Mapleton, stopping at Mapleton Falls to look out over the waterfall or hike the one-hour circuit walk.

On the beach, Noosa National Park

From the Sunshine Coast continue north to Hervey Bay, one of the best places to see humpback whales – they stop here on their annual migration from Antarctica, taking advantage of the calm waters sheltered by Fraser Island, and you can get very close to them on whale-watching tours. There are almost a dozen tour operators who run cruises in the bay during the season (June–Nov); for details, see visitfrasercoast.com.

SIDETRACK

Just because you have a car doesn't mean you can't head offshore. If you have a 4WD, take the car ferry to Fraser Island and spend a day or two driving along the beach and the island's sandy trails. If you have a 2WD, leave it on the mainland, jump on the ferry and simply relax for a day or two on this beautiful World Heritage–listed island; hire a 4WD on the island or take one of the dozens of tours on offer. Access to Fraser Island is via barge at Inskip Point, on the northern end of Rainbow Beach, or River Heads, south of Hervey Bay; or by ferry from Urangan Boat Harbour. All vehicles need an access permit (contact parks.des.qld.gov.au for details). For information on ferry crossings and car hire, see fraserisland.net.

😊 KIDS' SPOT

Take a ride down memory lane on the heritage-listed Pineapple Train through the sugar cane at one of Australia's sweetest big things, the Big Pineapple at Nambour. Trains depart every half-hour and an added bonus is that parents ride at kids' prices. Built in 1971, the 16m high fibreglass pineapple – highlight of countless Gen X childhoods – was one of the first of the 'big' roadside attractions. It's currently undergoing a renewal program and there's now a zoo here with more than 200 animals, a TreeTop Challenge high ropes and zipline course (bookings essential 1300 881 446), a host of special events and music festivals throughout the year and a cafe serving fair-trade Montville Coffee, as well as plenty of pineapple-themed goodies on sale (don't leave without trying a pineapple sundae). Future plans include a waterpark, brewery, RV park and glamping. 76 Nambour Connection Rd, Woombye; open Mon–Sun 8.30am–4pm; bigpineapple.com.au.

Bundaberg, roughly 90 minutes' drive north, is home to the famous Bundy rum, and you can tour the distillery and even join a class to blend your own rum (Hills St, Bundaberg; (07) 4131 2999; open Mon–Fri 10am–5pm, Sat–Sun 10am–4pm, tours on the hour 10am–2pm; bundabergrum.com.au). Other local activities include trips to offshore coral-cay islands such as Lady Musgrave or Lady Elliot, or evening tours of the Mon Repos turtle rookery, where sea turtles come ashore to lay their eggs between November and March; eight weeks later, the newly hatched turtles return to the sea. The best time to go is January, when you might be lucky enough to see both adults and hatchlings. (Mon Repos Conservation Park; 1300 722 099; turtle-viewing tours nightly Nov–Mar.)

Opposite top Stopping to admire the sights along the Grove Track, Eungella National Park *Opposite bottom* The famous white sand of Whitehaven Beach *Right* Tiny turtle hatchlings at Mon Repos Turtle Conservation Park

BUNDABERG TO AIRLIE BEACH

The twin towns of Agnes Water and Seventeen Seventy are about a 90-minute drive north. James Cook came ashore here in May 1770, inspiring the town's unusual name. Apart from a lighthouse, beachside caravan park and a few beach houses, not much has changed since – the beautiful inlet is surrounded by mangroves and white sandy beaches and there isn't a high-rise tower in sight. Take your last chance to surf: Seventeen Seventy has the northernmost surf beach in Queensland. Or jump aboard the pink Army LARC (Lighter Amphibious Resupply Cargo) vessel for a tour of Eurimbula National Park (1770 LARC! Tours; (07) 4974 9422; 1770larctours.com.au).

Check out the bull statues in Rockhampton, the beef capital of Australia, and taste the sweet life in the cane fields near Sarina and Mackay.

SIDETRACK

Head up into the hills to Eungella National Park (pronounced *yun-galah*). It is split into two sections, above and below the ranges, and both are worth visiting. Finch Hatton Gorge, just a few minutes west of Pinnacle in the Pioneer Valley, is part of the lowlands section and features two delightfully icy swimming holes fed by waterfalls. The highland section is a rainforest-clad plateau, usually several degrees cooler than the coast, and has some fantastic short walks, most of which offer spectacular views. If you only have time for one, make it the ten-minute Sky Window walk that leads to a stunning lookout over the valley below. But the main reason most people come to Eungella is to see platypus at Broken River. There are several viewing platforms strung out along the river near the picnic area and locals like to boast that it is one of the most reliable places 'on the planet' to see platypus in the wild.

Continue north to Airlie Beach, gateway to the Whitsunday Islands. The Whitsundays are a sailors' paradise, and numerous sailing tours are available, including bareboat charters (DIY skipper), at Airlie Beach. Most head out to Whitehaven Beach, a popular contender for having the world's whitest sands (whether it does is a matter of scientific analysis, but it's gorgeous anyway). One of the best things about Airlie Beach is that you don't have to spend money to get wet in style. Between the palm-fringed beach and the main street you'll find a massive artificial lagoon where you can swim stinger free, all year round. It's just like having your own five-star resort pool – but it's free!

SIDETRACK

It can be difficult to tear yourself away from Airlie Beach's magical water and beautiful islands, but the hinterland has some magnificent rainforest. A highlight is swimming in the crystal-clear, cool water below Cedar Creek Falls at the edge of Conway National Park, where a 12m waterfall cascades into a beautiful plunge pool.

Above Townsville Marina

AIRLIE BEACH TO CAIRNS

It's about a seven- to eight-hour drive from Airlie Beach to Cairns, so break the journey halfway at Townsville, where there is plenty to see and do. A top spot is the Strand, a 2.5km stretch of inner-city beachfront lined with cafes, parks, playgrounds, swimming enclosures and picnic and barbecue areas. Drive to the top of Castle Hill for views of the city (night-time views are spectacular) and nearby Magnetic Island, and then, if you can resist the lure of the beach or the shade of the Strand, head to Reef HQ, the world's largest coral reef aquarium and home to the only living coral reef in captivity (2–68 Flinders St, Townsville; (07) 4750 0800; open Mon–Sun 9.30am–5pm; reefhq.com.au).

Just next door to Reef HQ is the Museum of Tropical Queensland, which includes a fascinating exhibit on the wreck of HMS *Pandora*, the ship sent to find the *Bounty* and her mutinous crew in 1790. On her return voyage, having captured 14 of the mutineers in Tahiti, the *Pandora* struck the Great Barrier Reef. The wreck was discovered in 1977 and has been carefully excavated, with the artefacts on show at the museum. The story of the mutineers, their capture and the subsequent fight for survival after the wreck is fascinating. Kids will love the twice-daily loading and firing of the ship's cannon. (70–102 Flinders St, Townsville; (07) 4726 0600; open Mon–Sun 9.30am–5pm; mtq.qm.qld.gov.au.)

SIDETRACK

Jump aboard the car ferry to Magnetic Island. This large island is surrounded by marine-park waters and fringing reefs and more than half of it is national park. Features include rocky granite headlands dotted with hoop pines, sandy bays and pockets of rainforest. There are two ferry companies that travel to Magnetic Island from Townsville (near the marina at the eastern end of the Strand) and the trip takes about 30 minutes (see sealinkqld.com.au and magneticislandferries.com.au).

Leaving Townsville, the countryside gets greener as you head into the tropics for the last leg of this journey.

SIDETRACK

Take a 40-minute detour to one of the north's little known wonders, Wallaman Falls in Girringun National Park. Along with two falls in New South Wales (*see* p. 45), it claims to be the biggest single-drop waterfall in the Southern Hemisphere.

The stretch of coast between Townsville and Cairns is known as the Cassowary Coast, and Mission Beach – which is actually four villages linked by a 14km stretch of golden sand – is one of the best places to see these notoriously shy supersized flightless birds (Australia's heaviest bird) in the wild. Good spots to see them include the South Mission Beach Transfer Station (that is, the tip), and the Beachcomber Coconut Holiday Park (122 Kennedy Espl, South Mission Beach; *see* Best sleeps).

Another sight worth seeing is the Spanish castle ruins and rainforest gardens at Paronella Park, around halfway to Innisfail (1671 Japoonvale Rd; (07) 4065 0000; open Mon–Sun 9am–7.30pm; paronellapark.com.au). From here, it's just 120km to Cairns.

BEST EATS

- **Noosa Heads Surf Club** Located at the eastern end of Hastings Street, the club offers affordable meals and million-dollar views over the beach, and it's a great spot for lunch, particularly if you can nab a table on the deck. 69 Hastings St, Noosa Heads; (07) 5447 3055; open Mon–Sun for lunch and dinner, Sat–Sun for breakfast; noosasurfclub.com.au.
- **George's Thai on the Marina** Head here for quality Thai food on the waterfront. Mulherin Dr, Mackay; (07) 4955 5778; open Mon–Sun for lunch and dinner; georgesthaimackay.com.au.
- **Northerlies Beach Bar and Grill** Dine out with a view at this waterfront restaurant on the edge of Airlie Beach. The menu is seasonal, but there's always plenty of seafood and good steaks. 116 Pringle Rd, Airlie Beach; 1800 682 277; open Mon–Sun for lunch and dinner; northerlies.com.au.
- **Pier Restaurant and Bar** This à la carte restaurant specialises in seafood and has superb views of the city, harbour and marina. Sir Leslie Thiess Dr, Townsville; (07) 4721 2567; open Fri–Sun for lunch, Mon–Sat for dinner.

BEST SLEEPS

- **Noosa Hill Resort** The large self-contained apartments here have fantastic views and it's an easy five-minute downhill walk to Hastings Street – although the walk home up the hill is steep. 26 Noosa Dr, Noosa Heads; (07) 5449 2644; noosahill.com.
- **Kingfisher Bay Resort** This Fraser Island resort includes a 152-room, four-star hotel, 110 self-contained villas and the 180-bed Wilderness Lodge for backpackers and groups. The resort also offers a range of 4WD and guided eco-tours of the island and daily activities such as nature walks, bush-tucker talks and night-time animal-spotting. Kingfisher Bay village, Fraser Island; (07) 4194 9300; kingfisherbay.com.
- **Shelly Bay Resort** A great family option, the resort is opposite the beach in Hervey Bay and every self-contained apartment (except the studios) has a balcony with an ocean view. 466 Charlton Espl, Hervey Bay; (07) 4125 4533; shellybayresort.com.au.
- **Agnes Water Beach Club** Here you'll find good-sized apartments with a nice pool within walking distance to the beaches of Seventeen Seventy and local restaurants. 3 Agnes St, Agnes Water; (07) 4974 7355; agneswaterbeachclub.com.au.

- **Broken River Mountain Resort** The resort's comfortable motel-style cabins are within easy walking distance of platypus-viewing areas; there's also a pool and licensed restaurant. Eungella Dam Rd, Eungella; (07) 4958 4000; brokenrivermr.com.au.
- **Mantra Boathouse Apartments** Located in the middle of Airlie Beach, near the marina, this is a good option for families – it even has a children's playground. 33 Port Dr, Port of Airlie; (07) 4841 4100; mantra.com.au.
- **Oaks Metropole Hotel** This stylish serviced apartment accommodation in Townsville is in a great location with free parking. 81 Palmer St, Townsville; (07) 4753 2900; oakshotels.com.
- **Caravanning and camping** Almost every town on the coast has at least one caravan park. A top spot is the 1770 Camping Ground: it's not the flashest park (there are no swimming pools or games rooms and facilities are basic), but the lack of amenities is more than compensated for by the view (641 Captain Cook Dr, Seventeen Seventy; (07) 4974 9286; 1770campingground.com.au). If you're lucky, you may have a cassowary wander through your camp at the Beachcomber Coconut Holiday Park on South Mission Beach (122 Kennedy Espl, South Mission Beach; (07) 4068 8129; beachcombercoconut.com.au). Bargara Beach Caravan Park is the closest park to the Mon Repos turtle rookery, which can be handy as the turtles work to their own schedule and sometimes, if they are late getting on to the beach, a tour can end after midnight (25 Fred Courtice Ave, Nielson Park, Bargara; (07) 4159 2228; bargarabeachcaravanpark.com.au).

If you prefer bush camping and have a 4WD there are some fabulous camping spots in the dunes on Teewah Beach in the Cooloola Section of Great Sandy National Park. Fraser Island has eight campgrounds: all have water and toilets and most have gas barbecues. There are also informal camping areas with no facilities behind the dunes on Eastern Beach and Western Beach at Fraser Island, offering quiet wilderness experiences. You can also camp at Wallaman Falls near Ingham and in several of the national parks along the coast: see parks.des.qld.gov.au for details. Inskip Point Recreation Area has several great camping grounds right on the beach and offers good fishing and sheltered swimming on both sides of the peninsula. The facilities are basic, with toilets but no showers, and the camping grounds get very busy in summer holidays; but because it's a recreation area rather than a national park, dogs are allowed (parks.des.qld.gov.au/parks/inskip-peninsula).

Nicknamed Australia's longest shortcut, for those heading from Cairns to Perth (or vice versa), the Outback Way is not just the quickest and most direct route from the north-east to the south-west, it's also a truly amazing Australian adventure.

Outback Way, Qld, NT and WA

HOW LONG?

The Outback Way officially stretches from Winton in outback Queensland to Laverton in the Western Australian goldfields. Allow at least a couple of weeks to drive the whole way, more if you start in Cairns and finish in Perth. You can do the trip in ten days, but it will be rushed. Driving on unsealed roads is tiring – don't overestimate how far you can travel in a day (six hours per day is ideal) and avoid travelling at night as your chances of colliding with a camel, a kangaroo or wandering stock are very high.

WHEN TO GO

The temperature range is extreme and travelling through the central deserts in summer can be dangerous, and flies are in plague proportions. The best time to go is April through to October. Winter days may be warm, but nights (and early mornings) can be very cold, so take warm clothes.

NEED TO KNOW

You need two Aboriginal Community permits to drive the Outback Way – one to travel between Laverton to the Western Australian–Northern Territory border from the Department of Indigenous Affairs ((08) 6551 8024) and another from the Central Land Council ((08) 8951 6320; clc.org.au) to travel the Northern Territory section of the road from the border to Yulara. Sizeable sections of the trip are sealed – more than a third all up (about 1100km) – and more is being done every year: the whole thing should be a ribbon of blacktop by 2025. The longest distance between fuel stops is 300km – between Laverton and Tjukayirla Roadhouse – but carry extra fuel as sometimes roadhouses are closed for cultural reasons.

Drive rating
Moderate. Some unsealed roads with corrugations and bulldust – 4WD or SUV recommended

Distances
Total distance, from Winton to Laverton: 2800km (4615km if you go all the way from Cairns to Perth)
- Cairns to Winton via Hughenden: 805km
- Winton to Boulia: 362km
- Boulia to Alice Springs: 867km
- Alice Springs to Yulara (Uluṟu): 447km
- Yulara to Warakurna: 333km
- Warakurna to Warburton: 228km
- Warburton to Laverton: 553km
- Laverton to Kalgoorlie: 359km
- Kalgoorlie to Perth: 596km

Temperatures
January: 10–40°C
July: 4–25°C

More information
- Alice Springs Visitor Information Centre, cnr of Parsons St and Todd Mall, Alice Springs; (08) 8952 5800; discovercentralaustralia.com
- Kalgoorlie Goldfields Visitor Centre, 316 Hannan St, Kalgoorlie; (08) 9021 1966; kalgoorlietourism.com
- Winton Information Centre, Waltzing Matilda Centre, 50 Elderslie St, Winton; 1300 665 115; experiencewinton.com.au
- outbackway.org.au

Snapshot
This is one of the world's truly great transcontinental journeys. About 1000km or so shorter than driving Highway 1 and other main roads between Cairns and Perth, the Outback Way is not so much one road as a network of well-maintained dirt roads, such as the Great Central Road and the Plenty Highway. It might be the granddaddy of shortcuts, but with Australian icons, such as Uluṟu, Kata Tjuṯa and Kings Canyon, and some of our most fascinating outback towns, including Winton, Alice Springs and Kalgoorlie, on the route, this is not a road trip to do in a hurry.

Opposite top left Gormley statues at Lake Ballard *Top right* Driving up to Miners Hut, on the road to Boulia *Bottom left* The changing colours of Uluṟu at sunset *Bottom right* Dusty sunset on the Burke River, Boulia

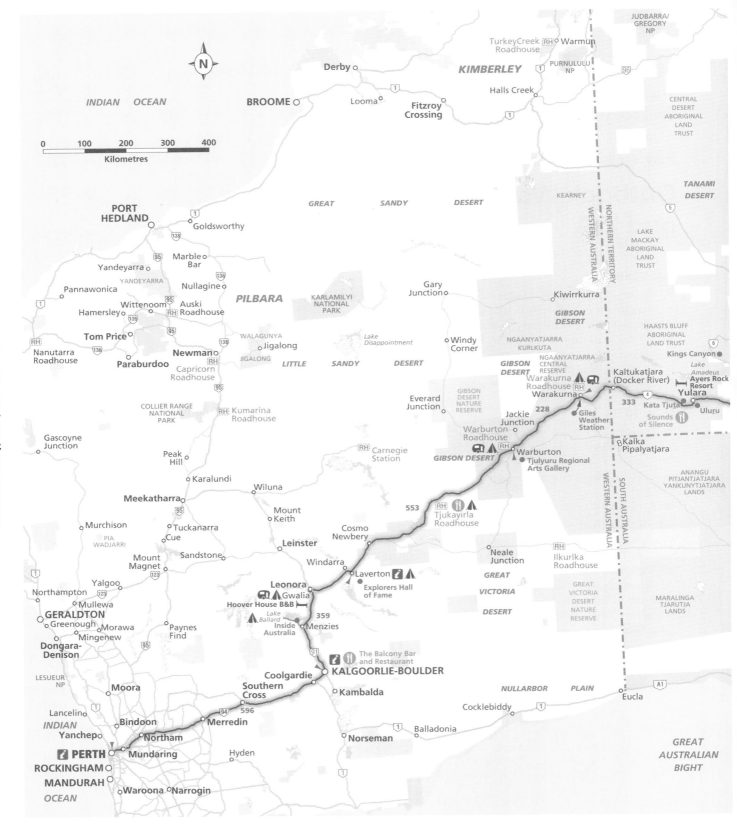

JUDBARRA/
GREGORY
NP

TurkeyCreek RH Warmun
Roadhouse

KIMBERLEY   PURNULULU NP

Derby   Halls Creek

INDIAN OCEAN   BROOME   Looma   Fitzroy
                                        Crossing

CENTRAL
DESERT
ABORIGINAL
LAND
TRUST

TANAMI
DESERT

PORT
HEDLAND   Goldsworthy

GREAT   SANDY   DESERT

KEARNEY

Kiwirrkurra

LAKE
MACKAY
ABORIGINAL
LAND
TRUST

Marble
Bar

Yandeyarra

YANDEYARRA

Nullagine

Pannawonica

PILBARA

KARLAMILYI
NATIONAL
PARK

Gary
Junction

GIBSON
DESERT

HAASTS BLUFF
ABORIGINAL
LAND TRUST

Wittenoom   Auski
Hamersley   Roadhouse

Kings Canyon

Tom Price

Newman

Windy
Corner

NGAANYATJARRA
KURLKUTA

Nanutarra
Roadhouse

Paraburdoo

WALAGUNYA

Jigalong

JIGALONG

Lake
Disappointment

LITTLE   SANDY   DESERT

GIBSON
DESERT

NGAANYATJARRA
CENTRAL
RESERVE

Lake
Amadeus

Kaltukatjara
(Docker River)

Ayers Rock
Resort

Yulara

Capricorn
Roadhouse

Warakurna
Roadhouse RH
Warakurna

333   Kata Tjuta

Uluru

Gascoyne
Junction

COLLIER RANGE
NATIONAL
PARK

Kumarina
Roadhouse

Everard
Junction

GIBSON
DESERT
NATURE
RESERVE

Jackie
Junction

228   Giles
Weather
Station

Sounds
of Silence

Kalka
Pipalyatjara

Warburton
Roadhouse RH
Warburton

Peak
Hill

Carnegie
Station

Tjulyuru Regional
Arts Gallery

GIBSON DESERT

ANANGU
PITJANTJATJARA
YANKUNYTJATJARA
LANDS

Karalundi

Wiluna

Meekatharra

Mount
Keith

553   RH   Tjukayirla
Roadhouse

Murchison

Tuckanarra
Cue

PIA
WADJARRI

Cosmo
Newbery

Neale
Junction

Ilkurlka
Roadhouse

GREAT
VICTORIA
DESERT

GREAT
VICTORIA
DESERT
NATURE
RESERVE

MARALINGA
TJARUTJA
LANDS

Mount
Magnet

Sandstone

Leinster

Windarra

Yalgoo

Laverton

Explorers Hall
of Fame

Northampton

Leonora
Gwalia

Mullewa

Morawa

Hoover House B&B

GERALDTON

Greenough

Mingenew

Lake
Ballard   359
Inside
Australia   Menzies

Dongara-
Denison

Paynes
Find

LESUEUR
NP

Moora

The Balcony Bar
and Restaurant

KALGOORLIE-BOULDER

Lancelino

Bindoon

Yanchepo

INDIAN

Coolgardie
Southern
Cross

Kambalda

NULLARBOR   PLAIN

Eucla

Northam

Merredin   596

Cocklebiddy

PERTH   Mundaring

ROCKINGHAM

MANDURAH

Hyden

Norseman

Balladonia

GREAT
AUSTRALIAN
BIGHT

OCEAN   Waroona   Narrogin

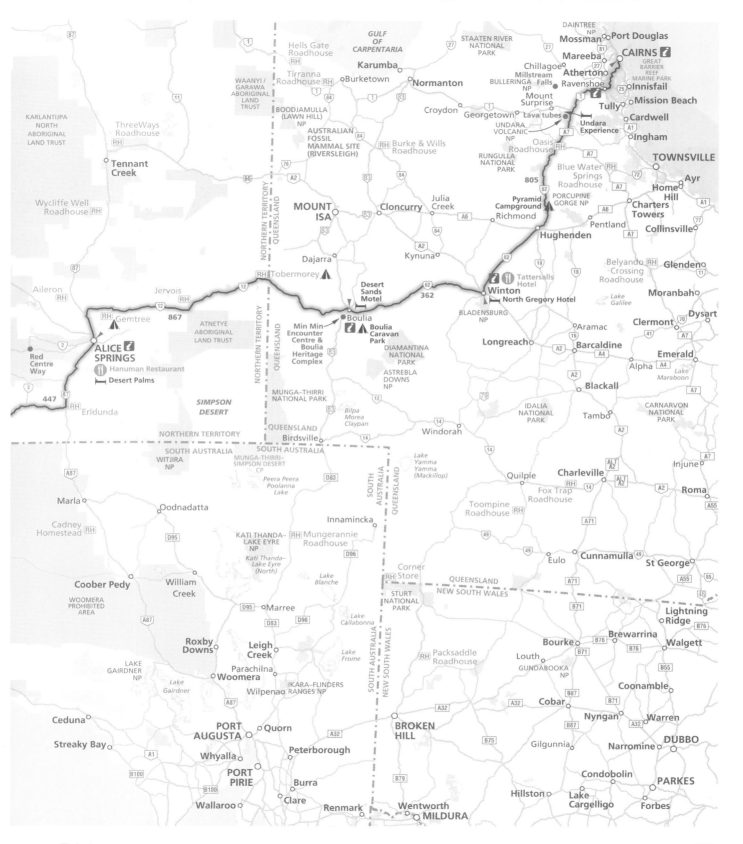

CAIRNS TO WINTON

The Outback Way officially starts at Winton, but if you are kicking off in Cairns head up over the range across the Atherton Tablelands to Ravenshoe, Queensland's highest town and home of Millstream Falls, the widest waterfall in the country (*see* p. 287). If you have time to spare take a small detour to Undara to explore some of the world's longest lava tubes – it's also a good place to overnight (*see* p. 287) – and then head south on the Kennedy Development Road.

The vast Mitchell grass plains of western Queensland can feel flat and monotonous at times, so coming across Porcupine Gorge, a massive sandstone-walled canyon with a string of deep permanent waterholes at its base about 60km north of Hughenden, is a welcome diversion. In some sections the gorge is 150m deep. It is stunning after rain or late in the day when the reflections are at their best. There is a swimming hole at the base of the rock formation known as the Pyramid but it's a steep walk back up (allow about 90 minutes return). An easier option is the 10-minute stroll to the lookout over the gorge.

From Hughenden, one of the stops on the Dinosaur Trail that winds through outback Queensland (*see* p. 269), it's about four hours to Winton, where attractions include the Waltzing Matilda Centre (the famous ballad was written and performed for the very first time in 1895 in Winton), the dinosaur stampede site at Lark Quarry and the Age of Dinosaurs Museum.

WINTON TO BOULIA

The road is sealed between Winton and Boulia and is a fairly easy drive across what seems like oceans of golden Mitchell grass. There's not much to Boulia, other than a pub and a couple of houses, but it's famous for the mysterious Min Min lights that appear after dark: floating balls of light that are said to follow travellers for some kilometres before disappearing. Depending on who you ask – and everyone you meet in Boulia will have a Min Min story to tell – the lights are clouds of bioluminescent insects, flocks of fireflies, fox eyes, fluorescent gases, Aboriginal spirits or even UFOs. According to the legend, anyone who chases the light and manages to catch it will disappear. Learn all about them at the Min Min Encounter Centre where the ageing animatronics, decked out in 1980s fashion, are so daggy they're good (18 Herbert St; (07) 4746 3386; open Mon-Fri 8.45am-5pm, Sat-Sun 9am-5pm Apr-Sept, 9am-1pm Oct-Mar). There are also some impressive fossilised plesiosaurs hidden away in a room behind the Stonehouse Museum, part of the Boulia Heritage Complex (57 Pituri St; (07) 4746 3386; open Mon-Fri 10am-3pm, Sat-Sun 10am-2pm Apr-Sept, Mon-Fri 10am-3pm Oct-Mar).

Above Porcupine Gorge

BOULIA TO ALICE SPRINGS

It's a long and sometimes dusty drive between Boulia and Alice Springs on the Plenty Highway; despite the rather grand name, it's mostly gravel, although it's usually in fairly good condition unless there has been recent rain. You can do this stretch in one very long day, but it's better to break the drive at one of the stations – Tobermorey, Jervois or Gemtree – along the way. All three offer camping and basic accommodation; Gemtree, which is closest to Alice Springs, also has fossicking, gem-cutting displays and entertaining Camp Oven Dinner shows.

It's also worth allowing an extra day or two to explore the East MacDonnell Ranges (East Macs) and the gold-rush ghost town of Arltunga on the way (*see* p. 24). For details of things to see and do in and around Alice Springs, *see* p. 19.

☺ KIDS' SPOT

Australia's longest shortcut also claims to be the world's longest treasure hunt. The Outback Way is a geocache trail, where small items – key rings, novelty toys or small mementos, usually concealed in a lunchbox or small tin – are hidden along the route and you have to find them using the longitude and latitude coordinates from your GPS. When you do find them you're expected to 'take a trinket out, put a trinket in' and leave a note in the logbook before replacing the cache exactly where you found it. Record your find and compete with others at geocaching.com/play. There are 35 cache locations each in a site of special natural, cultural, historic or scientific interest; download the cache locations from outbackway.org.au.

ALICE SPRINGS TO YULARA

There are two ways you can get to Yulara, the resort complex closest to Uluru. The easy way is to head south on the Stuart Highway to Erldunda Roadhouse and then west on the Lasseter Highway. It's fully sealed and the drive will take about five hours. The scenic alternative is the Red Centre Way, also known as the Mereenie Loop Road, through the gorges of the beautiful West MacDonnell Ranges and Kings Canyon. It's unsealed for large sections, and to do it justice you really need to allow several days, but it's one of the country's most spectacular outback drives (*see* p. 19, where you'll also find information on things to see and do and accommodation options at Yulara and Uluru).

YULARA TO LAVERTON

Before you leave Yulara allow at least half a day to do one of the walks at Kata Tjuta (the Olgas), which you'll drive right past as you head west on the Outback Way. This red dirt road between Yulara and Warburton, via Kaltukatjara (Docker River) and Warakurna, can be very dusty and a bit bumpy in sections but it's proof that you don't always need a 4WD to get off the beaten track (it's also being progressively sealed with new sections of bitumen added every year). Although it can look benign after rain when the countryside is speckled with delicate wildflowers, this is harsh country. Lots of people – explorers, gold diggers and adventurers – have died out here, including Harold Bell Lasseter, of the Lost Reef of Gold fame. The cave where he sheltered for 21 days in the summer of 1931 before he perished is signposted just east of Kaltukatjara near the Northern Territory–Western Australia border. Other highlights of this section of the trip include the stunning rocky ramparts of the weathered Petermann and Rawlinson ranges and the Schwerin Mural Crescent (another rocky range).

You're now in the heart of the western deserts – Gibson Desert is to the north, Great Victoria Desert to the south – and each of the roadhouse stops have fabulous collections of Aboriginal art for sale. Warakurna is also home to the Giles Weather Station, set up in 1956 to forecast weather conditions for nuclear weapons and rocket testing programs at Woomera. Watch the daily release of the weather balloon at 8.45am (Central Standard, or South Australian, time) from the weather station carpark, just up the hill from the roadhouse at Warakurna (warakurnaroadhouse.com.au). The site was selected by legendary surveyor and road builder Len Beadell, who with the help of his Gunbarrel Road Construction Party – which Beadell called the 'Gunbarrel Bush Bashers' – bulldozed more than 6500km of roads through virgin and sometimes unexplored territory in central Australia to service the Woomera rocket range and Maralinga nuclear-bomb test sites between 1947 and 1963. His grader, which trundled across more than 30,000km making these roads, is displayed beside the weather station, which is open for self-guided tours during business hours and features original murals painted by Beadell, also a talented cartoonist, on the walls.

Don't miss the Tjulyuru Regional Arts Gallery in Warburton; it's one of the world's largest collections of community-controlled Aboriginal art, with a focus on contemporary glass (Great Central Rd; (08) 8956 7966; open Mon–Fri 9am–4pm).

LAVERTON TO PERTH

Laverton's officially the end of the Outback Way, although most people continue on to Kalgoorlie and beyond to Perth (sealed all the way). Before you leave Laverton, stroll around the unrestored historic heart of the old mining town and spend some time at the Great Beyond Visitor Centre and Explorers Hall of Fame, which has lots of pioneer and Indigenous artefacts on display, and also serves the best coffee west of Uluṟu (5 Augusta St; (08) 9031 1361; open Mon–Fri 9am–4pm, Sat–Sun 9am–1pm).

Just an hour or so down the road is the beautifully preserved ghost town of Gwalia, established in the 1890s. When the Sons of Gwalia Mine – once one of the largest goldmines in the country – closed in 1963 the population shrunk from 1200 to less than 40 in just three weeks. As you wander through deserted streets full of grand old buildings and into abandoned houses that seem snap-frozen in time, it's easy

 KIDS' SPOT

A fabulous detour if you're travelling with kids is to head to Perth via Hyden and Kulin. It will add a couple of extra hours to your trip but the kids will love pretending to 'surf' Wave Rock near Hyden, a massive 110m long curve of granite shaped like a 15m high wave. They'll also love the wacky Tin Horse Highway. Here, on a stretch of road either side of Kulin, the local farmers have spent the past couple of decades trying to outdo each other by decorating the roadside with tin horses. At last count, there were more than 60, each bigger, better and more outlandish than the last. The first one mysteriously appeared at the turn off to the Jilakin race track in 1994, pointing the way to the annual Kulin Bush Races. The friendly rivalry has now grown into a fully fledged competition that attracts eight or nine new entrants each year, competing for a small pool of prize money and instant fame, at least around Kulin. Made in secrecy behind closed shed doors and erected under cover of darkness in the middle of the night, new horses begin to appear on the roadside in spring in the lead up to the October bush races.

to imagine that the townsfolk have simply left home for the day. The first mine manager was a young American engineer named Herbert Hoover, who later became the 31st President of the United States; visit his house (which is also a B&B; *see* Best sleeps), peer into the open-cut mine, and wander through more than 18 houses, mine offices and old shops. The Gwalia Museum tells the story of the town's boom and bust – and, a tip, it's pronounced *Gworlia*, not *Gwarlia* (16 Tower St; (08) 9037 7122; open Mon–Sun 9am–4pm; gwalia.org.au).

Menzies, 106km south of Gwalia, is also a ghost of its former self. In 1905 it had a bustling population of 10,000, thanks to the gold rush that was in full swing at the time, and it's now just one of several deserted towns littered throughout the goldfields. Menzies has, however, fared better than most with many stately buildings remaining, including the town hall with its 8.5m high clock tower and the railway station. The atmospheric cemetery, where many of the tombstones are made of tin, provides a sobering glimpse into just how harsh life was on the goldfields.

SIDETRACK

Before you leave Menzies, head north-west to Lake Ballard, a large white-salt lake in an otherwise featureless semi-desert and home to one of the country's most intriguing and otherworldly art installations. Here, scattered across the vast saltpan, flickering in the midday heat like a mirage, are 51 spectral sculptures of people – the work of internationally renowned British artist Antony Gormley. Gormley made laser body-scans of 51 of the Menzies locals and then created casts life-size in height but two-thirds in width. The resulting stick-like statues, now rusted and pocked by the harsh salt air, are scattered over 1000ha, each one standing alone about 750m apart from its neighbour, so that wherever you turn there's another on the horizon. Gormley called it *Inside Australia* (2003). It's spooky and eerie and, once you are out on the saltpan, everything seems to shimmer in the heat haze. The last 55km section of the road is unsealed but fine for 2WD cars when dry.

Kalgoorlie is about 90 minutes' drive from Menzies, and Perth is another 600km further west – for details on this section of the drive, *see* p. 27.

Opposite The 'Hilton' at Middleton may not be at the top of your accommodation list *Above* Catching a break at Wave Rock

BEST EATS

- **Tattersalls Hotel** This authentic outback pub serves good-value meals. 78 Elderslie St, Winton; (07) 4657 1309; open Mon–Sun for lunch and dinner.
- **Hanuman Restaurant** Alice Springs' best restaurant serves a spicy mix of Thai, Indian and Nyonya dishes. At the Hilton DoubleTree Hotel, 82 Barrett Dr, Alice Springs; (08) 8953 7188; open Mon–Sun for dinner, Mon–Fri for lunch, bookings essential.
- **Sounds of Silence** Yulara is around the halfway point on this trip so treat yourself to a special night out. The Sounds of Silence dinner atop a sand dune near Ayers Rock Resort is not your average bush barbecue: after a buffet dinner of fresh barramundi, lamb, kangaroo or emu steaks and delicious desserts, the lanterns are dimmed, the port poured and the legends of the southern sky are explained by a local astronomer. Absolutely worth the splurge. 1300 134 044; ayersrockresort.com.au.
- **Tjukayirla Roadhouse** Don't miss the chance to sink your teeth into a famous 'Chooka Burger' from the Tjukayirla Roadhouse (pronounced *Chook-a-yer-la*) between Laverton and Warburton. But don't be misled by the name: it's beef, not chicken. Great Central Rd, west of Warburton; (08) 9037 1108; open Mon–Fri 8am–5pm, Sat–Sun 9am–3pm; tjukayirlaroadhouse.com.au.
- **Balcony Bar and Restaurant** This upmarket pub restaurant does great steaks and has a wide selection of fresh seafood. Palace Hotel, 137 Hannan St, Kalgoorlie; (08) 9021 2788; open Mon–Sun for dinner.

BEST SLEEPS

- **North Gregory Hotel** This is the pub where 'Waltzing Matilda' was first performed. The rooms are basic but most have ensuites. 67 Elderslie St, Winton; (07) 4657 0647; northgregoryhotel.com.

- **Desert Sands Motel** Here you'll find comfortable motel-style units within walking distance to the centre of town. 50 Herbert St, Boulia; (07) 4746 3000; desertsandsmotel.com.au.
- **Desert Palms** The family-friendly self-contained cabins are good value. Relax in the pool surrounded by tropical gardens. On a long trip like this one the guest laundry is very handy. 74 Barrett Dr, Alice Springs; (08) 8952 5977; desertpalms.com.au.
- **Ayers Rock Resort** Six accommodation options are available here to suit varying budgets: the five-star Sails in the Desert; Desert Gardens (some rooms have views of Uluru); the family-friendly Emu Walk apartments; the mid-range Lost Camel and the Outback Pioneer Hotel for those on a budget; and the pet-friendly Ayers Rock campground with drive-through powered caravan sites and airconditioned cabins (shared bathrooms). 1300 134 044; ayersrockresort.com.au.
- **Hoover House B&B** Stay in former American president Herbert Hoover's old house in the ghost town of Gwalia, just 2km from the township of Leonora. 1127 Gwalia St, Gwalia; (08) 9037 7122; gwalia.org.au.
- **Roadhouses** Most of the roadhouses along the route offer motel-style accommodation – it may not be five-star flash but rooms are comfortable with airconditioning and ensuites, and if they don't serve meals there's usually a shared kitchen where you can rustle up your own from supplies sold in the roadhouse store. (See outbackway.org.au.)
- **Caravanning and camping** Many of the caravan and camping sites along this route are covered in other chapters: for details of where to camp in tropical north Queensland, *see* p. 155; Winton, p. 275; the Red Centre, p. 25; and the Western Australian goldfields, p. 33. Bush camping is available at Porcupine Gorge National Park near Hughenden. Boulia has a caravan park ((07) 4746 3320) or bush camp at the free riverside camping area near the racecourse – the Boulia camel races held in July are one of outback Queensland's big events and you'll probably see the camels going through their paces at the track in the early morning; there are no facilities here, but there are toilets and showers at the racecourse, a 15-minute walk away. On the Plenty Highway section of the Outback Way there are caravan sites and camping areas at Tobermorey, Jervois or Gemtree stations: facilities include hot showers. On the Western Australian leg of the Outback Way there are caravan and camping facilities with toilets and showers beside the roadhouses in Warakurna, Warburton, Tjukayirla and Laverton, and there is a free RV site near the museum at Gwalia. You can also bush camp at Lake Ballard, but BYO drinking water.

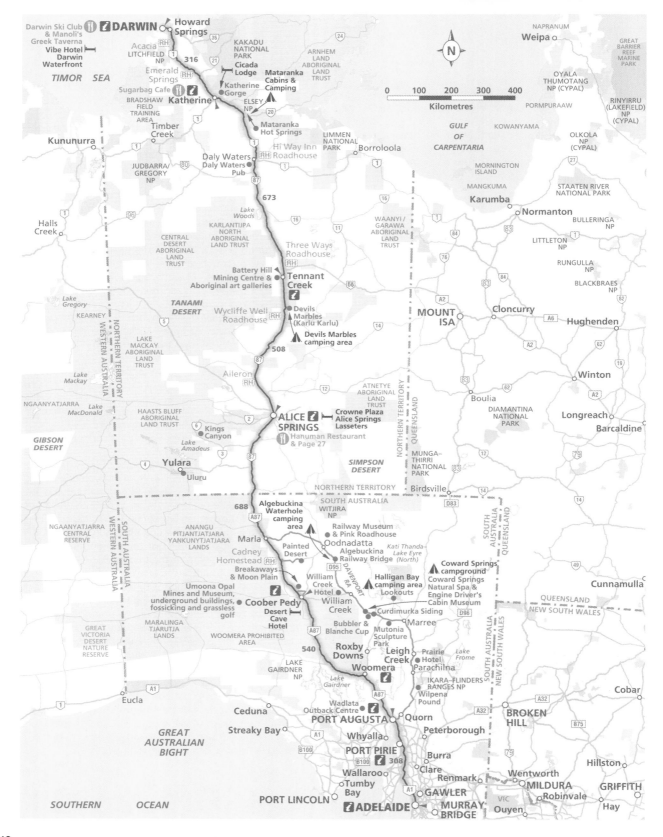

This great transcontinental drive from Adelaide to Darwin is an epic adventure through the red-desert heart of the continent.

Explorer's Way, SA and NT

HOW LONG?

Allow at least a week, twice that if you want to detour off the highway to visit Uluṟu and Kings Canyon or Kakadu. Other than flying part of the way, there are no short cuts!

WHEN TO GO

The temperature range is extreme and travelling through the Red Centre in summer can be uncomfortable, with flies in plague proportions and wet weather in the Top End. The best time to go is April through to October. Winter days may be warm but the nights (and early mornings) can get very cold, so take warm clothes.

NEED TO KNOW

This road trip involves some very long stretches, so share the driving and take plenty of rest stops. Wildlife is prolific: avoid driving at night and slow down when approaching roadkill to avoid hitting any feasting wedge-tailed eagles. Watch out too for road trains – move over towards the side of the road on approach and allow plenty of time to overtake.

Drive rating
Easy. Sealed roads with optional 4WD sections

Distances
Total distance, Adelaide to Darwin: 3030km
- Adelaide to Port Augusta: 308km
- Port Augusta to Coober Pedy: 540km
- Oodnadatta Track alternative route via Port Augusta, Parachilna, Marree, Marla: 1000km
- Coober Pedy to Alice Springs: 688km
- Alice Springs to Tennant Creek: 508km
- Tennant Creek to Katherine: 673km
- Katherine to Darwin: 316km

Temperatures
January: 22–37°C
July: 4–19°C

More information
- Coober Pedy Visitor Information Centre, Lot 773 Hutchison Street, Coober Pedy; (08) 8672 4617
- Darwin Information Centre, cnr Bennett and Smith sts, Darwin; 1300 138 886; tourismtopend.com.au
- Tourism Central Australia, cnr Todd Mall and Parsons St, Alice Springs; (08) 8952 5800; discovercentralaustralia.com
- Wadlata Outback Centre, 41 Flinders Tce, Port Augusta; 1800 633 060; wadlata.sa.gov.au

Snapshot
In 1862 John McDouall Stuart became the first European to lead an expedition across the continent from south to north – from Adelaide to just east of where Darwin is today – and back. His eight-month journey, through some of the harshest landscape in the country, opened the way for the building of the Overland Telegraph Line, which ultimately linked South Australia with England and the rest of the world in 1872. The all-sealed Stuart Highway pretty much tracks his original route. If you're looking for even more adventure – and have a 4WD – take the Oodnadatta Track from the Flinders Ranges and hook up with the highway near Coober Pedy.

ADELAIDE TO COOBER PEDY

Before you head north into the wild red yonder, visit the Tunnel of Time at the Wadlata Outback Centre in Port Augusta (41 Flinders Tce, Port Augusta; (08) 8641 9193; open Mon–Sun 9am–5pm), then spend some time in the beautiful Flinders Ranges (*see* p. 261).

SIDETRACK

If you have a 4WD and don't mind some dust and camping, the Oodnadatta Track is a fascinating alternative to the Stuart Highway. The track was blazed just ten years after Stuart charted the country, while the Overland Telegraph Line was built along his route. It was followed by the now-abandoned first Ghan railway line, which opened in 1929. All along the track you'll see remnants, reminders and ruins of both.

Once a major railhead, Marree is the jumping-off point for both the Birdsville and Oodnadatta tracks. Explore old train carriages still waiting at the end of the line and the crumbling ancient ruins of a mail truck in the park in the centre of town. Just out of Marree, a road to the right will take you to Kati Thanda–Lake Eyre (North) via Muloorina Homestead, where there are tracks to lookouts with magnificent views over the bright, white-salt vastness of Kati Thanda–Lake Eyre. Occasionally the lake fills with water and the dry saltpans become the breeding ground of an enormous number of birds, such as pelicans, silver gulls, avocets and gull-billed terns. Don't try to drive on the lakebed: although it looks firm, just below the shimmering, white, salt crust lies a slimy, black ooze that will swallow your vehicle in no time.

Stop for a rest at Mutonia, a quirky sculpture park 30km west of Marree. You can't miss it – you'll see the big dog made from an old water tank long before you get there. Reminders of the railway are never far away as you pass through places like Curdimurka Siding, a deserted but well-preserved stretch of rail, with fettler's cottage, water tower and water-softener tower still intact. A little further on are the Bubbler and Blanche Cup, the first two of several mound springs, where waters from the Great Artesian Basin bubble to the surface, creating small oases in the midst of red sandhills.

Built in 1888, Coward Springs was once a bustling community with a station, a hotel, stone-built railway workers' cottages and a hot artesian spa pool surrounded by date palms. The pub and pool made it a popular place to stop and, even though the pub was demolished in 1965 and the site was abandoned in 1980, nothing much has changed – the soothing, warm mineral waters of the natural spa pool are still a magnet for weary travellers. The old stone Engine Driver's Cabin is now a small but fascinating museum.

The track crosses ancient flood plains and undulating dunes, finally reaching William Creek, which is inside the boundaries of Anna Creek, the largest cattle station in the world at more than 3 million ha. There's a hotel here ((08) 8670 7880; williamcreekhotel.com) and not much else, but you can take a scenic flight over nearby Kati Thanda–Lake Eyre during the winter months ((08) 8670 7962; wrightsair.com.au).

Just before the town, there is a track to the right that cuts through Anna Creek to Halligan Bay, on the western shores of Kati Thanda–Lake Eyre (North) – a great place to camp for a few days. However, you must be self-sufficient, with gas stoves and plenty of water – and, if something does go wrong, under no circumstances should you leave your vehicle. Sign in and out at the William Creek Hotel before you go and when you return.

North of William Creek the landscape changes subtly, with creeks running down from the Davenport Range. From here to Oodnadatta, you cross the major channel system of the Neales River. The half-kilometre-wide Algebuckina Railway Bridge is an indication of how swollen the river becomes during floods. The old railway station at Oodnadatta has been turned into a museum and the landmark Pink Roadhouse is *the* place locally for supplies and information.

If you've stuck to the highway, your first stop after Port Augusta will be Coober Pedy, the largest opal-mining town in the world, where most of the locals not only work underground but also live there too. In summer, when outside temperatures can reach a sizzling 50°C, underground homes (dugouts) remain a constant 22–26°C. Renovations are easy: simply dig yourself a new cupboard, bookshelf or room – and who knows, you may even find some opal in the process!

Visit one of the five underground churches in town, as well as plenty of underground opal showrooms, most of them located along the main street. But to really get a feel for what Coober Pedy is all about, you need to get out to, or down, an opal mine. The Umoona Opal Mine and Museum is one of a couple of opal-mines-cum-museums in town. Tours begin with a 20-minute documentary on opals and how they were first found in Coober Pedy in 1915 by 14-year-old William Hutchison while searching for water. Also inside the museum are an Aboriginal interpretive centre, a gallery, an old opal mine and, of course, the ubiquitous opal showroom and shop. Entry to the museum is free – unless you succumb to opal fever and are unable to resist temptation in the showroom. (14 Hutchison St, Coober Pedy; (08) 8672 5288; open Mon–Sun 8am–6pm, tours at 10am, 2pm, 4pm; umoonaopalmine.com.au.)

If you do find yourself with the opal itch, go noodling on some of the mullock heaps around town. Noodling, or fossicking for opal among heaps of discarded rocks, is free, and occasionally visitors do find good-sized opals. There is a public noodling reserve in the centre of town.

Another fun thing to do is to play a round of golf on the unique grassless golf course. The 18-hole course has 'mod grass' (green plastic woven 'grass') greens, crushed-rock fairways and no water hazards – although the dry creek beds make great sand traps. The greens are oiled to stop the sand blowing away. If it's too hot, you can play at night with illuminated balls. (Coober Pedy Opal Fields Golf Club, 1509 Rowe Dr, Coober Pedy; cooberpedygolfclub.com.au.)

Opposite The largest lake in the country, Kati Thanda-Lake Eyre
Top Playing a round at Coober Pedy Opal Fields Golf Club
Bottom Old train at Marree railway station, SA

COOBER PEDY TO ALICE SPRINGS

It's a seven-hour drive from Coober Pedy to Alice Springs, with not much to break the drive apart from a couple of roadhouses and the following detours. So, before you leave town, stock the car with snacks, plenty of water and a picnic lunch to have along the way.

SIDETRACK

Take the dirt road north-east from Coober Pedy towards Oodnadatta for 15km to see the famous dog fence and the Moon Plain – the local nickname for the moon-like desert landscape along the fence. The 2m high fence, designed to keep northern dingos away from southern sheep, stretches across three states and is the longest fence in the world. Then follow the signs west to the Breakaways (32km north of Coober Pedy), a series of flat-topped hills, or jump-ups, that seem to have broken away from the Stuart Range. At sunset the sandstone pillars, pinnacles and gully edges glow pink, red, brown, purple, yellow and white – it's a great place to set yourself up with a picnic table, some nibblies and a nice bottle of wine to watch the sundown show. Continue west to return to the Stuart Highway.

SIDETRACK

About 150km north of Coober Pedy (100km east of Cadney Homestead Roadhouse on the Stuart Highway and 90km south-west of Oodnadatta) is the Painted Desert, a rather spectacular area of eroded, multicoloured, sandy hills that glow red, yellow, ochre and orange in the light of the setting sun. It's on Arckaringa Station, which also offers camping and hot showers ((08) 8670 7992; thepainteddesert.com.au). The road is unsealed and okay for 2WD and caravans when dry, but check current road conditions before travelling.

The turn-off to Uluṟu (Lasseter Highway) is 200km south of Alice Springs; *see* p. 19 for details, as well as information about things to see and do in and around Alice Springs.

ALICE SPRINGS TO DARWIN

It's about 1500km from Alice Springs to Darwin. About 100km south of Tennant Creek, the Devils Marbles (Karlu Karlu) are a collection of gigantic, rounded granite boulders – some are 4m high and almost as wide – that make for some great photo opportunities. The area is an important meeting place for local Aboriginal people and rich in sacred sites and Creation stories.

Stock up on supplies at Tennant Creek, the site of Australia's last gold rush, which took place in the 1920s and 1930s. Visit the Battery Hill Mining Centre (160 Peko Rd, Tennant Creek; (08) 8962 1281; open Mon–Sun 9am–5pm) and any one of several Aboriginal art galleries in town. Call in for a drink at the Daly Waters Pub, which is an outback icon, before soaking away any road weariness at Mataranka Hot Springs, where water rises from underground at a temperature of 34°C into a plunge pool surrounded by a paperbark and palm forest (Elsey National Park, 642 Homestead Rd, Mataranka; (08) 8975 4560).

It's worth spending a couple of days exploring Katherine Gorge and the waterfalls of Litchfield National Park and, if you have time, taking a detour out to Kakadu (*see* p. 277 for details). By the time you reach Darwin, you'll have seen a little bit of everything that Australia has to offer, from coasts and deserts to mountains, gorges and tropical monsoon forests, on one of Australia's greatest road trips.

Opposite No-frills waterfront views at Darwin Ski Club *Right* From the air, the landscapes of the Red Centre resemble an Indigenous dot painting

Explorer's Way, SA and NT

BEST EATS

- **Hanuman Restaurant** This restaurant has some of the best food in Alice Springs, most of it a spicy mix of Thai, Indian and Nonya dishes. In the DoubleTree by Hilton, 82 Barrett Dr, Alice Springs; (08) 8953 7188; open Mon–Sun for dinner, Mon–Fri for lunch, bookings essential.
- **Page 27** The outback is not renowned for its coffee, but the coffee served here is an exception. Tucked down an alleyway arcade off Todd Mall, this popular little cafe serves hearty breakfasts and a great range of light lunches. It's cash only, and you'll probably need to line up. Fan Arcade, 4/89 Todd Mall, Alice Springs; 0429 003 874; open Tues–Sun for breakfast and lunch.
- **Sugarbag Cafe** Find a table on the deck and enjoy the spectacular views over Katherine River at this licensed cafe inside the visitor centre in Nitmiluk National Park. 1300 146 743; open Mon–Sun for breakfast and lunch.
- **Darwin Ski Club** That's waterskiing, not sliding down the white stuff. Pull up a plastic chair on the beachside lawn and toast the sunset beneath fairy lights and swaying palms while you watch the sun go down over the bay. There's a playground for kids, live music on weekends and the food and drinks are cheap as chips. 20 Conacher St, Darwin, opposite the art gallery; (08) 8981 6630; open Mon–Sun for lunch and dinner.
- **Manoli's Greek Taverna** A long-time favourite with locals, this family-run old-school Greek restaurant is great value. Try the chargrilled octopus and the souvlakia. There's usually live bouzouki music on Friday and Saturday nights. 4/64 Smith St, Darwin; (08) 8981 9120; open Tues–Fri for lunch, Tues–Sat for dinner; manolisgreektaverna.com.au.

BEST SLEEPS

- **Desert Cave Hotel** Sample Coober Pedy's underground life at this hotel dug into the soft sandstone hillside under the main street. Rooms lead off tunnels and while each room is well ventilated and airy there are no windows or natural light. A good night's sleep is pretty much guaranteed – rooms are very quiet and pitch black when you turn off the light. If you don't fancy the idea of sleeping underground, there are some above-ground rooms available. Lot 1 Hutchison St, Coober Pedy; (08) 8672 5688; desertcave.com.au.
- **Crowne Plaza Alice Springs Lasseters** The best beds in Alice Springs are the premium rooms here; there's a great swimming pool and Lasseters Casino with its late-night bars, restaurants and entertainment is just next door. 93 Barrett Dr, Alice Springs; (08) 8950 7777; ihg.com.
- **Cicada Lodge** A luxury, fully Indigenous-owned eco-resort in Nitmiluk National Park, Cicada Lodge also offers a range of cultural and sightseeing tours. Nitmiluk National Park; (08) 8971 0877; cicadalodge.com.au.
- **Vibe Hotel Darwin Waterfront** This hotel overlooks the wave pool and lagoon in the heart of the buzzy waterfront restaurant strip. 7 Kitchener Dr, Darwin; (08) 8982 9998; vibehotels.com/hotel/darwin-waterfront.
- **Caravanning and camping** There are caravan parks and camping areas in most towns and roadhouses along the highway, as well as bush camping at Karlu Karlu (the Devils Marbles). There are unpowered caravan sites at Mataranka Hot Springs (Elsey National Park) and you can also camp in Nitmiluk (Katherine Gorge) and Litchfield national parks (*see* p. 277). There are several good bush-camping spots on the Oodnadatta Track, including Algebuckina Waterhole and Halligan Bay on Kati Thanda–Lake Eyre. Coward Springs has unpowered campsites, flush toilets and hot showers – although you'll need to heat the water yourself on the wood-fired heater and bring your own wood. It's also pet friendly.

Index

PHOTOGRAPHY CREDITS

All images © Lee Atkinson, with the exception of the following:

Front cover: Stocksy

Back cover: Destination NSW

Page ii, 2 (top right), 6, 9, 56, 58, 60, 67, 123, 125 (bottom), 126, 222-223, 224, 225: Visit Victoria; iv, vi, 34, 74, 98 (top right), 102, 103, 104, 105, 106, 268, 272, 275 (top), 298, 299 (bottom), 300, 306: Tourism and Events Queensland; x, 10, 40, 79 (top), 81 (bottom), 88: Alamy Stock Images; 2 (top left), 17, 68 (top left), 68 (bottom right), 71, 73, 82, 91, 98 (top left), 98 (bottom left), 98 (bottom right), 133, 139, 148, 161, 162 (top right), 167 (middle), 167 (bottom), 168, 169, 170, 192, 239, 241, 252, 286 (bottom left), 292, 302 (bottom left), 312: Tourism Australia; 2 (bottom left): Unsplash/Kevin Laminto; 7: Unsplash/Ben Kleant; 18 (top right): Uluru Camel Tours; 26, 33: iStock Photos; 32, 36, 42, 45 (top right), 48, 89, 94, 96, 97, 176 (bottom), 184 (top), 190, 191, 206, 208, 212, 214, 216, 217, 257, 259: Destination NSW; 41: Unsplash/Christopher Burns; 111: Mornington Peninsula Hot Springs; 114: NSW National Parks and Wildlife Service; 118: Unsplash/Kane Taylor; 120 (top right), 124: Phillip Island Tourism; 135: d'Arenberg Cube Surrealist Ball; 160: Unsplash/David Clode; 228: Unsplash/Laura Smetsers; 282: Tourism Northern Territory; 332: Bill McKinnon.

About the author

One of Australia's most experienced travel writers, and two-time winner of the prestigious Australian Society of Travel Writers Best Adventure Story Award, Lee Atkinson has been writing about her adventures on and off the road for Australian newspapers, magazines and travel guides since 1991. A self-confessed road trip junky who loves getting away from the crowds in wild and remote places, she believes "that any excuse to hit the road is a good one."

Lee is the author of 13 travel books and two smartphone apps about travelling in and around Australia and co-editor of two anthologies of travel writing, as well as a contributor to Explore Australia's *Camping Around Australia* guide and the road tripping bible, *Explore Australia*. Her most recent books published by Hardie Grant Travel are *The Definitive Bucket List*, *Australia's Best Nature Escapes* and *Explore Australia by Camper Trailer*. See www.leeatkinson.com.au.

Published in 2020 by Hardie Grant Explore, a division of
Hardie Grant Publishing

Hardie Grant Explore (Melbourne)
Wurundjeri Country
Building 1, 658 Church Street
Richmond, Victoria 3121

Hardie Grant Explore (Sydney)
Gadigal Country
Level 7, 45 Jones Street
Ultimo, NSW 2007

www.hardiegrant.com/au/explore

© Imprint and currency – VAR Product and PSMA Data
"Copyright. Based on data provided under licence from PSMA
Australia Limited (www.psma.com.au)".

Transport Data (Feb 2019)

The maps in this publication incorporate data © Commonwealth of
Australia (Geoscience Australia), 2006. Geoscience Australia has not
evaluated the data as altered and incorporated within this publication,
and therefore gives no warranty regarding accuracy, completeness,
currency or suitability for any particular purpose.

Assistance with research: The publisher would like to thank the following
organisations for assistance with data and information: Australian
Bureau of Statistics, Bureau of Meteorology, National Road Transport
Commission, Tristate Fruit Fly Committee; *New South Wales* Roads
and Traffic Authority, NSW Department of Environment Climate,
Change and Water, Destination New South Wales; *Australian Capital
Territory* ACT Planning and Land Authority, Australian Capital
Tourism Corporation; *Victoria* VicRoads, Department of Sustainability
and Environment, Victoria, Tourism Victoria; *South Australia* Transport
SA, Primary Industries and Resources South Australia, Department
of Environment and Natural Resources, South Australian Tourism
Commission; *Western Australia* Main Roads Western Australia,
Department of Indigenous Affairs Western Australia, Aboriginal
Lands Trust, Department of Environment and Conservation, Western
Australia Tourism Commission; *Northern Territory* Department of
Transport and Infrastructure, Northern and Central land councils,
Department of Natural Resources, Environment, The Arts and
Sport, Parks Australia, Northern Territory Tourist Commission;
Queensland Department of Main Roads, Department of Environment
& Resource Management, Queensland Parks & Wildlife Service,
Tourism Queensland; *Tasmania* Department of Infrastructure, Energy
& Resources, Parks and Wildlife Service, Tourism Tasmania.

A catalogue record for this
book is available from the
National Library of Australia

NATIONAL
LIBRARY
OF AUSTRALIA

Hardie Grant acknowledges the Traditional Owners of the Country on
which we work, the Wurundjeri people of the Kulin Nation and the
Gadigal people of the Eora Nation, and recognises their continuing
connection to the land, waters and culture. We pay our respects to their
Elders past and present.

Names in *palawa kani*, the language of Tasmanian Aboriginals, with
thanks to the Tasmanian Aboriginal Centre.

Ultimate Road Trips: Australia
ISBN 9781741176506

20 19 18 17 16 15 14 13 12 11

Publisher
Melissa Kayser

Project editor
Megan Cuthbert

Editor
Alexandra Payne

Trainee editor
Jessica Smith

Proofreader
Helena Holmgren

Cartographer
Robyn Hinchcliffe and
Emily Maffei

Design
Andy Warren

Typesetting
Megan Ellis

Index
Max McMaster

Prepress
Megan Ellis and Splitting Image
Colour Studio

Printed and bound in China by LEO Paper Products LTD.

The paper this book is printed on is certified against
the Forest Stewardship Council® Standards and
other sources. FSC® promotes environmentally
responsible, socially beneficial and economically
viable management of the world's forests.